Advance Praise for
Family Treasures Lost and Found

When a technology journalist turns her forensic skills to her own family, a unique detective story unfolds—crossing continents, following clues, undaunted by false leads and dead ends, buoyed by revelations. This beautifully written book, really two stories in one, is not only about what the author found. It is also a journey of discovery. Karen A. Frenkel demonstrates what truths can be revealed despite decades of silence and gaps in the record and inspires others to embark on their own journey. A must read.

—Barbara Kirshenblatt-Gimblett, Ronald S. Lauder Chief Curator of the Core Exhibition at POLIN Museum of the History of Polish Jews and University Professor Emerita at New York University

Karen A. Frenkel has gifted us with a deeply researched, profoundly moving journey before, during, and after the Nazi era of horror, death, escape, refuge. Her memoir is brilliant, gripping, haunting. With fascism, deportation, family separations, exploding across the globe, this book is the perfect read for this moment. Everyone concerned about humanity's ongoing struggle for empathy, survival, and human rights will benefit from Frenkel's vision, family love, and hope.

—Blanche Wiesen Cook, University distinguished Professor Emerita, John Jay College and the Graduate Center CUNY (or author of *Eleanor Roosevelt* and *The Declassified Eisenhower*)

AF619294

Karen A. Frenkel's remarkable memoir shifts the paradigm that assumed Holocaust survivors continued to be victims after the war. Readers are privy to the emotional experience of growing up with Holocaust survivors who embraced life. However, Frenkel's father's silence motivated her journey to meticulously research both parents' family histories before, during, and after the Holocaust. This beautifully written, riveting memoir is hugely ambitious, intensely engaging. Interspersed into the memorable family account is a social history of the time, which chronicles novel expressions of the rise of antisemitism in institutions of medical education, juxtaposed to individuals who risked their lives to save Jews. The tapestry Frenkel weaves with much persistence is inspirational.

—Eva Fogelman, author of *Conscience and Courage: Rescuers of Jews During the Holocaust*, and writer and co-producer *Breaking the Silence: The Generation After the Holocaust*

With the rise of active, global antisemitism, Karen A. Frenkel's *Family Treasures Lost and Found* is a most compelling and much needed work. While it presents a powerful and insightful story of a family's struggle to survive during and after the Holocaust, it departs from traditional survivor stories; a daughter of Holocaust survivors investigated their pasts and tells her parents' tales. This gripping memoir enables readers to absorb the most outrageous acts society can perpetrate on its members.

—Arthur Flug, EdD, Executive Director Kupferberg Holocaust Center, Queensborough Community College (Retired), Author, *Untermenschen: A History of Targeting Others for Inequality, Hatred and Suffering*

Family Treasures
Lost & Found

Family Treasures
Lost & Found

Karen A. Frenkel

A POST HILL PRESS BOOK
ISBN: 979-8-88845-956-0
ISBN (eBook): 979-8-88845-957-7

Family Treasures Lost & Found
© 2025 by Karen A. Frenkel
All Rights Reserved

Cover design by Don Morris Design (DMD)
Maps by Michael Lugo Holmes

This book, as well as any other Post Hill Press publications, may be purchased in bulk quantities at a special discounted rate. Contact orders@posthillpress.com for more information.

This is a work of nonfiction. All people, locations, events, and situations are portrayed to the best of the author's memory.

No part of this book may be reproduced, stored in a retrieval system, or transmitted by any means without the written permission of the author and publisher.

Post Hill Press
New York • Nashville
posthillpress.com

Published in the United States of America
1 2 3 4 5 6 7 8 9 10

Dedicated to my parents, lost relatives, and all the victims of genocide, and for Davida, Bret, Andy, Ali, Juliana, Ollie, Ava, Henry, Shana, and their descendants.

Table of Contents

Author's Note About Names xi
Preface xiii

Chapter One: Treasure 1
Chapter Two: Anatomy 9
Chapter Three: Anschluss and Absolutorium 26
Chapter Four: An Arrangement 38
Chapter Five: The Hovering Holocaust 54
Chapter Six: Letters, Literature, and Bones 71
Chapter Seven: The Land by the Bay 82
Chapter Eight: Coming of Age in Amagansett 95
Chapter Nine: Portraits 104
Chapter Ten: Gold and Prescience 112
Chapter Eleven: Never Worn 119
Chapter Twelve: Adrift and Betrayed 132
Chapter Thirteen: Insisting, Insisting, Insisting 147
Chapter Fourteen: The Soviet Occupation of Lwów 158
Chapter Fifteen: The Elder Finkelsteins Leave Berlin 169
Finkelstein Portraits, Photographs, Escape Routes, and Family Trees 179
Chapter Sixteen: The German Occupation of Lwów 199
Chapter Seventeen: More Insisting 205
Chapter Eighteen: A Sonata in Brooklyn 210
Chapter Nineteen: Resistance 214
Chapter Twenty: The Stamp of Life 220

Chapter Twenty-One: Aliens in the Catskills 228
Chapter Twenty-Two: The Fighter 234
Chapter Twenty-Three: In Transit 244
Chapter Twenty-Four: In the Belly of the Beast 252
Chapter Twenty-Five: Castles and Fairy Tales 257
Chapter Twenty-Six: Holocausted-Out 278
Chapter Twenty-Seven: Walking 289
Chapter Twenty-Eight: Dixieland, England, D-Day, and Normandy 300
Chapter Twenty-Nine: Doppelgänger 314
Chapter Thirty: These Hands 322
Chapter Thirty-One: Dear Mr. President 330
Chapter Thirty-Two: The Battles for France and Belgium 332
Chapter Thirty-Three: Liberation 341
Chapter Thirty-Four: Dachau 355
Chapter Thirty-Five: Un Château 360
Chapter Thirty-Six: A Reunion and a Kibbutz 363
Chapter Thirty-Seven: Chez Éclair 373

Epilogue 379
Acknowledgments 387
About the Author 393

Author's Note About Names

The city where my father was born changed names several times. Before World War I and while under Austro-Hungarian rule, the city was called Lemberg. After the Polish-Soviet war of 1920 it came under Polish control and was renamed Lwów (pronounced Voof). During WWII and the Soviet Occupation, it was renamed Lvov, and under the Nazis it was once again Lemberg. Today, now that it is in Ukraine, the city is known as Lviv.

The name Frankel is variously spelled depending on which country was in power and the official language at the time. As a result, my grandfather spelled his name Fränkel and my father Frenkel. My uncle spelled it Frankel. Ojzer, my paternal grandfather's first name, is the Yiddish equivalent of Oscar and is pronounced Oy-jer. My paternal grandmother's name, Michaela (pronounced Mee-ha-ella), is sometimes referred to as Mechla (Mehk-la) and Mechli. Dawid, Polish for David, is pronounced Dov-id. Irena, my mother's name, is pronounced Ee-renna. As for my mother's parents, Teofila is Teo-Phee-la, and Izydor is the Polish spelling for Isadore.

Occasionally, spelling across multiple languages and author-made transcriptions have rendered spellings of names difficult to confirm. I have chosen to include the Polish spelling of locations and rivers even though events took place during the Soviet and German occupations during World War II to avoid confusion and because in most cases we are in my Polish-born or Polish-identified relatives' points of view.

To preserve my mother's voice in her oral history for the Fortunoff Video Archive for Holocaust Testimonies I have declined to correct her grammar and inserted articles in brackets. There are no definite and indefinite articles in Polish, a source of endless confusion for my polylingual mother.

Preface

All Holocaust survivors' stories are extraordinary and precious because of the extremely unlikely odds of outwitting Hitler and escaping the Nazis' meticulous and murderous rampages. My parents' wartime tales are extraordinary for those reasons, too, but *Family Treasures Lost and Found: A Memoir* differs on several counts. First, my parents were not in concentration camps. Second, their strategic trajectories as they were hounded across Europe by exterminationist anti-Semites were highly unusual.

When World War II began, my mother was a sheltered fourteen-year-old living in Kraków. She and her parents fled east by train three days after the Germans invaded Poland on September 1, 1939. After zigzagging across Galicia (southern Poland), they ended up in Lwów, Poland, now Lviv, Ukraine. In the fall of 1941, she convinced her parents that they would not survive without false papers enabling them to pretend that they were Catholic Poles. She came of age sustaining this ruse and working as a slave laborer in Germany. My mother told my sisters and me about her survival, but only in snippets. She was selective in what she shared, and imparted different morsels to each of us according to what she thought each daughter could absorb.

I knew my mother's war story was unique in many ways. Very few Jews survived with false papers posing as Polish Catholics, as she had. Fewer still had made it thanks to that ruse *and by volunteering* to work as a slave laborer in Germany. She literally hid in plain sight in the belly of the Teutonic beast.

When I became a journalist in the 1980s, I tried many times to interview my mother. I would arrive at her home with my tape recorder, but she always demurred. "Oh come on, let's just talk and enjoy our tea," she would say. "Tell me how you are. What are you working on?"

In 1987, I urged my mother to record her testimony for the Fortunoff Video Archive for Holocaust Testimonies at Yale University. The Fortunoff archive preceded Steven Spielberg's Shoah Foundation project by about a decade. My mother was sixty-three and still in good health, although she had gotten a pacemaker a few years earlier. "They're interviewing survivors right on Austin Street," I entreated her, mentioning Forest Hills' main shopping drag. "Please, just sign up."

My mom overcame her hesitation and reluctance, gathered a few documents and photographs the night before, and recorded her oral history. She faced her two interviewers with characteristic forthrightness and irony, occasionally sidestepping questions that were too painful. She did not want to detail the abuse she suffered at the mercy of her "employers," who overworked and starved her. After the interview, she told me, "Maybe someday you'll do something with it." I had made a request of my mother and she in turn had given me an assignment.

One day in the early 2000s, I forced myself into reporter mode and sat on the couch in front of our VCR to transcribe her oral history. At first, I had trouble watching the tape. Ill at ease, stressed, and formal, my mother hardly resembled the vivacious, charismatic, and sociable woman I admired. I felt guilty that I had imposed upon her, even though she did not fault me. It took a long time to slog through my mother's testimony because her one-and-a-half-hour interview was full of Polish towns and cities I could not spell. I cut and pasted paragraphs of the transcript to get the chronology straight. Then I created a timeline and marked the towns and cities along my mother's long path to liberation through Poland, Ukraine, and Germany.

Delving into my father's past proved to be much harder. Four decades earlier—when I was fifteen—my father died unexpectedly at age fifty-seven. I remained hesitant and conflicted about delving into his past; I had been an obedient, dutiful daughter and had respected his privacy. But to better understand and memorialize my enigmatic father, I would have to defy him and uncover what he had not wanted me to know.

Growing up, all I knew of my father's life before he married my mother was that he was born in Lwów. And that he received his medical degree from the renowned University of Vienna Medical School, but I did not know when. Somehow my dad arrived in New York via Mexico before World War II. After he came to New York, he finished his medical training in Brooklyn before serving in the U.S. Army Medical Corps. He refused to discuss his pre-war life and refugee experiences with my two sisters and me. The little I knew I learned from my mother and my father's older brother. Shortly after my father died, my sisters and I learned that he had been married before he met our mother, that his first wife was the daughter of the owners of the famous dairy restaurant Ratner's, and that she was connected to the underworld of the Lower East Side. My father and his first wife divorced when he returned from serving in the U.S. Army.

As far as I know, three of my grandparents and my father's younger brother were never buried where they were murdered—in Nazi-occupied Lwów. There are no gravesites, no headstones, not even a cenotaph, a monument to a person or group of people buried elsewhere. An empty tomb. Not having been buried, my parents' parents' spirits float, dispersed in the air. There is wisdom in the Jewish tradition of sitting shiva and observing a period of mourning. Without it, I wondered how my parents could have experienced even a particle of resolution.

And so I love Lwów and I loathe Lwów. Birthplace of my father, killing grounds of my three grandparents, my uncle, his wife, and tens of thousands of other Jews.

As a witness of surviving witnesses—daughter of a refugee and a displaced slave laborer, granddaughter of a survivor, great-granddaughter of two refugees, grand-niece of two refugees, and as a descendent of those who perished: granddaughter of three murder victims, niece of a murdered uncle and of numerous great-aunts, great-uncles, and cousins—and in response to my mother's express wish, I felt obligated to research and recount both my parents' and paternal grandfather's wartime stories. These narratives recount the few, very unusual escapes from fascist genocide—and the fates of the vanquished eighty years ago.

In 2014 my career as a technology journalist was waning and I considered devoting myself to the project fulltime. I was about to turn sixty. In the spirit of the great Jewish sage Hillel the Elder, I asked myself: If I do not seek answers now, then when? I overcame my qualms and embarked upon a seven-year fact-finding quest so that I could describe how far my parents went emotionally, physically, and morally to save themselves during the Nazi onslaught. Using my skills as a journalist, I pieced together my father's pre-war life, medical school days, escape from Lwów, and tour of duty in the European Theater from scraps of information on forms and in documents my mother saved, interviews with newfound relatives, and the archives of the United States, Israel, the University of Vienna, and Ukraine.

Discoveries large and small enriched my understanding of what my parents and other relatives endured. I decided to disclose the precise details for two reasons: First, I had to come to terms with my parents' experiences in spite of their desire to protect my sisters and me from their travails and sorrows by remaining silent or speaking selectively about the war. I understand that they wanted new lives. They wanted to look to the future and not ruminate about the past and their losses, because the dead would have wanted it that way. Second, I want the world to understand what happened to them in a way that's real and relatable. Only then can such trauma be prevented from happening to others.

My parents' stories are important not just because they were my parents, but because—in contrast to those who survived the concentration camps—the trauma and loss experienced by displaced Jews and refugees remain largely untold. The same is true of their courage, cunning, and resilience. I did not anticipate that my parents' stories would become relevant again when the plights of 65 million refugees worldwide were reported in 2016. I was, however, acutely alert to the rise of authoritarianism here and abroad. With the worldwide refugee crisis having swelled to 123 million as of 2023, according to the United Nations High Command for Refugees, my parents' and grandfather's stories take on new relevance. *Family Treasures Lost and Found* shows that life and freedom are worth the struggle, and that they are precious and to be cherished.

In a sense, digging up facts and writing about my parents' stories is my response, my resistance, to those who want to rewrite history by claiming the Holocaust never happened, or insist that not that many people died, and that the Jews should just get over it. Before my quest, all I could do was retort with rhetorical questions: If that is so, then what happened to three of my grandparents? What were the fates of my Uncle Milek and his bride? Where are their graves?

But there are truths. There are facts. And I found them. I scoured the Internet, plumbed real-world archives, and retraced the steps of my parents, sole surviving grandfather, and other family members when I went to Europe in 2016. I visited Vienna, Kraków, Tarnów, and Lviv with the goal of leaving "no stone unturned," as my mother used to say. I needed to honor my relatives by learning more about them. When details eluded me, I filled in the blanks with conjecture, trying out scenarios based on what I already knew of my relatives' personalities and predilections.

With each discovery, I was rewarded with the most unexpected recompense: a deep sense of connection to the lost.

Chapter One

Treasure

"Be very gentle with Daddy this time of year," my mother cautioned one spring in the mid-1960s. "That's when he feels sad."

To my preteen mind, my father relished the greenery and rebirth that arrived with the season. Every April he welcomed "dilodaffs," as he playfully referred to his favorite flower, the first to bloom in our Forest Hills, NY, garden.

"Why does he feel sad?" I asked, puzzled by my mother's words.

She hesitated, then blurted, "Because that's when his mother took the poison." During World War II, my father's blonde, blue-eyed mother had tried to pass for a Polish Catholic. When the Gestapo stormed into her apartment in Lwów, now Lviv, Ukraine, she bit into cyanide rather than be deported to a concentration or death camp.

I accepted that the subject was untouchable and obeyed my mother. Except once. I was unendingly curious about the woman whose fair hair, fair skin, and figure I had inherited—as far as I could tell, at least, from the lone photograph with which my father arrived here in 1939. One evening I asked about my grandmother Michaela. The look of surprise and hurt in my father's blue-gray eyes showed me I had been intrusive, clumsy. He rose from his chair and silently left the dining room. I followed, apologizing profusely. He accepted. I tried again, asking what she was like.

"I don't want to talk about it!"

Understanding that he needed to be alone, I backed off and never again approached him about his past.

Displayed on my computer screen fifty years later was a charming, three-story townhouse with an amber-colored façade, its large windows fringed with beautifully crafted ceramic tiles. Cast-iron filigree balconies on each floor hovered over the lane below. A forged door echoed the motif of the lacy balconies. The building seemed inviting—a cordial shelter on a sunny, old-world street.

Every day on his way home from school, my father, David Frenkel, had pushed open that door and scampered up to his parents' apartment on the second floor. He and his family had gazed through those large windows at passersby below. Perhaps Michaela had sipped coffee and savored Linzer torte with a friend while seated on the balcony. In the smaller apartment next door, my grandfather Ojzer would have been toiling over his textile import business. And on one weekend while their parents were at the opera, the three Fränkel brothers, ever pranksters, swung from the dining room chandelier and crashed into their mother's china-filled cabinet.

Sitting at my desk in my Upper West Side apartment in the winter of 2014, with the help of Google Street View, I tilted up into the clear, Ukrainian sky that canopied Lviv. I understood immediately—and yet only partially—why my father had never described his beautiful home in this magnificent city when it was still in Poland and called Lwów. Previously named Lemberg and the capital of Galicia (southern Poland), the city had been the eastern center of commerce of the Austro-Hungarian Empire. Gazing at my father's childhood home, I sensed why style and aesthetics—from architecture to haberdashery to operatic and orchestral music—had been so important to him. The beauty before me also offered clues to who my grandparents were, their tastes and their sensibilities. More than before, I appreciated why my father could not bear to talk about what and who he left behind at age twenty-six in March 1939.

I was certain this was the right building because my father's older brother, Izak (who we called "Uncle Sydney"), had said it was one of two decorated with majolica tiles and inspired by the Secessionist Viennese architect Otto Wagner. Such tin-glazed tiles were first made in Renaissance Italy, which was why the house had a Mediterranean feel.

So this is where Grandfather Ojzer hid jewels in the basement, I thought. When my sisters and I were growing up, our mother said he had buried the jewels to hide them from either the Soviets or the Nazis. As a child, I imagined loose diamonds, earrings, and brooches—all of which my grandfather had bestowed upon my grandmother—wrapped in velvet cloth. I wondered whether, if ever recovered, the precious jewels would be encrusted from years in the damp.

Although we did not know exactly what my grandfather hid and when, we knew where to look. But the house had been inaccessible until 1991, when Ukraine declared its independence from the collapsed Soviet Union. Since then, it had not occurred to us to seek our property. And yet, how many families know of buried treasure and the possibility of a real live treasure hunt? The notion of finding what my grandfather had stashed away glimmered with intrigue.

As I stared at the majolica rosettes of ochre and white lilies, I longed to share this discovery. But my sisters were at work: Michelle was in meetings making decisions for the nonprofit she ran. Ivy, a therapist, was treating patients. My husband, Ed, was lecturing community college students about marketing or statistics.

I, too, worked. I was a technology journalist with a freelance gig covering cyberwarfare. Although I loved my beat, the zest with which I previously covered it was fading. Earlier in my career, I had crafted in-depth magazine features about computer science—but with the demise of print magazines, opportunities for long-form features were rare. I longed to submerge myself in deep investigative work. So that morning, although I had intended to take a short break from my freelance assignment, I could not tear myself away.

My discovery triggered a yearning to tell my parents, who were long gone. Like my father, my mother, Irena Goldberger Frenkel, was Polish. Unlike him, she had survived the Holocaust in Europe. I was certain she would have been intrigued and excited by the house. I was not as sure how my father would have reacted. He never confided in us about his hometown or the circumstances of his departure, and he died young when I was fifteen. I knew only that he loathed Poland, and that—unlike my mother—had never returned. I assumed part of the reason was the crushing anti-Semitism, but that also had been true of Vienna, where he studied medicine and which he loved and did visit after the war. The rest was deeply personal. It was too painful for my father to be reminded of Lwów—not only because his mother had died there during the war, but because of the way she had died. My father knew nothing about the fate of his younger brother, Milek. Perhaps it was better that way.

The morning of my Lviv discovery, I had searched several boxes of family documents my mother had saved—hers, my father's, and her grandparents'—now stored in a small room off my kitchen. As I pored over yellowing and crumbling Polish, German, Ukrainian, and English papers, I could taste the musky, decaying correspondence. Moistening my lips, I leafed through the files a little faster. Toward the back of one box, I found what I was looking for: a file labeled "David's Papers." Inside was a 1932 document titled "*Poświadezenie Obywatelstwa.*" Back at my computer using a "Polish-English Translator" I typed in the letters inaccurately, tripped up by the Ws, Ys, and Zs. Finally, up popped "Certificate of Citizenship," which my father probably had obtained before he went abroad to medical school. On the address line below, it said, "Rejtana 5."

Aha!

At first, online maps of Lviv in Cyrillic discouraged me. Then, I learned that after World War II, when Lwów became Lviv and was absorbed by the Soviet Union, all the streets were renamed in Ukrainian. I persisted and found a 1939 Polish map on Lviv Center, an urban architectural and historical site. Outlines of landmarks were inked in black and patches of green depicted parks with shadowed circles to suggest trees. Mustard-colored squiggly rings surrounded hills and other elevations.

Hoping to match the streets, I arranged my browser windows so that I could compare the maps, and zoomed in, keeping an eye out for parks and landmarks. The footprint of a large building partially labeled "Theat" caught my attention. Could this be the famous opera house, or Grand Theater as it was called when my father was a boy? Uncle Sydney said they used to walk to the opera. Just below was a wide promenade. I guided my cursor south, and there it was: Ulica Rejtana, nestled two blocks south and one east.

On the new Ukrainian map, Ulica Rejtana was no longer named for the Polish 18th-century painter, Tadeusz Rejtan, but celebrated a Ukrainian avant-garde theater director Les Kurbasa. I inputted "Kurbasa 5."

Et voilà, or *tutaj jest*, in Polish.

When I told my sisters, they, too, were awestruck.

"You think the jewels are still there?" I asked.

"I don't know…I doubt it," Ivy equivocated.

"It's unlikely that the basement remained untouched since Grandpa left," Michelle said. "That was so long ago."

"I'm not so sure," I countered. "People lived in poverty for decades behind the Iron Curtain."

"Yes, but Ukrainian yuppies live there now. Dirt floor in the 21st century?"

"But the building hasn't been well maintained. Maybe they did nothing," I said.

Michelle convinced me, for a while, that the basement had probably been renovated and that our heirlooms were gone. When my husband Ed came home, he was fascinated by the building and let me know in his usual, subtle way that he would support whatever I chose to do.

My sisters dampened my desire to go find the jewels, but I appreciated their pragmatism. I knew Ukraine had no policy for restitution of property to Holocaust survivors and their descendants. Besides, all we had was one document with the address, hardly proof of ownership. Treasure aside, if we pursued the matter and won after slogging through bureaucracy and accumulating legal expenses, the worth of the building would have to be divided into fifths because Uncle Sydney's two children, our cousins, are also heirs. Michelle knew of other children of survivors who had reclaimed property in Poland only to be slapped with costly bills and repairs because of years of neglect. I was satisfied for the time being, regardless of a monetary reward or not; just seeing my father's childhood home and taking the first step toward reclaiming his history was a gift in itself.

When next I "visited" Kurbasa/Rejtana Street, I took a virtual stroll down the street. I passed images of Ukrainians with blurred faces, and cars dating from the late 1970s to 2013, including some Soviet models. At the foot of the street, pink graffiti defaced a garage. To the right, a narrow street angled its way toward a lipstick-shaped building with an underpass that opened onto Legionow/Svobody Avenue, across from the opera house. Why not experience in 3-D Lviv's Theater of Opera and Ballet—the city's enduring cathedral for the arts, no matter who was in control.

But Google Street View would not allow me to enter the archway. I kept mousing toward white arrows and the shallow tunnel's entrance, only to be rebuffed. I turned around and rethreaded my way back. When I returned to my grandparents' house, I noticed more disrepair. Patches of tiles were missing and corrosion ate at the balcony supports. A sleek dentist's office and a computer store occupied the ground floor, but the front door's stone saddle was crumbling into gray powder.

And yet this gracious building is now a UNESCO World Heritage Site, a title bestowed upon remarkable accomplishments of humanity, and evidence of our planet's intellectual history. A tragedy within a tragedy: commissioned, designed, built, and owned by Jews, recognition came posthumously to most involved in its creation. I read in an article that the artisans of the ceramic tile workshop were murdered in 1943.

Who lives there now, I wondered. More cyber sleuthing revealed that the building is a co-op known as House of Austria. For a few Hryvnias you can lease my grandparents' renovated apartment with shiny, mint-green appliances and voile window treatments.

To its left stands a taller building of Gothic, gray-tinged stone that housed a small theater. The other side of my grandparents' house was flanked by a mid-19th century building with gabled windows. I did not yet know that these neighboring structures would prove to be important to my grandfather's story.

The next day, I googled "Rejtana 5." To my surprise, a photographer had created a site showcasing the building's exterior and vestibule. Above more tiles were peeling murals that had once depicted coastal landscapes—palimpsests of a lost world. Beyond the deteriorating mural panels, ghost-white sidewalls were interrupted by two portals—blocked up former entrances to shops. Friezes with spiraling vines and grape leaves crowned the former store entrances and the second vestibule door. Below it, smashed floor tiles obscured the original Polish address and the year of construction (1907). I stared, stupefied. Revisionist Ukrainians, with their sledgehammers, had succeeded in crushing the past.

During World War II, the Nazis, aided by their Ukrainian and Polish collaborators, exterminated local Jews and Jewish refugees. Toward the end of the war, the Soviets captured Lwów from the Nazis and later expelled the Poles. Now the house appeared as if my family had never dwelled there, as if my family had never even existed.

Beneath the initial thrill of discovery lurked a darker realization. I had not been gawking at a lovely townhouse that might or might not contain hidden loot. This place, the entire city, actually, was a crime scene. Here, my paternal grandmother Michaela was murdered; had the Gestapo not hunted her down, she would never have taken her life. My mother and her parents, Teofila and Izydor Goldberger, had fled here from Kraków. Like Michaela, my maternal grandparents hid and perished; Teofila was denounced on the street and picked up by the Gestapo. Just like that. Izydor jumped off a train bound for a concentration camp and vanished. For me the whole gorgeous city was fraught.

And so, I eyed those shattered tiles and seethed.

Just as it was impossible to reach the heart of Lviv by the virtual path I had taken with Street View, I could not grasp the details of my family's story for they had dissipated into smoke and ash. I did not expect to unveil official records of the fates of my murdered grandparents and other relatives. I assumed we would never know more than what my grandfather Ojzer had learned about Michaela's death, and what a family friend told my mother about Teofila and Izydor's murders. But I wanted to know where they had flourished and what their lives were like before the Nazi onslaught. Any fragment, any link of continuity, seemed utterly precious. I also wanted to resolve some mysteries about my parents, especially my father. I had no choice but to try.

Chapter Two

Anatomy

In the spring of 1933, with piercing war whoops, Austro-Fascist medical students at the University of Vienna stormed the lecture hall of a renowned anatomy professor. The intruders wore *Burschenschaft* caps, their fraternity hats, and were accompanied by invited reinforcements: Nazi thugs from Germany called "Brown Shirts." Hooting and screaming in solidarity, they charged down the aisles attacking students. They pulled out whips concealed in their coats and lashed out with unbounded ferocity at students seated in the top rows. Others brandished steel rods and rubber truncheons.

Swinging their weapons, the brawlers sang the "Horst-Wessel-Lied" song, the anthem of the Nazi Party. Hitler had been in power in Germany for several months and recently had decreed the song Germany's co-national anthem with "Deutschlandlied." Emboldened, the Austro-fascist students and the Brown Shirts sang boisterously to intimidate the professor's students, who were mostly Jewish and Socialists like him. The song glorified a murdered Nazi storm trooper who had led an attack on Communist Party headquarters, and proclaimed the Nazis' forthcoming revenge and triumph. As they descended the amphitheater steps, they screamed "*Juda verrecke*" (Death to Jews), and dragged Semitic-looking students from their seats and beat them mercilessly. One struck a student on the head. He sank onto a bench, clutching his temples with both hands as blood streamed down his wrists. The fascists brutalized classmates who came to his aid.

The professor was Julius Tandler, esteemed Chair of the university's Anatomy Department and author of a brilliant anatomy text. A Social Democrat not content just to teach, he was a healthcare reformer and the Commissioner of Health of Red Vienna, as the city was called between the wars when it was democratically governed for the first time by a leftist party. Tandler was also my twenty-year-old father's professor.

Such violence was the very reason my father, at age nineteen, had left Lwów. There, Polish and Ukrainian medical students attacked their Jewish classmates, brandishing long poles to which they had attached razor blades. Yet growing up, I knew nothing of the violence and persecution my father had been exposed to as a medical student. I read about the raid in *Fräulein Doktor*, a memoir by one of my father's classmates, Fanny Stang, and was utterly unprepared for the accounts of extreme violence suffered by Jewish medical students.

How did my father react? Had he vacillated between panic and outrage as he watched the fascists assault his classmates? Did he try to help them? Or was he among those who suffered bone crushing blows and bleeding wounds, their screams filling the air?

My father, with his fair complexion, gray-blue eyes, and swept-back strawberry blond hair, could have passed for an Aryan Eastern European. He resembled the aristocratic-looking Viennese actor, Paul Henreid (who, ironically, was actually Jewish). But what about his friend, dark-skinned Munio Distenfeld, whose yarmulke rested on brown, curly hair?

According to Fanny Stang, Professor Tandler entered through the faculty door, surveyed the situation, and assessed the intruders. He had seen such barrages before and kept a file documenting what he called "Chronology of Terror." He tore off his white coat and flung it on the table next to the podium.

"Unless all my students resume normal academic behavior, I will stop all anatomy lectures this semester," he bellowed in a cold fury. Everyone, even the Brown Shirts, froze. "You have five minutes to clear the theater and restore order." He stomped off. With that, the belligerents retreated, and a collective sigh of relief circulated in the lower amphitheater.

After his favorite Herr Professor Doktor returned and lectured from the podium, how could my father concentrate? He must have been rattled to the core. My father was so utterly devoted to healing that in spite of the violence, he was determined to finish his studies. His knowledge of Latin and Greek from his *gimnazjum* (high school) days helped him memorize a plethora of medical terms, and he had innate clinical talent. Then there was his considerable determination and drive.

"*Labor omnia vincit*," he would have told himself, remembering his Virgil. "Work conquers all."

And he proved it. My father followed his star no matter what he encountered. He thought of healing as a way to make the world a better place, a way to contribute to everyone's welfare regardless of their background. To heal the world one patient at a time. During his short career my father achieved much: He completed two residencies, one in pathology and the other in obstetrics and gynecology. As an attending physician at several Brooklyn hospitals—Brooklyn Women's, Unity, Kings County—he specialized in infertility. He was in the *Who's Who in American Healthcare* because of his pioneering research in pathology regarding the early detection of lung cancer, and he had devised a surgical technique to help infertile women conceive. In addition to two practices—one in Brooklyn, the other in Forest Hills—he followed Tandler's example by teaching. As a clinical professor at Downstate Medical School, he trained many OBGYN residents. He also had his eye on a new state university under construction on Long Island that was expected to be the Berkeley of the East. He was thrilled to be appointed clinical assistant professor of obstetrics and gynecology at the medical school of the new state university of New York, Stony Brook.

But back in Vienna, he faced daily barriers to get his medical degree. Another classmate, an American named Muriel Gardiner, referred to the March 1933 riot in her memoir, *Code Name "Mary,"* and described a May attack in the dissection hall. Gardiner, née Helen Muriel Morris, was a half-Jewish American heiress who had come to Vienna hoping to study psychoanalysis with Freud. She was the model for the protagonist in the 1977 movie *Julia* starring Jane Fonda and Vanessa Redgrave. Based on Lillian Hellman's short story in her collection *Pentimento* (1973), the film portrayed Gardiner's role in the socialist resistance and underground efforts to shield Social Democrats from the Austro-fascists.

I loved the film the first time I saw it and was aware that the beginning took place at the University of Vienna. In a harrowing depiction of a raid, Austro-fascists storm up a building's steps, hurl Jewish faculty and students down them and over the banisters, and beat everyone in their path. The marauders' screams ricochet off the marble pillars and stairs, as do their jeers and laughter, echoing loudly. Brandishing a pole, Redgrave's Julia runs down a corridor toward the fascists, only to be quickly overwhelmed. The scene then transitions to the *Anschluss*, the annexation in 1938 of Austria by the Nazis, by which time I thought my father had already left. According to my mother, he received his degree in the nick of time. He did not know until the last minute that he had graduated, she said, because he had taken a final oral exam in a taxi en route to the train station. From there he returned home to Lwów.

After I saw *Julia*, I discussed the on-campus violence with my mother.

"Ach. It was unbelievable," she said.

"At a university?" I replied, momentarily forgetting about the 1970 Kent State University shootings.

"Yes, at a university," said my mother, incredulous at my surprise. She paused. "And you cannot imagine the anti-Semitism. But your father had a favorite professor. And he was marvelous. There was a problem though. I no longer recall the details...."

I pursued them on my quest. Among my father's papers I discovered a worn gray booklet with faded German gothic characters proclaiming "Universität zu Wien." On the inside was a 1933 photo of my dad in his early twenties. Greenish pages followed with rows and columns bearing the names of my father's professors, their courses, signatures, and numbers from two to seven, which I assumed were grades. I scanned down the 1933 course column: "Physik," "Anatomie," "Chemie," and "Physiologie," returned to "Anatomie," and saw "Tandler" next to it—proof that my father was present at the March and May riots Stang and Gardiner had described. The realization was quite a shock. I suddenly remembered descending to my father's office as a teen. Skimming through his medical books, I was intrigued by a heavy three-volume set bound in deep red, written in German, and titled *Anatomie*. The spine said TANDLER in faded gold capital letters. I once admitted—a little sheepishly—to my father that I had looked at the books when he was not home. I was embarrassed because the illustrations were of nude bodies and I thought I might be invading my father's privacy by sitting in his office without permission. But he was pleased I took an interest and invited me to come down anytime to read his books.

Tandler's drawings, first published a century ago, were as innovative to his students then as computer-generated images and three-dimensional cartoons were to me when I was reporting on computer graphics during the late '80s and early '90s. On the fly on his lecture hall blackboard, Tandler recreated his textbook illustrations, editing the details so that students could appreciate and understand the miracle of the human form. He enabled them to see, from as many points of view as possible, the body's structure.

I returned from my reverie to my father's photo in the booklet. I had never seen him so young and yet he seemed very serious and wide-eyed. Below his photo was the Polish spelling of his first name, "Dawid," (pronounced Dov-id) for "David." I impulsively googled "Dawid Frenkel." To my amazement, I arrived at a virtual memorial book created by the University of Vienna to acknowledge and honor faculty and students the institution had persecuted and expelled during the Nazi Occupation. The university had commemorated this injustice in 2008, seventy years after the *Anschluss*, declaring its awareness of "the amount of shared responsibility it bears for this inconceivable atrocity perpetrated against its affiliates," according to the Memorial Book website. (The English translation seems to have been modified slightly since 2016.) I wished my father had lived long enough to see a new generation of Austrians, like those at the University of Vienna, willing to acknowledge the wrongdoing of their forebears.

The creators of the site, two historians, had also compiled a handwritten memorial book kept at the former Jewish House of Worship on the university's campus, which I visited in 2016. It listed 2,700 victims of National Socialism, including 200 dismissed professors and docents. Almost a quarter of the student body enrolled during the spring of 1938 right before the *Anschluss* left, but not all departed voluntarily. The university gave the names of Jewish students to the Gestapo to check whether "individual people should be arrested."

So far, the historians have identified 1,770 of the 2,230 expelled Jewish students, including my father. The page devoted to him displays photocopies of the administration's counterpart to the booklet I have. A brief paragraph stated where my father was from, named my grandfather and his occupation (merchant), and listed the years my father had been enrolled. Then it said: "He succeeded in finishing his studies and graduated on June 28th, 1938—because he was a citizen of a foreign country, he could not be restricted by the Nuremberg Laws. But nevertheless he was not allowed to practice as a physician in the territories of the Third Reich."

Well, that was pretty wild. For six years, a portion of my father's life—about which I knew nothing—was documented online for the world to see. I could so easily have missed it, I thought, and marveled at the serendipity of discovery. But how could my father have been expelled, given the dramatic tale of his oral exam in a taxi? That my father had been persecuted hurt me. I contacted the historians to express gratitude for the record the university had kept of my father's student days and to request clarification about the circumstances under which his degree was conferred.

The historians said our inherited booklet was called a "Nationale," and listed the courses my father had attended. The numbers were lecture hours per week, not grades, for which he had paid with stamps bought with Groschen (Austrian currency). As for the oral-exam-in-a-cab legend, the historians thought it unlikely because usually several professors had to be present, but they confirmed that my dad had not been expelled and had received his medical degree.

When I told my sisters of the online memorial book, Ivy recalled a photograph of one of our father's professors, "somebody Eppinger," she said, who had disappointed our father. I returned to the Nationale;

my father had attended Hans Eppinger's lecturers on internal medicine from 1935 to 1937. Again I scrutinized the list of professors and courses. Why had the Austro-fascists targeted Tandler's lectures and not those of other professors, I wondered. I wanted to know why anti-Semitic riots had erupted at the medical school, and why in the Anatomy Department in particular.

A history of the university revealed that the violence that morning in the anatomy amphitheater harkened back to unrest due to the influx of Jews to Vienna in the 1870s. By the mid-19th century, the university was one of the most prestigious in Europe; its hospital was a center for medical research. There, Ignaz Semmelweis had observed a connection between doctors' poor hygiene and the dreaded killer of new mothers: puerperal, or childbed fever. He found that hand-washing after dissecting corpses and before entering the obstetrics ward reduced mortality from 30 to 1 percent. There, Sigmund Freud had conducted his early neurology studies and lectured. There, four Nobel laureates had made the medical school their home: Robert Bárány won his prize for pioneering work on the inner ear, Hans Fischer for research on hemoglobin and chlorophyll, Julius Wagner-Jauregg for the treatment of paralysis by malaria inoculation, and Karl Landsteiner for discovering the A, B, AB, and O blood types and the Rhesus factor.

The Anatomy Department was at the center of a debate that raged among the faculty over types of scientific inquiry and anatomical differences between Aryans and non-Aryans. This dispute came to a head in 1888 over the appointment of a new Chair of the Anatomy Department. One candidate was Tandler's predecessor, Emil Zuckerkandl, who was Jewish and a pathologist. He appreciated physical variations among people, as well as what they had in common, and used anatomical knowledge to fight disease. His Catholic competitor emphasized physical differences between ethnicities, focusing on anatomical differences—like whether Austrians were pure Germans. These differences were inherited, he thought, and had nothing to do with food and the environment. Nature, not nurture. I could see the Aryan theory of racial superiority and inferiority germinating.

The students took sides and wanted to protect the turf upon which they would practice after graduating. Rather than taking disciplinary action when disputes arose between students, a long line of rectors permitted aristocratic students to exercise their "independent right of assault," as they put it, which was an Austrian tradition by the early 1930s. According to this code of honor, if someone insulted a student, the wronged student had to have satisfaction. That meant a duel, but only with those deemed qualified. Merchants and bankers were excluded, whereas those with academic educations were accepted. Proof of manhood meant participating in as many brawls as possible, so fraternities constantly provoked one another.

The university's solution was to split the Anatomy Department into two institutes. Anatomy Institute I emphasized anatomy in the service of treating patients. Anatomy Institute II focused on comparative anatomy and nomenclature, eventually aligning itself with fascism and eugenics. Therefore Jewish medical students like my father attended Anatomy Institute I.

There was a truce between the departments during *fin-de-siècle* Vienna, when society tolerated Jews in high places. In 1910, almost 60 percent of the faculty at the Medical University of Vienna was Jewish—one of the highest proportions in all European universities. The proportion of Jewish students rose steadily, too, climbing in a decade from 25 to 42 percent. But during the 1920s and early 1930s, students of the two institutes clashed violently, as they had intermittently for over sixty years. Although Tandler documented the attacks and protested to a string of university rectors, they were fascist sympathizers and gave him no support.

Under his tenure as Commissioner of Public Health for the Social Democratic Party, one third of Red Vienna's income was spent on social welfare and half of that third on children. New mothers received free milk and layettes so that their babies immediately received proper nutrition. My father had suffered from rickets as a toddler in Vienna, where his family had fled to escape the Tsar's army on the eve of World War I. The Fränkels were welcomed by my grandmother Michaela's uncles on the Lifschütz side, who owned and operated the famous Hotel Continental at the gateway to Leopoldstadt, Vienna's Jewish quarter. But immediately after the war, milk was so scarce that most children—regardless of how affluent their families were—suffered from this disease, which permanently weakened and damaged their bones.

And so I began to understand why my father had admired Tandler enough to haul his texts halfway around the world. But Tandler had made enemies; his reforms were expensive. He encouraged citizens to sculpt their bodies with exercise so that they were as healthy and physically fit as possible, arguing that his policy would ultimately curtail health costs. But not everyone agreed with such long-term thinking and planning.

My father had socialist leanings before he arrived in Red Vienna, so I could see why he would have been attracted to it as well as to the university. Back in Lwów during the late 1920s, when my father and his brothers Sydney and Milek were in their teens, an employee of their father raised their consciousness to the plight of the proletariat. At that time, Grandpa Ojzer, a serial entrepreneur, was importing textiles from Łódź to Lwów and ran his company from his house. The brothers were under the influence of Zionism because one of Ojzer's nieces, Golda, the daughter of his sister Soba, had married a Zionist. The couple made *aliyah* to Palestine where Golda opened a bakery. She had returned several times with tales of life on co-op farms called *kibbutzim* and taught her cousins folk dances and songs she had learned there.

Every day, the Fränkel boys saw their father's worker carry heavy bolts of fabric on his back, trekking up and down the stairs of their home. My father would have been concerned about the wear and tear on the worker's spine. As strong as he was, such lifting would take a toll. In contrast, Sydney was such a fervent Zionist that he challenged the worker about his politics—as I learned from an audio interview with Anita, his daughter and my cousin.

"What the hell?" Sydney said, recounting the anecdote. "With your strength, you could go to Palestine and build the Jewish homeland." He felt the worker was squandering his strength while Ojzer and others profited from his labor. But the worker was not content to passively accept his lot; he was a member of the Bund, the General Jewish Workers'

Union, and argued that this socialist organization promoted protection of all workers' rights. Thus, in their broad-minded way, Bundists indirectly combatted anti-Semitism. They were not Zionists, however, and opposed religious orthodoxy.

As Sydney read socialist works, his Zionist views evolved and he shared his readings with his brothers. All three came around to the Jewish Labor Bundist point of view. But at their *gimnazjum* (high school) where right-wing Polish politics were in vogue, it was risky to express leftist views. The few times they did, they were beaten.

In 1930, Sydney enrolled at Masaryk University in Brno, Czechoslovakia, to study mechanical engineering. Two years later, my father followed to study at the university's new medical school. By the time my father arrived, Sydney was active with the student arm of the Communist Party, which protested laws enacted to curtail workers' rights. He demonstrated and spoke at Communist Party meetings.

My father and Sydney shared a room until Sydney was expelled for his subversive politics. This was not advantageous for my father, who was steadier and more practical than his impetuous older brother. My father applied as a transfer student to the prestigious, six-hundred-year-old University of Vienna. He must have anticipated anti-Semitism, but probably reasoned that since it was everywhere, why not endure it at the most esteemed institution possible? And in the best location. The University of Vienna's medical school was as powerful a lure as Vienna itself.

The Medical School of the University of Vienna was renowned not only for its professors and research but its resources. One of its most treasured institutions was the Josephinum, an 18th-century military surgeons' academy that became a medical museum. There, students could study hundreds of Baroque anatomical models crafted from wax. Commissioned by Habsburg Emperor Joseph II, they were used to train medical students in an era when dissection was dangerous because the spread of disease was not well-understood and in some countries autopsies were illegal. The collection was also open to the public, to convey the beauty of a healthy human body and to encourage citizens to keep fit. Tandler was in sync with imperial preferences of the past.

My father must have been awestruck when he arrived on campus and first beheld the exquisitely detailed wax models. Fashioned in Florence, these edifying works of art had been transported over the Alps by mules and shipped along the Danube to their destination. The models were unlike others, especially those in England, which were grisly renderings of the corpses of prisoners. Instead, the Italian/Viennese models celebrated life and all its variety. When I saw them in 2016, I was fascinated by the artist's ability to combine beauty and accuracy—his respect for all that was human, for humanity itself. My father would have been, too. Perhaps he visited the models to take his mind off the constant harassment of the fascists.

Another draw would have been the world's then-largest collection of obstetric models. Early on, that specialty, as well as pathology, intrigued my father. The wax models my father would have most admired were two "Anatomical" or "Medicean Venuses," a brunette and a blonde. The latter—which even had eyelashes, a pearl necklace, and a gold headband—resembled Botticelli's goddess of beauty. She lay in her glass case, her chest and abdomen split open to reveal her lungs, digestive system, and reproductive organs. Her serene face and tilted-back head depicted sensual beauty. Perhaps the artist intended her to embody a passion and drive that had unwillingly succumbed to death. Eros and Thanatos; love, sexuality, creativity, the lifeforce in tension with aggression, sadism, violence, and death.

Trying to grasp my father's life-threatening experience of violence, my husband and I watched *Julia* again and replayed the riot scene several times. The specter of faculty and students too stunned to utter cries for help, abused and even thrown to their deaths, was so hard to take that we muted the DVD and watched the scene in slow motion, unable to tolerate the atrocities any longer without some sensory relief. Details that had slipped by quickly now became distinct; I realized that an "Anatomy" sign on a door marked the entrance to Tandler's amphitheater.

What does it take to bottle up memories of persecution and bloodshed? How had my father's experience, which would forever remain unknown, affected him in the long-term? Had my father not been exposed to such persecution in his early twenties, had he been able to just study under peaceful, collegial circumstances, would he have lived longer?

And yet, as family secrets go, this humiliation might not seem that terrible; my father was persecuted and traumatized just because he was a Jew and wanted to be a doctor. Nevertheless, he survived and achieved his wish to practice medicine. But as he continued to confront prejudice and persecution, his experiences in Vienna and the losses he endured could have had a cumulative effect. So did suppressing his memories of them. I know. I'm sure, because if we have *neshamah*, the Hebrew word for soul or breath, then mine is a feather brushing my father's. I feel his suffering.

My father was a handsome man with broad shoulders, strong arms, and an irresistible smile. But besides the harm rickets had done to his bones, my father had suffered a minor injury that had disfigured his right index finger. Most of the nail was missing. That, and the pain I imagined when it was torn off, had upset me since I was very little. When I was about eight, I asked what happened. We were sitting on the couch in our living room. Perhaps he had been watching *The Huntley-Brinkley Report*, or was relaxing as the great golf champion Jack Nicklaus putted on a green.

"My finger got caught in a window," he said blandly.

"But Mommy told me your finger got hurt when a door slammed on it." My mortified father said nothing.

Even then, I believed neither explanation.

I held my father's hand and said, "Daddy, I'll kiss it and make it better."

A few weeks after the March riot in Tandler's amphitheater, the university held disciplinary hearings. It found that despite a ban on campus, socialist students parading placards with party logos had provoked Austro-fascist students. Someone had placed in a display box an unapproved poster encouraging Jews to fight against Hitler, the "Jews-Murderer." That further aggravated the Austro-fascists. But two Jewish students testified that Austro-fascist students had stolen the key to the display box and pinned up the poster. The rector ordered locks installed at the entrances to the lecture halls.

My father and his friends must have anticipated recurrences of the violence anyway. After all, for centuries, officers of the law could not prosecute university marauders. The police and fire department were not allowed on hallowed campus soil. Ambulances could only receive victims who were escorted outside the university buildings after being beaten bloody.

The measures the rector took to prevent further trouble after the raid in Tandler's amphitheater proved weak and ineffective. Another invasion of Tandler's lecture hall occurred on May 10, 1933. A German newspaper article described students climbing out second-floor windows and escaping down a ladder. The ladder was provided only because passersby twice entreated a truck full of firefighters to rescue the locked-in students. The first time, out of respect for the university's jurisdiction, truncheon-wielding police bludgeoned the firefighters. Incredible and warped, yet it happened. The students' wounds at the hands of their Austro-fascist classmates were so serious that they required treatment at the emergency room. The wounded foreign students were Americans, Hungarians, and Poles. *Poles*? Was my father among them?

The Americans, three Jewish medical students from New York, returned home. According to a May 21, 1933 report in *The New York Times*, they had asked the American consul if badges to distinguish themselves from other students would protect them. They were advised that such identification would make matters worse because all American students in Vienna were Jewish, so wearing a badge would have invited an attack. Another group of students protested to the American Legion that Nazis always placed guards at every gate so that no Jew could escape. "The Jewish students just had to stay and fight," one young man said, "and when there were injuries reported, as a rule it was because some student had leapt from a high window to escape a beating."

I turned away from the papers and stared out my office window toward the patina cornice of a building across Broadway. I looked up at the pale blue sky, but saw only my father with other Jewish students at a long table dissecting a cadaver. Born left-handed, my father's elementary school teachers had insisted, as was the custom then, on training him to write with his right hand. Thankfully, he was ambidextrous. Dawid confidently makes incisions into a cadaver. He and his classmates are leaning over the corpse when suddenly they hear the blackguards' wild screams. Knowing their scalpels are no match for the intruders, the students grab the legs of their chairs to meet the charging, club-wielding Austro-fascists.

"Hey Jew, want to become a surgeon?" yells one brute. My father does not answer. "Here. We can help."

The bully pins Dawid's right hand to the dissecting table and the other smashes his index finger. They laugh and jeer, then turn to crush light bulbs with their bats and hoot some more as they approach the next table. Dawid and Munio run toward a window, fling it open, and climb onto the ledge. It is not that far down from the second floor, or so Dawid hopes. He clings to the sill, but fears the thugs will slam the window on his other hand. He lets go and hits the ground.

When Dawid opens his eyes he is in the infirmary.

A doctor approaches. "Frenkel? Frenkel. Hello there. You passed out, but you're going to be alright." He smiles reassuringly. "I've stitched up your index finger. The bone is bruised, and will take time to heal. You may lose the nail, but you'll have full use of your finger and hand. You'll be able to perform countless operations, if surgery is the specialty you choose."

The riots and persecution at the medical school diminished during the early summer semester of 1934 because of the short Austrian Civil War. Under Chancellor Dollfuss's "Fatherland regime," the university took more efficient measures against anti-Semitic terrorism and the Austro-fascist students quieted down because their side now had the power. Tandler went on sabbatical to teach in Shanghai. When news of the Austrian Civil War reached him in the spring of 1934, out of loyalty to his fellow Social Democrats and ignoring the personal consequences, he returned only to be arrested. In prison he joined 2,000 other Socialist Democrats, because the new regime branded all public officials associated with that party as criminals.

Dollfuss was assassinated in the summer of 1934 and succeeded by Chancellor Kurt von Schuschnigg. Although an Austro-fascist, his main concern was to preserve Austria's independence and to thwart Hitler's ambition to absorb Austria into Nazi Germany. But by early 1936, Schuschnigg had yielded to Hitler and German Nazi Party pressures. Vienna was but a faded shadow of its brief Social Democrat past.

Forced out of the university, Tandler left Vienna for an assignment in Moscow to show the Soviets his healthcare model. There he suffered a fatal stroke at age sixty-seven. Word was that distress over the executions of sixteen political plotters exacerbated his atherosclerosis. My father would have been aware of the unjust dismissals in Vienna, as well as Tandler's sudden powerlessness—despite having accomplished so much on behalf of his fellow citizens. They had rejected him, persecuting him because of his politics or Jewish heritage or both. Where were the moderates? Were there any moderates?

During those tumultuous times, where did my father turn to find solace and spiritual strength? In one of the oldest squares in Vienna west of Kärntner Strasse, the city's shopping district equivalent of New York's Fifth Avenue: Neuer Markt. At its center stands a fountain with a bronze Poseidon-like figure sitting on the rim of a basin, where several other statues keep him company. Each represents a tributary of the Danube overseen by a goddess-like figure on the pedestal in the middle. The Roman personification of foresight, Providentia, was believed to forecast and safeguard the supply of clean water vital to Vienna. During my 2016 trip to Europe, I listened to the burble of the splashing water and watched the play of light on the well-proportioned bronze forms. Designed and built in the late 1730s by Georg Raphael Donner, this Baroque work of art bears his name.

This was not the first time I gazed at the Donnerbrunnen. In the summer of 1961 my father presented a paper at a meeting of the International Society of Sterility Fellows in Vienna. My parents built an itinerary around the event and brought my sisters and me, ages twelve, seven, and five, to Europe with them. It was a great moment for my father to deliver a speech in the city of the university where he had been summarily dismissed.

Afterward, he took us to visit one of his favorite spots: the magnificent Donnerbrunnen. I distinctly remember that one of the bronze statues on the edge of the basin—of a muscular young fisherman straddling the rim of the pool and hovering over the water about to pierce a salmon with his trident—especially interested my father.

"Oh, after all these years he still hasn't gotten in," quipped my father.

I thought he was being silly. "Daddy, it's a statue."

The statue my father had wisecracked about represented the river Traun and its bounty. To my father, I thought in retrospect, it probably was a toned, wondrous example of the human form striving to achieve acceptance against the odds. It was about bias and rejection despite being qualified.

In 1903, the Jewish community commissioned a well-known architect to design an octagonal sanctuary on campus for Jewish patients. Over thirty years later, my father sits in the intimate synagogue in Court 6 near the Allgemeines Krankenhaus, the hospital of the Medical School of Vienna. He gazes at the vaulted roof thinking of the many dimensions of Tandler's brilliance. How quickly yet precisely Tandler had sketched illustrations on the blackboard, telling his class, "I prefer you to see an inaccurate diagram which portrays the correct idea rather than an accurate diagram which gives you the wrong idea." His renowned three-volume textbook, *Anatomie*, also spared students superfluous detail.

I believe my father wanted to be like Tandler—to see through the clutter, to perceive the big picture. To make a broad contribution and yet also experience the satisfaction and personal nature of clinical practice.

If ever there was a healer of the world, it had been Tandler.

Tikkun Olam, Tikkun Olam. Heal the world, repair the world.

But the prayer house's angular roof points to a heaven of which my father is increasingly uncertain. Above the ark and along the friezes of the eight walls was carved an inscription of Psalm 16, "A Michtam of David." "The Lord is the portion of mine inheritance and of my cup:

thou maintainest my lot....Thou will shew me the path of life..." (Psalm 16, lines 5 and 11.)

Where is God when a man like Tandler is banished from the country he loves and dies agitated and disillusioned? Where is God now for any Jew? Yet these are not the questions to ask, for Dawid knows humans are the source of the problem.

In a mournful haze my father wanders along the Ringstrasse. The beauty of the street, its trees, and the statues Dawid had so admired when he arrived seem to have vanished. The Fascists are winning, he thinks morosely. Now that the Social Democrats are out, there is no one to check them. It's all going to fall apart. He arrives at the Kärntner Strasse and quickly passes the opera house. The Aryans' circular avenue, their crescent-shaped seat of power, their blasted Teutonic Ring Cycle, their twirling, looping waltzes—where would they all lead him?

Dawid finds himself at his beloved Donnerbrunnen staring at the statue of the virile young man about to spear a fish. His striving body, his flexed arms and taut back, his leg ever-dangling on the outside of the fountain's rim.

On the periphery in perpetuity, Dawid thinks. For the first time, he fully recognizes the futility of trying to get in. The Herculean effort—no, the Sisyphean folly—of struggling for acceptance here.

Thou will shew me the path...

To prosper, my father would need an Appian Way straight out of German-speaking Europe where Jews were no longer welcome.

Chapter Three

Anschluss and Absolutorium

On March 12, 1938, the German army strutted into Austria. Chancellor Schuschnigg's government collapsed and Hitler arrived in Vienna two days later. He triumphantly toured the city in an open motorcade while delirious crowds lined the streets and welcomed him as a returning native son and hero. He declared the "entry of my homeland into the German Reich" from the balcony of the Hofburg Imperial Palace. Just beyond, in the public space known as Heldenplatz, 250,000 ethnic German Viennese gathered to celebrate. A parade that included the German Eighth Army, Sturmabteilung (SA), and Schutzstaffel (SS) units marched around the Ringstrasse accompanied by rolling tanks and overhead fighter planes.

During this so-called nonviolent annexation of Austria, the Nazis arrested 70,000 potential political opponents—Social Democrats, Communists, and Jews. The Northwest Railway Station in Leopoldstadt, the Jewish quarter, was converted into a makeshift concentration camp until those incarcerated could be transferred to Dachau Concentration Camp. Austria's 182,000 Jews—166,000 of whom lived in Vienna—were in despair.

The Nazis closed the university and usurped the administration. They immediately expelled Jewish and politically undesirable faculty. Every few days, the Nazis issued new orders concerning Jews; they could enter most buildings one day, but not the Anatomy Institute the next, for example. Jewish students wondered whether they were forbidden to go to the library, borrow books, or attend lectures. Until June, a Jewish student who had passed all his or her exams did not know whether a degree would be granted. My father was among those in limbo.

While my father agonized over his future, fascists gloated over the suicides of Jews, whose bodies filled overflowing morgues; Jewish suicides had increased twenty-fold since February. Cadavers, usually in short supply for anatomy class dissections, now exceeded demand. Austro-fascists resented that the Jews did not donate corpses of their own and perceived them as always ready to cut up Christian ones. They did not know that after death, Jewish law forbade bodies to be desecrated. If they had known, they would not have cared. Did they relish getting their hands on the corpses, hating Jews so much that they delighted in defiling insentient ones?

My father must have suffered crippling disappointment that made him feel old. And yet he was not quite twenty-five. In fact, his twenty-fifth birthday was a few days ahead, on March 17. His uncles Max and Simon, and brother Sydney, who had returned from hiking in the Alps, would have planned a little celebration. Had my father called his uncles, owners of the Hotel Continental at the gateway to Leopoldstadt, his distraught Uncle Simon would no doubt have described riots outside the Café Continental. Leopoldstadt was rife with looters and he would have advised my father to stay away. Now Sydney was doing everything possible to get out, braving long lines outside foreign consulates and applying for multiple visas.

The university remained closed for a month. In late April, the Ministry of Education limited Jewish students to 2 percent of the student body, effective the coming semester. This meant that 2,230 Jewish students—42 percent of the entire university student body—would be expelled.

When classes resumed on April 25, the Medical School was under the leadership of a new dean, Eduard Pernkopf, the Nazi former Chair of Anatomy II. Pernkopf reopened teaching by delivering a speech about

National Socialism and science, which he presented in the Anatomy I lecture hall. What a travesty it must have seemed to my father and his friend, Munio, as they sat in the auditorium and watched this Nazi stride through Tandler's professorial entrance. Then they were forced to look at a large photograph of Hitler that replaced a portrait of Nobelist Julius Wagner-Jauregg on the wall behind the podium. I have no doubt that to them, the red flags with spidery swastikas flanking the podium utterly degraded the dignity of the medical school.

Wearing SA regalia complete with the standard Brown Shirt uniform and kepi cap of Nazi stormtroopers, Pernkopf raised his arm in a "Heil Hitler" salute. With alacrity, the audience responded in kind. Then he articulated with pomp and triumphal tones that National Socialism must permeate education and science. He declared the merger of the two Anatomy Institutes. Freedom in the liberal sense leads to chaos, which is impermissible, Pernkopf stated, according to the weekly magazine, *Wien Klin Wochenschr.* The only useful goal of art and science, he said, is to serve the nation. "All disciplines in the medical faculty will work on the problem of race," he promised, and the curriculum will change to include race physiology, race psychology, and race pathology. The role of medicine in the new state was "to further the propagation of the fit" and "eliminate the unfit and defective" by controlling marriage, forbidding "breeding by individuals who do not belong together properly," and sterilizing the genetically inferior. My liberal-minded father, future infertility expert who believed everyone was entitled to be a parent, would have turned red with anger.

Like Tandler, Pernkopf had authored an anatomical atlas, which he began with four watercolor artists in 1933. The first volume, complete with swastikas and SS lightning bolts embedded in the illustrators' signatures, was published in 1937. With his new position of power and Tandler gone, Pernkopf could easily usurp the anatomy textbook market. The impact on medicine and the ethics of teaching with the complete set of this atlas, released in 1960, has been debated in many articles and books. Incredibly, the SS symbols were not airbrushed out until a few years later.

Pernkopf's proclamations would not have taken my father and his friends completely by surprise. They had heard a few weeks earlier that Pernkopf's first act as the new dean was to demand that all faculty declare their ethnic lineage—either as non-Aryan or Aryan—and swear loyalty to Hitler. Pernkopf sent the list of those who refused to the university administration, which dismissed them. Seventy-seven percent—153 out of 197 members of the medical faculty, including Nobel Prize winners—were purged, expelled either because they were Jewish or for political reasons.

The expunged included Professors Gabor Nobl, a skin and syphilis specialist, and Edmund Nobel, a pediatrician. Both shot themselves. Nobl shot his wife, too. Wilhelm Knoepfelmacher, a noted psychiatrist and head of the children's clinic, tried and failed to poison himself. After treatment at the Allgemeines Krankenhaus he had a stroke.

Nine others were my father's professors.

Arnold Durig, Professor of Physiology, was forced out. Professor of Medical Chemistry Otto Fürth, head of the Medical Chemical Department, suffered the same fate. Docent for internal medicine Leo Hess was expelled because he was a Jew. So was Heinrich Kahr (né Katz), Geburtshilfe und Gynakologie (obstetrics and gynecology) Professor Extraordinarius. Heinrich Neumann, Ohrenheilkunde (throat) Professor Extraordinarius, was arrested and thrown out. Professor of Pharmakologie Ernst Peter Pick, former Dean of the Medical Faculty, would be expelled later in May. Finally, Robert Willheim, Docent für Medizinische Chemie (medicinal chemistry), "*Raus.*" Out.

One of the Nazi faculty to thrive under the new regime was my father's Professor of Internal Medicine, Hans Eppinger, Jr., whom Ivy remembered had disappointed my father. Why then had Eppinger been hovering over my dad as he treated patients? I wanted to verify what he looked like, so I embarked on another digital hunt. I did not recognize images of the spectacled bald man with an unappetizing, asymmetrical mouth and chin. Neither did Ivy. The photo on my father's office wall was of someone else.

Because of his knowledge of the liver, Eppinger was held in such high esteem that the Soviets sought him out in 1936 to treat Stalin. The following year, Dowager Queen Marie of Romania became Eppinger's patient. Whether he appealed to the powerful or not, Eppinger's achievements were stained by his harsh and peculiar character. A kleptomaniac, he stole instruments from operating rooms and tore pages from journals in the university library, from which he was eventually banned. Eppinger also reputedly stole case histories and specimens from other physicians for his research, and had to be supervised while watching operations in case he walked off with instruments. In the lecture theater he once shocked students with his brutality by announcing a patient's end-stage nephritis and reducing him to tears. Nevertheless, Eppinger taught at the medical school from 1933 until 1945. Ivy's recollection of my father's disappointment was certainly confirmed.

My father's medical degree and professional fate were now in the hands of Nazis. It was anyone's guess whether they would pass an unfamiliar foreign student who was Jewish. To receive his doctorate, he had to be granted *Absolutorium*—proof that he had successfully completed the required semesters. The soonest he could receive *Absolutorium* would be late June, which must have seemed an eternity away. In the terror and turmoil, surely my father would have been desperate not to forsake almost six years of toil and to emerge from the chaos with his medical degree. Perhaps he felt guilty that his main concern was obtaining his degree when other Jews were losing their livelihoods—and even their lives. But it seems he had no choice but to stay. Were he to flee, even with his fine credentials, he might be discriminated against elsewhere. Circumstances might be even worse than at the University of Vienna, although that was hard to imagine.

At some point, however, my father learned that as a Polish national, even though a Jew, he was exempt from the Nuremberg Laws, which since 1935 had been gradually stripping Jews of their civil rights.

The next few weeks were grimmer and tougher to bear for Vienna's Jews. The Jewish Telegraphic Agency online archives documented the mayhem and persecution that April, including the treatment of Vienna's Chief Rabbi, Dr. Israel Taglicht. Nazi youths had surrounded the rabbi and forced him to picket two Jewish firms. For a quarter of an hour, the seventy-six-year-old rabbi had stood before a small Jewish shop on the Praterstrasse holding a placard above his head with an anti-Semitic slur. Then the thugs shoved and beat him for five blocks until they reached the Hotel Continental. In front of Café Continental, they again forced Dr. Taglicht to hold up the sign. To see their much-loved, honorable rabbi persecuted would have been shocking to the Lifschützes and Fränkels, as it was to all Viennese Jews. It was probably not a coincidence that the humiliation occurred within view of the very café Theodor Herzl, the father of Zionism, had frequented. The abuse ended when a patron stepped outside and volunteered to take the Chief Rabbi's place, which the mob allowed.

Only two months before, in February, small Nazi groups had roamed Leopoldstadt but the police had outnumbered them. Although his congregants felt nervous about political developments, Dr. Taglicht claimed the Jewish community had "the fullest confidence" in Chancellor Schuschnigg, as quoted in the Jewish Telegraphic Agency. "We do not believe the position of the Austrian Jews has already become as dangerous as for the Jews in Germany," he added. Why not, I thought furiously. The Nuremberg Laws had been in effect in Germany for two-and-a-half years and now Austria was part of the Third Reich. I wondered whether Dr. Sigmund Freud, born in Leopoldstadt and still living and practicing near the university, thought the rabbi was in denial. In June 1938, Freud fled for England. Taglicht followed a year later.

The vehement message the Nazis now sent by humiliating the chief rabbi of Austria's greatest city with its large population of Jews had far more force than sporadic anti-Jewish boycotts. It was clear that no Jew—neither the elderly nor helpless children nor anyone else, rich or poor—was exempt from the Nazis' savagery.

When I think of what my young father had seen and felt in medical school and during the *Anschluss*, when I contemplate what restraint it took to never hint at the traumatic, life-threatening experiences he must have had, or the toll it took to suppress those memories and emotions, I feel wobbly. It is the same kind of blinking, unsteady shock I experienced when the Space Shuttle Challenger burst into flames, when the Twin Towers fell, and when Trump was first elected president. But I witnessed these catastrophes from afar and I was much older than my father was. My dad's life was in direct danger for five years in his early twenties.

It must have been very difficult for my usually optimistic father to accept the sudden fall of his institution of learning and witness the monstrous plight of Austrian Jews. He made his assessment, a grave prognosis for Europe and for humanity. As I absorbed the details of the *Anschluss* in Vienna, I understood for the first time why this determined and quietly hopeful man had taught my sisters and me the value of pressing on, no matter what. When studying fatigued us and we still didn't know the material cold, he would command, "You will be tired later. If I wake you in the middle of the night and ask a question, answer it first. *Then* you can be scared." He learned this lesson in grit during and just after the *Anschluss* in order to pass his orals even as Jews were being beaten and Austria and Europe were falling apart: If my concentration flags, I will push myself to focus; if afraid, I will postpone my fear. He allowed nothing to stop him from graduating and getting out.

Besides my mother and us, my father's great love was practicing medicine and caring for his patients in accordance with the Hippocratic Oath:

> I swear by Apollo Healer, by Asclepius, by Hygieia, by Panacea, and by all the gods and goddesses, making them my witnesses, that I will carry out, according to my ability and judgment, this oath and this indenture.

Rumors had circulated through the medical school that the Nazi authorities would quietly drop the Hippocratic Oath from the graduation ceremony. Some students speculated that if the Nazis did offer the oath, they would forbid non-Aryans to take it. For days, the campus had been fraught with the far more disturbing concern that the June graduation ceremony would be reserved only for Aryans. These rumors turned out to be false. European foreign students—Jewish or not—were to graduate on June 28, 1938. And Pernkopf read the pledge.

I suppose my father thought omitting the oath would have been consistent with Pernkopf's warped philosophy of medical science and its purpose. But how did my father feel, knowing there would be no joyous festivities—no proud parents and relatives, no flowers, no celebratory dinner? Maybe my father was glad his parents would be absent because they could not have tolerated the compulsory Nazi salutes at the beginning and end of the ceremony. Nor could have Sydney, who had already crossed the Alps, arrived in Mussolini's Italy, and was miraculously working with an Italian engineering firm in Milan. Mussolini—Austria's supposed protector on whom Schuschnigg had depended to keep Hitler at bay—was now indebted to Hitler after having waged a misbegotten war against Ethiopia. Sydney was safe, at least for a while.

> Into whatsoever houses I enter, I will enter to help the sick, and I will abstain from all intentional wrong-doing and harm, especially from abusing the bodies of man or woman, bond or free.

What was it like for my father to hear these lines of the Hippocratic Oath from a Nazi whose voice sullied those very words? To receive his medical degree he had to shake hands with Pernkopf. Sometimes, under stress, Lefties instinctively extend the wrong hand. But my father had become a surgeon and surgeons know how to handle stress. He probably just wanted the ceremony to end and to have his medical degree in hand.

I know from my mother that my father did not like to hang his medical degree in either of his offices. But one day a patient had asked why my father's degree was not on the wall, and from then on he had to display it. My mother had saved a laminated, framed version of my dad's degree and the original degree, a yellowed, dusty board with the university's seal embossed on a paper fleurette with the image of Sapientia. The Roman goddess of wisdom held a book in her left hand and a scepter in her right. Underneath, in Latin, it said:

> ...after the customary examinations in the theory and practice of medicine confer on the distinguished gentleman Dawid Frenkel born in Lwów Poland the title in honor of Doctor of Medicine and the right to exercise the art of medicine by virtue of this document as confirmed by the seal of the University.

My father had stayed the course under the most challenging conditions. But next to the seal, the administration had stamped a prohibition in red letters stating that my father unconditionally relinquished the right to practice medicine in the region formerly known as Austria. Not because he was a Jew, but because he was a citizen of a foreign country. This was how, since 1912, the Austrians had controlled the medical market; they safeguarded their incomes by getting rid of the competition. The fascists enthusiastically perpetuated the restriction in the name of the *Reichsstatthalter* by applying it to Austrian Jews.

Forever after, through their signatures, the Nazis hovered over my father—intruding upon and plaguing him as he saw patients. They besmirched and perpetually branded my father's hard-earned, cherished diploma. But they did not blemish his career.

Although he intended to be a practitioner, my father hoped someday to pass along what his professors, especially Tandler, had taught him. And not just to sons. The progressive in him believed firmly that women in the professions benefited everyone. As I learned from an audio tape my cousin Anita shared of her interview with my uncle Sydney, our grandmother Michaela was as capable as my grandfather and her hotelier uncles. As a housewife, her quick mind was hardly put to full use and my father disliked wasted potential.

Back at his rooms packing his clothes, books, and degree, my father must have been devastated, loathing what Vienna had become. And yet, it was impossible for him to expunge his appreciation for its culture. Here he had achieved what he had wanted, what he had worked so hard for. But he was not free to practice medicine where he most wanted to.

What remained to admire? Where could he feel comfortable and safe? Did he *ever* feel safe?

My father arrived in Lwów's elegant train station. Built during the waning days of the Austro-Hungarian Empire, the palatial 1904 Art Nouveau station had proclaimed Lemberg the hub of several important trade routes. The grandeur of twin glass and steel arches—two onion-shaped structures covering the platforms like bosoms of southeastern

Poland—greeted my father as he alighted his train. The bent steel, balustrades, and railings resembled those of the Paris Métro.

Whereas once Lwów's station might have filled my father with awe, upon his return the whole city would have seemed provincial, a poor imitation of Vienna. In fact, when Lwów was absorbed into the Austro-Hungarian Empire, an imperial mandate required that no new building could be taller than any in Vienna. Although Poland's third-largest city with a population of 340,000 Poles, Ukrainians, and Jews, Lwów offered a diluted version of Vienna's urbanity. Still, he was coming home.

The lilting Austrian and more guttural German accents of persecuted and expelled Jews echoed throughout the cavernous station as these displaced, agitated, and forlorn refugees tried to orient themselves and secure lodgings. Many would rely on the beneficence of their *östlichen* (eastern) brethren—144,000 Lwówian Jews.

Weaving through the crowd, my father passed by the entrance of the First-Class waiting hall modeled on the ambiance of an English gentleman's club but furnished with dark, luxurious Viennese-style furniture similar to the Wiener Werkstätte. So, too, would he have disregarded Second Class, really a 19th-century Galicianer living room of leather seating, chandeliers, gilt mirrors, and a portrait of the Archduke Karl Ludwig, brother of Emperor Franz Josef. The Third-Class waiting room, decorated in the all-wood Zakopane style named for the Polish mountain resort, a nod to the motifs of Swiss and Austro-Hungarian chalets, might even have irked my father. Was there no escape from Teutonic influences?

His taxi approaches his childhood home on quaint, sunny Rejtana Street in the heart of the city. I imagine him stepping out next to the odd, gothic-inspired structure that houses the Bagatela Cabaret next to his parents' home, and the small Belvedere Hotel two stories above. Just beyond, my father glimpses through No. 5's first-floor windows, the proprietor of the grocery and convenience shop. My father waves, enters his father's small apartment building, and climbs one flight of stairs.

My grandmother Michaela rushes to the door, her large blue eyes twinkling. "Dolek!" she exclaims, using a Polish diminutive for Dawid. "Thanks be to God you are home!" After they hug, she steps back to admire the son who most resembles her. Both are so fair skinned that they cannot tan, although her hair is blonder and frames a wider face with a shorter, rounder nose.

My grandfather Ojzer rises from the dinner table and they shake hands. "Dr. Frenkel, my son. I am proud of you."

Milek, "the little one," approaches. Gentle and deferential, he greets and congratulates his older brother. Milek, too, will soon earn an advanced degree in civil engineering from Lwów Polytechnic.

Except for the architectural details of the station and the house, and the facts about Milek's education, all this is conjecture.

The Soviets did, however, gut the interior of Lviv's magnificent train station of which there is a record, and in so doing erased part of the culture of the eastern Austro-Hungarian Empire and pre-war Poland. When Ed and I arrived there in 2016 from Kraków by overnight train at dawn, we, too, walked from the platform through the palatial building to the main entrance. There was no hint of the magnificent interiors described above; post-Stalinist spaces and walls were filled with advertisements. From serfdom to enlightened despotism to proletarian ideals to fascism to communism to capitalism—all were reflected in this gateway between the East and West.

Like the lost architectural gems and the cultures they embodied, the circumstances of my father's return to Lwów and his departure are mysteries. I do not know if he came home because he wanted to, or if his parents beseeched him to. Did they try, like so many other Jews, to get visas but were refused because of the strict immigration quotas for Polish Jews in the United States? Even if Ojzer and Michaela saw the danger, where else could they have gone? They had a nephew in New York, but apparently he was unable to help. Maybe they considered joining Ozjer's niece, Golda, who had made *aliyah* to Palestine, but thought life there too rugged.

The events that unfolded by late September 1938—the discouraging news of the failed negotiations between Hitler and the president of Czechoslovakia, Hitler, in accordance with the Munich Agreement, adding the Sudetenland, the western part of Czechoslovakia, to southern Germany—would only have buttressed my father's point of view. If

Hitler took the rest of Czechoslovakia, Poland would fall next. Then, in early November, came *Kristallnacht*, the two-day pogrom in Germany during which synagogues and Jewish-owned shops were torched.

After my father's experience in medical school, and because of what he learned and the political climate on campus, it must have been abundantly clear that he had to get out of Europe. As a man of science, he acted on his diagnosis: the continent was moribund, infected with virulent anti-Semitism, Nazism, and other authoritarian regimes. He did not foresee a cure anytime soon.

Chapter Four

An Arrangement

"Mom, who is Rose Frenkel?" my oldest sister Michelle asked, holding a U.S. Army ID card that listed Rose as my father's beneficiary. My sisters and I were sorting through our father's papers in his home office, just off the kitchen. It was 1971, about a year after he died. I was sixteen.

After a long pause, my mother replied from the kitchen with studied nonchalance, "Oh, you know, your father was married before he met me."

What? I thought. How can this be? My sisters and I stared wide-eyed at one another, all six arched eyebrows inherited from our mother raised even higher.

Standing in the office doorway wiping her hands with a dish towel, she continued, "Your father married Rose in Poland. She was the black sheep of the family that owned Ratner's."

"Ratner's? The dairy restaurant on the Lower East Side?" Michelle said.

There were actually two dairy restaurants with that name famous for their kosher *milichg* (Yiddish for dairy) meals. The larger establishment was on Delancey Street, the other on Second Avenue at 7th Street. Both served delicious blintzes, smoked salmon, whitefish, and soups.

"When Daddy got here, he found out Rose had a boyfriend," my mother continued. "She assumed your father was such a greenhorn that he would front for them." After a pause she blurted, "Her boyfriend was a gangster."

This moment would go on to hover over me like the scent of steaming borscht with sour cream.

"When your father finished his residency, he enlisted in the Army and hired a detective," my mother added. The private eye gathered evidence of Rose's adultery. They divorced in 1946 when my father returned.

"Did they have children?" Michelle wanted to know.

"No."

My mother returned to the kitchen. That was all we were told about Rose.

As a young girl, I had reluctantly accepted my enigmatic father's silence. His right to privacy overrode my desire to know. When he died, his knowledge disappeared with him. During my young adult years, I could not defy him, even posthumously. Intellectually I made peace with the void, but emotionally it was impossible to accept.

In 1991, when I was in my thirties, the movie *Bugsy* was released. I became obsessed with it, not fully understanding why. Directed by Barry Levinson and starring Warren Beatty and Annette Bening, it told the story of the notoriously brutal Lower East Side Jewish gangster Benjamin Siegel, who envisioned and founded Las Vegas on a sand dune in the Nevada desert. I asked a friend who had grown up on the Lower East Side about Ratner's, which by then had closed. She said she knew it well and had eaten there many times. I revealed that my father had a first wife who was a gangster moll and wondered out loud whether she could have met her lover at her family's restaurant.

"That would fit," said my friend, "there was a backroom, a former speakeasy where they all hung out."

The "Kosher Nostra," in other words.

Looking back, I think I unconsciously suspected that Rose's lover was high up in the Jewish mafia. I sensed that my father never told us about Rose because any connection to the mob was dangerous. Here are the facts, as later found in documents my mother curated: According to their marriage certificate, Rose and my father were married on February

26, 1939. The witness on my father's side was Dr. Ignace Lifschütz, whom I had never heard of but who shared my grandmother Michaela's maiden name. The building where Rose had stayed was on the same boulevard as the opera house, and her host's backyard abutted those of the houses on Rejtana Street, where my grandparents lived. Literally around the corner from the Fränkel home, Rose was the girl next door… and yet not.

A yellowed envelope contained a July 1943 letter in Rose's handwriting and a small, high contrast photograph of her and my father dancing. In profile, Rose watches as he stares at the camera. On the back, she wrote: "Think of us often. Loads of love, Dolek—Rose." On the upper right corner, in the same ink my father added the date: March 11, 1939. From this, I surmised that soon after their wedding they parted. An accompanying note confirmed Rose's receipt of a check. She added that Sally's husband had arrived and that my father could write to him care of Ratner's. I had no idea who these people were.

Rose sailed back to New York City from Le Havre on April 19, 1939, on the luxurious ocean liner *Île de France*. She came home to 170 Second Avenue in the heart of the "Jewish Rialto" (the former Yiddish theater district in lower Manhattan). Three blocks from the Second Avenue Ratner's, it was next door to the Yiddish theater known as the Commodore that in the 1960s became the legendary Fillmore East rock and roll venue.

According to travel visa stamps inside my father's 1939 Polish passport, he went to the French Consulate in Lwów on March 16 and got permission to stay in France as a tourist until the end of the year. The next visa was stamped the following day, my dad's twenty-sixth birthday, at the German consulate in Kraków. I amused myself with the idea that he could have passed by my Kraków-born teenage mother strolling with her parents and their German Pointer Arko on the Planty, the park that surrounds the Old Town.

Three days later, my father entered Germany at Beuthen and exited within a few hours at Herbesthal, Belgium. In Paris on April 11 he got his Polish marriage certificate translated into English and court certified.

How and when my father got from France to the Western Hemisphere, what his destination was, and what happened when he arrived were much murkier because the crucial date of my father's departure was illegible. The hand of the police officer at the port of St. Nazaire must have been wobbly, or his desk uneven, because the embarkation date could have read May 6, 16, or 26. Another stamp below documented my father's arrival in Veracruz, Mexico, on May 31. To the left was a diagonal stamp: "Turista."

All my mother said about my father's voyage was that after he saved the life of someone ailing on the dock in Veracruz, he then talked his way out of returning to his ship by volunteering to work in a hospital until his American visa came through.

Rose and my father's 1942 separation agreement specified his financial obligations to Rose, which seemed excessive. That prompted a memory of my mother telling me when I was in my late teens that Rose had been vengeful; she tried to bilk him, a poor refugee just starting out, whereas she was from a well-to-do family. Interestingly, the divorce papers were missing from the file. All I could get from the Dade County, FL, court clerk was the July 1946 divorce decree, which said Rose divorced my father.

Finally, my mother had saved an October 1945 letter to my father from his girlfriend Mollie while he was serving in France. She said there had been a confrontation between Rose, her lover Joe, and his wife. But Mollie had no details and said she was discouraged.

Questions flooded my brain. Who travels to eastern Poland during the winter of 1939? What was Rose doing in Lwów? After *Kristallnacht* the preceding November, the consciousness of Jews around the world was raised by those horrific events. Could Rose have traveled to Lwów to save a Jewish man? I knew Jewish newspapers were filled with personal advertisements so that couples could be matched and Jews rescued. The fact that in Lwów Rose had stayed near the Fränkels suggested that the families knew one another. Wondering whether the marriage was arranged, I again inspected the back of the photo of my father and Rose dancing. "*Think of us often? Loads of love?*" That seemed breezy and casual, not the tone of a bride reluctantly parting from her beloved.

My mother had portrayed my father as Rose's victim, duped into a marriage for her benefit so that she could cover up her affair. He had been cheated on and, judging by the separation papers, could have been indentured to her for the rest of his life. My mother said Rose expected my father to be her cover, but from whom? Perhaps Rose's parents looked askance on her lifestyle. Had they pressured her to marry a nice Jewish boy? Did they threaten her inheritance?

I understood my father's plight and his desperation to leave Poland, but could he have married a woman without loving her? Or was he infatuated and misjudged her? Did he plan to extricate himself once he arrived here and was safe? Had he used her? Perhaps they were both using—or helping—each other. Ivy and I felt theirs was a marriage of mutual benefit, but Michelle was not so sure. None of us faulted our father for doing whatever was necessary to get out of Europe. Nevertheless, my sisters, Ed, and I endlessly discussed the circumstances and played out scenarios.

Had Rose been a gangster moll before, during, or after she married my dad? Maybe she got tired of waiting for gangster Joe, who was married, and tried to make a clean break when she traveled to Lwów but could not sustain it. Maybe she took up with Joe while my father was stranded in Mexico. Maybe, by comparison, my father was not exciting enough for her.

Uncle Sydney said Rose was a man hunter looking to marry someone with a prestigious profession, like a doctor. He said my dad was her victim, that neither he nor my father liked her, and they never lived together. But if their marriage was a sham from the start, how could my father have been the victim? If both were clear that this was an arrangement, then why did she turn on him and demand so much money in the separation agreement? I couldn't figure out the deal from Rose's point of view. She would save him, or help him save himself, and in return he would tolerate…what? Infidelity? And if he didn't cooperate, he would be indentured indefinitely? What about his life, his happiness?

Without more information, it was impossible to draw a conclusion. I would learn nothing more about Rose until further into my quest, when I connected with Rose's relatives, two of whom—I would discover—were also mine.

Until then, I struggled to reconcile these versions because I could not imagine my father being expedient. Then again, I could not imagine how far a desperate man would go to save himself.

On a frigid, late-January afternoon, my father sits alone on a bench near Wysoki Zamek, the High Castle park in the center of Lwów. My father anticipates that his route out of Europe will be complicated. He cannot see it clearly. But he must act. He asks himself: *Can I grow to love Rose? Will she love me? Could we make a go of it the way couples did back in the days of matchmakers?* Perhaps in advance of marrying, they would settle their differences, which is the meaning of "Shidduch"(arranged marriage). That was not so impossible. Young people had done so for centuries.

I am sure my father could never have imagined that his romantic life would come to this—a flat, realistic calculation, this desperate conflicted concession. Not that long ago, he must have felt the courage of a prancing wild animal, a lion, like Lwów's mascot. Now he was trapped into compromising himself.

Maybe my father, the optimist, simply hoped for the best. *I am her ticket back home and she is my ticket to freedom. Whatever happens, it's better than staying here, doomed. She's offering me a life raft I'm willing to take. I will manage somehow.*

For the last time, he descends the long staircase to the city streets below as icy and sharp winds slam the mount. After almost slipping, he makes sure to grasp the railing. At street level, he walks past Gunpowder Tower next to his *gimnazjum*, where he and his brothers had often played after school. One of several cylindrical towers along the medieval ramparts, the old city arsenal had stored grain in times of peace. Now it reminds my father of the University of Vienna Tower of Fools, an 18th-century asylum, and the lunacy of prejudice and war.

The next morning, Ojzer presses a handful of diamonds into my father's palm and clasps both his hands over his son's. Then he looks straight into my father's eyes and nods. At the train station, Michaela cannot conceal her grief. Ojzer confidently says he looks forward to being reunited and hearing in the meantime, by post, about my father's travels. Michaela grabs David's hand and says, "Dolek, remember to say the *Tefilat Haderech* (The Traveler's Prayer): 'May you guide our footsteps toward peace, and make us reach our desired destination for life, gladness, and peace. May you rescue us from the hand of every foe, ambush along the way, from robbers and wild beasts on the trip, and from all manner of punishments that assemble to come to earth."

My father hugs them as he holds back tears and says he will write as soon as possible.

Neither my mother nor Uncle Sydney could remember the name of the ship my father boarded, but both said it was well-known. The only famous refugee ship I knew of was the *MS St. Louis*; I had read about the horror of her German Jewish passengers stuck in Havana Harbor not being allowed to disembark in May 1939, her futile search afterward for a friendly port, that she was forced to return to Europe, that a third of the refugees were killed during the Holocaust. I thought it implausible that my father was on board; certainly my mother would have remembered the *St. Louis*, besides the liner had sailed from Germany not France.

On the United States Holocaust Memorial Museum's webpage I read that two more refugee ships, one French and one English, were in Havana Harbor at the same time as the *St. Louis*. The French ship was called *Flandre*. I again checked my father's passport and noticed something I had overlooked. To the right of the French departure stamp, someone had scrawled in blue ink, "*Flandre*." It was definitely not my father's handwriting—I am very familiar with his capital Fs. I was incredibly excited, but then I wondered whether my father's original destination had been Havana, not Veracruz. I determined that the French Lines owned the *Flandre* and that she was built in 1913, the year of my father's birth, and had been a hospital ship during World War I. This search was starting to seem charmed. I requested the May 1939 itinerary and manifests from the French Lines archivist. She intimated that no manifests were available, possibly because they were destroyed to protect passengers from the Nazis, but she emailed the itinerary. *Flandre* had sailed from St. Nazaire on May 16, stopped at several Spanish ports and had indeed arrived about a week later in Havana. Veracruz was her final destination. *Eureka.*

My father boards the modest liner, explores her decks and the First- and Second-Class dining and smoking rooms. He appreciates her Art Nouveau décor and is not the least bit disappointed in his tight Second-Class cabin. At dinner, he notices relatively few passengers, about one fourth the ship's capacity for over 400 people. That evening *Flandre* picks up 327 Spanish Civil War refugees at four Spanish ports, including former Prime Minister José Giral y Pereira of the Loyalist Regime.

Leaning over the deck rails, my father inhales the scent of the salty air and feels the strong sun, he admires El Morro—a 16th-century Spanish fortress perched on a promontory, its pink stone twinkling in the light. A little further in Havana Harbor looms a large, anchored ocean liner. As *Flandre* passes, my father makes out *St. Louis*, Hamburg. Small craft and rowboats encircle the ship.

After the deck hands tie up *Flandre* at the quay, some Spaniards disembark without incident. But the first Jewish refugees are turned back by immigration officials.

Flandre's passage to the Caribbean is mentioned in *The Voyage of the Damned* by Gordon Thomas and Max Morgan-Witts, which chronicled the fate of the *St. Louis*. The captain had instructions from his Nazi bosses to beat *Flandre* to Havana harbor so that the media would cover the *St. Louis* story. In addition to *St. Louis*' 907 German Jewish refugees, none of *Flandre*'s 104 Jewish passengers—nor those on a third ship, Britain's *SS Orduña*—were given asylum.

They did not know that their fates were entangled in a power struggle within the Cuban government. The Cuban president, angry that his Director-General of Immigration had excluded him from a cut of the landing certificate fees, decreed that entry to Cuba for passengers of any ship that sailed after May 5 now required written authorization from the Secretaries of State and Labor, and a $500 bond.

More insidious, however, was a carefully orchestrated Nazi publicity campaign to show the world that no country wanted Jews. The master

Nazi propagandist Joseph Goebbels sent agents in advance to Havana to foment anti-Semitism; to make Jews seem even more undesirable, the agents spread lies that many passengers were criminals. Soon Cubans saw Jewish refugees as a threat. The German agents organized protests. The crisis was timed to hit on the Pentecost, the seventh Sunday after Easter. The holiday extended over a three-day weekend, so the world was too busy commemorating the descent of the Holy Spirit upon Christ's disciples to be bothered with the fates of 1,200 Jews. German, English, and French diplomats saw no timely way to press the Cuban government to accept any passengers even though they had paid their ways in good faith.

I would never have gotten closer to the truth about my father and Rose if not for a newfound relative, Enrico Lamet (né Eric Lifschütz), who I happened upon in 2016 in the most circuitous, astonishing way. I had wondered where my father had roomed as a student, so I asked the University of Vienna historians for help. I knew from family lore that the Viennese side of my father's family, two Lifschütz great-uncles of my grandmother Michaela, had owned a large hotel but I did not know the name. During World War I, the Fränkels fled to Vienna and lived at that hotel, where Grandpa Ojzer worked and owned shares. After the war, Uncle Sydney had tried and failed for years to redeem those shares, but was vague with my sisters and me about the hotel's name and location.

The list of my father's addresses indicated that he had lived at the Hotel Continental during fall semester 1935. I was delighted to know the hotel's name until I considered that he might have moved off-campus because of the intolerable violence. The thrill fizzled further after I googled Praterstrasse 7, the Hotel Continental's address, and came virtually face-to-face with a modern skyscraper—Sofitel Stephansdom.

I found out that another hotel, the Goldenes Lamm, originally occupied the site on the corner of Taborstrasse and the Danube Canal. The gateway to Leopoldstadt, it welcomed people to the Jewish District, at the foot of the Swedenbrüche (Swedish Bridge). The four-hundred-bed Hotel Continental was built to accommodate visitors of the World Exhibition of 1873. When my great-great-uncle Maksymilian Lifschütz owned and operated it with his brother Simon, it was "the scene of a cosmopolitan way of life," on par with Vienna's other great hotels, including the Imperial Hotel where we had stayed during our 1961 trip and where Hitler had had a permanent suite.

The Hotel Continental had a colorful history. Besides its link to Herzl, a Jewish society called the Hallodri Association staged a cabaret for Purim 1902 in the hotel's ballroom while the Hall of Mirrors featured two dance orchestras. The Continental Quartet had played jazz at public tea dances during the hotel's golden age in the 1920s and 1930s. Maybe my father attended these as a medical student. Was this where he learned to Foxtrot, at which, according to my mother, he excelled? It was all so alluring and romantic.

The hotel fell on hard times in 1927 and stopped paying shareholders dividends. By then the Fränkels had already returned to Lwów. My great-great-uncles tried to improve the property by modernizing its sanitary facilities, investing in air conditioning, and remodeling the café.

But why was another hotel standing in Hotel Continental's place today? The mystery nagged at me, so I pursued it from another direction: my great-great-uncle Maksymilian, a reputed oil tycoon. Uncle Sydney said Max had made his fortune in two towns south of then Lemberg called Boryslaw and Drohobycz. The oil fields were so shallow that when young Max refitted a truck engine and drilled, he struck a gusher. It and seven other oil fields made Max rich, Sydney said. These towns were the center of a mid-19th century oil and natural gas boom. In the late 1920s, one oil refinery employed eight hundred people, ranking among Europe's biggest. When the shallow oil fields yielded less "black gold," as the oil was called, Max moved to Vienna and rolled his money into the Hotel Continental.

I asked Alex Dunai, a Lviv historian, genealogist, and guide, to check Polish business directories from the 1920s for Max's oil assets. A jocular, gregarious fellow, Alex's vast knowledge of Ukraine's State Archives and other resources proved invaluable. He found not eight but seventeen historically and literarily named wells, including "Pilsudski I, II, and III" (for the Field Marshall who ran Poland after WWI); "Kosciuszko" (for the Polish engineer who fought with American colonists against the British during the American Revolution); "Maurycy" (for Polish-Jewish painter Maurycy Gottlieb of Drohobycz, whose painting *Shylock and Jessica* won the 1876 Gold Medal at the Munich Academy); "Montana," and "Sienkiewicz" (for the Polish journalist and novelist Henryk Sienkiewicz who won the Nobel Prize for his novel *Quo Vadis*). Max seemed to have been an erudite and playful character loyal to his native Poland.

I shared this information with a professor at the University of Vienna, Jérôme Segal, who was researching a documentary about Galicia's Jewish oil barons. He responded that his great-grandfather Dr. Arnold Segal and my great-great-uncle Max had co-owned several wells, and that their business address was just across from the Vienna State Opera. Jérôme had been in touch with Max's two daughters, both of whom had died several years before, but Max and Simon's nephew, Enrico Lamet, was alive and well and living in the Berkshires. Did I wish to contact him? In seeking more information about Max, I had discovered another relative!

I immediately emailed Enrico, then eighty-six. His father, Markus Lifschütz, was the cousin of my paternal grandmother Michaela. Markus's and Michaela's fathers, Mojzese and Eisig (my great-grandfather), were Max and Simon's brothers. These four brothers were part of a thirteen-sibling generation. Enrico had lived in the hotel as a young boy, where Markus had worked, possibly alongside my grandfather Ojzer.

During the *Anschluss*, Max and his immediate family fled to their villa in Merano, a village in the German-speaking part of the Italian Tyrol. After Max died there in 1939, his widow and daughters went to Mexico. Simon stayed in Vienna, though, and after the Nazis extorted exorbitant rents from him, which he received from his properties besides the hotel, he was killed. I have found no record of how or where.

Most of the historic buildings along the Danube Canal were bombed during the Battle for Vienna in April 1945. When the retreating Nazis blew up the Schwedenbrücke, their munitions also struck the Hotel Continental, damaging it beyond repair and obliterating that side of my family's assets. But Enrico said that after the war, Max's widow negotiated compensation from the company that insured the hotel.

Enrico and his mother went to Italy and he chronicled his war years there in his memoir, *A Child al Confino*. In it, I was surprised to find a 1939 family photograph that included my grandparents, Ojzer and Michaela! Until that moment, I had seen only two—one when they were married and another of the family circa 1927. We did not even have a print of the family portrait—the low resolution image came electronically from Cousin Anita. It was exciting to see my paternal grandparents as they appeared to my father when he left Lwów, but Grandfather Ojzer was paunchy and Grandmother Michaela looked worn. Neither were smiling. I stared and stared at this gift, scrutinizing my paternal grandmother, her features, her expression, her body type, her posture, what she was wearing, her accessories—trying to find attributes each of her granddaughters could have inherited.

Other relatives in the 1939 photo included Norman Lifschütz and his fiancée Sally Ratner. *Ratner as in Ratner's the restaurant!* I gave Enrico a call and he explained that Norman was also known as Dr. Ignace Lifschütz. *The bridegroom who had been a witness four months earlier for my father's marriage to Rose!* Furthermore, Sally and Rose were cousins and good friends. Enrico put me in touch with Norman and Sally's daughter, another distant cousin new to me. She said her Aunt Rose was a character and had a mouth like a truck driver. My new cousin referred me to two of Rose's elderly nieces. Then I got an email from Rose's son, who I will call Lenny.

I was very nervous about speaking with Lenny. By then, I was certain Rose was linked to the most powerful Jewish mobsters. I had read that after Ratner's closed, the descendants opened Lansky's Lounge, a nod to the Delancey Ratner's backroom my friend had mentioned. I did not want to hurt anyone by dredging up the past. All I wanted was clarification about the circumstances of Rose's trip to Lwów in 1939and any clues that would shed light on whether her and my father's marriage was arranged, a marriage of mutual benefit, or something else.

I thanked Lenny for his willingness to talk on the phone and said my sisters and I were grateful that his mother helped save my father. "Whatever else happened between them, I want to acknowledge that," I added. Then I made a crack about being related "through unmarriage."

He laughed. I said I had seen pictures on Facebook of his silver standard poodle, Gemma, who could have been the sister of my poodle, Tiki (short for *Tikkun Olam*). We laughed again. He said he might have some pictures of my dad. He also remarked that we worked in the same industry; he was in personnel and hunted IT heads.

While we had some common ground, Lenny and I had heard very different versions of what had happened. Rose told him that she loved my father but he had not reciprocated the feeling. Lenny insisted his mother would not have married for anything but love, but he added that she was a "wild child," "very flamboyant," and that her parents had often sent her away. He also said Rose and my father traveled west by train together. That did not fit because of the March 11 date on the back of the photo, which I still thought showed they had parted in Lwów.

Lenny said his parents had met at the Delancey Street Ratner's, as I had suspected. Then he volunteered that his father, Joe, was a gangster closely associated with Meyer Lansky, Bugsy Siegel, and Lucky Luciano. He even disclosed his father's street name. His first name matched the one Mollie had used in her 1945 letter to my dad. I thought I might faint, because the connection to the Jewish Mafia was so close and high up, and because I had guessed correctly.

After Rose and my father divorced in 1946, Rose stayed with Luciano and his wife in Italy. When she returned to the States she married and divorced again in the late 1940s. She and Joe finally married after he divorced his wife and left his two sons in the early 1950s.

Lenny recalled being told that his mother and my father honeymooned in Havana, and he had a tantalizing memory of a photograph of my father wearing a light suit on a ship. He promised to look for it in his boxes and I promised to send him the photo of them dancing.

But if Rose had loved my father, why had she not joined him in Mexico after she submitted his U.S. visa paperwork in New York? I checked the ship manifests and flight lists and there was no record of Rose returning from Mexico at that time. And if Rose did have a married gangster lover, what else would she have told her family about her falling out with my dad? Once her agenda for a cover was foiled, it would have been handy to play the jilted woman.

I had searched for Rose on Newspapers.com, which archives many local American papers, but because I knew the site regularly added new newspapers, one day I tried again. Up popped a feature story about Rose and my father meeting in Havana Harbor. A Texas newspaper, the *Austin American-Statesman*, published a story on Friday June 9, 1939, by a correspondent in Cuba. He described Rose on the dock arguing with a Cuban immigration official:

> Typical of scenes at the refuge ship, as it anchored in the colorful Havana Harbor, was that between Rose Frenkel and her husband. With tears streaming down her face, she stood at the foot of the gangplank and pleaded with a stolid immigration official.
>
> "Why" she asked once again, "Why can't he land? His papers are all in order."
>
> The immigration official shook his head. "He is a Jew."
>
> "Yes." Mrs. Frenkel sighed, "he committed a crime the minute he was born."
>
> Dr. David Frenkel, promising Polish surgeon, was included among the refugees turned away at the very gates of their yearned-for haven.
>
> "Won't you let me speak to him for just a minute," the woman pleaded. "We haven't seen each other for such a long time."
>
> Circumstances had forced them apart last year in France. She had left for New York and later came to Havana when he joyously announced he had obtained a Cuban visa.
>
> The official listened silently to her, then motioned her gruffly up the gangplank. David met Rose halfway up. They had time but for a kiss and a hug and a few brief

> words before parting. She managed a brave smile from the dock as the ship backed out into the harbor and sailed for—destinations unknown....

How can I convey the astonishment I felt reading this? It was absolutely mind-blowing that my father's arrival and persecution were documented by a newspaper for the world to see. It also revealed Rose's character: fast-talking, unafraid of authority, sarcastic—an assertive, gutsy dame. Film Noir on newsprint. She spoke of my father's plight in terms of crime. She was also terribly upset.

My sisters and I could not get over this find. When I told them, each gasped, then sputtered with shock and amazement.

There was an inaccuracy in the article, however, that damaged Rose's credibility; she and my father had not stayed in France for a year, as the date on the photo and her perfunctory farewell showed. But perhaps Rose exaggerated to generate pity so that she could have a few words and a kiss on the gangplank. Although I had seriously reconsidered Lenny's narrative that they had traveled together west by rail, the article disproved a honeymoon in Havana. On the other hand, maybe they did have a whirlwind romance. But given how quickly things fell apart when my father arrived in New York, I wondered whether Rose had cried crocodile tears, or tears of frustration in Havana because now her plan to appease her parents with her proper, doctor husband might be thwarted. My husband was even more skeptical; he believed Rose deliberately misled the journalist and later cast herself before her family as the aggrieved bride.

My hypothesis is that Rose and my father each had a private agenda and did what he and she thought necessary—my father to escape the growing menace that was the Third Reich, and Rose to placate her parents while still carrying on her dalliance with her married gangster lover. Although my educated, elegant, gentlemanly father and fast-talking, vulgar Rose were mismatched, my father must have had good reason to marry her.

My father was incredibly fortunate that a medical emergency occurred on the dock in Veracruz, and to have been qualified to help. By saving a life he saved his own. The other passengers were not as lucky.

Flandre sailed back to Havana Harbor in June and was forced to return her "cargo" to France. It is not known how many of her passengers were killed during the Holocaust. Despite all that planning, had it not been for chance circumstance and how far he was willing to go to thwart the Nazis, my dad could easily have been among the doomed.

Whatever happened between my father and Rose, I am grateful to her. Without her, my father might not have been able to save himself. There were hard feelings, but they did not have to love each other to still be decent people. Still, who would have thought that verifying my great-uncle's oilfields in Galicia would have led me to substantiate my father's unwitting and unwelcome connection to bootleggers, loan sharks, and murderers on the Lower East Side?

After my father and Rose parted ways in November 1939, he settled in Crown Heights near Unity Hospital. Perhaps the brownstones with their bay windows and the smaller scale of Brooklyn's streets reminded him of the architecture of Lwów that he now missed. Unity was a nonsectarian hospital founded in 1924 that accommodated up to three hundred patients. It boasted a state-of-the-art, five-story maternity wing and made a name for itself in maternity services and as a teaching facility.

Half a year later in May 1940, my father received a letter Rose had forwarded from the National Board of Medical Examiners in Philadelphia. On the lower right, someone had typed, "In Care of Rutner's." What a country! I imagined him thinking. Here a secretary cannot fathom that a Jewish surname (Ratner) sounding like a rodent could possibly be correct. But sometimes a typo is just a typo.

My father certainly would have felt great satisfaction upon reading the letter, which stated that the Board was determining whether he was eligible for admission to the first parts of the National Board examinations. If they approved his credentials for Parts I and II, he could take Part III after completing his internship. But the next sentence revealed a downside. Because he had graduated from a foreign medical school, he could not progress automatically; instead, his case would have to be individually reviewed throughout each phase. If all went well, he would be licensed to practice in two years.

Chapter Five

The Hovering Holocaust

My parents met in New York in 1946 and married a year later at City Hall. No parents were present. Representing the twenty-two-year-old bride's family were her uncle, his wife, and their daughter. Next to the bridegroom, age thirty-four, stood a brother, sister-in-law, and a close friend and his wife. It was Thursday, July 3, a day before America's 171st birthday. The 95-degree heat was grueling and most New Yorkers were looking forward to the long weekend.

My father, wearing linen, gazed at his stunning bride, so elegant in her yellow silk gabardine suit, which showed off her narrow waist. A corsage of lilies of the valley was pinned to her left shoulder.

They settled in Forest Hills, NY, and moved into a garden apartment. After my sisters were born, my parents rented a house. When my parents were expecting me, they moved to a larger house on the northern side of Queens Boulevard, where my sisters and I grew up. The main requirement when they were house hunting was that part of the basement could be remodeled into a medical office. My father wanted two practices, and his larger, already established one was in Brooklyn on Eastern Parkway near the Brooklyn Museum. Every Saturday morning while he saw patients downstairs, we were not allowed to practice piano in our living room, which was just above his waiting room.

Our house was built on an old cherry orchard. Two beautiful Queen Anne trees formed an arch at the back of our lawn, and we harvested cherries every June. My mother cultivated roses and lilies of the valley in the almost-black flower beds that edged our lawn. Years of rotting cherry tree leaves accounted for the fertile soil, she explained. My specialty was growing tomatoes by the driveway on the other side of our house. I loved to sniff the pungent fragrance the stalks emitted when I pruned them. Then I washed my hands at the kitchen sink and watched the suds turn chartreuse.

My parents built an assimilationist life amid the shadow of the war and the trauma of enormous loss. For my sisters and me, that often meant growing up in the penumbra of what we sensed and could not fully know. English was the main language spoken at home, however, at dinner, when my parents wished to discuss something they did not want us to understand, they switched to Polish.

During one dinner while my parents were speaking Polish, I poked and dawdled over a tough piece of beef, unable to finish my meal. My mother told me to eat.

"*To jest flaki*," I blurted, meaning "This is gristle."

My parents briefly stared at each other until my mother exclaimed, "*Kicia* (a romantic diminutive meaning kitten), our first child to speak a full Polish sentence."

Snapping out of sentimentality, they then corrected me. "Kareny, it's '*flak*,' not '*flaki*.'" I glanced at my sisters and smiled. We knew our parents had said "*flaki*" many times.

At first they welcomed our comprehension, but as we continued to catch on, my parents switched to German. My father did so reluctantly even though it was his first language, whereas my mother often spoke German with her relatives and friends. As we began to decipher that, too, they substituted Russian but lapsed back to Polish. I began to daydream at the dinner table, deliberately tuning out Polish to show my parents that they spoke too fast for me to understand. That way, my father would not have to speak German. Without knowing it, I was protecting him from his own feelings.

Late at night in our living room, behind closed French doors, my parents often engaged in lively arguments about politics. One night, they raised their voices so high that I came downstairs clad in my panties and slippers, and walked into the living room without knocking. As I sat on one of our mid-century modern armchairs, they continued on in Polish until I fell asleep. Before they went to bed, my father snapped a shot with his Polaroid of me sprawled across the armchair. I saw it on the end table in the morning when I awoke with a crick in my neck.

Later that day, I observed my parents being friendly with one another as if nothing had happened. That was the norm in European circles, I learned; you smoked and drank and discussed. Passionately.

In an effort to recreate the cultural life they had enjoyed in Europe, my parents went out most Saturday nights either to the Metropolitan Opera, the Philharmonic, or the theater. They often attended parties, or dined out with their many friends and my father's colleagues. My father instilled in us a love of classical music and music generally. I grew up listening on our hi-fi to Brahms, Beethoven, and Juliette Gréco singing about the skies of Paris. I was as mesmerized by Gréco's throaty, sensuous voice as I was taken with Brahms's Violin Concerto in D Major, Opus 77. While happy to attend the opera and concerts, my mother was not as captivated by music as my father and told us she often used the time to think. She preferred plays and literature.

Before my parents went out, my sisters and I frequently kept my mother company in their bedroom as she dressed and put on jewelry and lipstick while seated at her vanity. Those were the days when opera audiences arrived in formal regalia. "Will you wear the black or the pink?" I asked once, after my mother had hired a seamstress to sew a shocking pink satin gown. (It was the sixties.) Usually, the black won out. My mother was glamorous without being showy. I suppose most people think their mothers are beautiful, but mine really looked like a movie star. She underplayed her beauty, though, especially when we were adolescents.

I once pressed her as to why she would not acknowledge her good looks even though many people compared her to Ava Gardner. My exasperated mother finally blurted, "So what? So I was beautiful. My appearance prevented me from staying with my parents in Lwów."

My mother did not have the positive memories of a carefree, pretty young woman. For her, beauty was associated with trauma, helplessness, humiliation, and the hazard of being conspicuous. Also, having been raised until age fourteen in Kraków, a university town filled with intelligentsia, she was aware of the elegant, understated fashion sensibilities of her mother and aunts compared to women from Warsaw, who she told us were "flashy." And so twenty years after the war, she rarely wore her smashing pink gown.

My mother's parents were not observant and rarely attended synagogue. My mother went to synagogue for the first time on her own at age thirteen. She did not say why, but judging by her age, she may have had friends who were Bar Mitzvahed and so she went out of curiosity. When my parents were first married, my mother wanted to celebrate the Sabbath, but my father—who had attended cheder and was quite learned about the Talmud—did not. The Holocaust damaged his faith. "How can I believe in a God who allowed such things to happen?" he asked. As a result, I grew up in a secular household. We attended Sunday school so that we would have some formal instruction and we celebrated Jewish culture. None of us were Bat Mitzvahed, though, because my parents considered that "an American invention." We observed Rosh Hashanah, Yom Kippur, Chanukah, and Passover, but that was all. When we were very young, we celebrated Passover with my mother's side of the family, the Finkelsteins, who had lived in Kraków and Berlin before World War II. Seders were held at our great-aunt Lucia and Uncle Sholek's apartment in Washington Heights. Lucia, my grandmother Teofila's younger sister, had survived the Warsaw Ghetto. Their brother, my uncle Max, his wife Stefi, and their daughter Vera, were the relatives on my mother's side who attended my parents' wedding. They had settled in the Heights when they arrived in 1938 from Berlin. Max had desperately tried to get visas for the entire family, but succeeded only in bringing over his parents, my great-grandparents Sara and Heinrich Finkelstein.

Holiday celebrations shifted to our house after Uncle Sholek died. I always sat next to Max and Stefi, who I thought a great storyteller. I once praised her to my father and he surprised me by retorting that she was long-winded. My father rarely said anything negative about anybody and always put people at ease when my parents entertained, which was often. Max and Stefi had taken in my orphaned mother when she arrived here in the summer of 1946 on one of the first Liberty ships from Germany. As a welcoming gift, Stefi bought my mother a cheap pair of sandals from the now-defunct department store A & S for $1.99 ($27.00 in 2021 U.S. dollars). Max and Stefi let my mother know in this and other ways that she had to immediately find work, so she held various jobs—as a clerk at a publishing company, receptionist for the east coast office of a movie studio, and as a receptionist at her cousins' diamond import firm. At night, she took classes at George Washington High School to learn English and earn her high school equivalency certificate.

My father thought Max and Stefi feigned hardship and never forgave them for not hosting a wedding reception for him and his orphaned bride. A luncheon, perhaps, nothing grand, would have sufficed. My mother thought it was punishment because my father had not preferred their daughter, Vera, or maybe because my mother got married before Vera.

In retrospect, my parents, sisters, and I hoped for more affection and involvement from our Finkelstein relatives—either as surrogate parents or surrogate grandparents. I do not remember *not* knowing that three of my grandparents had been murdered during the war because they were Jews. To cope with the void, I thought of grandparents as distant relatives. Even our language reflected that they were unfamiliar. I rarely spoke of my murdered grandparents Michaela, Teofila, and Izydor. When I did, I referred to them as my father's mother, my mother's mother, my mother's father. I never called them "Grandma" and "Grandpa," nor were the words "bubbie" or "zayde" part of my vocabulary. My sisters and I only referred to our father's father as "Grandpa Ojzer," but he died when I was a toddler so I do not remember him. Ivy recalls only that he was affectionate and enjoyed her rendition of the Mr. Clean ad jingle. Michelle has more detailed memories, like that Grandpa rose at dawn every Saturday to travel from the Bronx to pick her up and bring her to ballet school in Manhattan. All for the joy of seeing her plié and point her toes. I do remember my grandfather's second wife, my step-grandmother Rifka, a Russian baker who lived with us for six months after he died in 1960 of esophageal cancer. We were very attached to Rifka, but she had grown children of her own in Israel and returned to them.

I only met one of my friends' grandparents. Mrs. Canada, grandmother of my best friend Susan, fascinated me. I was amazed that someone that old could move. In fact, she often complained about her "arthuritis." Susan and I had many playdates and sleepovers at their St. Albans home, and Mrs. Canada was always there to greet me with a hug and smile. Once when Susan and I were quite young, about six or seven, I asked Mrs. Canada, who Susan called "Ma" (Pronounced "Maaaah" with a flat "a"), if I could call her that too, and if she would be my grandma. She chuckled and said, "Sure, honey." I was not quite certain of a grandparent's role, though. I see now that Mrs. Canada helped keep house and cooked because Susan's mother worked, and that grandparents stepped in when parents were too busy.

I saw Mrs. Canada more often than I saw Max and Stefi, who visited only on holidays. I adored my great-uncle Max, who was gentle and soft-spoken, and his daughter Vera told me when I was an adult that he loved me. In retrospect, I did not know him well, yet I wish he had filled in and been our surrogate grandfather. Vera had no children, so it's not as if we would have been competing for his grandfatherly attention.

Max and Teofila's sister, my great-aunt Lucia, was a talented sculptor, severe, competitive, stunning, and unhappily married. I saw her smile once and that was a spectacular event. My mother said Aunt Lucia had had an affair with her father, Izydor, Lucia's brother-in-law and my grandfather. She also thought Teofila knew or sensed it. I suppose Teofila and Izydor's marriage was typical of upper middle class European unions in which the husband strayed and returned, strayed and returned. My mother said Teofila considered Izydor's transgression a mere peccadillo;

after all, Izydor always came back to her, therefore she was the one he truly loved.

Teofila could have been rationalizing. There were other women. Izydor even introduced one of his mistresses to my mother, angering her. The only explanation for such inappropriateness I can conjure is that Izydor intended to communicate to his girlfriend that he was and would remain a family man. I wonder what would have happened to that marriage had there been no war.

Despite her father's dalliance with her aunt, my mother liked Lucia and strove to please her. In retrospect, it is strange that Lucia was so disinterested in and critical of us. Perhaps Lucia's rejection of us, grandchildren of the sister she had betrayed, was connected to her and Izydor's ended affair. Secrets secrete in unexpected ways. Did we remind her that she was not, ultimately, the one Izydor chose? But wouldn't my mother have reminded Lucia of that, too? Like Max, she could have been a surrogate grandparent, but clearly that was beyond her capacity. In any case, Lucia was withholding and had generous words only for her granddaughter, Susie. "Look what a perfectly straight nose my Susie has," she would say and look down her equally fine nose at mine.

We did not see these few relatives often enough for their roles in our lives to be substantial. Their lack of generosity disappointed my sisters and me. The fact is, that although the Finkelsteins were learned and elegant people, they were neither affectionate nor attentive, as my parents were.

Although not as cuddly as my father, my mother was very loving and devoted. She allowed nothing to hinder her dedication to us and our educations and worked around barriers, especially when we started school.

Michelle's first school was P.S. 196, an elementary school on the other side of our driveway. I used to stand with my fingers clutching the chain fence as I searched for her during recess. One day she came home and refused to tell our mother about her homework. My mother probed. "Teacher says we don't have to tell you our homework assignments," Michelle responded. My mother began to suspect that the American public education system was not for her kids. This was reinforced when Michelle entered Halsey Junior High, which was not strong academically.

My mother researched private schools in our neighborhood. She did not want to send us to yeshiva because we were not religious, and she thought a private school called Kew Forest too small and provincial. Friends who lived in Forest Hills Gardens sent their daughter to the United Nations International School, so my mother interviewed the headmaster. Then we all took admission tests. Ivy and I attended the elementary school branch in Parkway Village on Union Turnpike, where the U.N. had housing for its staff. Michelle traveled to Manhattan to the junior high in an abandoned public school building on First Avenue and 70th Street. Attending a private school cost us our playmates on our street, though, who felt we were snobs. "Our school isn't good enough for you?" one asked. They no longer wanted to play with us.

The U.N. school, or UNIS, as it is called, was established in 1947 by United Nations employees for their children. Its goal was to provide an international education while preserving students' cultural heritages. In keeping with the spirit of the U.N., it made no distinction as to race, gender, language, or religion. British and French headmasters ran it when we attended. If a child made a prejudiced remark, he or she was thrown out. Period.

On our first day of school, a hurricane churned into New York, which usually meant that our basement flooded. But my intrepid, conscientious mother ignored all that. So did two other mothers, Dorothy Jackson and Goldie Blanksteen. Mrs. Jackson drove through the storm from the Black middle class neighborhood of St. Albans, and Mrs. Blanksteen arrived from Queens Village. Their daughters, Susan and Janie, became my closest friends and remained so through most of high school. Our other friends were Chinese, Continental Indian, Czech, Ghanaian, Italian, South African, Turkish, and on and on. Many were the children of diplomats. So many parents were foreigners that mine did not stand out and I thought of them as simply European. The phrase "Holocaust survivor" was not used then, if World War II was discussed at all.

My second grade teacher, Miss Maria Rheinshagen, was a Swiss blonde goddess with a flawless Beehive, as we called that updo then. She introduced a star system on a chart that she posted on a wall for everyone to see; perfect spelling and arithmetic were rewarded with stars. I lagged in the spelling department, whereas Janie and Susan excelled. Janie tried to coach me. She sat behind our primer, with its cover of orange and white flames, while I tried to recite the right letters.

I preferred to stare at Miss Rheinshagen's strands of natural, shiny platinum, which swirled across her forehead and swept over her ears into a perfectly formed cone. I wished I looked like her. I yearned for her to uncap her blue magic marker and draw five-pronged stars next to my name on the chart. But I did not earn her stars as often as I wanted and felt frustrated. But I also did not like how public the chart was and that it encouraged a competitive climate.

After school, my mother waited for us in her fabulous, baby-blue Citroen station wagon with its frog-like nose, and greeted us with her dazzling smile as she leaned across the front seat to wave hello. The seats were upholstered in golden-beige, plastic imitation caning. We jockeyed to sit on two little face-to-face seats in the far back because they were special and private; my mother could not hear our conversations well. But that was unnecessary when my mother offered lifts to our teachers to Queens Boulevard so that they did not have to take both the Union Turnpike bus and subway back to Manhattan.

Before our 1961 trip to Europe, my parents had bought the French car to replace my mother's little yellow-and-white Metropolitan Nash, which we called "the shopping car" because she mainly used it to buy groceries at Bohack. My mother arranged for her Israeli cousins, Olga Mandel, a linguist, and her husband, the journalist Amnon Kapeliouk (also spelled Kapeliuk), who was an Israeli correspondent for French newspapers, to pick up the Citroen. In exchange for the favor, they got to joyride across France. Then the car was shipped to the States on an ocean liner while we flew home.

My mother loved that car. What style, what pizzazz. Heads turned throughout Queens to watch us zip by. My mother was fascinated by cars and often mentioned that her great-grandfather, the first to build a watch factory in Breslau, now Wrocław, Poland, had owned an automobile at the turn of the 20th century. She even had a picture of her great-grandfather Herman Lewy in his splendid car seated next to his chauffeur. In the back seat, his daughter, Sara, hugged her Dachshund. I later learned the car was a German-made Argus, circa 1905. How I wished I could have told my mom!

Our Citroen was a lemon from the start, needing constant attention and expensive replacement parts. My mother eventually accepted that and got a cream-yellow Mustang. This too was fabulous and sexy. Like my mother. My horsey friend, Lisa, who rode every Saturday in Kew Gardens, was ecstatic. Nothing could beat that galloping logo with its flying tail.

Miss Rheinshagen's star system alerted my mother to a persistent difficulty that beleaguered my sisters and me. Regardless of my father and Virgil's dictum, we were bad spellers and misread words; I mistook "soldier" for "sailor" and vice versa, for example, and I could not see the difference between "president" and "presidant."

My mother was also an atrocious speller. She mangled words in all six languages she spoke—Polish, German, Russian, Ukrainian, English, and French. "My parents could not understand why their capable daughter was not at the top of her class," she told me years later. And in her oral history for the Fortunoff Video Archive for Holocaust Testimonies she said, "I was not a very outstanding student. I never learned how to spell and the opinion in schools was how come such a bright girl who knows everything verbally makes spelling mistakes? And I always sort of wondered, 'Maybe I'm stupid after all.'" By the age of ten, though, she became an avid reader. "With development, dyslexia improves and by the time I found myself in Soviet schools I was an A student."

My father, a Lefty who was forced according to European tradition to be a Righty, saw nothing wrong with us, however. He was so ambidextrous that when he operated and requested a clamp from a nurse she would respond, "Yes, right away Dr. Frenkel. Which hand?" He also may have wanted to prevent us from using our disabilities as a crutch. His message was to toughen up.

My mother thought he was behaving like an ostrich. Ever the realist, she ignored him and tenaciously tried to solve what she recognized as a problem. She sought advice from psychologists and reading experts. Then one day she read a magazine article about dyslexia that mentioned Columbia University's Optometry program. That lead her to one of its graduates, Dr. William M. Ludlam, a vision and learning disabilities specialist. He examined and diagnosed us. We were dyslexic, as was my mother.

"So we are dyslexic," she told us afterward. "Anybody can spell. But my girls know how to think."

We were given eye exercises and with time, improved. Certain quirky behaviors now made sense. At nap time one day at Flushing Progressive Nursery school, my teachers had called me over from my cot.

"Why are you writing your name backwards?" one asked. I had no idea what she was talking about. "You signed all your paintings "neraK." The other one pointed to the bottom of several crayon drawings on construction paper. I still did not understand, or rather see, what was wrong. What I had done made sense: Righties' hands moved from the midline of their bodies out to the right, so Lefties ought to write from the midline out to the left. And I was a Lefty. I think at first they thought it was a prank, but it became clear that I was unaware that my letters progressed in the wrong direction. I may also have flipped them, so that the letters were mirror images of themselves. The teachers reported my weird signature to my mother.

Several years later, Ivy and I sent out faulty birthday party invitations. We were planning a treasure hunt with clues in our garden and cherry trees, so we asked our guests to dress casually. But we spelled "wear" "ware." Susie, our cousin and granddaughter of our great-aunt Lucia, was among the guests. Unlike us, Susie was an excellent speller, and Lucia embarrassed my mother over our mistake. In turn, my mortified mother chastised us.

"Why didn't you look it up in the dictionary?" she fumed.

"How can we look it up if we don't know how to spell it?"

She had no answer.

I liked my elementary school homeroom teachers, but clashed with my particularly authoritarian French teacher, Madame Grunberg. Every week she inspected our textbooks, which we had to cover to protect. Most of us simply cut up brown paper bags for this purpose, but they often tore. My mother bought clear plastic covers that slipped on, but they, too, had a disadvantage: pencil and eraser dust clung to them, turning the plastic gray and preventing me from seeing the pretty cover. Afraid one week that I would not pass inspection, I slipped into the bathroom a step away from my desk to wipe off my plastic cover. (Our classrooms were converted apartments, so the bathroom was nearby.) Madame Grunberg called me to the front of the classroom. I tried to explain why I had left my seat without her permission, but she interrupted and said she would not listen until I apologized. I felt this was unjust and that she was making an example of me for no good reason. I was unable to articulate then that she had shamed me in front of everyone. Instead, I balked and refused to apologize. A standoff lasted for about a week, during which I was invisible. I did not tell my parents right away. When I confessed, my mother said I had to do as the teacher said. Madame Grunberg out-endured me; I could not bear to be shut out and ignored. In the end, I apologized teary-eyed and humiliated in front of my friends. All this was in French. She accepted my apology, but I was revolted when she hugged me.

Clearly, I had a problem with authority. My parents had never demanded blind obedience and always explained why they wanted us to do something. They seemed to have come to a consensus about this aspect of our upbringing. In my mother's case, I think this was because she had had an equal say in family decisions before and during the war. Her parents included her in discussions and there had to be unanimous agreement about strategy. My father, on the other hand, had had to submit to and obey his father, with whom he did not get along, and who was tough, demanding, and, at least after the war, manipulative. My grandfather Ojzer was, as I understand it, typical of his generation of Austro-Hungarian men—they expected children to be seen and not heard. I believe my parents thought it more effective to gain our cooperation and affection by explaining their requests rather than ordering us about. That may also have been a result of the long shadow of the Holocaust and their experiences under authoritarian regimes. To a large extent, by not requiring blind obedience they preempted knee-jerk teenage rebellion. The flip side was that I would not obey unless I understood the underlying logic of a directive. To this day, I do not regret having stood up to Madame Grunberg. But later, in college and during my career, this defiance cropped up again—and not always to my advantage.

I learned that there are many kinds of resistance and resilience. In the wake of my French teacher episode, my mother noticed that I was a bit defiant and likened my personality to her mother's, my grandmother Teofila. "She had a temper," my mother said. "It would suddenly flare." But when I listened to my mother's oral history, I discovered that she herself was no angel in school. "I was not aware of the fact that I was Jewish until I went to school," she said, "which was the first time somebody called me a dirty Jew. And I didn't know what that meant." The interviewer asked when she became aware that there was something wrong with being Jewish. My mother answered:

> In *gimnazjum* (high school) I was attacked and I always fought back. I was not a quiet sufferer. I don't remember if I was physically attacked, but I have a vague recollection that I retaliated physically.

My mother smiled. I could see a glimmer of the feisty girl she had been: My teenage mother swings her fist at the jaw of her nemesis, probably a lanky boy with short blond hair and a snub nose. He stumbles backward from the blow while she stomps off saying, "Serves you right. How dare you call me that!" And a moment later she would have reeled around to add, "Say it again, and you'll see what happens."

And yet, she was called to task for something else:

> I belonged to Jewish scouts, which were part of the Jewish veterans of WWI, and it was forbidden to be a member of an organization outside of school. Sure enough, I was called to the Director. I remember how

> vehemently I accused the school that I was not allowed to join the scouts because I was not Catholic. They let it go.

The scene plays out in my mind. The *gimnazjum* director's call to his office was reserved for the most serious offenses. The formidable director sits behind his desk. "Young lady, it has come to my attention that, contrary to school rules, you are a member of a particular organization of scouts." How daunting he seems as he stands and towers over my mother. If his height and stern voice scare her, she does not show it. She thinks: *What does slugging an anti-Semitic classmate have to do with the Jewish Scouts? Who informed on me?* True, she and her friend Anula Dawidowicz had been especially active recently; with the arrival of Austrian Jewish refugees after the *Anschluss*, they and other Jewish Scouts were doing their utmost to find temporary lodgings among members of Kraków's Jewish community.

"Do you know that I can suspend you for disobeying our rules?" he thunders. The embodiment of subtle and underhanded Polish anti-Semitism, the director faults my mother, the victim. Instead of punishing the other kid for his aggression and prejudice, he faults my mother for not obeying the school's rules. But, of course, the rules are biased.

Just as she perceived manipulations when I was growing up, my mother saw right through him. She argues her case with the skill and logic of a daughter who must convince her litigator father of her point of view in family debates. I hear her saying, "It follows from the school rules that because I am not Catholic, I am not allowed to join the School Scouts, so you see, Sir Director, actually I *am* obeying the rules."

My mother beat up a kid for insulting her. She out-argued a powerful man. Tough and assertive, she let no one push her around. Like grandmother like mother like daughter.

When my sisters and I entered junior high, both our parents, especially our father, emphasized that we were to study, "make something" of ourselves, and become professionals. As we progressed and had to memorize facts, my father invoked the be-scared-later rule and Virgil's adage, '*Labor omnia vincit*' (Labor overcomes all)." At dinner, my mother chimed in with, "And what have you accomplished today?" We all felt like strangling her. If we brought home a B+, my father praised us but said next time it would be an A-. Same for an A-; it would become an A. Equally important was his message that we were here to make the world a better place. *Tikkun Olam*. Heal the world. He was not severe, but he made his expectations quite clear.

My teen school years therefore were filled with homework, exams, and satisfying my parents' requirement that I achieve. In the summer months, the pressure lessened, but it was always there. During the school year, if I had had trouble with fractions or later, with quadratic equations, I had to set aside time in the summer to work through a math exercise book. Now I'm grateful for my parents' standards and the breadth of experience they offered my sisters and me in the fine arts, as well. We all took ballet lessons, studied musical instruments, and were encouraged to draw and paint. My mother regularly took us to New York's great museums as soon as we were old enough to walk through the galleries.

In the late '60s, Michelle was already away at college. Ivy and I studied on weekends while our parents were out, and we sneaked in our favorite television shows. These evenings were not entirely carefree for my father, who found his answering service unreliable. Ivy was phone phobic, but after a few trials he decided he could count on me. "Daddy says you are absolutely reliable," my mother said proudly. He made me feel important, like I was his special assistant, and I took my job seriously. Before leaving, my father always confirmed that he would call during intermission. His office phone had a slightly deeper ring then our other line, perhaps because it stood on a table in the crook of our staircase and the ring echoed a little. I awaited his call and rushed from the living room to the phone no matter if Flipper was rescuing Bud from danger, or the dolphin itself was stranded on some shoal. After the call, Ivy and I watched Colonel Hogan ridicule Colonel Klink on *Hogan's Heroes*, a farce about prisoners of war in the fictional Stalag 13 during World War II. We had to watch *Hogan's Heroes* clandestinely because my mother could not tolerate that we found anything about the Nazis funny.

One evening, my father did not call. I became agitated because a patient had called twice to say she was spotting. I had no idea what that meant nor that she was describing a symptom, but during the second call I assured her that my father would receive her messages. When the phone was silent through intermission, I felt concerned. I waited up for my parents, worried that my father had not called because something bad had happened. But he said he had called his patient anyway to check on her. I was relieved.

In 1967, when I was twelve, my parents bought me an electric typewriter, a taupe Smith-Corona Coronet. When I turned it on, the carriage return jumped, as did I, but then the machine settled into a soothing hum. At first, we put it on a metal typing table, which my father brought up from his office, and placed it in front of the radiator. That way, in between sentences and commas, I could gaze at Willow Lake, which was just past P.S. 196 and Grand Central Parkway. But the table wobbled under the typewriter's weight and vibrations, especially when I shoved the manual return, and one of the collapsible wings was broken, so my mother bought a steady wooden table. Now I could stack my *World Book, Book of Knowledge*, and other books from the library on one side. Hand-written drafts of my term papers rested on the other. It was heaven, working this way. And I loved the black and red ribbon.

To celebrate the gift the evening after it arrived, I typed a phone message to my father on a square of turquoise paper from a psychedelic swirl pad, the kind with paper twisted into a multi-pronged star like a rainbow pinwheel. I proudly left the message on the telephone table so that he would see it upon returning. Of course my father noticed, and asked why I had typed my message even though we had spoken during intermission. I shrugged and said I just wanted to show how much I loved my typewriter. I was a reporter filing a story, but I did not yet know it.

Looking back on my school days, I see how natural it was for me to write and that, partly because of my parents' early and subtle guidance, it made sense that I would become a journalist. My father was empirical, observing how I handled messages and testing my interest with newspaper reading assignments. Once when he asked me to pick an article in *The New York Times* and write a summary, I chose a short piece about new strapless bra designs that enabled women to wear strapless evening gowns. When he praised me, I expressed embarrassment over the topic, but he did not mind. "The important thing is that you did it," he said.

In 1939 when my dad was waiting in Mexico for his United States visa, he met an AP reporter and they became lifelong friends. Eventually the journalist became a medical reporter and medical newspaper publisher. I have the feeling that my father consulted him on how to encourage me. And the typewriter was the perfect gift. But I was lucky to have been born just before the Information Revolution and to benefit later from all the writing tools personal computers offer, especially Spellcheck.

My parents placed great value on education and demanded that my sisters and I strive for success in that arena more than any other. Sports and the arts were important, but the pursuit of excellence in scholarship was paramount. My father endured great risk and even life-threatening circumstances in *gimnazjum* and medical school to get his degree. My mother's high school education was interrupted by the war and although she got her high school equivalency and enrolled in college, she never graduated. No wonder there was so much emphasis on academic achievement.

Chapter Six

Letters, Literature, and Bones

When my parents married in 1947, my father, already in his mid-thirties, wanted children right away. My mother was in her early twenties, and in retrospect felt she was not quite ready. But they had a tremendous desire to rebuild family life because they had lost so many relatives. Within a decade of having children, though, my mother returned to another great passion—literature. In 1956, she enrolled part-time at New York University to earn her bachelor's degree. Even with fulltime help, commuting to campus could not have been easy, given the needs of an eight-year-old, a toddler, and a baby. My mother's energy was split, so three years later she opted for the university's new distance education program, Sunrise Semester. This program was the 1960s precursor to interactive television, which never took off, and to online learning today. Sitting in our living room in her plaid bathrobe at 6:30 a.m., my mother tuned in to CBS to attend literature, history, philosophy, and archaeology courses. Then she cooked breakfast and brought us to school. Throughout the semester, she wrote and sent in papers, and took final exams in-person at the Washington Square campus.

In the family archive stored in our small spare room I found her term papers and essays. Very gingerly, she had begun to write memoir-like snippets about the war and its impact on her impressionable teenage mind. She also examined and critiqued post-war literature. I skimmed through an out-of-order stack of mostly unstapled, yellowed originals. Some were fastened with rusty paper clips, but not their carbon copies on brittle tissue paper, nor marked-up versions with my mother's edits or her professors'—and my father's—corrections. My mother struggled with the grammar and peculiar spelling of the English language, which affected her grades. Like many middle and eastern Europeans of her generation, including my father, my mother was polylingual. Polish and German, which she spoke with her parents, were equally her first languages. Often and emphatically she told us that her *Hochdeutsch*, that is, literary or high German, was crucial to her survival. She spoke without a Polish inflection, but most important, without a Yiddish accent, which endangered many Jews during the war.

While a refugee in eastern Poland after the Soviets invaded, my mother learned Russian in Soviet schools. In Lwów, before the German Occupation, she attended Ukrainian schools. Thus, English was her fifth language. She learned it when she arrived here and had a mild accent, unlike my father, who studied King's English while in *gimnazjum*. A born mime, people assumed that whatever language he uttered was his native tongue. Having learned English at a young age, he spoke with a mere inflection.

My sisters and I did not hear our mother's accent until we went to college and spoke with her long-distance on the telephone. Somehow the wires enhanced her accent, or perhaps not speaking with her daily made it stand out. We were always well-aware of my mother's uncertainty about when to use definite and indefinite articles because there are none in Polish. Sometimes that resulted in confusing instructions. "Call me on telephone the next week," she would say and get frustrated when I asked, "Which week?" Also, my mother often mixed metaphors or garbled the latest slang to hilarious effect. When I was a teenager, I cackled after she said, "I have to pull my ass together," a conflation of getting her ass in gear and pulling her act together. She laughed, too. Often, a ricochet of giggles lasted several minutes.

But sometimes, friends called attention to my mother's accent in a hurtful way. One college friend spent part of mid-semester break at my house in Forest Hills and in describing her visit to her family, focused on a meal my mother had prepared. Of particular interest was my mother's pot roast.

"Potrose, *potrose*?" mimicked my friend. "I had no idea *what* Karen's mom was talking about," she added with a laugh. Her parents and sister joined in while I flushed with anger that my mother's accent, which was not even thick, was the butt of a joke. This girl from a depressed town in western Mass is making fun of my mom? I thought. Who are they to laugh at my cosmopolitan mother, who reads Voltaire for fun?

As I looked at her term papers, filled with a mix of typos, phonetic spelling, and wrong synonyms for the context, it was clear that she struggled. Though not as hampered as some dyslexics, she remained a terrible speller. Her writings, nevertheless, are vivid and conceptually sound.

I picked out four gems. In one essay, excerpts of which are lightly edited here, my mother discussed her response to post-war Holocaust literature. She had declined to read Anne Frank's *The Diary of a Young Girl*, which had been translated into English a few years earlier, perhaps, she said, because the picture on the cover looked too much like her own from that era. She read Leon Uris's *Exodus* and commented only that it was "very informative." Next, she read the Dutch author Jan de Hartog's *The Inspector* and found it good but flawed; his ending, which evidently advocated turning the other cheek, was neither a credible nor palatable solution to her.

Finally, she read Meyer Levin's *Eva*, one of the few books, even today, about a Holocaust survivor who, like my mother, had false papers and worked as a slave laborer in Germany. But Eva was found out and sent to a concentration camp, which my mother was not. I had eyed the book in her bookcase and asked about it. "Ach. Levin got it all wrong," she said. "He made Eva begin to lose her sense of identity." My mother was very clear about who she was; she never wavered in that regard, and found that part unbelievable. In her essay, she dismissed the book as sincere, but not literature. By that, I think she meant that it was well-intentioned but not written in a literary style and voice. While on my quest, I read *Eva* too, and agreed.

Frustrated, my mother requested that her cousin, Henryk Trammer, a professor of law at the University of Warsaw who had survived Buchenwald, select and send her Polish post-war literature. Of that, my mother most appreciated the work of Tadeusz Hołuj, even though some of it smacked of communist propaganda. A Catholic Pole from her native Kraków, Hołuj had been in the Polish resistance and was interned in Auschwitz. His short story, "Sol," was based on what he had witnessed. It chronicles the story of Herman, a German Communist who had fought in the Spanish Civil War and is an orderly at the camp "hospital" for women. Brutal to those on his ward, Herman viciously beats a Greek professor of law for stealing bread meant for the sick. He is so ferocious that Hołuj has trouble pulling him off. But Herman falls in love with a sixteen-year-old Greek Jew named Sol with wheat-colored hair that shines in the sun. He smuggles food to her in tiny boxes tied with beautiful ribbons. He tries to save her from fertility experiments intended to annihilate whole societies and races through mass sterilization. Herman fails.

My mother found this shred of humanity within a monster realistic and interesting. Although this tale resonated with her, still on a wave of literary letdown, she concluded, "None of these stories about Hitler's horrors are any good."

In April 1961, my mother saw a televised preview of Adolf Eichmann's trial in Israel, which was to be broadcast internationally in June. The footage included liberated concentration camps. Shaken by the experience, my mother grappled further with why she found descriptions of the Holocaust futile. "I saw on the screen the living and dead skeletons. I had mixed emotions: All this is absolutely incredible. It must have been somewhere on the moon, or better yet, on Venus," she wrote. "Then came my anger. How could we all permit this to happen? Both these thoughts, and emotions, I realized were totally absurd. Because how can I think it happened on Venus, when for all I know I am looking at my mother or father, so changed that I don't know them?"

A surge of repulsion coursed through me as I envisioned my mother watching this. Whenever I watched documentaries of pre-war Poland or the Holocaust, I too, full of anxiety, searched for her parents among the doomed. But I was a generation removed and I cringed at the hypothetical horror of seeking *my parents* in such newsreels.

Some may conclude that my mother was struggling with "survivor's guilt," which was first identified and defined in the 1960s. I have always found that label facile, even shallow. I sought definitions. One professor of psychology said Holocaust survivors' guilt is peculiar in that it is "guilt without perceived wrongdoing" and carries a burden of its own. "Survivors don't feel guilty because they did something wrong," he said. "They feel guilty because they *lived*." My mother never felt guilty that she lived. She was heartbroken that her parents had *not* lived. The loneliness of surviving without them and pain of having been orphaned in such a cruel way was sometimes unbearable. She never accepted her loss. I understood this from a very early age, as well as the idea that there are some things you never get over. I don't see why or how my mother could have gotten over it. And what does it mean to get over something?

Searching for reasons for why she survived and others did not, my mother contemplated the dehumanized and persecuted and the role of luck: "I am most certainly looking at my cousins, friends, the kids I played hopscotch with," she wrote. "Is the reason I am not there among them mere chance? It was a split-hair of difference then. So how could I possibly be responsible at age 14 for not stopping this madness?"

She was amazed and even marveled that luck had favored her—but not her parents, not her community. She felt her life was a gift and that her parents would have wanted her to enjoy it to the fullest because their lives were stolen. My mother did cling to the misguided and even grandiose conviction, however, that if she and her parents had remained together, she could have prevented them from making mistakes that led to their capture. These emotions existed simultaneously and had little, if anything, to do with guilt.

In the 1990s, "survivor's guilt" was renamed "survivor syndrome," or "concentration camp syndrome." Again, this did not apply to my mother because she was not interned in a camp. I have read that those who hoarded crumbs in the camps later felt guilty for not having shared. I have also read that many selflessly shared their last bits of nourishment out of love for fellow Jewish prisoners. My mother was spared such dilemmas, and much more, because she was not tortured and imprisoned. Therefore, she did not carry the guilt of those who had to make unbearable choices.

Similarly, Jews born in Palestine or Israel, and perhaps Jews in the States, looked askance at female survivors, assuming they must have prostituted themselves (the language of the time) in order to survive the camps. Although my mother may have escaped such suspicions, it is possible that as a slave laborer she was sexually exploited. Why would she not have been? After all, she was young, beautiful, and entirely at her "employers'" mercy. She never spoke about this directly, but as I delved further during my quest I recognized clues.

Psychologist Stephen Joseph of the University of Warwick recently parsed three types of survivor's guilt experienced not by Holocaust survivors but by survivors of combat, natural disasters, and terrorist attacks. His list: guilt about staying alive while others died; guilt about things they failed to do—these people often suffered post-traumatic intrusions as they relived the event again and again; guilt about what they did do, such as scrambling over others to escape. The second seems somewhat to apply to my mother, but she was not present when her parents were in mortal danger. Still, she imagined what she would have done had she been with them. Such scenarios intruded again and again and again.

Throughout my life, I heard some variation of what follows. This version appears in her Fortunoff oral history:

> Unfortunately I am as dark as I am. If I were blonde and blue-eyed, I could have stayed with them [her parents]. And I would never have permitted my mother to go to work. I would have kept her under lock. I had far more sense of reality to danger than they did. And that's completely irrational because how can a 16-year-old girl think she could save her parents? That, of course, has had a terrible impact on my whole life. The regret that I was unable.

And so I look up the definition of "regret" to prove to myself that it is not the same as guilt: "Regret is the emotion of wishing one had made a different decision in the past, because the consequences of the decision were unfavorable. Regret is related to perceived opportunity. Its intensity varies overtime after the decision, in regard to action versus inaction, and in regard to self-control and at a particular age the self-recrimination which comes with regret is thought to spur corrective action and adaptation," according to Psychologist N. J. Roese of Northwestern University. He further describes regret as "an aversive emotional state elicited by a discrepancy in the outcome values of chosen versus unchosen actions." Marcel Zeelenberg of Tilburg University, Netherlands, says regret differs from remorse "in that people can regret things beyond their control, but remorse indicates a sense of responsibility for the situation." Writing about moral dilemmas, Canadian philosopher Terrance C. McConnell of the University of North Carolina at Greensboro, notes a person can feel regret that people died during natural disasters but cannot feel remorse for that situation: "'Agent regret' is the idea that a person could be involved in a situation, and regret their involvement even if those actions were innocent, unintentional, or involuntary."

The involuntary part of my mother's situation was the crux. Her parents forced her to separate from them. She had no choice but to obey. And so the fact that they saved her by forcing her to leave them was a blessing and a curse.

Like my mother regarding early Holocaust literature, I feel that words inadequately describe the emotions—the trauma and loss—of a Holocaust survivor *not* in the camps and instead undercover in the enemy's midst. Perhaps it is that so few survived the way she did that they have not been extensively studied.

My mother also tried to refute the notion that the Jews had been punished because of original sin. She was referring to the general Christian doctrine that humans inherit a tainted nature and a proclivity to sin from birth, and that God made the Jews suffer for it. "Surely it is not [so]," she wrote. "It is perhaps the awareness that no matter how we search, there are no rules for life, or how it is supposed to be."

She recognized that the norms of behavior were forever altered. Our perception of what humans are capable of had reached beyond the comprehension of sane minds. She appreciated Hołuj mostly because of the appalling nuance in his depiction of the co-existence of good and evil: "Along with the greatest cruelty there exists tenderness. It comes mixed in different proportions in all of us," my mother concluded. "This is what 'Sol' is all about."

And so I wondered, had someone been both cruel and tender to my mother? Yet nothing in her oral history alluded to such an experience.

Referencing contemporary atrocities, when troops of the then Republic of the Congo attempted to crush the secession of South Kasai in 1960, my mother commented: "It is so much easier to weep about one crucifixion than for the starving Kasai province. Individuals respond to individuals, not to multitudes. That is why I feel the dying on the screen are strangers and Sol and Herman are not."

My mother connected the displaced of all creeds who had left their homelands to start lives elsewhere, with the inadequacy of post-war Holocaust literature:

> We Poles who left Poland—Jews, Christians, or non-believers—were told to forget what happened. It's an absurd notion. That is why neither from Israel nor the United States has come any real post-war literature. To me it came from my hometown of Kraków, where people cannot forget, they must live with it, many of them, anyway. Surely Tadeusz Hołuj [does].

She attacked the prescription handed to survivors back then—*move on*. Today, with advances in neuroscience and our understanding of post-traumatic stress, we know loss and trauma are not easily erased from the amygdalae of eyewitnesses. This part of the brain is responsible for so-called flashbacks of shocking events. These are symptoms of Post-Traumatic Stress Disorder and must be treated. They cannot be ignored. Or forgotten.

Looking at literature and the larger picture, my mother concluded her essay with: "The artist's role is not only to mirror life, it is also to anticipate things to come and the ability to perceive what is happening elsewhere." I wonder what she would have thought about today's

Holocaust bookshelf; there are memoirs, novels loosely based on true stories, and historical fiction. How much do those works ring true to Holocaust survivors? Now there's a topic for a PhD dissertation.

"American artists like Tennessee Williams are trying to disturb the public," my mother wrote in the same essay, "a public that so often has strange notions, like Harry Golden (a journalist, critic, and champion of the Left), who says, 'I don't understand why so many nice people go to the theater to look at characters that are not nice at all.' Who is nice?"

What a question. Who, indeed?

Correspondence among her papers indicated that she intended to translate "Sol," whether or not nice people wanted to read about not-so-nice characters like Herman. She asked her favorite New York University literature professor, Floyd Zulli, Jr., whether he would accept her translation *in lieu* of a term paper. He said he would. Then she wrote to Tadeusz Hołuj, asking to meet during her visit to Kraków in the end of August. My mother's urgent wish to return to Poland during our 1961 trip was not just about visiting her few remaining relatives in Kraków and Warsaw while they were still well. She had a business appointment lined up. She returned to Vienna in the middle of the Berlin Crisis with a letter signed by Hołuj, granting her permission to translate, adapt, publish, and sell his novels, plays, and other works. I felt proud of my mother's activism and entrepreneurial spirit.

That fall, upon the conclusion of Eichmann's trial, my mother wrote a term paper about how Herman Melville developed Captain Ahab's lunacy in *Moby Dick*. In the final paragraphs, she said she identified with Ishmael because, like him, she had outlasted a vicious madman. Again, to preserve her voice, I've minimally edited her words:

> ...It is not the fact or action, but an individual's reaction to them that matters. Ahab was far indeed from accepting the will of God the way Job did. Tragedy could be viewed as God-sent punishment, or as the reality that must be faced. The main question remains: Can we live with our tragedy? Ahab's inability to face his mortality,

> and with it his human frailty, became a compulsion to find Moby Dick and death.
>
> Call me Ishmael, since I am one in a way and have also survived a madman's destructiveness. However, little is known in this country about people who, like me, lived for years under cover of false identity. Death was expected every minute, not only one's own, but of the heroes that tried to help. Even though giving shelter to a Jew meant the death of a whole family, many took the chance and helped. Asking then for a roof over one's head became an act of potential murder of the innocent. We were guilty of being alive, while, according to the law, we should have been dead.

Ah, an entirely different reason for the guilt of a Holocaust survivor.

From an early age, my mother understood that literature saves lives because it portrays peoples' plights and how they responded. Books she read as a child later helped my mother save her life. As to being unable to protect her parents, here is what she said in her oral history:

> I knew my parents died on July 7 [1943]. At least my mother did. Gestapo took my mother and father disappeared. And that was all. And that I never really did get over. When I came here, my grandfather said it was all his fault that he let his children stay in Poland. And I looked at him like he was out of his mind. It was my responsibility to save them and I failed.

One of her two interviewers echoed what my mother had said: "You failed. You felt it was your responsibility." When my mother affirmed this, the interviewer asked, "How could you have done that, as a very young person?" She replied:

> I had the perception that we were in danger, which nobody around me had. I spent a lifetime trying to

> understand why I had that perception. Perception is a responsibility.

My mother's sorrow and extreme frustration at being thwarted despite what she discerned never faded. Nothing could comfort her that her parents' decision to send her away, a choice that saved her life, meant she could not safeguard them. The exchange was unacceptable.

Chapter Seven

The Land by the Bay

One morning in 1962, while kneeling and tying his shoe, my father turned to tell my mother something. In mid-sentence, he howled with such pain that we heard him through the closed door of their bedroom and down the hall to ours. His agony was so intense that he could not move. My mother called an ambulance and told us our father was going to the hospital. When the medics arrived, she said to stay in our rooms. My room was at the top of the stairs, which turned at a landing and then descended to our foyer. After the medics passed the landing, I poked my head out and watched them carry my sedated father on a stretcher down our long stairway. I was only seven, but I knew our lives had changed forever.

Even after an orthopedic surgeon treated my father's severe sciatica by removing a herniated disc in his lower back, he got no relief. He consulted other New York orthopedists, but they found nothing wrong and considered him a psychiatric case. My parents flew to Minnesota to consult experts at the Mayo Clinic. They, too, were unable to help. My father became addicted to Miltown, a powerful painkiller, and later struggled to shake it.

Somehow my father finally found an orthopedic surgeon in New York who helped. After examining my father and while he dressed, Dr. Tarnower told my mother, "I cannot imagine how Dr. Frenkel withstood such pain for so long." The doctor believed the wrong disc had been removed and recommended a second operation. Back then, there were no MRIs to confirm damaged soft tissue like discs, only X-rays that showed fractured bones and arthritis. Although disillusioned with his colleagues, my father took a leap of faith and agreed to a second surgery.

Young children were not allowed in the hospital, but my parents wrangled permission for me to visit. I arrived with my mother at Flower Fifth Avenue Hospital at 106th Street, now Terence Cardinal Cooke Rehabilitation Center, wearing a black and white houndstooth party dress. Underneath the gathered skirt was the itchiest petticoat imaginable. I was thoroughly uncomfortable but did not say a word.

My father was lying in a strange bed in a noisy place with a tiny window. I noticed a black box at his side on the bed.

"This is my tape recorder," my father said as he patted his Norelco, one of the first cassette recorders. "I'm telling it a story."

A story? A story! And yet I did not ask what it was about.

The day before my father returned home, my mother set up a daybed in our playroom, which was just off the kitchen. She covered it with a beautiful new blue corduroy bedspread. I grabbed a pair of scissors and cut it in a few places. My mother was astounded and demanded an explanation, which I was unable to give.

The next day when my father arrived, again I was speechless. Lying on the bed, he bellowed, "Irene, what did you tell the children? Kareny doesn't know who I am."

Before my mother could run in from the kitchen, I answered, "I know it's you, Daddy. Mommy said not to be loud because of the hospital."

I must have been terribly anxious about the coming change at home because I did not know what my father would be like. The last few times I had seen him he was immobilized and helpless; I didn't understand that pain could strike and then disappear with healing. My explanation probably caused him pain of another kind. Nevertheless, he gently took my hand and motioned for me to sit next to him. I hesitated, afraid that even if I sat on the edge that would disturb him.

"It's OK," he reassured me. "Sit and tell me how you are."

After my father's long recovery, he did leg lifts and strengthened his abdominals every morning before work. Sometimes I joined him on the lush, gold-colored rug in my parents' bedroom. He was so disciplined and determined; he never missed a day of his routine.

Eventually, he learned through the medical grapevine that during another botched surgery, this time on a child, the first surgeon was unable to continue. The surgeon suffered a nervous breakdown and stopped practicing shortly thereafter. If only that surgeon, who had removed the wrong disc, had admitted his mistake. My father might have been spared the stigma of hypochondriasis and self-doubt between operations, and would have avoided dependence on an addictive painkiller. How lonely he must have been, suffering terrible pain with no one to turn to, and feeling betrayed and abandoned by his peers. But he was resilient enough to follow through with the recommended rehabilitation.

In the summer of 1966 when I was ten, Michelle graduated from high school and went off to England. Planning for the rest of us, my father asked my mother to find a house to lease near water so that he could swim laps and strengthen his back. My mother piled Ivy, our mutt who was innovatively named Pooch, and me into our Mustang. Off we went to the eastern tip of Long Island. Pooch, who had never been on a long car trip, howled the entire way. Sitting in the back with him, I tried everything to pacify him or quell his nausea, if that was the problem. I hugged and kissed him, I stroked his sleek torso, I massaged his velvety ears, I clenched his snout when I could no longer bear his yelping. I dared not offer Milk Bones, though. We kept all the windows open, hoping the cool air would soothe his nausea. No, he brayed like a coyote at the moon.

At Manorville Road, the exit from the Long Island Expressway toward Sunrise Highway, my mother slowed down. Pooch took this as an opportunity to escape. In a flash, he lunged for the triangular back window to freedom.

"Mom, Poochy jumped!" I screeched.

"So, hold him down!" she retorted, irritated.

"No, he jumped out."

"Out of the car?" She slammed on the brakes.

Trotting nearby, Pooch had evidently landed like a cat, and seemed perfectly happy though a little stunned.

After what seemed like an eternity we finally arrived in East Hampton, with its glorious Village Green and pond fringed by huge elms.

"Rather impressive," was all my mother said, as we absorbed the lush grandeur. On either side of Main Street stood old estate houses mostly hidden behind huge, manicured hedges. Here and there we got a peek at those New England-like, Gilded Age "cottages" where New York City's blue bloods summered. As we passed the still water and those dignified homes, my mother glanced around, embarrassed that the owners might overhear our mongrel and disapprove. White churches presided over the center of town, and there was a theater as well. At the far end, we approached East Hampton's iconic windmill. I wanted to know whether it was used to mash grains. To this my mother had no answer.

About fifteen minutes later, we entered a sleepy village with a name I could not yet easily pronounce—Amagansett.

"It's an Indian name," my mother explained, sounding pleased. "Pequot or Montaukett."

Gradually we noticed the air was different and that it relaxed us. Later we learned that as crashing waves met land, they ionized the rising molecules of salty air. Thus, the transformed air made us drowsy, extinguishing big-city worries. And the light. A soft shimmer, a lazy shine, made everything somehow more vibrant.

Amagansett was hardly even a village. It was a hamlet, really—a pause between stately East Hampton and tinselly Montauk. With no diner or deli in sight, we entered the IGA in search of sandwiches. Back then, the quaint store was on Main Street and had wooden floors and narrow aisles. Nearby was the Post Office, a sporting goods store called LaCarrubba's, a library, little inns, and lots of real estate offices. All were in old, musty wooden houses that had once been dwellings of early settlers from Massachusetts and Kent, England, with names like Lester, Edwards, Miller, Bennett, and Osborn.

Toward the end of the strip stood the firehouse, one of the few red-brick buildings, and next to that a nightclub called Martell's with navy-blue table umbrellas. Across the highway was an elementary school and playground, but there weren't enough kids to attend a high school, so local children commuted to East Hampton High.

As we passed through, the highway veered to the right toward Amagansett East, now Beach Hampton, a neighborhood of shacks inhabited by Lefties, card-carrying communists, artists, and writers. The northern fork led to The Springs, where Jackson Pollock had lived and died in a car crash. Beyond was Barnes' Landing where the Accabonac Cliffs edged Gardiners Bay. Local workers, especially fishermen, were pejoratively referred to as "Bonackers," a reference to the magnificent heights and the superb fishing and clamming, the bounty of the bay that enabled them to earn their livings.

Most exciting of all was Bluff Road, which we took when we returned to town. It was dotted with old whaling captains' houses that overlooked a floodplain to the Atlantic. Little towers above their shingled rooves served as lookout posts. When the adventurers who lived in these homes spotted spray and black fins, they rushed to the beach and rowed out to harpoon their prey.

We learned all that at the Whaling Museum. We also learned the lore of the Hurricane of '38, which had carved out the bluff for which the road was named. The storm, also known as the Long Island Express, had rushed up the East Coast like nature's aquatic locomotive in September 1938 and devastated the East End and New England. Years later when I was in my twenties, an old man who ran a country store described to my mother and me how the water had surged and churned, whipped by 160-mile-per-hour winds. The furious surf washed over Old Montauk Highway, temporarily splitting Montauk from the rest of the South Fork. The man and his neighbors were caught unawares, he said, partly because the storm had surged so fast that the weather service could barely track it.

But there was another reason why they were not forewarned.

"Before it hit—before the worst—we were glued to our wireless, because they were reporting about Chamberlain and Hitler negotiating," he had recalled, shaking his head and looking down at the worn shop counter. "Yep. And we were so darn scared of another world war, we stayed tuned to that station. The storm warnings came in on the other channel. And them seas—they melted those sand hills just like you pour hot water on sugar."

"Ach, the Sudetenland," my mother had said as we drove home. "Such a betrayal. We were listening to that news, too, in Kraków. We couldn't believe it—that Chamberlain actually thought Hitler could be appeased."

"People already knew there was no stopping him?" I asked.

"Some. Some did. Not *knew*, but had a sense. Especially after speech Hitler made at Nazi rally in Nuremberg. That was few weeks earlier." She was dropping more articles than usual, I thought, as she reached back to her early teens in Poland. "And yet…who could imagine…what would happen to us…"

My mother glanced away from the road for a moment, peering toward some wetlands. She was checking for an osprey nest on one of the tall poles conservationists had placed in the marshes to help the endangered birds reproduce. She spotted the nest and returned her attention to the winding road, grasping the steering wheel hard.

"Nah. It never occurred to me that listening to news *here* could be dangerous," she said.

"What, Ma?"

"Just by choosing one station over another, I mean. So strange. Strange they had no idea such onslaught was coming."

But back to our exploratory 1966 trip. My mother rented two rooms in a motel and we spent the next few days noodling around with a real estate agent, looking at houses for rent. My mother favored artsy, Red Amagansett over better-heeled, social register East Hampton. She chose the most modern house of all, a transparent, one-story box right on the beach in Amagansett East. We turned off Marine Boulevard, to the driveway, and saw through the house's sliding glass doors cobalt and sapphire streaks of horizon. Giant, precise brushwork heralding the Atlantic.

"You can jump out of bed in the morning and take a swim," my mother said. And so we did, all summer long while Pooch cavorted at the water's edge.

It was a summer of many firsts for us all. Pooch's was the first first. While chasing a seagull he ran into the ocean and got wave-smacked. He never wetted his paws in the salt water again, but Ivy and I had no fear, even without a lifeguard. We played on the beach in the afternoons. Mornings, before it got too hot, were devoted first to tennis lessons on the town courts, where our patient instructor John presided. He tossed balls from the other side of the net to warm up Ivy and me. Then she and I switched places to practice our backhands. I had the advantage because I was a Lefty and even though I was weak, I could compensate with strategic ball placement and steadiness. Ivy was strong but erratic, with an occasional smash so powerful I could not return the shot.

Afterward I did my dreaded eye exercises. Then we practiced typing with a record droning out the letters. Ivy and I took turns punching the blue- and red-covered keys of our Hermes Rocket, the first "streamlined" really light portable typewriter.

My father arrived for the first weekend of the season and tried to hide his frustration. My mother had mistakenly thought he could swim laps beyond the surf, but to return to shore he had to battle the undertow. While we delighted in checking the new mood of the waves each morning and body surfing later, my father quietly began to toodle around The Springs.

Sometimes he joined Ivy and me at tennis, but I worried the whole time about his back, especially when he twisted and ran. And yet I admired how well-coordinated and strong he seemed, striding across the red and green asphalt. He preferred golf, perhaps because it was slower and more predictable. He brought me along to caddie at the local course, across the Long Island Rail Road tracks. I didn't lift his bag or hand him irons, but as soon as I was old enough, I relished driving around the course in an electric cart. The course was split by Barnes Hole Road and I felt so adult when I navigated across to the next hole. Greens fascinated me. I stooped to brush the compact, mint-colored growth while my father fussed over the best position from which to putt and then rocked sideways in his spiky shoes.

My father did not have the greatest sense of direction so several times we missed our turn and took another fork to the right. The first Sunday morning this happened, my exasperated father's face reddened and he was silent as the anti-Semitic Devon Yacht Club on the shore of Gardiners Bay came into view. I thought he was upset because the club reminded him of persecution during the war but did not dare to ask. As we turned around, I tried to cheer him up, saying we had plenty of time to golf before lunch and that the course was unlikely to be crowded before noon because the locals were at church. His jaw set and he said nothing.

His silence troubled me for many years; it was striking and unusual, given his jocular nature. In my research into his tour of duty in the U.S. Army, I read about a catastrophic D-Day rehearsal that took place at Slapton Sands near Devon, England. When I saw photographs of the tall cliffs overlooking the English Channel, I understood why East End colonials had named the southern coast of Gardiners Bay after the original Devon. The English cliffs were much higher, but the similarity was obvious.

To keep the operation secret, 3,000 local residents of farms and villages had been hastily evacuated from Devon, England, in November 1943. The area became a collection of ghost villages. In early 1944, during a secret night exercise code-named "Operation Tiger," a convoy of eight landing ship tanks (LSTs) carrying 30,000 troops tried to simulate landing on Utah Beach. The Sands were chosen for their likeness to Normandy—wide beaches and cliffs. A British corvette, a British destroyer, three torpedo boats, and two gunboats escorted the convoy. Torpedo boats also monitored Cherbourg where lurked German Kriegsmarine *schnell* boats, fast-moving hunter-killers that the English and Americans called E-boats for short.

On the morning of April 28, the commander of a field hospital in Southampton received a phone call from headquarters. Then he ordered his staff to prepare to receive patients. He did not say why.

Communication problems had plagued Operation Tiger; because of a typographical error, the corvette and the Royal Navy's headquarters ashore were on a different radio frequency than the LSTs. When a British ship spotted a German torpedo boat, the report quickly reached only the British corvette. The commander assumed the LSTs had been informed, so he did not alert them. As a result, nine German E-boats easily attacked the barely defended convoy. One torpedoed LST exploded into flames and sank within six minutes. A third listed for forty-five minutes as sailors and soldiers struggled with firefighting equipment that was useless because of a power failure. That LST also caught fire but made it back to shore.

The chaos was ghastly, the carnage gruesome. Over 900 American and British servicemen died that night. Many deaths of those who abandoned ship could have been avoided, but ill-trained and panicky, the servicemen incorrectly put their lifebelts around their waists instead of under their armpits. When they jumped into the water, their combat packs flipped them onto their backs and dragged their heads under. Many others drowned in the 45-degree water while awaiting rescue for five hours.

The field hospital staff was ordered by the commanding officer to keep the incident top secret. "You are to treat these soldiers as though you are veterinarians," he said. "You will ask no questions and take no histories. There will be no discussion. Anyone who talks about the casualties will be subject to court-martial." The doctors treated these patients in weird silence.

I knew my father had been stationed at a field hospital in southern England just before D-Day. Was he one of the medical officers who had treated survivors in shock from immersion compounded by explosion wounds? Was he still keeping quiet, as commanded? Perhaps I had uncovered the reason why our detour so upset him. If so, it must have reminded him of the terrible, unnecessary loss of life during those early days of his service. If not, he probably overheard whispers about the disaster from colleagues. Seventy years later, the hush still screams at me.

Sometimes on the way home after golfing, we went sightseeing, which meant house gazing. Our summer rental was part of an aesthetic trend; architects everywhere on the East End were experimenting with Modernism. They played with clean lines and minimal ornamentation, creating cubic, mostly white and gray wood structures. Charles Gwathmey led the pack, having become famous for a house and studio he had completed on Bluff Road for his parents the year before. His father was a painter, so a little deeper into the lot the son built a mini version of the house as a workspace, an architectural echo. A narrow, white chimney bifurcated a bright yellow horizontal stripe on the house and a triangular peak reached for the sky. A witty takeoff on the captains' houses; you could climb up to the roof to overlook the houses on the floodplain and admire the ocean beyond. We always slowed down to admire the pair. All along the bluff and below, Gwathmey imitators and competitors were throwing up similarly stark, sharp-edged houses. My father was delighted to watch the week-to-week progress of each construction site.

One day, my father spotted an even more unusual house. This one was a two-story octagonal, built in height to catch a glimpse, of course, of the ocean. It had casement windows that you cranked open, which was a new concept to me. But why an octagon? Wouldn't such an unusually shaped house be hard to furnish? I did not realize that my father was dreaming of building a house of his own, and that several plots of land he coveted on Gardiners Bay were for sale.

As the summer waned, hurricane season arrived and we experienced the effect of the Caribbean on the mood of our watery backyard. One bright windy day, Ivy and I were body surfing in waters that at first seemed manageable, and then turned treacherous. An undertow challenged us as we tried to return to shore. Every time we thought we were getting closer, we were sucked back to the breakers, where our toes felt the eerie cold. We knew we were too far out and stayed close together. Ivy said we had passed by too many houses too fast. My parents must have been watching from the deck, or perhaps we had been gone for a suspiciously long time, because I saw my father briskly walk to the beach and wildly gesture at us. We could not hear him because of the kicked up, roaring surf. As he ran east along the beach keeping abreast of us, I kept waving, trying to signal that we were alright.

Ivy was the first to make it in. She told me later that my father was frantic.

"Go back and get Kareny," he ordered, but Ivy was too exhausted and unsteady to obey. Meanwhile, I saw that the waves were breaking on the sand at a diagonal. I summoned all my energy and tried to swim across counter-diagonally, staying as near to the surface as possible. I tried and failed many times. I floated a bit. A huge wave smacked me and I tumbled closer toward the beach, sand swirling around me. I felt the grit inside my bathing suit. I knew another wave would follow soon, strike, and wring me like a washing machine. I judged the sacrifice necessary. Anything to propel me closer to shore. I was beginning to flag out there, alone.

When I emerged, I staggered toward my relieved but still frantic father.

"Didn't you hear me? You didn't hear me? My heart was pounding. I thought I was going to have a heart attack."

My heart. You want to give me a heart attack?

I don't remember what I said right away, but we were contrite.

My father calmed himself, sitting and chain-smoking charcoal-filtered Tareytons on the deck while listening to Beethoven and Brahms.

It seemed we had been caught in a rip current. From then on, we swam only at lifeguard-protected beaches where a red flag warned swimmers when the ocean was too rough.

Food shopping one day at the fancy new IGA, I ran into a UNIS classmate, Alicia Sullivan, who invited us to join her and her parents at Atlantic Beach, one of two public beaches. On the fine-grained sand sat Alicia's mother, Ginny, who had been a soap opera actress. Her husband, Joe, played the policeman in *Fiddler on the Roof.* Clad in a leopard one-piece, Ginny sat on the sand with excellent posture. The daughter of a Jewish financier who had lived in Germany after the war, she and my mother occasionally spoke German. Ginny did not like doing so, but according to my mother her German was "not bad." She told my surprised mother that sailors from a Nazi submarine had landed on that very beach in the summer of '42, but that the FBI had caught the saboteurs.

A station coast guardsman had played an important role in the Nazi submarine incident. Early in the morning of June 13, 1942, he encountered four Nazi agents who had landed a U-boat on the beach. He returned to the station to report the incident. Later, the Chief Boatswain's Mate brought four boxes of explosives into the boat room, which his team had found buried in the sand. The Nazis' intention: to blow up power stations. After one would-be saboteur turned himself in to the FBI, the others were apprehended and tried. The episode led to the establishment of the Coast Guard Beach Patrol, which grew to 24,000 men who were important to coastal defense during the war.

As the summer wound down, my parents discussed real estate.

"*Kicia*," my mom said to my dad, using the Polish diminutive for kitten, "this is the only place where you can take Long Island Rail Road all the way, get off, drop your things at home, and then walk to the beach."

"It's a sleepy, little nothing village," my father responded. "The houses in town are hot. I want a view."

My mother, who suffered from hay fever and migraines with every September crop of ragweed and goldenrod, retorted, "But houses near ocean have breathe. And no pollen."

"Breeze, *Kicia*, breeze," my father corrected. "Nah. It'll be impossible to get insurance. Or exorbitant. What, you want to buy a house that could get washed away?"

We looked at many huge, musty old houses with sagging attached pantries and added on bedrooms in Amagansett proper, including the one Elie Wiesel eventually bought. My father nixed every one. My brilliant mother, still thinking about the distance from the station house, lobbied for buying land and building in town. She would have bought up all of Amagansett if we had had the money.

Then one late August weeknight after my father returned to the city, my mother was awakened by Pooch whimpering and pacing along the glass sliding doors in the living room. My mother thought the pounding surf unusually loud but ignored it and encouraged the dog to come back to sleep in her bedroom. He was too agitated to obey. My mother peered into the night.

"With the lights off and moonlight, eventually I made out ocean," she told us the next morning. "Surf was too close. I saw foam in the dark."

In the end, my father got what he wanted partly because I broke the stalemate.

"Mommy. I've been thinking."

"Yes, darling. What?"

"If we build a house by the ocean, Daddy will be unhappy. Right?"

Nothing.

"If we buy in town, Daddy will be unhappy. Right?"

She hesitated for a moment. "Right," she answered with a rising inflection.

"But if we buy land by the bay and build there, you won't be unhappy."

My mother looked at me contemplatively. "You are right," she said and hugged me. "My little one. So logical. Such a diplomat."

And that was that. They bid on the land on the Accabonac Cliffs overlooking Gardiners Bay.

Chapter Eight

Coming of Age in Amagansett

After many weeks of wrangling between lawyers, the property was ours. The first time I saw it was at the end of the summer of 1966. We drove along Barnes Hole Road, with as many twists and turns as the real estate negotiations, until we arrived at Waters Edge Road. Up and up the car climbed until we reached a dead end. Instead of picking our way through the thick oak forest shrouded in vines, a short dirt road from the cul-de-sac enabled my father to slowly drive toward the water. Here it was so different from the ocean beach only fifteen minutes away; insects buzzed, bluebirds flew between branches. Then sea gulls announced the rapturous blue calm before us that stretched all the way to Montauk. Mid-way between us and the horizon was a bright spit of sand sprinkled with vegetation, a sandbar, really, called Cartwright Island. The large, verdant sickle of Gardiner's Island dominated the north side of the bay, and a promontory tapered toward and flirted with Cartwright so that they almost touched. Beyond Gardiner's Island and Peconic Bay we glimpsed Connecticut's smokey, blue shores.

My father stood at the edge of the bluff and gestured toward the sea with what became known as his "to conquer" pose, memorialized by a shot I took with my Brownie Fiesta camera. My father then tested a name he was considering for our property.

"Scirtetsbo. Has a Scandinavian ring, doesn't it?" he asked, looking at us quite seriously. Then he laughed with delight. "It's 'obstetrics' backwards." We all thought that was hilarious, though a bit eccentric.

The 80-foot sea cliff severed our patch of green paradise and plunged toward another kind of glory—our beach. Ivy, Poochy, and I scampered down the precipice without considering the erosion we would accelerate. Carefree, we romped barefoot and miraculously did not get jabbed by desiccated branches that occasionally poked through the sandy soil. My parents followed more slowly, sidestepping their way down.

Warm water kissed white sand, shells, and finally our toes. The quiet water lapped and lapped and lapped. Here and there it deposited leafy seaweed with frilly edges and branchy, floppy tree-like sea tangle. We inhaled the musty celadon scent of drying sea lettuce and dead man's fingers, as I later learned this alga and fungus were called. It was low tide and large barnacled boulders skulked, half-submerged. We waded in, and on closer inspection noticed mussels clinging below the waterline.

We turned to visit our neighbor's jetty, which jutted into the water from a wood and tar structure, a seawall or bulkhead that seemed to have made our neighbor's part of the cliff slope more gently than ours. On it, I saw random clumps of fallen land with bushes growing on them. Other green patches were even homes to pink dune roses. Between them flourished rows of beach grass.

My parents had now reached the beach and joined us at the jetty, where Ivy and I noticed funny little gray bumps on the planks of wood.

"Mom, what are these little knobs?" we asked. My mother picked off a grayish one with a spiral and cradled it in her hand. My parents conferred in Polish, but neither could think of the English word.

"These are little snails," she said. (The mollusks were actually periwinkles.) "*Slimaczku, Slimaczku, Wywstaw rogi, Dam ci sera na pierogi,*" she recited. "*Jak nie sera to kapusty. Od kapusty bedziesz tlusty.*" Then she translated, "Snaily, snaily, bring out your feelers, and I promise to give you a cheese pastry. If not cheese, then cabbage. Cabbage will make you plump." The one my mother held poked its little head as far out as it could and nodded and bowed and stretched its feelers. "See, they come out to greet you."

On the way home, my mother helped me memorize the Polish ditty, which I can still recite today.

Because our view extended as far as Montauk, we decided to visit it. I tasted my first lobster at Gosman's Dock at the mouth of Montauk Harbor. Dinner was in a fisherman's shack that booked no reservations, used wooden barrels as chairs, and was incredibly noisy. While eating, you could watch the fishing boats putter in with their catches. We all loved the informal, family-oriented joint. I was a "skinny little marink," as Michelle called me, and simply could not gain weight no matter how much ice cream and potato chips I ate. So when my corn on the cob and lobster arrived, my parents were delighted that I ate with gusto.

"Ooooh, there's meat in the claws, too?" I said.

"That's what the nutcracker is for," said my father. "Let me show you." He split one open to reveal the pink-white flesh.

"It has spidery legs." I brushed my finger against the little brown hairs along the limbs.

"Yes, use the nutcracker and the little toothpicky tool to get at the meat inside there, too." Eating that meal was like an explorer's expedition. Then came the sweet-scented hand wipes that cut through the melted butter and fishy smell on our fingers. My parents never mentioned that some Jews considered shellfish "treyf." In fact, I did not hear that term, meaning food that was not kosher, until college.

Not long after that culinary first, I witnessed my first touch of sexism when Yale Repertory Theater came to East Hampton and performed at the John Drew. Barbara Damashek, the stepdaughter of one of my father's colleagues, was in the play and might have been going out with the director, Robert Brustein. I no longer remember what the play was—it may have been written by Brustein himself. I do remember him pacing the stage and describing a woman, possibly the character's wife.

"What could be pinched and plucked then only stretched and drooped now," he said with a sneer and a studied pause. I turned to my mother, who had tittered with the rest of the audience, but now seemed embarrassed that she had. I didn't like the joke one bit. What gave him the right to snicker at an older woman, to make that joke at her expense?

I was at that stage when girls are turning into preteens and they start noticing that the world does not regard them as equal to boys.

But there were other, fabulous performances at the Drew. I distinctly remember the enchanting dancer and choreographer Carmen de Lavallade, who moved like a big, graceful cat in a light blue, stretchy costume.

One time my father glimpsed Barbra Streisand roaming the IGA aisles with her son, Jason, sitting in the shopping cart. She was surprisingly small, pretty, and blonder than he had expected. My parents were to attend a Democratic fundraiser and she was going to be there. My father went to East Hampton, which I don't think even had a record store, and somehow returned with her latest album, *On a Clear Day You Can See Forever*. It must have resonated with how he felt about our magnificent view.

After the event he presented the signed album to us.

"You went up to Barbra Streisand?" Ivy asked.

My father nodded. "I did."

"Tell us, tell us!"

"I said, 'Ms. Streisand, I am a celebrity doctor. I am unbelievably famous and I have three equally well-known daughters. I know they would be just thrilled if you were to sign this for them.'"

"Daddy! Really?" said Ivy.

"What did she say?"

"She laughed. She was very nice."

We were also into Joan Baez and The Singing Nun. While Ivy sang the melodies, I harmonized on the fly—"Sweet Sir Galahad" and "Dominique," nique, nique, and all that. My father listened to "Jerusalem of Gold," with its new final verse which reversed lamentations in the original opening. Instead, it referenced shofars sounding from the Temple Mount, as happened after the Israelis captured the Old City from the Jordanians in June 1967 during the Six-Day War.

My father tracked down the polygon-loving architect who had built the octagonal house in Amagansett East. George McAuliffe arranged for us to see two of his other creations. One was a larger, newer house not far from the glass box we had rented that first season and was also on the ocean. Its central living room was hexagonal and the roof was supported by a star configuration of dark beams that reached out to the vertices. Oddly, the fireplace was smack dab in the way of the ocean view. My father frowned. The other house was on Lion's Head Beach, a northern inlet of The Springs, and it, too, had hexagonal rooms. Built-in furniture in primary colors filled the peculiarly angled corners. All the houses had cedar paneling inside and out. Frank Lloyd Wright with a pinch of Japanese.

My parents hired McAuliffe and when we returned to Forest Hills that fall, the process of designing my parents' dream house began. Meetings with the architect and the construction of the house were the greatest adventures of my childhood. Every few weeks he arrived with a new set of blueprints. My father not only included me in the meetings, he welcomed my opinion. I wanted to know why the plans were called blueprints, which actually looked more purple to me, but no one knew. I was fascinated by the stylized handwriting the architect used to label rooms, and by the little half-moon arrows that indicated which way a door would open or close. And how could he get such large copies so that he could leave them with us and take another set home? Perhaps my father was empirically exposing me to architecture to see if it resonated with me. In fact, I think if I had not fallen in love with words and become a journalist, I seriously would have considered architecture.

My father wanted as many rooms as possible to have a view of the bay. At one point, our living room was to be octagonal, but eventually gave way to a hexagon. There were design reasons for this change, having to do with how walls of the hall and guestroom could abut the living room. My father resisted. My mother impatiently said, "David, enough with your octagons."

In 2014 when I landed on the memorial book site of the Medical School of the University of Vienna, I saw a photograph of a restored building that housed the leather-bound print version of the book. The building was a small octagonal Jewish prayer house nestled in one of the medical school courtyards. I asked the historians for more information about the original structure and they sent me a journal article about the architect, who had built several other Viennese synagogues. As I looked at the blueprints of the tiny 1903 synagogue and photos that illustrated the article, including one of its ceiling of wheel-spoke rafters, I realized that my father's fascination for the eight-sided beach house was not an eccentric quirk. Within his dream house, with its soaring, two-story-high hexagonal living room, he had re-created that little sanctuary. Better yet, he built his own sanctuary—its form and structure the result of a joyous act of defiance.

I can only guess what details my father learned of the fate of the university's prayer house in 1961 when he returned to Vienna to give his talk on infertility. My father must have seen or been told that the Soviets had desecrated the prayer house; during the 1950s, they destroyed its interior fixtures to use it as a transformer station. Who knows what the Nazis did before them, considering that they torched all the city's synagogues. The university reconstructed the prayer house and in 2005 dedicated it as a *Marpe Lanefesh* (Hebrew for "healing the soul"). All destroyed elements (roof, porch, Torah-alcove) were replaced with glass, following the architect's original plans. Now a monument and "site of remembrance and thought," people can contemplate names, including my father's, listed within the fine blue leather memorial book. I wonder what my father would have thought of the university's effort to take responsibility for policies in the 1930s and '40s that destroyed so much. Would he have accepted the gesture of recognition? Would it have comforted him?

We broke ground for our house in the winter of 1968. I was upset that so many trees were lost, and the bulldozer's tracks seemed careless and brutal. But the oldest and largest tree on the property was spared; McAuliffe said he had stood guard in front of it. We built our deck around it, and for many years it thrived until a Nor'easter tore off a major limb. It never quite recovered and we quaked each time one of those strong winds blew in from Connecticut and the placid bay became grim and choppy. These winds and high tides could and did splinter the boards of our new bulkhead. Then the sand poured out, as if through a sieve. Twice, the force was so great that the tide pulled the bottom steps off our stairway to the beach. Not only were repairs incredibly expensive, their environmental impact had to be assessed before permission to repair might be granted.

The next spring, when I was twelve-and-a-half, construction was fully underway. Plywood covered the foundation, transforming it into a basement. Leo Hall, a Norwegian contractor, and his brothers hammered in two-by-fours. My father and I could sense the dimensions of the rooms and the view from each when we went out on weekends to monitor the progress.

One weekend, my father stood on top of the newly poured foundation, checking whether it was high enough for him to admire Gardiners Bay. I was petrified that he might fall and injure his bad back.

"Be careful Daddy," I ordered, as he walked across a wobbly wooden plank back to the forest floor. "It's bouncy. Don't fall."

"I won't fall, I promise."

The next summer, while my father practiced in the city on weekdays, my mother tried to supervise the contractor, who treated her like a buzzing black fly rather than his employer.

"I just wanted a little place in the village that would be easy to maintain," she told us girls. "Or a shack in the dunes. Or a pre-fab." With the last alternative she was referring to another architectural movement that had taken hold on the East End—relatively inexpensive, pre-designed and factory-built houses. You chose various dimensions and combinations, and these arrived in parts—the basement cinderblock, the kitchen appliances and sheetrock, and the wood-paneled bedroom walls, for example, which a contractor then assembled.

Both my parents had hoped we would be able to spend at least the end of the summer in our house, but that was not to be, as construction progressed more slowly than expected. My restless mother took us exploring, driving around Napeague. This was the narrow spit that had flooded during the Hurricane of '38 so that Montauk was temporarily detached from the East End. In fact, the name of the lurking lowland means in Montaukett "land overflowed by the sea." On a clear day from our cliff, or later with a telescope on our deck, you could see past Napeague and glimpse a streak of the Atlantic.

"Come, let's see what Cranberry Hole Road is all about," said my mother. And we discovered Napeague's tall creeping dunes and shallow little bays crowded with wind surfers and Sunfish sailboats. We also visited Sag Harbor, which she said had influenced Melville's description of a whaling village in *Moby Dick*. On the way back to Barnes Landing, we always detoured to drive by a little game preserve and orchard, Quail Hill. Once we glimpsed a fox trotting along, its bushy tail bobbing, the gold light shimmering on it. A sense of peace and closeness to nature always engulfed me when we passed that spot.

In Forest Hills, in an effort to hear alternative news, my mother would often bring her shortwave Zenith radio up to the attic where the reception was better. She would sit by one of three gabled windows that faced our lawn and tape the antenna to the glass. Now she transferred this habit to Atlantic Beach and tuned into whatever Russian channel she could get. The static was tremendous, but she claimed she could decipher words between the crackle. When *The Russians Are Coming, the Russians Are Coming* came out, she practically ran to East Hampton's movie theater. It was one of the few American films in the Cold War era to portray Russians in a positive light and did so with deft satire and superb comedic actors. That it took place in a small New England town much like ours added to the attraction. My mother laughed so hard that it was almost embarrassing. But I know why she loved the film; its message was that whether Communist, Socialist, Capitalist, or none of the above, we all want our children to be safe.

Ultimately, my mother adored our new summer home, but she believed it attracted attention and spawned jealousy. She taught my sisters and me not to covet possessions and quoted Thorstein Veblen about "conspicuous consumption." She felt the house made us seem more affluent than we really were. There were constant expenses. For years, my parents sent money to our relatives in Poland and Israel. And my father was rebuilding his practice after his back surgeries.

These summers were opportunities for me to scrutinize the adult world. I realized that our family was different from others not just because my parents were European Jews, but because of their moderate religious observance, values, as well as their artistic inclinations. They observed few rituals; we did not attend synagogue and only celebrated our favorite holidays. Their interests were intellectual and aesthetic and they loved nature, as evidenced by the house they built. My parents neither designed nor thought of their new home as an investment. There was no thought of keeping up with the Joneses; they did not choose a style or size to impress anyone, but created a haven that pleased them aesthetically. Throughout the house were nods to styles of the regions in Poland, for example, the herringbone cypress wood paneling above my parents' bed. I learned later that this motif was often seen on doors in Zakopane, the Tatra Mountain resort where my mother's family hiked in summertime. Perhaps it even was on the walls of the Third-Class waiting room in Lwów's train station.

Our house reflected the way my parents brought us up. Both understood from experience how you could lose everything. We were to follow our own stars, not look over our shoulders to see what others were doing. If we did what we loved to the best of our abilities, the rewards would follow, they said. We were not to aim only to amass wealth because it might be here today, and could be gone tomorrow. Although both were politically liberal, my mother was a non-conformist, a hippie before the hippies. My father believed in the American dream and loved our country. She was more critical of it. He wanted to assimilate and looked to the future rather than the past and all that had been lost. She did not desire to fit in as much as my father. She knew she could not leave the past behind and that it had shaped her. She regarded every day as a gift. Both believed in enjoying life to the fullest. Together, they found the right balance.

Chapter Nine

Portraits

At the end of the summer of 1968, when I was about to turn thirteen, my great-aunt Lucia died of a brain tumor. The Washington Heights apartment she had lived in had also been the home of her parents, my great-grandparents, Sara and Heinrich Finkelstein. My mother and Franca, Lucia's daughter and my mother's cousin, began going through Lucia's belongings. Grimly, for several days in a row, my mother left home early and did not return until late. While clearing out a closet, she found three plastic garbage bags and was astonished to discover four life-size family portraits: two rolled up oils on canvas and two pastel boards, all dated 1912. She also found two large oval photographs circa 1870, one of a bearded man with laughing eyes wearing a top hat, and another of his wife, who wore a modest gray dress. In addition, my mother found several butter cookie tins filled with family photos, documents, and correspondence.

Franca did not want any of it, so my mother brought everything home. She inspected the paintings, and later, with great care, took them to a trusted artisan who cleaned and framed them.

The most spectacular oil portrait depicted Sara at age forty-four wearing an Edwardian aubergine dress with an ivory rose pinned to her waist. Beneath a huge black hat with a titanic brim, she seemed to look confidently and with interest at whoever viewed her. The work had a subtle, almost unfinished style that the artist had insinuated with a dry-brush, gray-aubergine background. I never knew Sara, who died a few months after I was born. My mother loved her. With pride she told us that Sara had declined to have a matchmaker select her husband. Instead, this proto-feminist attended the equivalent of junior college in Breslau, now Wrocław, Poland. "Unheard of back then," my mother exclaimed, "and she married for love at the scandalously old age of twenty-three." Sara's *bashert* was my great-grandfather Heinrich, who was from Kraków. His oil portrait was less successful than hers—a bit too dark and brooding, my mother thought, though apparently that was how he was even before the war. She said the painting was a take-off on Manet's portrait of the French journalist and statesman Georges Clemenceau.

My mother saved my great-grandparents' 1940 passports, so I knew Sara was born in 1868. The daughter of a wealthy man, Chajman Lewy, Sara was raised in Breslau in the largely German-speaking part of western Poland known as Silesia. At some point, Chajman changed his first name to Herman, perhaps to fit in. He is the watch factory entrepreneur I mentioned who was so prosperous by the turn of the 20th century that he owned an automobile.

In addition to their own portraits, my great-grandparents also commissioned pastel portraits of their four children. Their oldest, my great-aunt Isabella, did not survive the war and her portrait was lost. The portrait of her brother Max in his World War I uniform showed him hunched over, wide-eyed, chin on hands and facing the viewer. A thinker. Max brought the pastel to New York when he left Berlin in 1938 and it is magnificently preserved. His daughter, my mother's cousin Vera, inherited it.

The third and most important portrait to my mother depicted my grandmother Teofila and great-aunt Lucia, who were then ages fourteen and thirteen. Alas, this one was damaged; the plastic must have abraded and smudged Lucia's favorite feature, her fine, straight nose. My grandmother's face was intact, though; innocent in her coiled braids, her slightly downcast blue eyes do not meet viewers.

The portraits were painted by Stephan Zarnecki (whose real name was Goldfinger) while the family still lived in Kraków. He contracted syphilis, my mother said, and committed suicide at the age of twenty-eight.

My mother slowly organized the photos into twelve albums. Among them we found several shots of Teofila and Lucia that might have been studies taken in preparation for the pastel. One shows them in large hats like their mother's, but with big bows. They appear a little older in two faded sepia postcards taken in a studio in Zakopane, the Tatra Mountains resort where the family vacationed. Avid hikers, they got their exercise by exploring glacial lakes like the Eye of the Sea and other landmarks.

Two years after the family portraits were painted, on the eve of World War I, the Russian Army reached Kraków, so the Finkelsteins fled with their daughters to Berlin. Max, who had just graduated from law school, was conscripted and sent to the Eastern Front at Bessarabia, in the Kingdom of Romania near the Black Sea.

In Berlin, Heinrich turned from the family diamond business to cultured pearls and was one of the first, if not the first, to import them from the Orient. He, Sara, and their daughters lived very comfortably as they absorbed German culture during Weimar. I know no details of my grandmother Teofila's upbringing, though, just that her pet was a beloved German Shorthaired Pointer named Arko, as several photos show.

Because the three Finkelstein daughters "married back to Kraków," as my mother put it, there was much trafficking between the two cities and the family celebrated the Jewish holidays in Kraków. Teofila was a lady of leisure from an artistic family who took singing lessons, though she never sang opera professionally. My mother found Teofila's voice shrill and blamed that on bad training. She said Teofila was very lively, fun to be with, and the life of most parties, but my mother resented her volatile temper. My mother gave no details about what triggered it. Maybe Izydor's infidelities were the reason for Teofila's irritability.

Lucia, on the other hand, was both moody and accomplished. Her sensuous odalisque sculpture lounges in my dining room, seeming to harbor secrets. Off-white clay contrasts with an odd, dark wood pedestal, an old drawer that once might have contained lead type or the cards of a library catalogue. Another surviving piece, a badly cracked bas-relief, is clearly an idealization of Teofila; her nose is a little smaller and her less frizzy hair swirls romantically like a Greek maiden's. Among the photos we found a shot of another bust of Teofila, more realistic and older, with a bun at the base of her neck. But it shows only her profile. Whenever I look at the photograph, I wish I could walk around the bust to see my grandmother's likeness face-to-face and in 3-D.

Six years after the family portraits were completed, the world they depicted—of leisure and parties and plumed, wide-brimmed hats and feeling part of society at large—came to an end. But one day in Berlin in the early 1920s, another magnificent work of art literally fell into the Finkelsteins' hands. A messenger knocked on their door, confirmed that theirs was the Finkelstein residence, and shoved a large flat package at whoever answered the door. It was a portrait by one of Russia's greatest artists, Ilya Yefimovich Repin, which became the *piece de resistance* or I should say *Stük Widerstand* of the elder Finkelstein's art collection. In the 1970s, my mother bought the painting from Max, who told her it was a portrait of the opera singer Chaliapin in the role of Mephistopheles. There was no provenance so my mother tried to have the work assessed, but communication with Repin experts behind the Iron Curtain was difficult. Eventually, my sisters and I showed one of those experts the work. She pronounced it authentic in writing and said the painter had portrayed his friend, the Russian actor Grigoriy Grigoryevich Ge , in the role of Mephistopheles in a play based on Goethe's *Faust*. It was the only painting the Finkelsteins hung in their Washington Heights apartment, where the diabolical image—especially its calculating yet frenzied eyes—terrified us great-grandchildren, who tried to avoid looking directly at it.

Aunt Lucia's death was the first experience of loss my parents did not shield us from. She either succumbed to cancer quickly, or we were not told of her illness until it was clear it was fatal. We sat shiva, but I did not mourn Lucia because she had been critical and dismissive of my sisters and me.

A cascade of deaths followed, or so it seemed to me. Later that summer, my best friend Susan's grandmother, Mrs. Canada, died too. When we paid a call to the Jacksons at their St. Albans home, I was surprised that Susan and her mother seemed to take their loss with great poise and regarded it as a natural event.

Soon after, Mrs. Hildt, a Polish aristocrat from Warsaw and neighbor across our street in Forest Hills, also died. My mother was friends with her daughter, Marta, a champion skier. In contrast to the Jacksons, Marta was inconsolable. During the church service, she draped herself over Mrs. Hildt's casket, stroked the gray cloth of the coffin, and whispered and wept. It was wrenching and awful to see. What could anyone do to help her find solace?

For my mother, the loss of Lucia was a major blow but she did not cry. She pursed her lips and was quiet. Later, when she talked more about the portraits, I could tell she was surprised and hurt that for twenty-two years since her arrival here in 1946, no one had told her that a likeness existed of her mother as a young girl. Their silence proclaimed psychic damage and continued to wound; my relatives were so traumatized by loss that they could not share a precious artifact with my orphaned mother. And yet I still cannot accept that they failed her so deeply, failed to overcome their own sadness for her sake. She who had lost both parents while so young. I think Sara and Heinrich were so shattered by the loss of two of their daughters, Isabella and Teofila, that silence was the only way they could communicate their sorrow. Nevertheless, the unspoken and unseen found a way to be heard and viewed.

My great-grandparents were in their seventies when they fled Berlin in November 1940. They boarded a locked train transport with only the food and water they could carry, and traveled through Germany, France, and across the Iberian Peninsula to Lisbon. Their steamer trunks were shipped in advance to relatives in New York but one was lost along the way.

Twenty-seven years later, the arrival of the portraits to our home triggered my family's preoccupation with facial resemblances. When Michelle returned from college one weekend, she glanced at the rendering of Teofila and Lucia in the dim, cherry-tree shadowed dining room. With the tone of one who felt excluded, she asked, "Ma, you had Ivy and Karen painted?" My surprised mother scrutinized the work and concluded that despite my light hair, which was darkening as I approached puberty, I resembled Teofila. But she said I had Lucia's brown eyes. I was not pleased with this combination and it confused me because all those years, everyone said I looked like my father. My mother resembled Teofila too. Yet my parents looked nothing alike. So how could I look like all three of them? Not only that, Ivy also took after Teofila, which was fitting since she was named for her and Izydor—Ivy Teresa. She looked like Teofila in a different way, sharing exact coloring—blue eyes and almost black hair. Genes are truly mysterious.

The great debate in my family about who looks like whom continues among my sisters and me and extends to their children and grandchildren. Before and during holidays we discuss which features we do and do not have in common. Of course, each wants the others to agree that she resembles our stunning mother. Then we segue to my father's side of the family and speculate, based on the lone blurry photograph my dad brought with him in 1939. His mother, Michaela, is seated and looks at us from a three-quarter point of view, light hair parted to the side, tightly combed back and pinned up. Unlike the Finkelstein women, she has a soft chin and full lips and is voluptuous in her flowered blouse and long solid-colored skirt. Ojzer stands behind, a little to her right, in his best suit. Michelle announces that she looks just like Michaela, and has her nose, lips, and chin. We listen and nod. This is our ritual; it tightens our bonds. But we never debate who looks like Ojzer, the only grandparent to have survived. So it seems to me now that we are grasping for any detail in order to relate to our murdered grandparents—Teofila, Izydor, and Michaela—because we have so little else to go by. We have no other way to connect with the intangible, the unburied, the shiva-less and thus the improperly and incompletely mourned.

In the early 1980s when she was writing her will, my mother bequeathed the portrait of Sara to Ivy. Michelle inherited the portrait of Heinrich, which now hangs in the parlor of her Brooklyn brownstone. When Vera, Max's daughter, died, Michelle acquired his portrait. Ivy loves the painting of Sara, but does not have room for it on her apartment walls. So I live with the portrait; Sara watches from above my living room couch while I play the flute or do Pilates. Teofila and Lucia see Ed and me as we dine. I gaze back at them and their mother in wonder.

The portraits reveal how important family was to the Finkelsteins. They were valued enough to be smuggled out of Nazi Germany at great peril because Jews were not permitted, under the Nuremberg Laws, to keep works of art. And yet Sara and Heinrich had taken such a risk only to end up burying their treasures. At what point were the paintings banished to that closet? Immediately after my great-grandparents Sara and Heinrich unpacked, I believe, amid the torturous uncertainty about their daughters and their families left behind.

These works of art also represented a lost way of life. As elderly refugees supported by their refugee son, who had money to reframe those portraits? And although the elder Finkelsteins were grateful for shelter here, their apartment in Washington Heights must have been quite a comedown; judging from the eighteen-place china settings they transported in their trunks, their Berlin dining room was very large and the apartment opulent.

In 1946 and until the 1980s, when refugees, survivors, and extended family not in Europe gave up hope of finding missing relatives, euphemisms like they "did not make it" were preferred to the brutal term "murdered" that people rightly use today. So I'll say it: When it was clear that my grandparents Teofila and Izydor, my great-aunt Isa, and her husband my great-uncle Tobek, had been murdered, the once-treasured portraits became reminders of unendurable loss. They were also emblematic of the loss of a culture, the milieu of European assimilated urban Jews. The treasured artifacts that had memorialized pre-war times had to remain hidden in the back of a closet, shrouded in black garbage bags until the elder Finkelsteins died. And joined their lost loved ones. They had to remain unseen until their one surviving daughter, Lucia, rested with them all. I feel certain that those portraits were never hung because they made the journey whereas my grandmother, great-aunt, their husbands and children did not. Displaying the portraits would have required facing that the family was broken, and that the European Jews now existed as mere remnants.

What is the likeness of a fractured family? I have always thought that the worst loss a person can endure is the death of their child. It is utterly unnatural for parents to outlive their child or children. But what if your outlived children were victims of the most unfathomable onslaught against a minority ever perpetrated by one so-called civilization? What if your family was shattered by an event unique in history? How can you recover from both calamities? Why should you get over them? Some barbarisms and the resulting heartache are impossible to surmount.

But treasures are mutable; their values change over time. Because of their pain, my great-grandparents and great-aunt Lucia squirreled away their treasures and kept secrets from my mother. And secrets, when revealed, can feel like lies, undermine trust, and cause pain. My mother probably felt a little of all three, but she cherished and exhibited the paintings, and organized the photo collection so that her daughters would grow up with them and love them. They gave us a sense of history and, of course, intrigue.

But I was denied the experience of sitting on my grandmother Teofila's lap and feeling her caress. I never heard about her favorite paths to stroll on Kraków's Planty with my mother and Arko. Nor did I get to ask which Lieder she enjoyed singing most. My grandfather Izydor could not share with me his World War I stories, nor his triumphant court cases, nor later when I was old enough, explain his allegiance to the Polish General Jewish Labor Bund and his simultaneous attraction to German 19th-century philosophy. All this and so much more that I could not conceive of remained unknown and unknowable.

Chapter Ten

Gold and Prescience

When I was growing up, my mother and I tried several times to build the Finkelstein family tree, which was a huge task because it was a very large clan. Jewish families flourished in the mid-to late-19th century because they were allowed more rights and so could earn better livings and feed their children more nutritious food. As a result, more survived. My great-grandfather Heinrich was one of eleven siblings, six brothers and five sisters. My mother knew the New York and Antwerp brothers and could name most of the five sisters, who had settled in Antwerp. But our tree, crowded onto three pieces of scotch-taped together paper, was incomplete. Another branch, distant geographically but not emotionally, was in California. But my mother did not know who the first relative to emigrate was nor his exact relationship to the Kraków line. All she knew was that he had left Kraków when gold was discovered in northern California in 1848. Complicating matters, the "forty-niner" and other relatives who followed had changed their last names and chose different variations on the original for their new ones. I had their correspondence with my great-grandmother Sara, but they never signed with their last names.

My mother met several of these great-uncles during their 1937 visit to Kraków. In her oral history she mentioned them first in the context of borrowing money from them for visas and false papers. Then she added that one wanted to adopt her:

> I knew that we had very wealthy relatives here—my great-great-uncles came during the Gold Rush, and my great-uncles, who visited Krakow in '38 [sic]—I knew them. One wanted to take me to Stockton, California…

This prescient great-uncle was I. F. Stein, one of Heinrich's younger brothers. In my mind, he had taken on almost mythic import because he had tried to save my mother. I also knew he had been a successful businessman and active citizen who greatly influenced the growth of his town and that he eventually became the Kraków line's benefactor. I yearned to know more about this intelligent, attuned, and generous man who had never married.

It also surprised and intrigued me that the first settler had gone gold prospecting in the mid-19th century. A Polish Jew in the American El Dorado. What a story.

In 1983, I wrote to my great-uncle Max to ask about Uncle I. F. and the rest of the West Coast clan. His reply was a delightful and precious letter, full of direct translations from his native German, which accounts for his unusual sentence structures. He said the gold prospector was the younger brother of our forefather, my great-great-grandfather Abraham Finkelstein (the fellow with laughing eyes photographed in the top hat). Because news traveled slowly to Kraków in those days, Max said, goldsmith and watchmaker Markus Finkelstein and twenty other "young adventurers" sailed a little late to California and arrived in pre-canal Panama in 1850. Young Markus and his buddies traversed the Isthmus alternately by foot and by boat along the Panama Lakes. All succumbed to Yellow Fever, except Markus.

Delayed further by the epidemic, he arrived in San Francisco in 1851, after it had been devastated by a big fire. Few thought the city had much of a future so Markus settled 40 miles north in the prosperous town called Stockton. There he changed his last name to Marx and started a watchmaker business. He befriended a German Jew who owned a cigar store in the same building and married his daughter.

They had four children, presidentially named Fillmore and Monroe, and Hattie and Jenny.

In 1870, Finkelstein/Marx returned to Kraków, where Abraham was struggling with his jewelry business. Abraham gladly accepted his brother's offer to import his eldest son, Martin, to America. But Martin was bookish, so Markus sent him to college and requested another nephew. Max wrote:

> My father Heinrich was supposed to be the next emigrant to America. My father Heinrich never got to Stockton, he was too important help in support of his mother and 5 sisters in Kraków. The next one, Maurice, was gainfully employed with a jeweler in Vienna. The choice was Ignaz, who gladly followed the call. Ignaz was an extrovert and needed less than a year for a complete acclimatization. He and brother Martin changed their name to Stein and became Martin F. Stein and I. F. Stein. I. F. used probably only on official documents the Stein name, but in business and private life he was known as I. F. The brothers formed an Ice & Fuel Co.; Martin speculated also in real estate and gained and lost fortunes. He married his cousin Hattie Marx, but they didn't have children....Fillmore married Gussie Fox, a S. Francisco society girl. They had 2 daughters and 1 son, a beautiful home and lived far above the means of Fillmore.
>
> In the meantime, I. F. was making lots of money not only from Fuel and Ice, but from his Brick Co. He never married, died too young, and left in his estate besides his companies some 20 buildings, among them the only skyscraper in Stockton the Medico-Dental Bldg.

By 1939, all the Finkelstein brothers except my great-grandfather Heinrich had died. When Uncle I. F. died the year before, he left his estate to Heinrich's heirs, and to his five sisters and their heirs. Because many of the beneficiaries were caught in Europe, I. F. appointed his nephew and business partner, Fillmore, manager of the estate. After Fillmore died in 1949, thirty-two heirs received their inheritances. "In retrospect, the war years were hard for foreigners," commented Max, who represented the European side when the estate was disbursed in 1949, "but I. F.'s money gave every one of us a foothold." My parents used my mother's share of his estate for the down payment on our house in Forest Hills in 1955 when they were expecting me.

As a reporter covering technology, I often made business trips to Silicon Valley. Before I flew west, my mother would suggest that I try to find our relatives there. I couldn't find them and was frustrated. Because I relied on Max's letter, there was no reason to check the spelling he gave for our relatives' changed last names. In 2005 when I was in San Francisco with a friend, Kate Patterson, I mentioned my missing relatives. "The last name is Marx. I must be doing something wrong."

Kate had an acquaintance who worked in development for the Jewish community. She told me that since my relatives arrived in the mid-19th century, they were probably involved in the local synagogue. She contacted Temple Israel in Stockton and their oral historian responded that my relatives had been past presidents of the congregation, and that Marx was spelled "Marks." Uncle Max had gotten the spelling of the last name wrong. The find was wonderful and yet a little disappointing, because I harbored a fantasy that I might be related to Richard Marx, the rocker. (I later found out that one of the Marks descendants, Jessica Baer Mears, had the same fantasy.) But overall, I was thrilled. The suspense was heightened though, because the son of one of the past presidents, Fillmore Marks, Jr., was in Europe. I had to wait until he returned to see if he wanted to know me.

One day in the mid-2000s, while waiting for Fillmore Jr. to return from his trip, I Googled the Finkelsteins. Up popped a family tree, which didn't even resemble the one my mother and I had tried to draw on three sheets of scotch-taped paper. It looked like a list of names with dates; each generation was indicated by a few keyboard space bars to the right, and men were denoted by Xs and women by Os. Dan Hirschberg, a computer scientist at UC Irvine, had built the Finkelstein tree based on birth and death records stored in a Mormon library. The Church of Latter-Day Saints had acquired these documents to beatify the Jews of Kraków who had been murdered during the Holocaust. After building his own family tree, Hirschberg decided to tackle all 700 root Kraków families. For fun. Then he incorporated census records from Kraków's municipal archives. The trees are available through his website at University of California, Santa Barbara, and on JewishGen.org as the Dr. Dan Hirschberg - Kraków Collection. Other census records are in the *Archiwum Główne Akt Dawnych* (Central Archives of Historical Records), also known as the Warsaw AGAD.

Our tree not only revealed that the Finkelstein clan dates back to the 1790s, but corrected mistakes Uncle Max had made. My line showed that my great-great-grandfather Abraham was born in 1824. (It was his and his wife Laja's photographs that my mother inherited in 1968.) Abraham had an older (not younger) brother, Mozes (not Markus) Finkelstein, born two years earlier. They were the sons of Markus Finkelstein. Mozes was the forefather who had arrived in the promised land of the California Gold Rush.

Fillmore Jr. returned from his trip and was delighted to hear from me. He said he had just been lamenting to his wife Barbara (née Mayer of Chicago) that she came from a large family, whereas his side was so small. He filled me in on his branch's history; Mozes Marks was his grandfather and had chosen his new last name in honor of his father, Markus. Max had conflated father and son. Mystery solved.

Fillmore Jr. shared some colorful lore, like that a madam in a Panama City brothel had nursed Mozes back to health during the epidemic, which delayed his journey a year. But Fillmore Jr. had no idea that his original family name was Finkelstein. He also was unaware that Uncle I. F. had tried to adopt my mother, but mentioned that the family had adopted a German boy. We stayed in touch and exchanged more information and documents. When Fillmore and Barbara visited New York a few years later, we had a lovely brunch.

I shared the electronic tree with Fillmore, who passed it along to his sons Doug, Will, and Brad; we have all since filled it in. Will visited New York and brought a xerox of a photo taken in 1900 of Mozes and Fillmore Sr. on the rooftop of one of their buildings, perhaps the Miller Warehouse, with two workmen wielding hammers. All except Mozes wore cowboy hats to shield them from the bright California sun. Mozes sported a dapper bowler instead. Will also shared fascinating newspaper clippings about Martin Stein's many businesses, including investments in almond and wheat futures, and a 1950 article about I. F.'s estate, the city of Stockton's largest at the time.

Doug and his family went to Kraków and visited the New Jewish Cemetery at the foot of Miodowa Street in Kazimierz to look for Markus's grave. Instead, they found Abraham's headstone, a large gray stone slab topped by a brown cornice. I found out that the monument did not mark Abraham's grave, however, because during the Occupation the Nazis removed such monuments at the front of the cemetery and threw them into a pile. They used the flat monuments to pave the way to Kraków-Płaszów Concentration Camp, which was depicted in the movie *Schindler's List*. Perhaps that's why I could not find Laja's headstone. Now it is the full-time job of a grave keeper to try to return the headstones to their original plots according to old cemetery maps.

Before leaving New York, I had asked a Warsaw AGAD researcher to find out where my maternal grandparents had been married. Up the street from the cemetery, I stood in the magnificent 19th-century Progressive Tempel (German spelling) and burst into tears as I admired the bima and imagined Izydor and Teofila's wedding there in 1923. For an instant, I tried to envision them standing before a rabbi as he blessed their union. Top hat, lace veil, cream white shoes. But I could not linger. I turned away to the rust-red walls with painted flowers and the gold-trimmed columns. Why had the Nazis not destroyed this magnificent treasure, I wondered, as they had so many Jewish houses of worship?

Later I determined through ship manifests on Ancestry.com that my great-great-uncles Paul and I. F. visited Kraków in 1937 and returned to New York from Rotterdam. Maurice of Antwerp may have accompanied them to Kraków, but since they probably traveled by rail, there is no record. Because of the Nuremberg Laws, my great-grandparents Heinrich and Sara could not leave Berlin and join them.

Uncle I. F. visited Kraków on the fiftieth anniversary of his departure. Perhaps this perceptive, brilliant businessman understood the danger threatening European Jews because he had analyzed it from afar. What heartbreak he must have suffered when Heinrich and Sara spurned his offer to adopt my mother. But like father like son; Abraham would not allow Heinrich to leave Kraków, therefore Heinrich forbade his daughter Teofila and son-in-law Izydor to part with their only child. This, despite Teofila's willingness to do so. As my mother continued in her oral history:

> ...One [great-uncle, I. F.] wanted to take me to Stockton, CA. And it seemed unbelievable that my mother said, "Yes. You take her." My grandmother objected strenuously and didn't allow it. But mother said, "If she gets out, we will get out."

Wealthy, generous, prescient, powerful Uncle I. F. was foiled by his older brother. And my frustrated, cowed grandmother Teofila appreciated I. F.'s offer but had to obey her less-discerning elders.

Chapter Eleven

Never Worn

During a late-summer storm in 1970, the older and bigger of our two Queen Anne cherry trees was struck by lightning and split in two. The graceful, aged tree had bifurcated long ago, enabling it to spread its glorious branches and blossoms over the part of our lawn farthest from our street. The arch its branches made with the other, smaller cherry tree seemed like a floral vaulted ceiling. Cathedral-like, it graced the entrance to our more private backyard.

Before we began spending summers on Long Island, Ivy and I would climb into the big tree's nook and play. Every late June, when the bloom faded, we watched the little white petals flutter down to our lawn like incongruous summer snowflakes. Come July, we inched up from the nook along the branches to harvest ripe, yellow-orange cherries. If a bird had not picked at them, they were juicy and sweet, but the taste was tangier than Bings. As we got older and heavier, our parents forbade us to climb, for our safety as well as for the sake of the damaged trunk. Instead, after exhausting the low hanging fruit, we got a ladder from our basement so that we could reach and forage amid the shiny, deep-green leaves.

We had done everything we could to prevent the water that collected in the big tree's cranny from rotting the lower trunk—tar, cement, gravel. Nothing worked. This next-to-last vestige of the cherry orchard became more and more vulnerable.

My father ordered Tony, our gardener, to cut down the charred and ruptured trunk. "Do it so that no one will ever know a tree grew there," he said. Ivy and I looked at the torn, raw wood, and felt stricken.

"Why did you tell Tony that?" I asked.

"What should I have told him? We can't leave a stump."

I had no answer, but a feeling of desolation lingered inside of me.

"The flavor of Lwów and its culture is tart," the Polish poet Józef Wittlin wrote in his 1946 memoir, *Mój Lwów* (*My Lwów*), wistfully adding that it was like the taste of an unusual fruit, the *czeremcha*, a wild cherry that ripened only in a suburb called Kleparów. "Nostalgia even likes to falsify flavors too, telling us to taste nothing but the sweetness of Lwów today. But I know people for whom Lwów was a cup of gall."

Struck by Wittlin's words, I connected them to our cherry trees and my father. I emailed Alex Dunai, the Lviv guide and historian, to ask if he knew of the cherries Wittlin had described. He said his wife's family resides in that area, now called Klepariv (in Ukrainian). "She recalls two cherry trees, that, according to her grandpa, were the remnants of those famous Klepariv cherry orchards," he wrote and added that they were predominantly gone after World War I.

How odd, I thought. Four cherry trees, two defunct orchards.

Unfortunately neither the species nor the Latin name are known, Alex continued. "Now they may be completely extinct." Then he corrected the name Wittlin used for the cherries. "*Czeremcha* is a completely different plant and means sour bird cherry," he said. He claimed the proper name is *czereshnia*. "Those cherries had a rich sweet and sour taste, almost reminding some of red wine," Alex explained, really getting into it.

It seemed uncanny and not coincidental that my father had chosen a house on the site of an erstwhile cherry orchard. And even though I understood my father's reasoning about the stump, it pained me that our magnificent remnant had to be obliterated. Sheared to the ground and grown over. Blanked out, like my father's memories of his hometown. No nostalgic *czereshnia* wine for him.

My father's back was better, but my mother was constantly ill, as if somehow it was her turn. Periodontal surgeries for chronic gum disease, a consequence of not being allowed to see a dentist during the war, flattened her. She lay in bed for days with debilitating headaches only to learn years later that she had developed an allergy to the penicillin packs her surgeon applied to prevent infection while she healed. During these bouts, I kept her company and we read together in my parents' bedroom. We "laughed ourselves silly," as she used to say, over Voltaire's *Candide*. My mother was tickled by any joke having to do with buttocks, which in Polish are called *dupa* (pronounced doopa), itself a funny-sounding word. Her delight accelerated as she read to me of the poor old woman, daughter of Pope Urban X and the Princess of Palestrina.

"Half a *dupa*? Half-assed! Voltaire is absolutely marvelous. What an imagination!" she remarked and then roared. She thoroughly appreciated every page of Voltaire's satire, headaches or not. At first, I worried about the old woman's pain, but my mother relished the metaphor. Her laughter bounced around the room, spreading a sense of hilarity so contagious that I joined her. She said my grandmother Teofila used to laugh uncontrollably, too. *Dupa* jokes, evidently a family affinity, were also her favorites.

"Do you suppose sense of humor is inherited?" my mother wondered. We giggled so much that we alarmed Pooch, who sat up suddenly and tried to climb into bed, which was forbidden.

On a warm early fall evening, I entered our living room where my father was lying on the couch. From where I stood, his face seemed unusually pink.

"Dad, it's dinner time. Wake up," I said as I approached. He did not answer and just lay there, beads of sweat dotting his forehead. Now at his side, I repeated myself. Nothing. I touched his shoulder. No response. I waited a few seconds and then terror slammed me. I bent over and shook him.

My father's eyes sprung open. "Daddy, didn't you hear me?" I glared. "You scared me!"

"Give me a kissy, Kareny." Relieved, I kissed his drenched forehead. As he rolled onto his side, the way he had been taught to protect his back, and pushed himself up from the sofa, my nerves again overtook me.

"Why didn't you answer? You didn't hear me?"

My father looked drowsily at me. "Don't tell Mommy."

"Mommy, Daddy's playing jokes on me!" I shrieked. I had just turned fifteen, but in my anxiety, I regressed.

"What *is* it? Everything is getting cold," my irritated mother yelled back from the kitchen. I knew that tone. It meant, "Is it too much for everyone to come straight to the table when I have carefully prepared our meal?"

"Don't do that ever again," I said to my father as I stalked out. I remained mad at him throughout the meal, refusing to engage in conversation no matter what he said.

Then there was the blowout on my father's commute home from Brooklyn when one of his tires ruptured on the Brooklyn-Queens Expressway. He called my mother and asked her to come get him. My mother did, and when she returned home, had a conniption.

"I don't know what's wrong with your father," she fumed, as she hurriedly finished making dinner. "He calls me when he has an accident?"

"What should he have done?" I asked as I made the salad. I had not yet taken Driver's Ed and knew nothing of cars and the rules of the road.

"He was supposed to call Triple A. You call them and they tow you. Triple A! He calls his wife, not Triple A." I had never seen my mother this agitated and exasperated with my father. "Something's not right," she said as she put the pressure cooker under the kitchen tap to cool.

Two weeks later, on a Saturday morning, my father and I were in our Lincoln Continental bound for one of the hospitals where he was an attending. He had asked me to accompany him to Brooklyn Women's where he would make rounds.

We passed by burned-out apartment buildings with boarded up windows. I was aghast at the rubble and litter everywhere. And the poverty. The buildings looked like shelled hulks of brick and limestone. No one entered or emerged. Skinny stray dogs trotted along the cracked sidewalks. While we stopped and waited for our light to change, ragged men on a corner warmed their hands around flames that licked the rim of a metal garbage can. Burning Brooklyn garbage imitating the incinerated South Bronx.

"Dad, why are we going through this neighborhood?" I was alarmed and even felt imposed upon. "I don't feel safe."

"We are safe. We're going this way on purpose," my father answered. "I want you to see."

"Why? Why do I have to see this?"

"I want you to look because I want you to know what can happen to entire neighborhoods."

The streets were unrelentingly desolate. The buildings appeared bombed out. What was his point? World War III?

"But why are there so many empty buildings? Couldn't they stop the fires?"

"It's not clear that they can. Or that they want to. Some people think it's a wave of arson. Others say the landlords burned their buildings to get insurance money."

I looked at my father in amazement. Then I became indignant. "Isn't that illegal?"

"Sure it's illegal. But they can get away with it. And the destruction you see, all this is why it's important for you to study. That homework you left to the last minute, that chemistry final and the others coming up—" He lifted his right hand from the steering wheel and gestured with a panoramic sweep. "*This* is why you must study. So that when you grow up, you have a profession. Earn a living so that you never have to live in a place like this."

I sulked and then asked, "You think I might have to live in a slum?"

"Not if you make something of yourself," my father reassured me. "But you must study and work for that. So you can make the world a better place. Contribute to society."

My father had never spoken to me so seriously. I turned to him and listened.

"You probably hear from your friends about all kinds of recreational drugs. Never mind all that. Do you understand? Marijuana—"

"Pot, Dad."

"Whatever you want to call it. Lots of people are on drugs now. But I'm telling you as a medical doctor, as your father, don't start."

"But it's just a plant."

"Don't talk nonsense. Plants are not meant for smoking." *Oh maaaan, what about your Tareytons*, I smirked internally. Tobacco is a plant. I turned toward the window. "And no matter what anybody else says," he continued, "I'm warning you, one drug leads to another. I know. And then you don't feel like doing schoolwork."

I turned back again to watch him closely. So that was the connection. Study to make something of yourself so you can heal the world.

"You try marijuana," he continued, "and the thrill wears off. Before you know it, you're trying something else."

"Like what?"

"Doesn't matter what. Don't take it."

"OK, Dad. OK."

We arrived at the hospital and my father told me to wait in the lobby while he visited his patients. A nurse approached and greeted him with a smile. He introduced us.

"This is Birdie Williams," my father said. "We've worked together in surgery for many years." He gestured toward me. "My youngest, Karen."

"I thought so. Hello Karen." She smiled again, this time at me. I was still in my awkward, gangly phase, having grown very suddenly. I shyly smiled back. "This one looks just like you."

Birdie must have met Ivy, who had already been on rounds with my father several times. Clearly, Birdie liked and respected my father and I was impressed that she knew about my sisters and me. How personal a hospital community is, I thought, the staff chats about their families. Is she the operating room nurse who, when my ambidextrous father asked for a scalpel, asked which hand? Or was she the one who, according to my mother, asked him to operate on her when she had a gynecological problem? "Yah, that's how loved your father is by the OR nurses," my mother once said. "They see what's what, right there on the operating table. There is no higher compliment for a surgeon."

I began to wonder what I could do when I grew up that would help those less fortunate than me.

The next Thursday night I was sitting on the rug in my bedroom, amidst my class notes and two chemistry textbooks. I leaned against my bed answering practice questions. My door was open a few inches and my father entered.

"Kareny, I don't feel so good," he said. All week he had been complaining of a sour stomach and had been eating antacids.

"Did you take your Maalox?" I asked without looking up.

"Yes, but it's not helping." He seemed down.

"Maybe it needs more time." I turned around to face him and said I thought I finally understood the concept of chemical equilibrium. He didn't react. "But Dad, my final is next week, alright?"

My father apologized for disturbing me and returned to my parents' bedroom down the hall. I immediately felt guilty, but I shunted that aside and tried to concentrate on reviewing a few more questions. I needed to finish the chapter before going to bed. I wanted to do well and bring home not an A minus, but an A to my father.

The next evening right before dinner, my father got a call on his office phone. A patient had gone into labor and he left for Brooklyn Women's. My mother had asked him to cut back on delivering babies and to delegate to his residents, and he had, but apparently he was concerned enough about this patient to want to be present in the operating room. I heard him backing his car out of our driveway. Bye Dad, I thought. When he returned later that night, I would shout as usual to the rest of the family, "Daddy's home," and hurry down the stairs to keep him company at the kitchen table while he ate a late, warmed up soup-meat dinner.

Instead, while Ivy and I were watching television, my mother's line rang. She called up to us from the foyer to say that she would be gone for a while. We heard her make a phone call before she left.

Standing in the doorway to my parents' bedroom several hours later, my mother told us our father had died of a massive heart attack.

Ivy and I burst into tears and my mother backed away. I don't remember much about what happened next. At some point I found myself downstairs in the kitchen where my mother's friend Goldie stood crying at the table. I think my mother was on the phone in the dining room.

I neither remember when nor who told me about my father's last moments. He had stopped by his favorite bar, where he regularly lunched, and asked for a glass of grapefruit juice. He felt nauseated and asked the bartender, who knew him, to call the hospital for an ambulance. My father went to his car to wait. By the time the ambulance came, he was slumped over the steering wheel. His body was still warm when my mother arrived at the hospital.

My father should have been surrounded by family when he died. That would have been no less devastating for us, but at least my father would have died while we held his hands. After all that he had been through, all that he would not tell us, why was this small comfort not to be?

Later that night, Ivy and I gathered around our mother in the bedroom as she called Michelle, who was newlywed and living with her husband, Alan, in Portugal.

"Your father is not well," my mother said, "You have to come home." I was surprised by this.

"What do you mean he's not well?" Michelle asked.

"You have to come home."

"Is he alive?"

"No."

My mother handed the receiver to Ivy and then to me.

I whispered only, "Hi Michelley."

"Hi Kareny," she said. When I heard her sob, I, too, lost my composure. She asked me to hand the phone back to our mother. After she hung up, my mother sipped her vodka until she became sleepy and we tucked her in, as we later would do every night.

I asked Ivy if I could sleep in her room, like I had when we were little. "Or do you want to be alone?"

"No. I *want* you to sleep here with me," she replied without hesitation. The extra bed, which had been mine, was still there. Without disturbing my mother, we got the sheets and blanket from the linen closet and made the bed.

Ivy and I either could not sleep, or cried so much that we slept from exhaustion.

Why? Why did this have to happen?

And this was just the beginning of mourning.

The next day, my mother was dazed. One of her friends took her address book and started notifying everybody. Michelle and Alan's flight out of Lisbon was canceled because of fog. They considered taking the train to Madrid, but discovered that much of Europe was fogged in. The funeral, which was scheduled for Monday, was postponed until they arrived mid-week.

The funeral was at Schwartz Brothers on Queens Boulevard. My mother left the side parlor and went to view the open casket. For a second, I watched her unbearably sad face tilting down toward my father. I felt I was intruding and had to look away. She returned and brought us back with her. This does not look like my father, cannot possibly be my father, I thought. My father's strong chin had been pushed back and there was a gash above his upper lip, the result of the force with which he hit the steering wheel. The wound terribly distressed me, but that was nothing like the nonabsorbable fact that my affectionate, brilliant, and kind father, who had been so devoted to his family, friends, and patients, had died alone in his car. Alone, alone, alone. Alone in the cold.

I clutched my mother's hand.

The place was packed. So was our house throughout the weeklong shiva. All I remember were callers entering our foyer and their hushed tones as they said "Irene" and embraced my widowed mother. Widowed at age forty-five after twenty-three years of marriage.

One afternoon, Aunt Mary, a friend of my father's who was an executive secretary at CBS, came to see Ivy and me upstairs. She hugged us and asked me why I was crying. How can she ask that, I thought, but I could not be rude to my father's friend so I blurted, "Because Daddy is dead and Mommy will never be happy again." Tears welled up in Aunt Mary's eyes. But at that moment, my mother was passing by Ivy's room and Aunt Mary repeated what I had said. It happened so fast that I couldn't stop her. I had not intended these words for my mother. She paused and turned away so that I could not read her reaction. Later, my mother told me it was excruciating to see her children mourn.

When I did not cry myself to sleep, I stayed awake long into the night, staring into the darkness and worrying about my father in his dark grave. I fretted about him being all by himself moldering away in his beautiful pine casket, with its Jewish star on the shiny outside over his chest and folded hands, his head on a little pillow.

In a flash on December 11, 1970, whatever joy had thrived in my family was obliterated, wiped out. Our family life was demolished, my parents' love affair destroyed. My mother was near collapse as reality—her newly disintegrated, mangled, cracked, splintered reality—began to sink in. Grief paralyzed my sisters and me. At ages twenty-one, sixteen, and fifteen our hopes and dreams were wrecked. We understood how unstable everything is. We learned that loved ones could disappear in an instant. Suddenly, I saw how brittle and delicate and easily busted life was. Fractured, shattered, smashed, forever.

My father had been relieved not to have had three sons. He and his two brothers were rascals and he thought girls were easier to handle. Now he would never see Ivy and me grown. Nor would he take pride in the accomplishments all three of us would achieve as professionals, for which we were so carefully prepared. I was not sorry for myself—that I felt orphaned, I mean. I grieved for my father because he had had so much more living to do. At fifty-seven he had plenty of gusto. He was still young. He had been deprived, cheated. My sorrow felt like searing pain in and behind my eyes. My throat seemed to be perpetually closing, as if I was choking because my father's life had been throttled. I cried and gagged and cried.

My mother asked Michelle and Alan to post notices at Brooklyn Women's and the other four hospitals where my father had admitting privileges. They also posted at Downstate Medical School where my father had taught gynecology as a clinical associate professor.

The New York Times ran an obituary: "Dr. David Frenkel, Infertility Expert," but I have no memory of seeing it. Even now, I cannot bear to read it. My father had authored or co-authored nine journal articles and was preparing four more research papers when he died. He had realized his dream to teach and his residents fanned out across the world. My father was especially proud of having invented a surgical technique for women who suffered ectopic pregnancies and subsequent infertility. The idea was to clear and suture their fallopian tubes so that scar tissue grew only on the outside. For this pioneering surgical technique and his first paper on pneumonia, he was included in the *Medical Who's Who.*

My mother called UNIS and spoke with the headmaster, who waived our final exams. We would not return until the end of the school holiday break.

At dinner I could not look for long at my father's empty chair at the head of the table near the lone cherry tree outside. I stared at my plate. We started eating in the kitchen.

Barely a year before, at my parents' New Year's party, jolly friends had congregated to drink and dance. In my head I heard their laughter after my father cracked a joke. They admired my beautiful mother in her teal satin, boatneck dress as she served hors d'oeuvres. My parents and their guests fox-trotted in our living room and spilled out into the foyer, balancing their champagne flutes.

I wandered into the living room like a sleepwalker and saw out of the corner of my eye the empty spot on the couch where my father used to watch *The Huntley-Brinkley Report* before dinner or Arnold Palmer putt on Saturday afternoons. I floated over to our upright piano. My father used to sit on the bench and play either the "Moonlight Sonata" or "Für Elise." When he felt too confined, he relaxed by improvising with whimsical, jazzy musical jokes. He would single out a motif, exaggerate it to the point of caricature, and then laugh his head off. His versions were quite convincing and I was not always certain which was the original. What a charming and courageous way to respond to Beethoven, perhaps Germany's greatest composer—with affection and generosity in the wake of what that culture wrought more than a century later.

Two years earlier, when I yearned to play the flute, for six months I had to convince my father I would not quit, as I had piano. Satisfied, he took me to 47th Street to buy the instrument. He played the piano well but grew curious about the flute. I taught him what I learned from my teacher, and we bought another student flute. My father made me feel so special and confident because I could share something I knew with him, rather than the other way around. Eventually we got good enough to play duets. On the music stand rested the *Album of Flute Duets* we had played the weekend before. I remembered that my father had had trouble controlling his fingers; they shook as he tried to cover the key holes.

"Daddy, what's the matter?" I asked.

"It's nothing," he said. Although not out of breath, after a while he suggested that I continue without him; he would watch and listen. I registered that something was wrong. I think I sensed that subconsciously, just as I had been so alarmed that late summer moment before dinner, when I could not rouse my slumbering father. Yet instead of saying something either to him or my mother, I basked in his attention as I played alone. Later, I berated myself and asked why I had reported nothing. But it turned out that my mother already knew; after weeks of cajoling my father, he had finally made an appointment to see a cardiologist. It would have been the Monday after the shiva.

My father's flute rested on the piano top where he had left it. I packed it up. Sheathed in its case, I hid it. I did not pack up my flute, but I could not touch it for many months.

I ran upstairs to my room and shoved my navy-blue dress with its princess seams and puffy sleeves to the back of my closet, so that I would not have to look at what I had worn to my father's funeral. My father's funeral? How could there have been a funeral for my father? How could my father be dead?

I stepped into my parents' walk-in closet and looked at my father's suits. Together we had bought three at Field Brothers just a few weeks ago. My father felt he had splurged, but his usual gray glen and houndstooth plaids were a little worn, he said. And he wanted something different. After he had made his selection, I watched the tailor, chalk in hand, mark where to adjust the shoulders and how much to take in the waists. A week later when we arrived to pick them up, my father tried on his suits in front of the tall mirror. Now my fingers grazed the fabric of the new, deep-brown suit with tiny beige dots that he had hesitated to buy; he thought that compared to his other suits it was dark, a little somber and severe.

Now none would ever wear out.

Chapter Twelve

Adrift and Betrayed

Ivy and I returned to school in mid-January of 1971. We took the crowded subway, with its torn rattan seats that always shredded our stockings, from Forest Hills to midtown Manhattan. As we walked east along 53rd Street, much seemed changed yet some constants persisted. The building that had been under construction on the corner of First Avenue was now sealed, but we knew the hard hats who had ogled us during lunchtime would return. In the fall, they had sat on the sidewalk with their legs open and the soles of their yellow, lace-up boots pointing at us, while they commented on our bra sizes.

On the second floor of our school, my friends and I had hung out between classes on the hump of a ramp that bridged two buildings. The incline extended the main hallway from the library and science labs to slope down into classroom spaces defined by movable, 6-foot-high wooden partitions. Some faculty had enclosed offices against the outer wall on the right. It was all very innovative and très Mod.

At this juncture between classes and during recess, we monitored the school traffic to and fro. We eyed each other's bell-bottoms and deliberated whose were wider. We speculated over whether our calculus teacher was dating the principal's secretary. We anticipated upcoming parties and debated Simon & Garfunkel's "Bridge Over Troubled Water" versus The Jackson 5's "I'll Be There," and what a drag that both "weren't danceable."

At the beginning of the school year when Ivy and I were in tenth and eleventh grade, UNIS had moved from an abandoned public school on First Avenue and 70th Street to these refurbished warehouses on York and 54th. The walls and ceilings were white, but assorted sections had been painted psychedelic colors: neon turquoise, dayglo orange, and acid yellow. Even the bathrooms seemed dipped in kitschy, electric tones. In the fall, I had stood at the mirror of the bright blue girls' room on the first floor with my friend, who I'm renaming Monique. As the scent of french fries wafted in, she put on mascara and announced in her most sophisticated voice, "You know, of course, that my father is having an affair."

"What? That can't be."

"Why not?" she retorted. "I showed you the photo of him with that blonde on his lap. Remember? In the top drawer of his desk."

I refused to believe it. "If he were having an affair, he wouldn't have brought that photo home."

Monique glanced at me with utmost disdain. "Ugh, Frenkel, you are so naïve," she said archly. "Look, let's just drop it." Then she applied blush.

She was right. I had grown up with the secure feeling, the luxury even, that my parents' marriage was quite happy even though of course there were stresses and strains. Proof came not long after Monique's comment when one night my mother got a phone call on my father's line.

"Mrs. Frenkel? You don't know me, but I knew your husband very well," a woman's voice said. My mother waited. "I was in love with him," the woman continued with a tone that revealed she was not sober. "I told him so when we were in Bermuda at a medical conference. But I didn't stand a chance because he was madly in love with you."

"What do you want?" my mother snapped.

"A photograph of him." My mother hung up.

Then I remembered another photograph that revealed my father's jealousy. Someone had shot a Polaroid of my mother dancing with one of my father's handsomest friends at a party. The way he held her and my mother's smile betrayed sexual attraction. My father threw a fit. He knew his friend and his friend's wife, both doctors, had an "open marriage. " My mother never danced with that gentleman again.

Returning to school, I tried to blend in with my friends and classmates. At first, I felt as conspicuous as the garish décor. I longed to slink away into a muted background where I did not have to pretend that I did not feel different. But in fact, I did act different and withdrew. The year before in assembly, we had seen Ingmar Bergman's *The Seventh Seal.* Back then, death was distant, hooded, and holding a sickle. A scary, pale, mean chess player in a chilling, weird movie that Ivy, our classmates, and I were too young to understand at ages fourteen and fifteen. But now I knew more. I could not relate to the happy-go-lucky flirtations of teenagers in my midst; they saw Bergman's great opus and that was all. It was removed from their experience, but not from mine. I was living it. Even before my father died, I would not have been one of those silly, carefree girls, but I certainly could not join them now. They could joke, laugh loudly, and feel confident that even if they were sad, the feeling would pass. They got over their sadness the next day. I could not.

I lingered on the sidelines. I felt that my classmates, except for my friends, were secretly thankful that they were not in my shoes. I sensed this when I approached a clique and their voices lowered, or hushed completely, and they turned from each other toward me and back again. The expressions on their faces indicated that they were sorry for me, but also relieved that their fathers—at work, as always—were safe and coming home for dinner. I could see this in their eyes; it was clear they didn't know what to say to me. Their awkward silence showed me that I was tainted. A downer. It was so much more fun to talk about their latest crushes.

The whole upper school knew what had happened. Between Ivy and me, the older siblings of our classmates and the younger ones of Michelle's, word got around. Older kids who had never said hello before while passing in the hallway now nodded in recognition, and with a sympathetic glance, continued on. That made it harder, even though I knew their intentions were kind. In retrospect, I think these momentary interactions were constant reminders of my loss when, for an instant, I might not have been feeling it. They broke my reprieve, my need to not feel like the girl whose dad had dropped dead. Those temporary, miniscule moments helped me to not feel abnormal, so that I could keep going.

The shock of my father's death began to wear off. As I gradually absorbed the fact of his permanent absence, anger and envy detonated slowly inside me, threatening to alienate the friends I still had. I was forced to grow up fast in some ways and I was left behind in others, especially social ones.

Our teachers offered us make-up exams and gave us much-needed leeway to take them when we felt ready. Of course, that was never. Yet I plunged myself into this work—both as a distraction and to honor my father's parting instructions. *Make something of yourself, make something of yourself, make something of yourself.* I clung to this mantra, but had difficulty concentrating. I also did not want to burden my mother with worry about my schoolwork, on top of everything else she had to handle. Ivy was not doing well and was under tremendous pressure as the second round of SATs loomed.

My chemistry teacher, Alan Honeyman, sent word that he wanted to see me. An energetic, short and blond Yorkshireman with red sideburns, he doubled as our soccer coach. He even voluntarily held practice in Central Park on Saturdays. We had a special rapport because he understood my visual difficulties; in fact, his eyes were not perfectly aligned either. One day in chemistry class, he called on me to copy chemical equations from my notebook to the blackboard. I stood there with my back to the class and tried to make the transfer but kept losing my place when I tried to focus on my book. With my right hand holding it and my left grasping a piece of chalk, I could not put a finger on the page to guide me. I made one mistake after another. Mr. Honeyman understood that my visual challenges were preventing me from easily switching from close print to the blackboard and vice versa. I had poor near-far accommodation, as Dr. Ludlum, the eye doctor who had given me visual training exercises, later explained. While I smarted, Mr. Honeyman behaved as if my mistakes were the most natural thing in the world, said it was OK, and in his Northern England accent commanded my tittering classmates to "Shoooot oop." Then he called on someone else.

Mr. Honeyman was attentive to Ivy as well. He loaned her a special workbook about S and P orbitals, the spherical and hourglass-shaped clouds in which electrons spin around an atom's nucleus. He spent extra time helping her, for which she was very grateful, she said later, because she was far better prepared than her college classmates when she took chemistry.

I knocked on the faculty lounge door, fearing the attention that waited on the other side. Another teacher—who had never taught me—answered and hugged me. But the comfort of this stranger seemed hollow to me. Seated on a beanbag further in, Mr. Honeyman rose quickly and greeted me. With tears in his eyes, he said he understood because he, too, had lost his father when he was young. I turned sideways to try to hide my tears. For once in my life I had a tissue in my pants pocket. I quickly dabbed my eyes and asked how old he had been.

"Twenty."

You've got to be kidding me, I thought. The expression on his face told me he knew he had erred; there was really no comparison. But he had been only one year younger than my sister Michelle was now, so I understood his intention and thanked him for his condolences. He said I could do my final exam at home and take all the time I needed.

Mrs. Caroline O'Neil, my favorite English teacher, handled my return completely differently. I loved English class. All I know of world literature, I learned from her. Mrs. O'Neil loved Shakespeare and *King Lear* was her favorite play. And so it became my favorite play. Mrs. O'Neil demanded high standards not only for term papers, but class participation. She had this sense of humor that was just on the edge of smug; we all knew that if we said something superficial, we might generate a caustic yet amusing remark from her. I liked that. She was gentle but assertive. What an example to set for a teenage girl.

Mrs. O'Neil often sat on one of the student desks waiting to welcome us to class. I picture her now with her graying, straight brown hair and lipstick, wearing a crew neck, plaid skirt, and loafers. I didn't know then that she had gone to Vassar and that this was typical preppy garb.

One day I skipped break and came early to class. She appeared pale to me so I asked whether she was feeling OK.

"Yes," she said. "Why?"

I hesitated and blurted, "Because you're not wearing lipstick."

She chuckled and said, "Why do women put on lipstick anyway?" But she continued to wear it. Her influence on me was huge. She gave me the confidence to sit alone in a room and write, whether it was a book report or anything else.

Upon my return to UNIS, Mrs. O'Neil had the grace not to ask how I was doing. I believe she understood that doing so would have burdened me with having to reply.

Then there were the teachers who acknowledged nothing, like Mr. Fenn, who taught biology. Once I confessed that I was having trouble focusing, and he insinuated that I was looking for an easy way out of a homework assignment.

At home, suddenly there was no income. Our financial situation remained uncertain for a long time. In the meantime, my mother relied on cash my father had stored in our safe in the basement. The first call my mother made after the shiva was to my father's lawyer, accountant, and friend, David Safer. When they met, he made a pass at her. She was amazed at the man's gall. "I know and like Ceil!" my mother exclaimed to me later, referring to his beautiful and diminutive wife. The Safers had been our occasional dinner guests and attended my parents' parties.

This was just the first crude blow my mother took from the men my father had entrusted with his finances, who he had expected to respect and protect her if something happened to him. Instead, they tried to take advantage when she most needed loyalty and support. She had to put up with that cretin Safer until my father's will was probated and executed. As soon as possible afterwards, my mother found another lawyer to advise her. That guy, Leon Swerdlik, promptly propositioned her, too. But they wouldn't have dared while my father was alive. I was beginning to understand what Monique had been talking about.

It got worse. When my mother contacted my father's stockbroker and financial advisor he refused to do business with her because she was a woman. She found another firm which had a branch near us on Queens Boulevard, and transferred my father's account there.

Another unexpected betrayal occurred after my mother handed over my father's Brooklyn practice to Dr. Otto Knoller, an Austrian who had been my father's classmate in medical school. They had had a congenial relationship and shared an office in Brooklyn on Eastern Parkway. Dr. Knoller agreed to give my mother a percent of the income he earned from my father's patients, but after he got the patients' files and treated them, he reneged. Lotte Knoller sat at our kitchen table and bemoaned Otto's behavior. "What can I do?" she asked. "He is my husband."

Even our mailman, Mr. Gaskill, who doubled as our house painter and handyman, offered to service my mother. According to her, he said, "Mrs. Frenkel, you know how sorry I am about Dr. Frenkel. You are still a young, beautiful woman, though, and you have certain needs. I can fill them for you." My mother said no thanks, and nevertheless continued to employ Mr. Gaskill. She explained to us that if anybody else pulled anything, she wanted to be able to count on a strong man who could throw around some weight and protect us.

I thought, why are all these sons of bitches alive, and my honorable, ethical father is dead? His dear friend and medical school classmate Munio suddenly had died of a heart attack too. What the hell is going on? I thought. Some drop like flies from clogged coronary arteries and those who don't have the hots for my mom?

But the pre-#MeToo moments my mother suffered were not the worst shocks. One day my mother was searching for Bufferin in a kitchen closet where my father had stored medications. It was so stuffed that we jokingly called it "The Pharmacy." Instead of finding relief for her migraine, my mother found a bottle of digitalis, an extract from the dried leaves of the plant with the same name. The dainty, elongated bell-shaped flowers of this magenta foxglove prompt some to call it "Lady's Glove." To me, it was hideous; the drug it yielded was prescribed for patients with congestive heart failure caused by arteriosclerosis or hypertension. It was supposed to strengthen heart contractions and slow the rate of atrial fibrillation when heart muscle becomes uncoordinated and cannot contract effectively. But digitalis had to be carefully monitored to avoid heart palpitations, diarrhea, and vomiting. Vomiting? My father had been nauseated for at least a week before his death.

Apparently, my father had believed for some time that his heart was failing and he was secretly self-medicating. My mother was livid. So was I. What could possibly have been going through his mind? He knew better than to diagnose and treat himself. He had told me that doctors cannot treat members of their own families, much less themselves. That is why, when my mother had an ovarian cyst, he did not operate on her. What hubris, then, for my dad to have assumed he could be objective enough to treat his own heart. I asked my mother about this. She said that after his botched disc surgery seven years before, he had become so disillusioned that he could not again entrust himself to so-called "experts." That was why it had taken her so long to convince him to see a cardiologist.

Despondent, I looked at the closet shelves packed with bottles and boxes of medical supplies. There were Band-Aids and ace bandages for our scrapes and sprains when we had tripped and fallen on our sidewalk or patio. Vicks VapoRub for our congested lungs and cough drops to soothe our sore throats. Gentian violet, which my father had applied with Q-tips to yeasty bellybuttons we had forgotten to dry after a bath.

I stepped back, furious. How could my father have been so cavalier with his health? With his life? He had been weak and irresponsible. Just because he had had the misfortune to be operated on by a mentally ill orthopedic surgeon did not mean no cardiologist could be trusted. Besides, the second orthopedic surgeon had operated successfully. I could not accept that my father had fallen into the trap of self-diagnosis, that he had succumbed to denial over the seriousness of his condition, that he had taken unnecessary risks. That he had, as a result, abandoned us.

But I knew he loved us dearly, and that in the face of adversity, he had often been cheerful. He saw the sunny side, as I read in the letters he had sent to my sisters and me when my mother took us to Israel in 1961 before we reunited with him in Europe. Alone in the summer evenings, my father wrote to us.

"I know you have arrived in the ancient land so new to you," he wrote Michelle, perhaps sitting in our backyard under the glass awning, "and that you have many impressions of it. Would you share those with your 'Old Man?'" I imagined him savoring a martini olive before reporting on our half-mutt, half-poodle, Duke: "He walks around with his tail hanging down, wondering what happened to his playmates." After all that moping, our dog was probably lounging on our flagstone patio. "The streets of Forest Hills are deserted," my father continued, "as the children have all left. The house is big and empty without my Cookheads and I miss the noise and clatter that was ever present when all of you were here." I smiled as I was reminded of this term of endearment derived from two others—"Cookies" and "Smoosh Head," which he sometimes called Michelle. "I'm looking forward to seeing my big young lady very soon. In the meantime, I kiss you and love you very much. Your Daddy."

Next, he praised Ivy's letter and self-portrait showcasing her long brown braids with red bows at the tips. "It is very beautiful," he commented, "and I know exactly where the ship was when you wrote." Then he recapped her latest report card, in which her teachers noted that she was good in math and French. He closed with, "I hope to see you soon, and kiss your little nosey."

"Dear Daddy, I will see you soon," I had written. "I am having fun. Soon we will be in Israel." Below I drew a tiny ship and jagged lines from left to right, depicting, I suppose, our passage through the waves. At age five I could barely write, but my father found a way to encourage me. "How is my little Kareny? Your letter was fine with big letters and a pretty picture. It is on my night table and I look at it often." He then asked, "Did you see the captain of the boat? Isn't the ocean big? And did you do any ocean fishing? How do you find your cousins in Israel? Please write to me. Dukey sends his best barks to you and your Daddy kisses and hugs you a million. Love, Daddy."

How wonderful, I thought, reading through these letters almost sixty years later. He was so attuned to his daughters that he addressed us each with a special voice. I am sure we felt his love. I felt it again.

All through tenth grade, I lived in a state of constant fear; my mother was not functioning as she used to. I was obedient and tried not to add to her woes and stress. She could not sleep and drank vodka every night and swallowed valium by day. I threw myself into my schoolwork partly because of my father's directive. Too young to fully understand sexual politics myself, I was bewildered by the treachery of his friends and associates. I was still so innocent, but I was observant. While I knew nothing of cheating husbands, suspicious wives, and how they would betray a friend to protect their lousy marriages, I saw that in 1970s America it was crucial for a woman to keep her man. The worst fate was to be widowed; left, shunned, isolated, trampled. A woman alone was fair game for roving eyes, hungry hands, and randy pricks.

But Mr. Gaskill, the mailman and handyman, was right about one thing—my mother was lonely for male companionship. In the spring of 1971, friends of my parents introduced her to a doctor, an anesthesiologist at a Queens hospital who I'll call Selig. They started dating. When I met Selig, I thought him a worm of a man, short in stature with shifty dark brown eyes. I couldn't believe that my mother found him in any way attractive. She said she thought he had a nice smile.

My parents had arranged a summer trip to Europe for Ivy and me with a UNIS program run by our assistant principal. They had already paid for it, and my mother wanted us to have some semblance of stability and normalcy, so she kept the plan in place; we were to attend French classes at L'Université de Poitiers in Tours and then travel to Belgium, Germany, Italy, and the Netherlands.

After Ivy and I returned, my mother told us she was marrying Selig and that he and his teenage son and daughter would be moving into our house. Ivy and I were stunned. I thought this very sudden but did not challenge my mother even though we had corresponded for six weeks and she never hinted that her relationship with Selig was serious. In her letters, she asked questions about how Ivy and I were. To show her that I was alright, I wrote about the elderly French couple hosting me, described their charming house and garden, offered amusing anecdotes about my French teacher at the university, and detailed the châteaux our group visited on weekends. I reported on each Son et Lumière, the sound and light shows châteaux curators present to tourists that convey the sites' historic significance. I described winding stone staircases cool in the shadows despite the summer heat, walking through ancient quarters that bridged quiet rivers, and exploring a moat in a rowboat with Ivy. My mother filled her pages by enumerating activities with Michelle and Alan, who had returned from Portugal. She offered no information about Selig. Later, when I asked why she married him, she said that as a woman alone she needed protection, and she thought we needed a father. But Selig was an alcoholic and he was turning my mother into one. I would fly into a silent, impotent fury when I heard the clink of bottles as he climbed the stairs with a bag full of booze. And one night, also on the stairs, Selig and his son got into a fist fight.

Suffice it to say that the marriage was mercifully short-lived; unbeknownst to me, my mother hired a smart female divorce attorney with whom she devised a plan that would play out over the next nine months.

In anticipation of school letting out for the summer of 1972, I mentioned Cornell's Advanced Placement program for high school juniors and my mother encouraged me to apply. Ivy attended the Hartt School of Music summer program at the University of Hartford in Connecticut. In April, Ivy was accepted to Barnard College and the University of Rochester. My mother said Ivy had to go to Rochester because she wanted Ivy out of the house. When Ivy and I returned from our summer programs, my mother announced that she and I were bringing Ivy to school. Ivy later told me she figured something was brewing with Mom and Selig.

We drove upstate through a late-summer storm and as the sun broke were heading down a hill. Our front and rear right wheels suddenly lifted as we hit the water, hydroplaned, and spun across the oncoming lane. An experienced driver, my quick-minded mother steered into the spin. We landed with a huge thud and three tires on a guard rail and one on the highway's shoulder. Unscathed, we all got out to see that the car was perched over a deep gully on the other side of the rail. My mother had not seen a large puddle in the outer lane and shoulder of the highway because the reflection made the water match the asphalt.

We heard the wail of a state trooper's siren and a car door slam. He rushed over to us.

"Ma'am, are you all OK?"

"Yes," said my mother with eerie calm.

"I am so sorry," he said. "I checked the drain a short while ago and cleared it of high grass. You know the grass and reeds here grow so tall. It must have just clogged up again."

"No, we do not know. We're not from here."

"Ma'am, I saw the whole thing. It's a miracle you didn't flip over."

Years later, my mother revealed that she blamed herself for speeding down that hill and endangering us. She had been ruminating furiously about an argument she'd had with Selig. My mother told me that before our trip she had been wavering about ending their marriage, but immediately after the accident concluded without a doubt that it was time to do so.

With her attorney's coaching, my mother gradually introduced Selig to the reality that our blended family was a disaster. Perhaps they ought not live together, but that was no reason why she and Selig could not continue seeing each other, she appeased him.

Back home late at night when I could not sleep, I often longed to hear my father's voice and laughter. When I could conjure neither his soft tenor nor the chuckle I had grown accustomed to when he was telling a joke or playing a musical prank, I was appalled. They were fading away. I would have given anything to have had one conversation with him and to feel him hug me and tell me everything would be alright.

My mother let me spend any number of sleepovers at my friend Monique's on the Upper East Side. That provided some respite from the insanity at home, but I was, nevertheless, terribly lonely. I often called Ivy, who was also a bundle of anxiety.

I was so stressed that I did not perform well on my PSATs and SATs, although I aced my Achievement Tests. UNIS offered International Baccalaureate courses for students who wanted to apply to colleges abroad. Those who planned to remain in the States could opt for a partial I.B., as I did. I got high grades on my four I.B. classes. But after the summer school classes I took at Cornell, I told my mom that I didn't want to go to college because my teachers at UNIS were just as good and I hadn't really learned anything new. While waiting outside the UNIS guidance counselor's office the previous spring, my mother had struck up a conversation with a classmate of Ivy's who felt as I did. She said the only school she would consider was Hampshire College, the new experimental brainchild of faculty from Amherst, , Mount Holyoke, Smith and UMass in western Massachusetts. Modeled on the English tutorial system at Oxford and Cambridge, students worked at their own pace with the guidance of their faculty. There were no grades and instead of written exams, they had to pass orals. I applied Early Decision.

My mother rushed up the stairs one December morning and handed me an envelope. Her jade-green eyes zeroed in with great intensity as I unfolded the letter. I was accepted! She immediately called her cousin Olga in Israel and asked that her husband, Amnon Kapeliouk, by then a well-known journalist , visit us for a week, all expenses paid. When Amnon arrived, she told Selig it was time to fly to Las Vegas for a divorce. Amnon did not leave until Selig and his kids moved out without incident.

The veiled threat of publicly shaming Selig by having a member of the press present was quite ingenious of my mother. All completely in character. She and her attorney organized and orchestrated a plan and thoroughly outsmarted her adversary.

I arrived at Hampshire College in the fall of 1973 in a state of suspended mourning. I missed my mother all the time. Haunted by flashbacks of what had gone on under our roof and petrified that Selig or his son would take revenge on my mother for the breakup, I called every night to make sure she was safe. Then she departed for Israel, where she planned to stay with relatives for a month. When the Yom Kippur War threatened to break out, my mother called to tell me she was OK. Still half asleep and immersed in campus life, I had no idea she was in harm's way. With her nose ever attuned to danger, she then left for the airport. While awaiting flight information, she struck up a conversation with a gentleman and his wife sitting at a table in a café. In roundabout terms so as not to alarm his wife, the man indicated that if my mother was lucky enough to get a seat—any seat to New York—she should take it. My mother flew home on the last plane out of Israel. The gentleman was President Carter's Chief of Staff, General Alexander Haig.

I made many new friends at Hampshire but for two years I rarely let any guys near me. When I did, I was distrustful. I had boyfriends in graduate school and throughout my twenties and thirties, but for twenty-seven years did not find a man in any way comparable to my father until I met my husband Ed. In college, I questioned everything, especially the Holocaust and religion. Hampshire offered the first college course ever taught about the Holocaust called "Thinking the Unthinkable." I stayed away; I wanted to leave it behind. If there was a God, how could the Holocaust have happened? I asked, unconsciously echoing my father. When someone said that people are the problem not God, I was satisfied for a short while until a friend responded that that let God off the hook too easily. How could I believe in a patriarchal God that demanded a prayer from men every morning, thanking Him for not creating them women? How could I pray to a God that permitted hypocritical, lascivious men to victimize women? What kind of God was I supposed to worship when malicious behavior went unpunished? How could God allow my father's untimely death?

My father did not live long enough to see me become an adult, read any of my articles or see my films, praise or critique the work, give his blessing when I married a good man. I never got to talk to him about his youth and his family. No words of wisdom were ever passed down from his parents to us. The void never abated.

Through my early teens, I thought of my mother as charming, charismatic and a tough, no-nonsense woman who was courageous, frank, assertive, and demanding in a way American women of that era generally were not. (Her Polish women friends were like that, too, to varying degrees.) She set a precedent to fight for what you believed and, above all, to think several steps ahead when danger seemed imminent. She taught my sisters and me that we could reach family members and other individuals with logic and convince them of our point of view. We were not to assume a man knew better and never to capitulate if we felt our assessment was more astute and could protect us from harm. That was why I was so distraught and disoriented when she would not react to Selig's transgressions. I saw an unfamiliar side of her that I did not understand, the side that went under the radar when necessary. It was discreet and used only when someone needed protection from the truth. Sometimes she applied it to family, but more often she applied it to the world beyond because she distrusted crowds and the cruelty of the masses.

It took that potentially lethal accident near Rochester to snap my mother back to her alert and vigorous self. Several times I had confronted her about Selig's alcoholism and abusiveness.. I insisted that she act. I was imitating her, proving that she had taught me well. This lesson—not to unquestioningly submit to authority or bad judgment even if doing so was easier, and to strategize and stay several steps ahead—was useful throughout my young-adult years. The other lesson, about when and how to *lie low*, I learned later. Both were, of course, rooted in my mother's wartime experiences.

Chapter Thirteen

Insisting, Insisting, Insisting

t dawn on September 1, 1939, the Germans invaded Poland. Twenty years later in an NYU essay, my mother described her and her family's response in Kraków:

> In spite of the obvious signs that something was about to happen, we were taken by surprisc on Friday September 1 at dawn. When I opened my eyes, I saw a plane between the right side of my window and the roof of the next house. My experienced father walked into my room, and said, 'It seems our boys are exercising.' In the meantime, a few bombs fell and the probability of maneuvers was eliminated by the radio broadcast of President Ignacy Mościcki making a patriotic speech.
>
> We were being attacked by Germans. It seemed to me that everyone was very optimistic at least for the first few hours. They said, 'In no time at all our boys will be in Berlin.' We were very much afraid of poisonous gas and for a day or so tried on the ghastly, necessary masks.

The next day, the Goldbergers went to the Town Hall to obtain permission to leave the city. "Because my father was a lawyer, everything had to be correct," my mother explained in a college essay, but "there were thousands of equally proper people also trying to leave legally." The Germans bombed Kraków again. "This time it was petrifying. As we stood in the wide, wide hall of the Old Town Hall on Szczepańska Street, suddenly and for the first time, I was afraid. I looked at my brave but pale father and something froze inside of me."

After they got the "wretched permission papers," my grandfather took my mother to the best store in town. My mother wrote:

> He said, 'You need a pair of good and sturdy shoes, the kind that would protect your feet through war.' Frankly, I was not too impressed with the shoes Father bought, which were brown and indestructible. My father, it seems, was not at all aware of the fact that I was a young lady of 14 looking forward to a long-promised pair of navy-blue pumps. The sturdy shoes on my feet did not even vaguely resemble pumps but looked like what my parents wore during their frequent hikes in the Tatra Mountains. All my young life, I had been waiting to be big enough to join my parents on their excursions, so these shoes somehow promised adventure.

This glimpse into my mother's adolescent mind on the eve of war revealed an interesting mix of childlike and womanly sentiments. She never described the German invasion to us, but our shoes were always very important to her; they had to be well-made and durable but also stylish. Every spring my mother bought my sisters and me navy blue shoes to match our navy blue, white-trimmed coats.

I was surprised by her remark that her new boots inspired her to regard leaving Kraków as an exploratory ramble, as if the Goldbergers were not really fleeing for their lives. She had told us that she owed this sense of adventure to the stories of the German writer Karl May, famous for his tales about the "Old West" and Native Americans. May was not well-received here, though, because American children detected inaccuracies in his depiction of the frontier. In fact, May never visited the United States.

My mom was nevertheless captivated by the friendship of Old Shatterhand, a German émigré who became blood brothers with an Apache chief, Winnetou. But it was the plight of the Native Americans that truly resonated with her; she was horrified by the fate of the conquered Apache in May's Winnetou trilogy. In the opening scene in the first Winnetou book, Old Shatterhand meets a gunsmith who is fashioning a new firearm with a twenty-five round repetition carbine. May raises the moral question of whether the gunsmith would be an accessory to murder, might even be as bad as a murderer, if every villain acquired his weapons. The Indians would be annihilated—slaughtered everywhere, Old Shatterhand argues—on the prairies, in the forests, in the canyons. My mother concluded that the main issue for May was the destruction of all Indian tribes and collusion in that crime. She saw this even more clearly when she read *The Last of the Mohicans*, by James Fenimore Cooper, who had strongly influenced May. In her oral history she said, "Maybe I had the perception [that she and her parents were in danger] because I read about the American Indians and I could recognize the symptom of people that are doomed."

These authors—as well as teenage boredom with her routinized life in Kraków—stirred my mother's initial excitement as she traveled east into the unknown. More important, though, these books shaped her thinking about practical matters and emboldened her decisions during the next six years. Almost twenty years later, recalling the German invasion and the following Sunday afternoon, my mother wrote:

> My father closed the door of our apartment without even bothering to lock the safety lock. I looked at the door for a brief moment and felt that I will never see it again. We all had knapsacks on our backs, coats on our arms, and the family silver. Somewhere along the way [to the station across the Vistula River] we got hold of a peasant with a wagon. I was put on top of the cart with all the knapsacks. I thought I should really not be treated like a child, but I remained on the cart, reflecting. The sun was setting behind Kraków and the

> churches were slowly disappearing in the oncoming darkness. We spent that night in a mail compartment of an East-bound train.

Such lovely writing, I thought with pride. Yet my mother had kept this to herself, as well as what happened the following morning after the Germans bombed the train:

> We all ran to the windows. Right behind me stood a handsome young fellow about 17 years old. I tried to flirt with him. But my father pulled me down to the floor and pushed me under the bench. He said, "Do not run."
>
> At this moment, a bomb exploded right next to our car. The handsome young boy was hit in his neck with shrapnel. Just a few seconds ago, I had been standing in his place. My father covered my eyes and said not to look.
>
> I ran and ran and panicked. The train stood in the village underneath the trees. There was moaning and death.
>
> After a while we were all in the train again. I shivered for hours in the heat of the afternoon. My father pointed out that the train was really safer than the roads because the aim of the pilots was not good and the likelihood that a bomb would hit a train was comparatively small. On the other hand, while running away from the train, we could have been mowed down by machine gun.

My grandmother Teofila coaxed my mother, as she always had on unpleasant occasions like swallowing cod liver oil, tolerating an injection, or having a cavity drilled: "Be brave, Irka. Remember, your father is a war hero. Have courage like he did during the Great War."

My mother stopped trembling.

The earliest memory I have about my mother's fraught wartime relationship with my grandfather Izydor Goldberger and her great love for him was when I was twelve. One evening, I could not get the logs in our living room fireplace to ignite. The wood was damp from snow that had drifted down the chimney, so the logs needed more than the usual kindling to catch. On an end table next to the couch, I spotted a newspaper that appeared to have been read, so I figured I could use it. I had seen other editions around the house and noticed that the paper was different from the bone-colored newsprint of *The New York Times*; this paper was thin, a crisp white. I stuffed it between two logs and lit it with a long match.

A while later, my mother inquired about the newspaper. As I started to answer, she interrupted. "Don't tell me. Don't tell me," she wailed.

"I thought it was OK. I thought you'd read it," I said.

"I did, but I wanted to check it again." Now her tone was plaintive, even a little whiney. Definitely not the usual confident voice to which I was accustomed. I apologized and suggested that maybe we could buy another copy.

"Don't you know these newspapers are hard to get? They come all the way from [the] Soviet Union." She pointed to a brown paper loop on the table that I had overlooked. "Via Air Mail. See?" Sure enough, the wrapping said, "Par Avion."

These news digests from behind the Iron Curtain were very important to my mother—not because of the headlines or articles, but because of the photographs. She was searching for her father.

I had always known my mother's father Izydor was extremely brave because she often spoke with pride about his military service during World War I. A decorated war hero, he had served on the Italian Front in the Dolomites. In one of four gems she had written for her Sunrise Semester classes, she described what happened when he and his orderly pushed ahead of their battalion to scout out some caves. The version below combines what she told my sisters and me, and her Fortunoff interviewers:

> I vividly remember the story of how he and his orderly captured part of the general staff of the Italian army. He stood there in the mouth of a narrow passage leading to a cave pretending there was a division behind him. As he shouted orders into the cave in different voices and dialects, his orderly responded in varied tones of voice. Their voices bounced off the cave walls and echoed, so the Italian contingent became convinced it was outnumbered. The enemy climbed up a cliff and over the ridge one by one and stood with their hands up. Then my father requisitioned delicacies including oranges, which I remembered because they were very rare and expensive in Poland. Also, in our salon, a living room used only when company came, stood a magnificent beautifully carved ivory box. It contained a huge amount of war pictures.
>
> Of course, we were all hero-worshipers then, not only Catholic Poles but we Jews, too. For as long as I can remember, on unpleasant occasions my mother would say, "Remember you are your daddy's daughter and you know how brave he was."

I was filled with pride about the cunning and courage of my mother's father and the example he set. On the other hand, it amused me that Teofila used her husband's big picture heroism, which had had historical consequences, for mundane and practical purposes like dental hygiene. But I never thought of him as my grandfather.

Other than my mother's stories, I knew little about Izydor and had only a vague sense of his appearance. Among the photos my great-grandparents had saved was Izydor and Teofila's engagement portrait, which my mother had reproduced and enlarged in 1964. Elated, they stand in a park smiling at one another; they are in profile, and the photos in albums always showed my grandfather in later years with a mustache and a fedora that shadowed his eyes.

In investigating his education, I guessed that Izydor had earned his law degree from Kraków's Jagiellonian University. This center of learning founded in the 14th century was one of the oldest universities in the world. The esteemed astronomer Nicolaus Copernicus called it his alma mater. I emailed the press officer inquiring about law school alumni. An archivist responded that my grandfather received his Doctor of Jurisprudence in 1916, right on time to be drafted into military service. The archivist also wrote, to my surprise, that my great-grandfather, Ignacy Goldberger, was a manufacturer in Nowy Sącz. Now I knew my great-grandfather's full name. The archivist added that Izydor had attended *gimnazjum* there. This was news, because my mother said he was from Wadowice, at town about 30 miles southwest of Kraków. Evidently the Goldbergers had moved to another town the same distance away but in the opposite direction.

There was also a portrait of an unidentified young man in military uniform which had fallen out of an album; because I didn't know where my mother originally placed it, the clue to his identity by association with other photos was lost. I returned to the albums and the displaced photo of the military man, this time examining it with a magnifying glass. On the lower left corner I noticed an embossed stamp of the photographer's studio and location—Nowy Sącz. I studied how the young man's eyes were set, speculated how they would look if jade-green like my mother's, and imagined her eyes before age twenty. There was no question that the dapper young man in uniform was my grandfather Izydor, probably just before he shipped off to the Italian Front. The future war hero in his prime. I was extremely pleased.

Curious to know more about his service in the Austro-Hungarian Army, I wrote to the Kriegsarchiv in Vienna which sent copies of not one, but two citations for bronze and silver medals. Also included was a five-page commendation by my grandfather's commanding officer describing his heroics in old-German, military terms. These were peppered with stamps of approval of four more senior officers petitioning Kaiser Wilhelm to honor my grandfather for his valor during the 11th Battle of Isonzo, and at Mt. Saint Gabriel in the fall of 1917. Little symbols in the shape of a crown, the Kaiser's seal, appeared throughout.

Kaiser Wilhelm conferred the awards to my grandfather and promoted him to lieutenant on May 11, 1918.

To think that my grandfather's awards had been sitting in an Austrian archive for a century and all I had to do was ask for them! At first, I could not contain my exhilaration and shared this thrilling find with my family and friends. But then, as with my discovery of the house in Lviv, sadness drowned my excitement. I wished I could share the information I had retrieved with my mother. That, and knowing the risks my grandfather had taken for the Kaiser and how the Germans, whose culture he revered, had treated him afterwards, gnawed at me. With remorse, I envisioned the award certificate hanging in their salon in Kraków, my grandfather gazing at it and his medals for the last time, then leaving them as well as his collection of war photos in the large ivory box. I vacillated like a pendulum, drawn to the past and recoiling from it. For this find *was* reason to celebrate. Although my grandfather Izydor's heroism could not save him later during World War II, his exemplary courage helped save his daughter.

My mother and her parents stayed on the train from Kraków until the end of the line and got off at Tarnopol, now Ternopil, Ukraine. There a Jewish family, the Helmanns, took them in and gave them a room. Utter chaos overran Tarnopol when the Soviets invaded two weeks later, on September 17, 1939. In the turmoil, my grandparents incorrectly assumed the border was closed and abandoned their original plan to go south to Romania. Everything might have been different if they had followed through with their original strategy.

From Tarnopol my mother wrote to Anula Dawidowicz, her best friend from Kraków with whom she had worked as a Jewish Scout when German-speaking refugees arrived after the *Anschluss*. Anula was living in Lwów with her parents. After my mother died, Anula kindly sent me my mother's correspondence, which I then had translated. As before, words of eighty-odd years ago let me into my mother's adolescent mind on the cusp of adulthood, flitting in and out of comprehending her situation. In a postcard, after asking for Anula's news, my mother wrote that she hoped to visit Anula after exams, as if leisure travel was still possible. Her words expressed her longing for the quiet, normal life they had lived in Kraków.

Under the Soviets, my grandfather Izydor refused to work as a prosecutor, having been a litigator before in Poland. Instead, he worked as the manager of the main grocery cooperative. The hardship for everyone in Tarnopol, Jewish or not, was getting enough to eat; long lines for food started at 4:00 a.m. at the poorly supplied Soviet food co-op. But my mother noticed that the Helmanns worked there and made quite a bit of money. So too could have her father, had he been willing to sell goods on the black market.

She asked why he did not use the severe food shortage to his advantage.

"If I were to take, what example would I set for others?" he answered.

As a result, the Goldbergers never had more than a cup of sugar and my mother was constantly hungry. It occurred to her that despite their intellectual accomplishments, her parents were ill-prepared to deal with war. "Certainly as manager of the grocery we could have lived in our own apartment rather than with the Helmanns," my mother told her oral history interviewers, "but that was how my father was. These were the values with which he wanted to raise me." He also was supposed to provide for his family, I thought. This did not seem to me to be the right time to demonstrate exemplary behavior to strangers. On the other hand, he had to live with his conscience.

This was the first of several disagreements between my mother and her father as the Goldbergers made decisions during the early war years that had huge implications for their survival.

My mother and her parents remained in Tarnopol until spring 1940, when the Soviets offered Polish refugees the option to become Soviet citizens or to return to German-occupied western Poland. Still an officer in the Polish Army Reserve, my grandfather did not want to go back because, if captured, the Germans would surely imprison or kill him. There was no good choice.

Ultimately, the Russians reneged and instead deported the Jews who opted to return to western Poland to Siberia. It was too early to know that the terribly harsh conditions in Siberia would be better than those in ghettos and concentration camps under the Germans.

My mother and her parents chose to become Soviet citizens, but their new ID cards contained a clause forbidding them to live anywhere within 100 kilometers of the frontier or in a large city. In May 1940, they backtracked a little west to Złoczów, a town between Tarnopol and Lwów. Grandfather Izydor got work in the office of an engineer in charge of building the new Lwów-Kiev highway. Again, the Goldbergers were taken in by a Jewish family whose home was on the outskirts of town, as required. Although the house was small, the room my mother shared with her parents was far larger than in Tarnopol and, to her delight, faced farmland with wildflowers.

One afternoon, pen in hand, my mother again wrote to her friend Anula. "We live wonderfully, literally outside of town in the fields," she wrote, cramming her words into a two-page letter. "You will see it all yourself, when you visit." She reported having fallen a little behind her classmates because she had started school a week before exams, but she had already passed biology and German. Then she confided about a "tall, dark, and handsome" boy named Edek, who had already graduated high school. She expected "to happily fall in love for the first time ever" and yet managed to break a date with him. But she added that Złoczów was so small that two random villagers could tell her about Edek's whole day and help her find him. She also spoke wistfully about being a refugee and feeling different from her classmates:

> They are so free. I feel so old and experienced in comparison to them. It worries me that perhaps I will never be able to act as freely and childishly as them. It seems to me that you are down as well, and your letter doesn't really say why. Is it because of politics?

She wanted to know what Anula's family had decided regarding the Soviet offer to return home. "Have you registered for coming back or for staying in Lwów?" she asked. Flitting from one subject to the next, she declared:

> Writing to you has made me feel so much better, physically and emotionally. Because I have become an optimist, I have learned—or rather I am starting to learn—to enjoy my life as much as I can. As you see, my writing is rather chaotic, please forgive me. I also became so used to saving. That is why there are no spaces in my writing.

A year earlier, she and Teofila had gone to the dressmaker in Kraków. That night, my mother dreamt she hardly had anything to wear—just a blouse and a faded skirt. Now resources were very scarce indeed.

Although my mother tried to accept what came, she could not tolerate her father's announcement that the farmhouse was two kilometers too close to town and that they again had to move. And again, my mother perceived that her parents—especially her father—lacked the pragmatism she had at age fifteen. It exasperated her that for him everything always had to be so honorable, so morally correct, very straight and very legal. He had taught her to think like a lawyer and argue her point of view, so she made the case that they were not refugees because before she was conceived and when she was conceived, her parents lived as newlyweds in Borysław (the same town where my oil tycoon and hotelier great-great-uncle Maksymillian Lifschütz had made his fortune). This town, rich in oil, was south of Lwów near the Carpathian Mountains which divided then-Poland and Hungary. The young couple had registered there as Polish citizens, and that area, too, was now Soviet-occupied Poland. Therefore my mother's parents were indigenous Poles of that region, she argued, so they could live near any large town or city.

"I remember how heartless I was. I just said, 'You just have to do it. We have to get out to a main town,'" she recounted in her oral history. She insisted and insisted and insisted until her father relented. Unbeknownst to her, though, he had to bribe and coddle an official to get the necessary registration documents: Soviet I. D. cards supplemented by papers showing that they really were not refugees from western Poland. In August 1940, the Goldbergers left Zlochów for Soviet-occupied Lwów not knowing what awaited them.

Chapter Fourteen

The Soviet Occupation of Lwów

The rape of eastern Poland by the Soviets began by snatching and shipping her means of production to the Soviet Union. During the first two months, trade continued while merchants' stocks lasted. Polish currency, the złoty, remained legal tender until the third week of December 1939. But in late October, the National Assembly of western Ukraine and White Russia met in Lwów's nationalized Grand Theater, which the Soviets renamed the Lvov State Theater of Opera and Ballet. There they passed a motion to nationalize the largest and best equipped of the region's 9,000 factories. Ukrainians regarded themselves as liberated from factory owners and the yoke of all Polish capitalists. Up-to-date sugar factories southeast of Lwów, electric works, fine spinning jennies and looms in mills all disappeared. Sometimes entire factories, one of wireless receivers, or an oil plant, for example, were simply taken. Workers occasionally went with them. The Soviets emptied the railway workshops in Lwów and snatched the equipment and furniture of the Agrarian Bank and other institutions. The same was true of agrarian and mineral assets; Ukrainian peasants felt they had been subjugated by the Polish landowning elite and took revenge by plundering large estates. Timber from Polish State forests; hay and straw from estates of the Polish former nobility; reserves of grain sugar, tobacco, spirits, cement, hides, textiles, iron, and coal—all were confiscated. The

Soviets appropriated medical supplies, such as cotton wool, bandages, and iodine. Anything movable was filched.

But they weren't finished. Suddenly, on December 21, the Soviets simply withdrew the złoty from circulation. Bank deposits above 300 złoty were seized. Overnight, 1,500 million złoty—or $1.5 billion in today's dollars—literally evaporated. Prices soared and there were food shortages because country people would not sell their produce for a currency they distrusted. A system of barter developed and the standard of living plummeted.

Simultaneous with sudden impoverishment, the Soviets nationalized commerce by seizing goods from wholesalers and carrying them off to Russia. The value stolen from Lwów alone was about $2.2 billion in today's dollars. Of the city's 8,500 shops, 6,500 were closed. Only 500 stayed in the hands of their Soviet-connected proprietors; the remaining 1,500 were transformed into co-operatives subject to the whims of the Soviet Central Committee and its bureaucracy.

Although suspicious of all religions, the Soviets trusted Jews more than Ukrainians. At first the regime bestowed upon Jews important bureaucratic positions in the realms of culture, science, and the economy. But by the fall of 1939 the Soviets had to ensure that the Ukrainians and Poles would not think the Jews were taking over. As 1939 drew to a close, Ukrainian nationalists grew disgruntled and pressed for their own state, so the Soviets wooed and appeased them. They declared the Ukrainian language, which had been prohibited in pre-war Poland, an official language. Ukrainians received preferential treatment in government offices and were appointed heads of most administrative departments. Fewer and fewer Jews had high-ranking positions; nevertheless, people perceived and spoke of a "Jewish regime."

I'm certain that whatever my grandfather Ojzer Fränkel's entrepreneurial enterprise was upon the invasion, the Soviets swiftly nationalized it. He must have been among the 6,500 shop owners whose stores were shuttered. As it became impossible to live on a Soviet salary of a couple hundred rubles a month, most of the merchant middle class suddenly struggled to make ends meet; a kilogram of bread cost one ruble, a kilogram of sugar two-and-a-half rubles, the same amount of beef went for seven to eighteen rubles. For shoes, one paid fifty to eighty rubles, not to mention the cost of coal and heating oil.

I knew from my mother that Grandfather Ojzer had been a black marketeer during the war, but she did not say under which Occupation. Now knowing the economic circumstances under the Soviets, I'm sure his bank savings dissolved, but I also know he was shrewd and probably squirreled away cash when he buried jewels in his basement. I also understood from my mother that Ojzer would have done whatever he had to when the Soviets arrived. He was the kind of man to beat the corrupt Soviets at their own game. If they could nationalize his business, pay him unsustainable wages, seize his bank account, and devalue Polish currency to the point that it was worthless and his life savings had disappeared, then he could hijack supplies before they reached the damn proletariat. And sell them at a profit "at the back door."

And so I see Grandpa Ojzer climbing the stairs to his second-floor apartment at Rejtana 5, bread hidden under his coat. He opens the door, hands the loaf to my grandmother Michaela, and embraces her. Formal and educated as I know the Finkelsteins were, I assume the Fränkels were affectionate and playful because my father was. In another pocket Ojzer carries two cans of sardines, which he also presents to my grandmother with a flourish and a second kiss.

What goes on inside Ojzer's head, as he feels the softness of Michaela's cheek plumping with her smile? Perhaps he thought: So I am becoming a *shvarts markater* (black marketeer). So be it. *Noit brecht eizen* (Necessity breaks iron). A *ganef fun a ganef iz potter.* (It's no crime to steal from a thief.) These sayings didn't come from nowhere. He must have despised the Soviet bureaucracy and the idiotic restrictions it imposed. The Soviets knew nothing of business and the market for anything in Lwów—food, dry goods, furniture, clothing. Furs. But he knew. How dare they just march in and order him to give up all he had built—his loyal customers, inventory, and staff—because of some ill-founded, centralized, corrupt system that arbitrarily decided who would get what, from whom, and when.

In 1901, at age thirteen, Ojzer left his parents' home in Busk 36 kilometers east of Lwów, then Lemberg. It had taken years of experience for him to understand and predict his customers' needs. He had run businesses first as a wholesaler and later as a retailer. After serving in the Austro-Hungarian Army, he became a cigarette manufacturer. In those days, cigarette suppliers had to have a license to sell, which was difficult to get. But Ojzer wrangled one and he and Michaela rolled cigarettes on the kitchen table. Little Sydney, their assistant, filled the cartons with cigarette packs. Ojzer delivered the goods to stationery stores with his beautiful wagon pulled by Shivek, his trusty horse.

In my imagination, every day on their route Ojzer and Shivak pass by the new Grand Theater to marvel at its beauty and admire the embodiment of an engineering feat. Due to the Pełtew River, the site had been marshland. The solution was to enclose the river underground with a concrete foundation, a first for any building in Europe. It was also Lemberg's first building with electrical lighting, which was provided by a German company called Siemens. Ojzer turns on to Hetmańsksa Avenue and catches a glimpse of the Neo-Renaissance building's columns, balustrades, and statues of muses. As he and Michaela had approached for their first performance, they looked up in awe of the central sculpture atop the cornice—Glory, the patinaed angel, holding a semicircular golden fern, a partial crown above her head. On opening night in 1900 an Armenian archbishop blessed the new building in the presence of a rabbi and a Protestant pastor. The architect was a Pole, as were the finest painters—Catholics, Protestants, Jews alike—who collaborated on the exterior and opulent interior. Ah, the mosaic that was Lemberg.

Glory now for whom? I fancy my grandfather Ojzer asking himself in 1940, if he had had the time to gaze at the huge posters hanging from the opera house's arches advertising the season: *Eugene Onegin, Natalka Poltavka, La Traviata,* and *Aida.* He might have wondered what fabulous performance Soviet officers and their accomplices, the Ukrainian Militia, would enjoy that night with their wives or mistresses. They would marvel and applaud, while the Jews in Lwów—whose population had doubled to 220,000 because of Western refugees—quaked in filthy, over-crowded rooms.

After the Great War, when the Fränkels returned from Vienna, Ojzer turned to retail. He and Michaela owned a shoe store stocked with styles from a Czech supplier, an army veteran with whom Ojzer had served. It took some time to know the local housewives' and businessmen's buying habits and tastes in footwear, but after a while Ojzer knew which of the finest oxfords to order for Mr. Moszkowicz, the owner of the building next door. His building housed a hotel and the Bagatela, a cabaret in the round that originally had been a theater known as Casino de Paris. Michaela tastefully arranged the displays with pumps she knew would appeal to her friends. Next, Ojzer went into business with Michaela's uncle and together they bought a construction equipment factory.

Knowing so little about my paternal grandmother—only that she came from a large family—I asked Alex Dunai to search the Ukrainian State Archives. In my grandparents' marriage record, Michaela is referred to as Mechla, or Mechli Lifschütz, born in 1886, two years before my grandfather Ojzer. Her father, Eisig Lifschütz, was one of several sons of Abraham Lifschütz, a large prosperous family that lived in Lemberg.

Eisig's two younger brothers, Szymon (Simon) and Mojzesz (Max), were my great-great-uncles who owned and ran the Hotel Continental in Vienna. Eisig was not to achieve such material success, however. He moved from Lemberg to a shtetl called Zuków (Zhukiv today), where he lived in House 99 as a "petty trader" and "day worker," according to the documents. With his wife, Frimi Leder, he had three children, Dawid Meyer, Chuwe Scheindel, and my grandmother who was the youngest. In 1889, when she was three years old, Eisig died at age thirty of typhus. So did Chuwe four years later. Alex was unable to determine what happened to Dawid Meyer, for whom I assume my father was named. I had no idea that my grandmother was orphaned and had lost her siblings, too. Eisig's widow, my great-grandmother Frimi, remained in Zuków and married again.

To my surprise, by finding the names of Eisig's siblings, Alex solved the mystery of mine. When I was born, my sister Michelle suggested my first name. My father added my Hebrew and middle names, Chana (Ann) in memory of his favorite aunt. But that is all I knew. When it came to choosing my byline, I included my middle initial "A" in honor of Chana and because my father's middle initial was also "A," for Allen. I learned that Chana was born in 1860 just before Eisig and over a century before me. I hypothesized as to why she was dear to my father. Maybe Chana had looked after my orphaned grandmother Michaela. Maybe they had been close despite being twenty-six years apart.

On a map of western Ukraine, I found Zuków 20 miles southeast of Busk, the shtetl where Grandpa Ojzer was born. Was this scrap of information a clue as to how my grandparents met? Since their families lived in neighboring villages perhaps they were introduced by relatives and friends.

I never determined which of Eisig's other brothers was Ojzer's business partner, but he perished from a shrapnel wound during the Polish-Ukrainian war in 1920. According to my uncle Sydney, upon learning this, my grandmother shrieked and tore at her flying blonde hair.

Now on his own, Ojzer turned to importing textiles from Łódź. Ojzer had learned grit and persistence from his father, my great-grandfather Leiser, a flax merchant. Strong and determined, Leiser carried bags of flax on his back for many kilometers to make a sale. He was considered a tremendous hero in Busk, where it was widely known that he successfully fought off a wolf with his bare hands. Although not deeply religious and he did not *davin* in the morning, Leiser was a Chassid. Ojzer had left behind his father's religious orthodoxy but maintained a respectful observance of Judaism. He loved when his father visited and taught his young sons Chassidic songs. It would have pained Ojzer terribly, therefore, to pry off the mezuzah from the entrance to his building when the Soviets arrived.

Ojzer's success extended beyond his customers, though. Due to his fine reputation among other merchants, he had been elected head of a merchants' association—no small feat for a Jew. So it must have surprised him that all three of his adolescent sons became socialists, when—not so long ago—they had exercised the competitive instincts of capitalists like him. Their neighbor, a business competitor, had provoked Ojzer by illegally building a tall wall that blocked the backyard light. In retaliation, Ojzer hired a crew to demolish half the wall overnight. Then, knowing his competitor needed his furnace on day and night, Ojzer, my father, and his brothers inserted hoses down the fellow's chimney to squelch the fire. The neighbor went to the authorities, but as the head of the merchants' association, Ojzer had their ear.

I believe Ojzer was not surprised when Sydney's affinity for Socialism weakened after he worked in Moscow in 1936; Ojzer knew his oldest son would never build factories, railways, and a life far from the luxuries he had so enjoyed in his beloved Vienna. Trans-Siberian Railway? *Vos umzin* (What nonsense). Milek, on the other hand, seemed to be more dedicated. Not that he was a zealot. He was a true idealist who passionately hoped for a classless society. He and his bride Feiga were pursuing their engineering degrees at the Polytechnika. It remained to be seen whether Milek's politics would change once in the working world and blessed with children. And Dolek, well, he was a healer with only slight socialist leanings. He seemed to remember that profits from his father's various enterprises had paid his tuition. Dolek was destined to be a fine researcher—a scientist, that one. It was so hard not knowing how his older sons were doing in America. It made Ojzer ache all over.

Knowing that Soviet citizens were allowed little space and privacy, I assumed that the Fränkels were required to share their apartment with strangers and that Michaela fretted over the intrusion.

Sydney told my sisters and me that Ojzer had hidden in his camouflaged attic during the German Occupation with ten other Jews, so as soon as the Soviets invaded towns and cities further east, Ojzer surely assessed the situation and concluded that at any moment the environment could become dangerous for Lwów's Jews. But perhaps by the early days of the Soviet Occupation he had already prepared a hiding place, a crawlspace under the slightly inclined roof. The rise could not be detected from the street; you had to know to look for the window, as Ed and I did when we visited Lviv in 2016. From a particular angle, we saw a small, grilled window peeking between the two gabled dormer windows of Rejtana 7 next door. I envision my beleaguered grandfather planning to build shelves to camouflage the way in to the attic. First, however, he had to acquire supplies—planks, nails, paint—but gradually, to avoid suspicion.

I had assumed that my paternal grandparents, Uncle Milek and his wife Feiga, were allowed to stay in Rejtana 5. I had imagined the Gestapo storming up the steps for Michaela and Feiga. That was why virtually discovering the house in 2014 had been both joyful and devastating. But as I learned more about the Soviet Occupation, I questioned my assumptions. I wanted to know more about Uncle Milek and wondered whether, like the University of Vienna, Lviv's Polytechnic Institute still had his records. I also wanted to know more about his wife, my aunt.

In the spring of 2021, I asked Alex Dunai to search for my uncle Milek in the archives of the Polytechnic. The seventeen-page dossier he found included a wealth of information about the Fränkels' circumstances from 1939 to 1941. I learned that Milek and my father were only two years apart, whereas I'd previously thought Milek much younger because my father and Sydney always spoke of him as "the little one." After graduating from *Gimnazjum No. 8* in 1933, for two years Milek was not accepted to the Polytechnic mechanical engineering program, possibly because of anti-Semitism under the Poles. When the Soviets arrived, he was specializing in energy and automobiles. Did he agonize over whether he would be allowed to graduate, as my father had at the University of Vienna Medical School during the *Anschluss*? Probably not—Jews fared better under the Soviets.

The matriculation form also provided the name of Milek's wife, Feiga Aizenbach-Frenkel, and information about her and her family. Until July 10, 1940, she had worked in the food trade. They lived in Apartment 5A of Klaynivska Street (its Russian name), No. 3. Feiga's father, a former realtor, and my grandfather Ojzer were employees in the confectionery of Food Factory #2. Ojzer's previous occupation described him as a handicraftsman who had finished and sold furniture, making his "class before the October Revolution wholesale merchant third category," according to a form in the file. Now as a "warehouseman" at the candy shop, he earned 170 rubles a month on which he supported my grandmother Michaela at their home, No. 7, Volnosti Street (Russian name).

The Fränkels had been thrown out of Rejtana 5!

With the help of my favorite 1939 online Polish map of Lwów, I determined that Volnosti Street was the former Polish Wolnosc Street, near the Jewish Hospital and about eight blocks from my grandparents' former home on Rejtana Street. The Polish name of Milek and Feiga's street—a tiny lane next to the music museum and across the park from the university—was Sykstuska, known today as Kamenyariv Street. The building no longer exists. Neither does the building my grandparents had moved to; it was destroyed and the paved over site is part of a modern complex. During the Nazi Occupation, when the Gestapo came for Michaela and Feiga, the secret police had not stormed up the wooden stairs of Rejtana 5. Four years later, however, they *did* rage up three flights of those steps in pursuit of Ojzer and his cohort in his attic.

Pleased as I was to have gathered this information and to have honored Milek by finding out whatever I could, I was distraught when I saw his student I.D. photo. Until then, the only picture of him I had seen was the family portrait circa 1927. Seated in the middle, Milek is only about ten or eleven. In the back row his adolescent older brothers tower over him. His face is round and wide, his jaw slightly asymmetrical, his expression contented and gentle. Sepia hides whether his hair is fair or dark. But in the Polytechnic photo, at age twenty-five, Milek strikingly resembles my father and is incredibly handsome. The same high forehead, big, bright, light eyes, and fair hair. The expression in Milek's eyes is full of hope. And love. The love of a newlywed.

Ivy and I discussed the likenesses of our father and younger uncle. Our father so easily could have been in Milek's place and destroyed by the Nazis. It shook me the way a wave smacks you hard so that you stumble on the sand, reminding you that you are a mere speck whacking about among the forces of nature and evil. That the shore is not by any means safe. It is breathtaking to be confronted with the embedded imperative that—according to the plan of some maniac who usurped immense power—you are not supposed to be here. I felt this again and again on my quest. It is not clear to me whether this strange recognition and the satisfaction that came with each discovery, large or small, will ever balance out.

During the Soviet Occupation, in another part of town I know not where, my mother's family struggled alongside thousands of Jews who had fled to Lwów from middle-Europe and western Poland. Although Grandfather Izydor again found work in a food co-op as an assistant bookkeeper, it was a demotion. He continued to refuse to cook the books or sell merchandise on the black market, even though my mother and Teofila went hungry. My mother told him he put in many, many hours for very little money, just like in Tarnopol, but that in Lwów the bakers and restaurateurs reported to him. Couldn't he request a promotion or finagle a little, she asked, so that they would have more to eat?

Grandfather Izydor would not hear of it. "I cannot work as a bookkeeper because I would have to be in cahoots with the buyer," he said, as my mother reported in her oral history. "Sooner or later the Soviets would discover that and send us to Siberia."

My mother doubted he was right. It reminded her of his impractical reluctance when they were starving in Tarnopol, and where he had held a higher level position.

And here is a remarkable coincidence. The food co-op buyer with whom Grandfather Izydor refused to collaborate was my paternal grandfather, Ojzer. Between October 1939 and the fall of 1940, Ojzer must have gotten a promotion from "warehouseman" of Food Factory #2's confectionary to "buyer" for the whole organization. Unlike Grandfather Izydor, Grandfather Ojzer did not hesitate to take advantage of his position. He answered to the general manager, a Communist Party member, who also needed to earn a living somehow. So Ojzer had no choice but to collude with the manager. If he had not, the manager would have refused to assign supplies to the co-op. No supplies meant no turnover and then the store would have been shut. And so corruption trickled up and down the hierarchy.

When Grandfather Ojzer and my mother met a decade or so later in New York, he admitted to the risk he had taken and affirmed what Grandfather Izydor had predicted. "If the Germans had not invaded, the Soviets would have sent me and the bookkeeper to Siberia. No question."

My mother was determined to find a way out. In late November 1940, she ran into a friend from Kraków, as my mother recounted in her oral history:

> On my 16th birthday, I came across a friend from Kraków, Olek Auerbach. I found out that they just received papers from United States, with passports [sic] to Guatemala or Dominican Republic, don't remember which. I came home and I said, "For $500, if our family in New York will pay it, we could get the papers and get out." Because by that time, whatever enthusiasm I had about the Soviet schools—it vanished.

But Grandfather Izydor refused to ask for the money. What a coming of age. My mother's teenage rebellion consisted of deploying her intellect to convince her parents to act in the face of increasing hardship. Her testimony became a catalogue of arguments as she and Grandfather Izydor repeatedly clashed over the ethical and the practical—even as conditions in Lwów grew harsher. Such an acrid sweet sixteen.

Chapter Fifteen

The Elder Finkelsteins Leave Berlin

Meanwhile in Berlin, my great-grandmother Sara Finkelstein, my mother's grandmother and the grand lady whose portrait had been stowed away in a closet until 1968, was packing up her few remaining belongings. Ever since 1935 when the Nuremberg Laws were enacted to strip German Jews of their civil rights, the elder Finkelsteins had been trying to leave. The plan was for their son, my great-uncle Max who was in New York with his wife Stefi and daughter Vera, to sponsor Sara and Heinrich. But again and again, their U.S. visas were denied and the elder Finkelsteins put on the next year's list. Then, miraculously, on December 19, 1940, the visas were granted.

In the scene in my head, great-grandmother Sara sits at her Biedermeier secretary in a Berlin apartment she and Heinrich moved to when they were thrown out of theirs. Sorting through the contents of each little drawer, she finds her box of calling cards. They are printed in an elegant, elaborate typeface, that is a variation of an ancient font called *Schwabacher*, meaning square black letter, widely used in medieval times.

In a few weeks, Sara and Heinrich would travel in a locked special transport train through Occupied France and Spain to Portugal. From Lisbon they would sail to New York where Sara's calling cards would be useless vestiges of a defunct way of life and social position.

No longer "Frau Finkelstein," matriarch of a wealthy clan of far-flung and prosperous jewelers, she would just be "Mrs. Finkelstein," refugee. Nevertheless, Sara took her calling cards. They might come in handy in Lisbon. Who knew what lay ahead?

I'm sure Sara worried about how she and Heinrich would fare during the long train ride and voyage across the Atlantic. No doubt she vacillated between that concern and her lingering agony over her three daughters, sons-in-law, and four of her five grandchildren stranded in Poland. How did she keep calm, I wonder, for I assume anyone as dignified as she in her large, elegant hat and aubergine gown did maintain her composure. "Trust in Max," she must have repeatedly reminded herself. "He will get visas for us all."

In May 1939 Max wrote to his sisters Isa, Teofila, and Lucia in Kraków. His daughter, my mother's cousin, Vera, shared his letter with me:

> New York, May 9, 1939
>
> My Dear Ones,
>
> …I spent the entire day today in the waiting room of the German Jewish Refugee Health Committee on the matter of our parents. For my petition, a few more documents were necessary. At the same time, our parents write in a letter that the London Committee has requested that they send birth records etc. I have great hopes that our parents will be able to depart in the coming weeks. Once in London, it will not be difficult for them to move to Belgium, but I hope they can come here very soon. Assuming that we still have peace. For weeks everything has been fraught with nervous tension although storms are threatening from such a distance. We, who are so closely tied to all of you, tremble at every piece of news. But ultimately the hope for peace is stronger.

> In the face of that, all of our little daily concerns disappear. What does it mean if business is not good for a couple weeks? That the apartment is too hot; that the work for Stefi is sometimes too hard and Vera wants to change schools? Those are our personal concerns. There is not a day when we forget how lucky we are despite everything…

As I contemplate Sara packing, I wonder why she never placed her many family photos in albums. But then I realize that she must have removed them from albums because they would have taken up too much space in the trunks. When my mother filled her own albums, she began with a photograph of Sara's mother, Tina Lewy, clad in a black beaded dress that showed off her tiny waist. She had died young, and next to her photo my mother placed another of Tina's headstone in the Jewish cemetery in Breslau, now Wrocław, Poland.

I knew from Sara's birth certificate that the Lewys were originally from Piotrków, in central Poland, where Sara was born in 1868. Warsaw's AGAD archive contains the birth and death and marriage registries for all of Poland, so I hired a Polish researcher. To my surprise, the records he uncovered were in Cyrillic script because that part of central Poland had been in the Pale, under the control of the Tsar from 1815 to 1917. But there were three early 19th-century records in the Latin alphabet, including the birth of my great-great-grandmother Tina Lewy, who was born in Łowicz as Tauba Sztyft:

> On August 11th, 1841, at 8:00 in the morning came Samuel David Sztyft, age 32, from Łowicz, and in the presence of witnesses Davida Halania, age 48, and Mosiek Aaron Rotszberyn, age 45, also from Łowicz, declared that today at 4:00 in the morning his wife Laja, age 22, gave birth to a baby girl. The baby was named Tauba. After, the declaration was read and signed by the witnesses.
>
> —Clerk's office of Łowicz

The clerk had taken the trouble to compose a little story welcoming a new life to the community, which I found endearing; it showed the gentle pace of life at that time. And talk about calligraphy—the handwriting flowed with voluptuous Ys, Ps, and Js.

Next was the marriage of Tina and Hermann, aka Tauba and Chajman. Looking at the map of central Poland, I see that he traveled 45 miles from Piotrków to Łowicz to court his bride. The clerk's crowded hand yielded a wonderful surprise that sparked an old, dim memory. When we were young, my sisters and I had asked our mother about our first and middle names. We knew that "Ivy Theresa" was in memory of Izydor and Teofila, but why, we asked, had my mother chosen the unusual British first name? She said she did not like the name Isadora—it seemed old-fashioned, and she did not want to name my sister Isabella because that would have been naming my sister for Aunt Isa. My mother consulted Sara, who remembered an Ivy in the family several generations back but nothing more. Sara gave my mother her blessing. In fact, the Iwy mentioned in the wedding announcement above was Tauba's mother-in-law, Sara's grandmother, and my great-great-great-grandmother.

Another surprise was that a Jew was president of Łowicz. A quick look at the history of the town on JewishGen.org showed that in 1795 almost a quarter of the population was Jewish. The third document the researcher found was the birth record of my great-great-grandfather Abraham Finkelstein, son of Markus, father of my great-grandfather Heinrich (Sara's husband) and his five brothers and five sisters. The entry yielded two surprises. The first was a reminder of how quaint cities were in the early 19th century and how quickly they grew; the 1824 record, exactly a century before my mother's birth, only listed Markus Finkelstein's house number. Evidently there were so few streets then that only house numbers were necessary, whereas a century later, his great-great-granddaughter, my mother, lived in a three-story apartment house with an address that included a number and a street. I was also surprised that there were illiterate Jews in the early 19th century. I thought all the people of the book were readers.

I was thrilled that the researcher also found the record of the marriage of my grandparents Izydor and Teofila. They were thirty-two and twenty-seven when they took their vows at the Progressive Tempel (German spelling) on Miodowa Street, on October 7, 1923. They were married late and I wondered how they had met. Why had Teofila moved back to Kraków, where she was born, and left her parents in Berlin? Perhaps she was living with Isa, who was already married. I figured that Izydor returned to Kraków after his WWI service because he had gotten his law degree there. Maybe he needed legal experience, or to pass the bar before he could present himself as capable of supporting a wife.

This, too, was probably the case with Izydor's future brother-in-law, my great-uncle Max, who also had just received his Doctor of Jurisprudence when he was conscripted to fight on the Bessarabian Front. Two years later, he was captured and imprisoned in Sapozhok, Russia, just 150 miles southeast of Moscow. Yet as a POW Max was allowed to correspond with loved ones. He sent two letters to his uncle, Martin F. Stein (Heinrich's older brother and my great-great-uncle, who had emigrated to Stockton, California). Martin informed a local paper, which reported in mid-October 1916 that the Russians were treating twenty-three-year-old Max very well and that he was using his time in captivity to study English. "We are visited often by the Redcap Cross and each time are made very happy," Max wrote, and the officials distributed clothes and money. He spent some of the cash on paper and colored pencils and created beautiful drawings while he waited out the war. When I was a teenager, I saw those drawings, with green, leafy swirls and black outlines, on a wall in Max's Washington Heights apartment.

Max was fighting in Bessarabia when the Soviets threatened to besiege Kraków and his family fled to Berlin. They settled in the Wilmersdorf district at Prinzregentenstrasse 86 in a fine, large apartment. I amused myself with the thought that because "Sara" means "Princess," the address was perfect; my great-grandmother was the Princess of Prince Regent Street.

When Max was set free, he joined his family in Berlin, practiced law, and fell in love with Stefanie Werber, a beautiful but materialistic German-Jewish girl. Heinrich and Sara disapproved and sent Max to

New York to work for Heinrich's brother Paul and his nephew Frederic in hopes that Max would be smitten by an American. When that did not happen, he returned to Germany and married Stefi.

Sometime between 1935 and 1940, Sara and Heinrich disobeyed the Nuremberg rule to surrender works of art and shipped three steamer trunks of goods to New York. They may have sent them with Max in 1938, or sent them earlier to Uncle Paul. Whenever it was done, it was an audacious act of defiance. The Finkelsteins separated the family portraits and the Repin from their frames and rolled up the oils. The pastel boards and two large photographs of Heinrich's parents Abraham and Laija could lie flat on the bottoms of a steamer trunk. On top of that, they piled as many other belongings as possible acquired during fifty years of marriage: a silk tablecloth; a diaphanous curtain with a matching mesh border, both of which Sara had crocheted; two down comforters that I brought to college to ward off New England winters; an eighteen-place setting china collection with matching platters and a gravy dish—all white trimmed with gentle gold swirls. We use these today for our seder.

These treasures were sent from the Germany the Finkelsteins had loved and where they had been proud German citizens. But in fall 1940, Heinrich was "Heinrich Israel" in the eyes of the Third Reich, and it said so on his passport. "Sara Sara" was on his wife's. These so-called supplementary names, Israel and Sara, were imposed on Jews in August 1938 by the Law on the Amendment of Family and First Names.

A Nazi *Oberstleutnant* had selected the best of their property and carted it away. Before that, the Finkelsteins gave up their car because Jews were not allowed to drive. Their telephone had been confiscated, and with neither a free Jewish press nor the radio, their isolation was almost complete. Finally, in 1941, Jews were not permitted to own birds under the First Decree on the Implementation of and Addition to the Law on Carrier Pigeons. Can't have those dirty Jews exploiting Aryans' feathered friends by sending messages through the air. But by then, my great-grandparents were gone.

Sara leafs through her most precious stash of memorabilia—congratulatory telegrams from family in Kraków, New York, and Stockton,

California, on the occasion of her and Heinrich's fortieth wedding anniversary in 1931. And above all, loving, illustrated letters in recognition of various birthdays from their grandchildren, then in their middle-school years: "Dear Grandma, I wish you lots of happiness on your birthday," my mother wrote. "I send you a lot of kisses." Below, Teofila had jested in German: "For two months she has used your fountain pen and that accounts for her penmanship!"

Sara takes these mementos with her. *Tak, absolutnie.* Yes, absolutely. She presses the letters against her breast. It has been so long since she heard from her darlings. Now Rena, Franca, and my mother Irena, the three granddaughters still stranded in Occupied Poland, were the same age Sara and Heinrich's children had been when their portraits were painted. The contrast between their lives then and now was unbearable, yet she could not have avoided thinking about it. Lucia managed to send a letter from the newly formed Warsaw Ghetto. Isa, her husband, and Rena were still in Kraków, but in a few months would be confined to its ghetto. Their son Leon had escaped to Palestine to study engineering, thank God. Teofila, Izydor, and Irena were now in Soviet-occupied Lwów. Would they ever be safe? Would she ever see them again?

Heinrich sleeps on the couch on the other side of the wall. Maybe he had been reviewing, for the umpteenth time, a contract titled *Verhandelt* (Negotiated). A large *Parteiadler* (eagle symbol of the Nazi Party) hovered over the title of the document:

> I authorize herewith the businessman (dealer or trader) Georg Israel Weck, Berlin W 50, Augsburgerstraße 21 (street) as my assignee and give him the power of attorney to take care of all my business affairs. He is entitled/authorized to handle any legal business, and legal act, which I myself could do, and for which an attorney legally is acceptable, on my behalf and with the same effect as if I had conducted it...

He was entrusting his wholesale jewelry business and bank account to a friend. It must have deeply distressed Heinrich to bring this document to the notary public. Had he procrastinated? Yes, I believe, and I picture him dreaming of how he used to end a satisfying day at his office, having negotiated and arranged for the delivery of hundreds of strands of cultured pearls he would sell to jewelers. Restrung and finished, they would then be ready to decorate the necks of countless German ladies.

Afterwards, he might have met a friend in Volkspark Wilmersdorf by one of the lovely duck ponds and enjoyed a game of chess. How he adored the battle of wits, the rigor of thinking as many steps ahead as possible, the clack of his bishop against his opponent's queen. And then, "*Schachmatt* (Checkmate)!" Word got around in chess circles that Herr Finkelstein was not a man to be trifled with. And he loved that. It had been one of his great pleasures to teach his children and grandchildren the game, but only Irena had caught on.

What did any of that matter now? How could he not have seen this coming? At the beginning of the regime, many Jews were convinced they would face hard times, but Heinrich could not have imagined how intolerable their situation had become. They can condemn us to go hungry, but not to starve, he probably thought at first, as did so many in his circle. After all, one could live under any law. But lawlessness on the part of the state was inconceivable.

Heinrich got the Aryanization paper notarized and delivered to Georg Weck, to hand over after they were gone. After the humiliation and hardship of four days locked in the special transport, they arrived in Lisbon in January 1941. They were to board the American Export Liner *USS Siboney* in mid-February.

The last open European gateway to the Atlantic in the early war years, Lisbon was inundated by one million European refugees. Secret agents pursued them and the Gestapo-like secret police of the neutral Portuguese regime were ever on the prowl. Spies perused bars and restaurants of the grand hotels Avenida Palace, Victoria, and the Britannia because the Nazis needed Portugal's tungsten for munitions. Of course, they also coveted its gold. The Allies wanted to prevent the Nazis from acquiring these minerals. Both sides threatened Portugal with sanctions or worse for dealing with the enemy. Prime Minister Salazar played off the competitors and Portugal's balance of trade soared. Intrigue and double-dealing permeated the place much as it did French Morocco's

Casablanca. The Jewish JOINT Distribution Committee relief agency provided shelters and soup kitchens and chartered ships and funded rescue missions amid a torrent of paperwork and bureaucracy.

Sitting in a café surrounded by other well-to-do refugees awaiting passage, the Sara of my imagination picks up an old German newspaper and browses through it. An article about a decree by Hitler banning the Schwabacher typeface catches her eye. Hitler has deemed the most-used typeface since 1530 "Jew-letters of Schwabach." Sara fingers her calling cards in her purse. She and Heinrich find the decree so absurd and malicious that it strengthens their resolve about leaving, excruciating as that is.

Her attention is diverted by the news that Her Highness Princess Marie-Luise Croÿ of Dülmen, Germany, will be on board *Siboney*. The father of the elegant twenty-two-year-old was the 13th Duke of the House of Croÿ, and her mother the daughter of the former United States Ambassador to Germany and former president of Carnegie Steel. Marie is on her way to New York to marry the son of the former New York City Comptroller.

The nobility of Europe has all the choices imaginable, but Sara wonders how many chose marriages of convenience or mutual benefit to escape. How ironic that she, who had eschewed a matchmaker in the late 19th century, now regrets that her granddaughters are too young for such arrangements and cannot use the institution of marriage to save themselves.

On February 15, *Siboney*'s second day at sea, 100-mile-an-hour gale winds struck, buffeting her for three days. The storm was so forceful that the ship nearly capsized. The raging water swept the vessel fore and aft, but her 1,300 tons of cargo helped steady her. The forecastle and kitchen galley flooded and the cooks stood up to their waists in water as pots and pans washed out on deck. For two days they could not prepare food.

One hundred of the ship's 342 passengers suffered cuts and contusions, including Sara, who broke her arm as *Siboney* rolled and swooped at the mercy of the waves. But the pain would have been nothing compared to how she felt knowing her three daughters and their families were marooned in Poland.

Siboney arrived three days late to Bermuda and then steamed up the coast to Pier F in Jersey City, NJ, where Max, Stefi, and Vera greeted Sara and Heinrich. I assume that for Sara, the family reunion would have been joyful yet mingled with pain. When Max embraces her, she shivers.

"What is it?"

"I cannot stop thinking of our other dear ones," she says.

Heinrich does not radiate the joy with which Sara greets their son and his family. He hugs and kisses them, but says nothing, so paralyzed is his heart.

Finkelstein Portraits

Great-great grandparents, Abraham and Laja Finkelstein. Date unknown, Kraków.

Great-grandfather Heinrich Finkelstein, oil, Stephan Zarnecki, Kraków, 1912.

Great-grandmother Sara Finkelstein, oil,
Stephan Zarnecki, Kraków, 1912.

Great-uncle Maksymilian Finkelstein, pastel,
Stephan Zarnecki, Kraków, 1912.

Grandmother Teofila and Great-aunt Lucia Finkelstein, pastel, Stephan Zarnecki, Kraków, 1912.

The Finkelsteins. Clockwise: Unknown soldier, waiter, grandmother Teofila Finkelstein, great-aunt Lucia Finkelstein, great-grandmother Sara Finkelstein, unknown soldier, friend or relative who was a soldier, great-grandfather Heinrich Finkelstein. Berlin, 1917.

Maternal grandparents Izydor Goldberger and Teofila Finkelstein, upon their engagement in 1923.

Irena Goldberger, age 14, walking with her mother, Teofila Finkelstein Goldberger, to the dressmaker. Their last photo together before World War II. Kraków, May 1939.

The Finkelsteins, Goldbergers, and Wexners in Zakopane, the Tatra Mountains resort. Clockwise: Lolek Wexner*, Sholek Wexner, Teofila Finkelstein Goldberger*, Izydor Goldberger*, Lucia Finkelstein Wexner, Cila Goldberger, Yaqob Singer, Irene Goldberger Singer, Irena Goldberger, Rena Wexner, Franca Wexner. Photographer possibly Isabella Finkelstein Wexner*, circa 1936.
*Lost in the Holocaust

The Fränkels/Frenkels

Paternal grandparents Ojzer and Michaela Fränkel. Possibly their wedding day. Lwów, Poland, now Lviv, Ukraine, 1910.

The Fränkels. Clockwise: Paternal grandmother, Michaela Fränkel*, Sydney (né Izak), my father, David, paternal grandfather, Ojzer, Milek (né Samuel)*. Photographer unknown. Mid-1920s, Lwów, Poland, now Lviv, Ukraine. *Lost in the Holocaust

Meldungsbuch

Aufgenommen für 2 Semester

in der ... Fakultät

der

Universität zu Wien.

Known as a *Nationale,* this booklet lists my father's courses and professors at the Medical University of Vienna from spring semester 1933 through spring semester 1938, during the *Anschluss.*

My father, David Allen Frenkel, perhaps on vacation between semesters in medical school, judging by his hairline. Photographer, date and location unknown.

My exhausted father rests after treating the wounded during The Battle of the Bulge. France, Christmas 1944.

Irene and David Frenkel at the Copacabana nightclub. Photographer unknown. New York City, Late 1940s.

Mozes Marks (né Finkelstein), forefather of the California clan, with his son Fillmore Marks, Sr., possibly their warehouse rooftop. Photographer and date unknown, Stockton, CA.

My Mother's False Papers

Arbeitskarte

für Arbeitskräfte

aus dem Generalgouvernement Polen

und

Bescheinigung

über eingezahlte Lohnersparnisse

Danuta Milewska

Nbg. 10000. 2. 42.

Umschlagblatt Va 5760

This document is the cover Arbeitskarte (work card) issued in Nazi-occupied Kraków. Stapled inside are three smaller work cards, revealing her "employers" in Bavaria.

Dioecesis: Leopoliensis r.l. Palatinatus:

Parochia: St. Nicolai E.l. Districtus: Leopoliensis

N-rus: 761/42

Testimonium nativitatis et baptismi.

Ex parte officii parochialis rit. lat. Ecclesiae sub. tit. St. Nicolai E.l. *notum testatumque fit, in libris metricalibus natorum hujus Ecclesiae destinatis pro* urbe Leopoli

Tom. XV. *Pag.* 533 *reperiri sequentia:*

Annus 1925 Mensis VI. Dies 20a nativitatis	Locus nativit. et N-rus domus	NOMEN	Religio	Sexus	Thori	Parentes: Nomen, cognomen et conditio	Patrini: Nomen, cognomen et conditio
Anno Domini Millesimo nongentesimo vicesimo quinto die 20a Junii nata est. baptisata est die 24/XII 1925	Leopoli, Mochnackiego 26	Danuta Stanislaa (bin.)	rom.-cat.	puella	legitimi	Ladislaus Joannes (bin.) Milewski, offic. priv., fil. Joannis et Franciscae Falkiewicz. Casimira Kuśniecz, fil. Lucae et Alexandrae	Stanislaa Nowakowska, ux. Leonardi. Mieczislaus Milewski, offic. priv.

Sacerdos baptisans: R.D. Stanislaus Sokołowski, parochus.

Obstetrix: Monasterska

Annotationes: —

Quas testimoniales manu propria subscribo et sigillo Ecclesiae parochialis munio

Leopoli *die* 5 Septembris *A. D.* 1942

Urząd Parafialny ś. Mikołaja

Makarew

G. 11796 — 22.7.42.

Certificate of Baptism. Signed by a priest, or forger, September 5, 1942. Because my mother escaped the Tarnów Ghetto immediately upon receiving the papers, she evaded an aktion five days later that ended with the second deportation of 8,000 Jews to the Belzec death camp.

Siedmio -klasowa Publiczna Szkoła Powszechna
żeńska Nr: 35 imienia Klementyny Tańskiej
we Lwowie (powiat: Lwów miasto).

Nr 33 Rok szkolny 1935/36

ŚWIADECTWO SZKOLNE

Milewska Danuta

urodzona dnia 20 czerwca 1925 r. we Lwowie
(powiat: Lwów miasto, religji rzym. katolickiej)
uczennica klasy czwartej otrzymuje za rok szkolny 1935/36

stopnie następujące:

ze sprawowania się	dobry
z nauki religji	bardzo dobry
„ „ języka polskiego	dostateczny
„ „ języka	—
„ „ języka	—
„ „ rachunków z geometrją	dostateczny
„ „ przyrody, a mianowicie: z przyrody żywej	—
z fizyki i chemji	—
z higjeny	—
„ „ geografji i nauki o przyrodzie	niedostateczny
„ „ historji	—
„ „ rysunków	niedostateczny
„ „ robót ręcznych	zwolniona na podst. rozporządzenia Insp.
„ „ śpiewu	dostateczny
„ „ ćwiczeń cielesnych	zwolniona na podst. rozporządzenia Insp.
„ „ robót kobiecych	—

Liczba opuszczonych dni szkolnych 24, z czego nie usprawiedliwiono 1
Liczba spóźnień 1, z czego nie usprawiedliwiono 1

Wynik ogólny niedostateczny

we Lwowie, dnia 20 czerwca 1936 r.

Helena Żołnicka — Opiekun oddziału
Tafasiówna Antonina — p. o. Kierowniczka szkoły

Drukarnia Państwowa Nr 82992. 25.III.36. Świadectwo szkolne dla szkół powszechnych 6 i 7-klasowych (P. 1). Cena 8 gr.

This school certificate shows that my mother's alias, Danuta Milewska, completed the 1935–1936 academic year at a Polish school in Lwów.

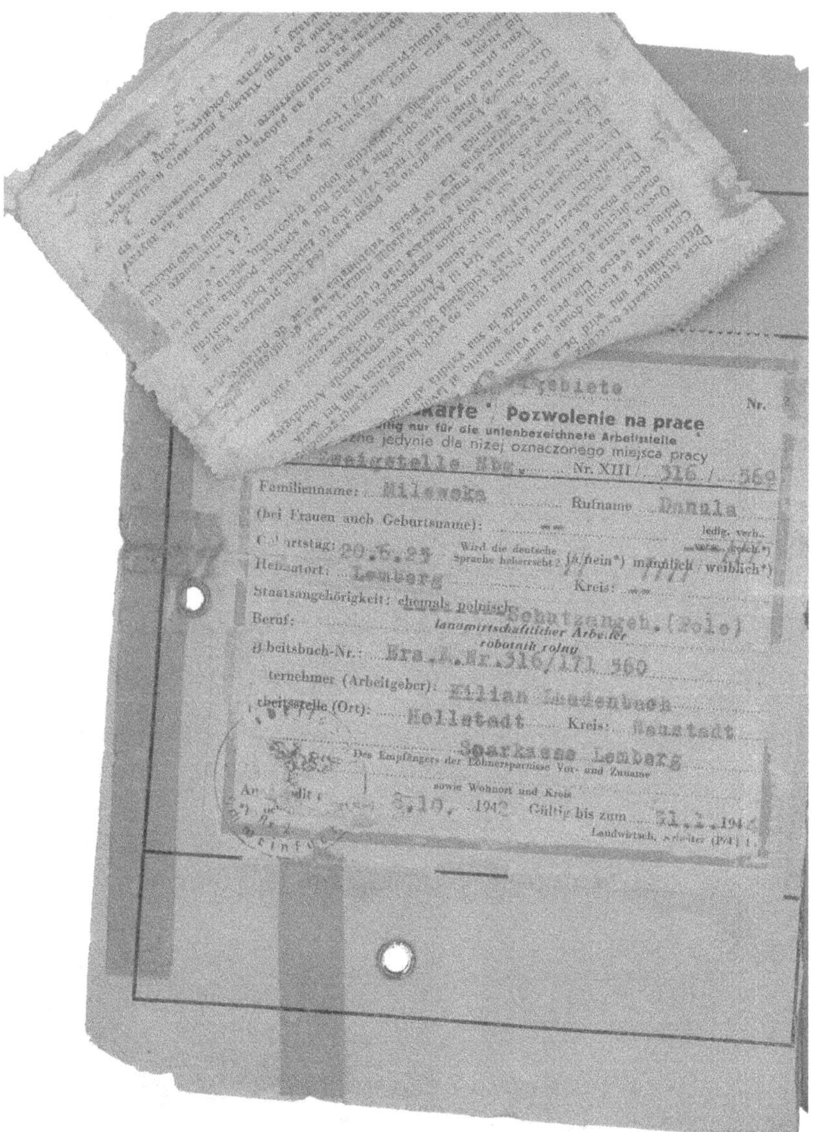

karte", Pozwolenie na prace
gültig nur für die untenbezeichnete Arbeitsstelle
ważne jedynie dla niżej oznaczonego miejsca pracy
Nr. XIII/ 316 / 569
Familienname: Milewska Rufname Danuta
(bei Frauen auch Geburtsname):
ledig, verh.,
Geburtstag: 20.6.25 Wird die deutsche Sprache beherrscht? (ja/nein*) männlich / weiblich*)
Heimatort: Lemberg Kreis:
Staatsangehörigkeit: ehemals polnische
Beruf: landwirtschaftlicher Arbeiter
robotnik rolny
Arbeitsbuch-Nr.: Nr. 316/171 560
Unternehmer (Arbeitgeber): Kilian Laudenbach
Arbeitsstelle (Ort): Hollstadt Kreis:
Sparkasse Lemberg
Des Empfängers der Lohnersparnisse Vor- und Zuname
sowie Wohnort und Kreis
3.10. 1942 Gültig bis zum 31.1.194
Landwirtsch. Arbeiter (P/4)

Work card showing that my mother worked for Farmer Kilian Laudenbach of Hollstadt from October 10, 1942, through the first frost.

Genehmigungsschein für den Betriebsführer

Herkunftsland: Generalgouvernement Nr. 5

LAA. Nordbayern

Zweigstelle Nürnberg des LAA Bayern Nr. XIII ... 316

Familienname: Milewska Rufname: [illegible]

(bei Frauen auch Geburtsname): ledig, verh.

Geburtstag: 20.6.25 Wird die deutsche Sprache beherrscht? ja/nein*) männlich / weiblich*)

Heimatort: Lemberg Kreis: Lemberg

Staatsangehörigkeit: [illegible]

Beruf und Berufsgruppe: [illegible] – 22 a 1

Arbeitsbuch-Nr.: [illegible] 316/271 560

Unternehmer (Arbeitgeber): Gärtnerei Oppelt

Arbeitsstelle (Ort): Bad Neustadt Kreis: Neustadt

Angestellt am 5.4. 1943 Gültig bis zum 27.12. 1944

*) (Nichtzutreffendes streichen.) Ausländer 17

Work card for the Gärtnerei Oppelt (produce nursery) from April 5, 1943 to December 27, 1944.

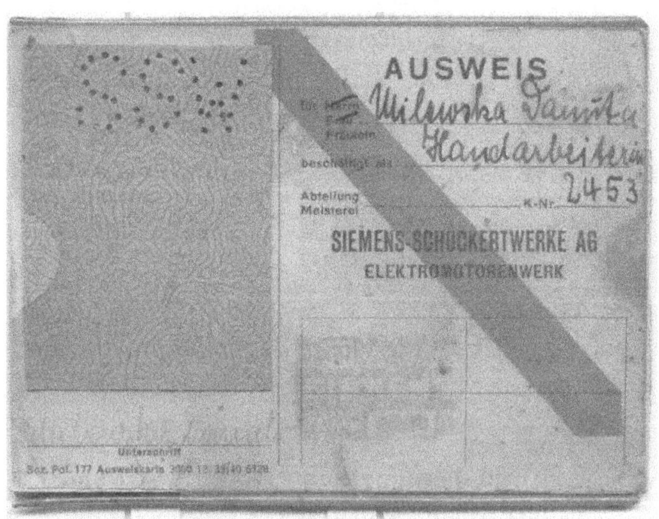

AUSWEIS

für Herrn Frau Fräulein Milewska Danuta

beschäftigt als Handarbeiterin

Abteilung Meisterei K.-Nr. 2453

SIEMENS-SCHUCKERTWERKE AG

ELEKTROMOTORENWERK

Unterschrift

Soz. Pol. 177 Ausweiskarte

Siemens Schuckertwerke AG work card, January 1944 to Liberation, April 7, 1945.

Family Trees

Finkelsteins of Kraków

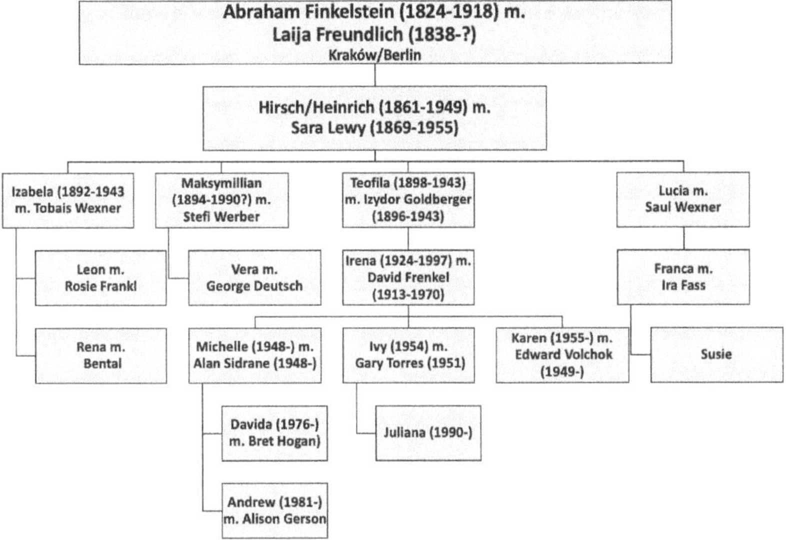

Abraham and Laja Finkelstein's Sons

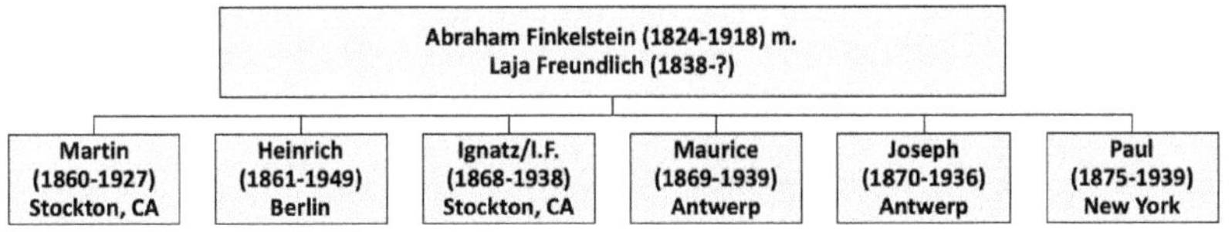

Goldberger — Wadowice

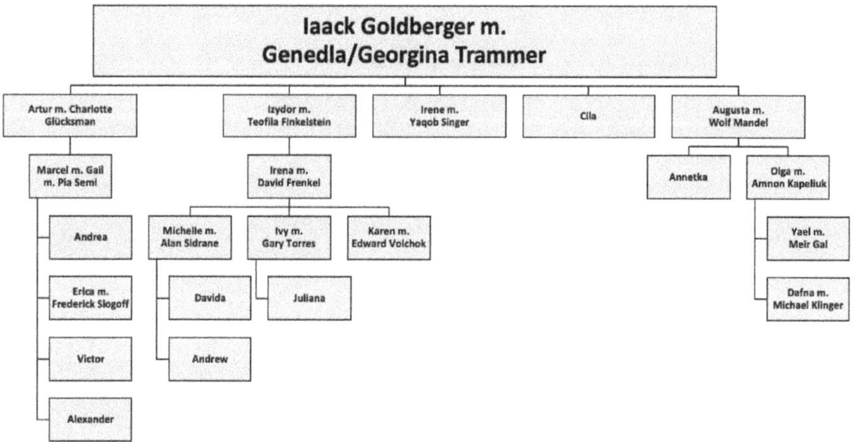

Lifschütz — Lemberg/Lwów

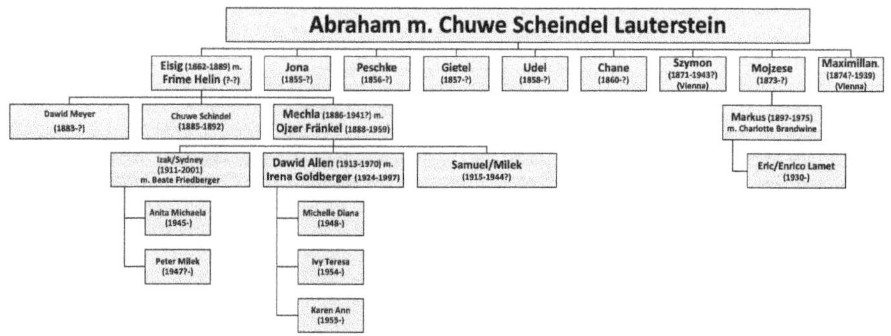

Trammer — Wadowice/Tarnów

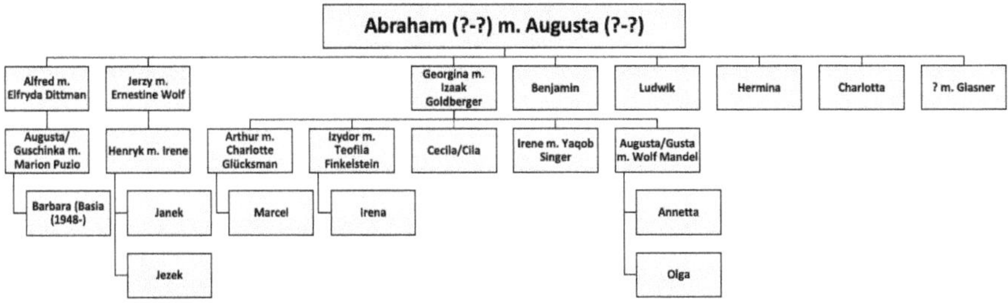

Finkelstein — Stockton, CA

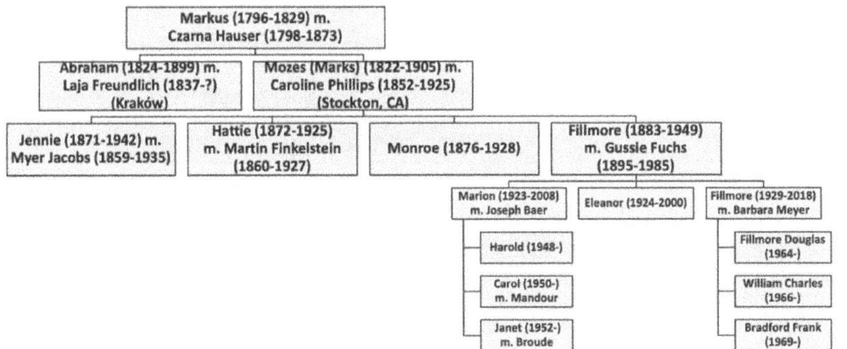

Escape Routes

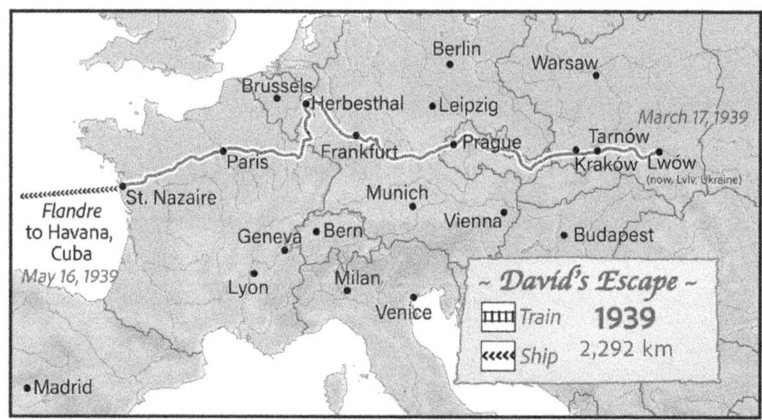

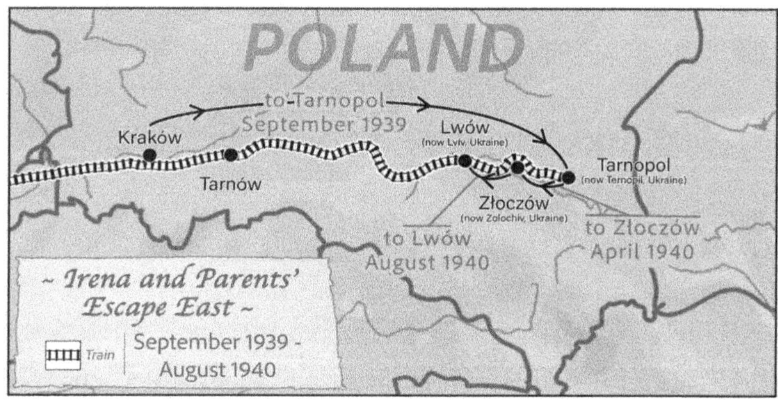

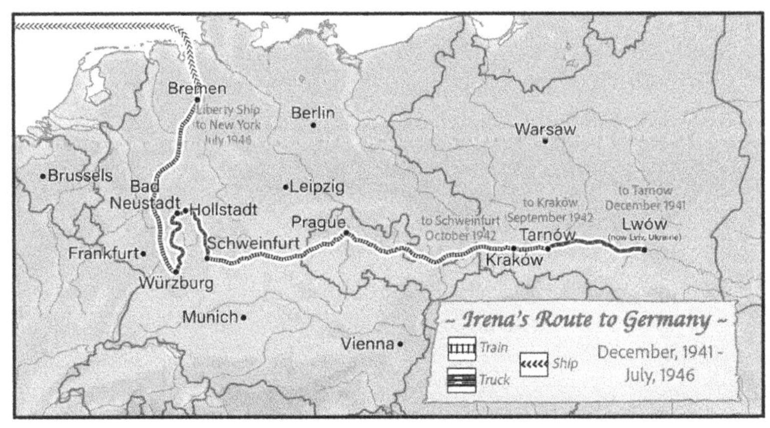
Bremen
Liberty Ship
to New York
July 1946
Berlin
Warsaw
Brussels
Bad
Neustadt
Hollstadt
Leipzig
Prague
to Schweinfurt
October 1942
to Kraków
September 1942
to Tarnow
December 1941
Lwów
(now Lviv, Ukraine)
Tarnów
Kraków
Schweinfurt
Frankfurt
Würzburg
Munich
Vienna
~ Irena's Route to Germany ~
Train
Truck
Ship
December, 1941 -
July, 1946

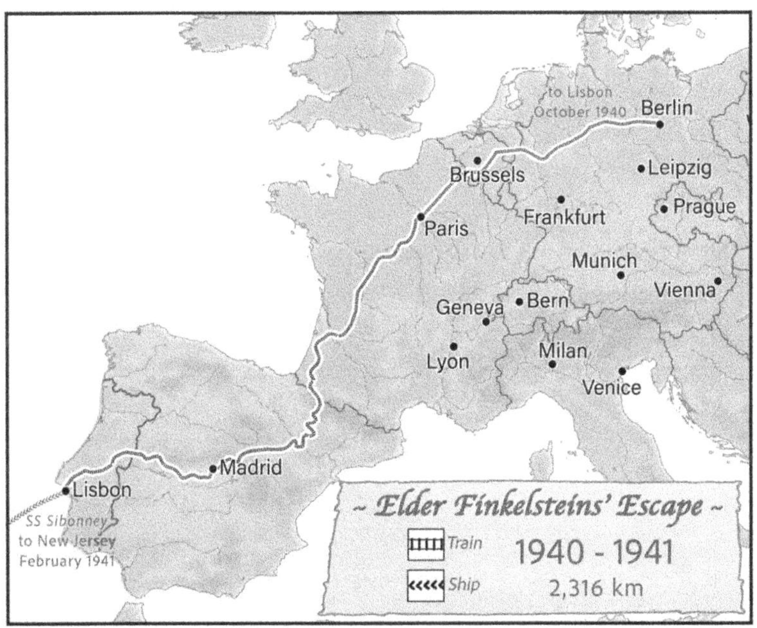
to Lisbon
October 1940
Berlin
Leipzig
Brussels
Frankfurt
Prague
Paris
Munich
Vienna
Geneva
Bern
Lyon
Milan
Venice
Madrid
Lisbon
SS Sibonney
to New Jersey
February 1941
~ Elder Finkelsteins' Escape ~
Train
Ship
1940 - 1941
2,316 km

Tarnów
Kraków
Lwów
now Lviv, Ukraine
Carpathian Mountains
Fled October 4th, 1943
Budapest
August 3rd, 1944
Constanta
Morina to Istanbul, August 1944
THE BLACK SEA
Belgrade
Bucharest
Istanbul
Adapazau
Tartus
Beirut
Haifa
Arrived August 14, 1944
~ Ojzer's Escape to Palestine ~
Train
Ship
Foot
1943 - 1944
3,252 km

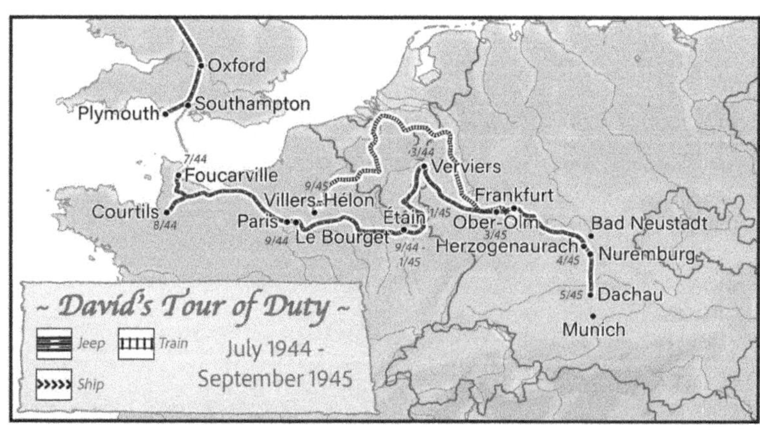
Oxford
Southampton
Plymouth
7/44
Foucarville
Courtils
8/44
9/45
Villers-Hélon
Paris
9/44
Le Bourget
Étain
1/45
Verviers
Frankfurt
Ober-Olm
3/45
Herzogenaurach
4/45
9/44 - 1/45
Bad Neustadt
Nuremburg
5/45
Dachau
Munich
~ David's Tour of Duty ~
Jeep
Train
Ship
July 1944 - September 1945

Chapter Sixteen

The German Occupation of Lwów

On June 22, 1941, the Germans invaded Soviet-occupied Poland and the Soviet Union. Seven days later, the *Wehrmacht* entered Lwów from the west, driving its motorcade toward the heart of the city. Forming a pincer, tanks arrived a little further south, trailed by parading, singing infantry. As the Germans clamped down on the opera house at the head of the main avenue, the former Fränkel residence on Rejtana Street was wedged between them. The paraders turned toward Rynok Square, accompanied by a Ukrainian legion called the Nachtigall Battalion, which German military intelligence had established and trained. The Ukrainians now regarded fascists as their allies and liberators from the rule of the Jews. Posters all over the city incited inhabitants to smash Jews and Communists. Ukrainians hailed their leader and the Führer, chanting in one breath, "Long live Stepan Bandera, long live Adolf Hitler!"

When the Germans and Ukrainians arrived at the square, they toppled the Soviet red star from the City Hall tower and hoisted a swastika and the blue and yellow Ukrainian flags. Along the streets, Ukrainians and Poles welcomed the Nazis with flowers, just as the Viennese had upon the *Anschluss*. The cobblestoned streets of Lwów were blanketed with petals.

More German units arrived at the Jewish cemetery and suburbs. At midnight, three armored trains filled with German soldiers pulled in. By dawn, German guard units were everywhere. Next came *Einsatzgruppen C*, one of four murderous units whose mission was to shoot Jews throughout Poland.

Some Jews still believed the Germans would behave as the Austrians had during their 19th-century tenure in then Lemberg. The disciplined procession in the streets amid signs in German reminded them of this recent past. They consoled themselves and one another, saying that elsewhere Jews live among the Germans—and so would they.

I am certain Grandfather Ojzer was not among them, judging by what I've heard of his character, but I have no proof. The only fact I know is that within five weeks, the Gestapo arrested him, according to a document in the Arolsen Archives (formerly the International Tracing Service), which are available online and housed at the United States Holocaust Museum in Washington, DC, and several other repositories. When my grandfather sought restitution from the German government in 1954, he said he was transferred to "GH Lemberg" where he lived from September 1941 to October 1943. I believe "GH" is shorthand for ghetto. He also said he "then lived illegally in Poland." The form and accompanying cover letter by an attorney named his parents. I already knew my great-grandfather's name was Leizer, but I did not know my great-grandmother's: Beila. What a way to learn it.

Did Ojzer witness the arrival of the vicious *Einsatzgruppen* and the cheering crowds? Did he realize he was facing a cataclysm, and understand immediately that he and Michaela could not survive together? At some point they separated, my mother told me, because his heavy Yiddish accent was a liability. It would have given him away when he spoke Lwów's subdialect, a mishmash of Polish, Ukrainian, German, Yiddish, Hungarian, and Czech. *A mentshn derkent men in zayn redn* (a person is recognized by his speech).

I hated every minute of my research into the massacres and the Lwów Ghetto, which cumulatively took many, many hours. I read every memoir by survivors from Lwów that I could find, and many accounts by eyewitnesses and historians. Only 800 of the 250,000 Jews in Lwów survived but I had to reread their material, make notes in the margins, and attach Post-Its to maintain my concentration because every paragraph made me wonder what outrages or terrifying acts had traumatized my mother and all four of my grandparents.

My mother, then sixteen, described this reaction to the Germans' arrival:

> The Germans came in June of 1941. My impulse was to run and my father said I can't and it really was not possible because the roads were jammed. And the Soviets had enough trouble evacuating their own people. So the escape, without going through the fields, was not possible. The German army was motorized and moved very quickly so we stay in Lwów.

During the Soviet Occupation, the Soviet secret police (NKVD) had executed about 8,000 inmates in Lwów's prisons. Shortly after the Nazis overran the city, they opened the prisons and revealed the scale of murder. They then used that to incite fury among the Ukrainians and Poles against the Jews. The Nazis plastered propaganda throughout the city, pinning posters on buildings and distributing leaflets that declared the Jews not only responsible for the murders of Ukrainian and Polish prisoners, but also for starting the war.

A series of pogroms followed, perpetrated in collaboration with the Ukrainian auxiliary police. Mobs chased Jewish men in the streets and ferreted them out where they hid in their homes, basements, and attics. The Ukrainians sent them to prisons under the pretext that they were needed to remove the decomposing bodies to the prison yards. After the Jews did the work, they were massacred. The walls as high as the second floor of the courtyard of Brigidka Prison were covered with Jewish blood and brains. Several thousand died. Luckily, my grandfather Izydor narrowly escaped that fate:

> Right away in the beginning, my father was visiting his cousin, Ignaz Szancer was his name. As he [Izydor]

> left the building, he was caught by some Ukrainians. He was put against the wall, but he escaped. He knew how to run away. After that, I insisted he should stay at home.

My mother often told my sisters and me that during WWI her father had learned as a soldier to foil the enemy by running away in a zigzag; a meandering target made it hard to aim and shoot accurately. Grandfather Izydor must have used this technique on the Ukrainians either during the "lightning" pogroms, or in the midst of the Petliura pogroms in July.

After a two-day respite, the "lightning" pogroms, so named because of the speed with which they struck, continued. They were also called "*aktionen*," in German. Two thousand Jewish men were tortured by the Gestapo at the courthouse and the 1,400 who survived were taken to a nearby forest and massacred. The July pogroms were named for Symon Petliura, a Ukrainian from Tarnopol who had led the region's struggle for independence after the Russian Revolution. A Jewish anarchist assassinated Petliura in May 1926 and the Ukrainians, at long last, exacted their revenge. The Nazis gave the Ukrainians *carte blanche*, declaring it was the anniversary of Petliura's murder even though it was not. For three days, the Ukrainians hunted down and murdered 2,000 Jewish men and raped Jewish women. They brutally beat another 5,000 to 7,000 Jews. The Nazis executed 3,000 more in the municipal stadium.

After Grandfather Izydor's narrow escape, and because Teofila looked Semitic, my mother insisted that they stay home. She became the sole provider.

One day, my mother came upon several abandoned Russian trucks on the outskirts of town:

> I had a job selling soya beans on black market. The Soviets left carloads of Soybeans—must have come from outer Mongolia—and when I sold all day, I had enough for us to eat. Each time I look on the soya bean sprouts, I say, "Ah, I wish I knew!" Because soya beans,

> if they are boiled takes hours. Could have sprouted them. Didn't know.

Had they cultivated them in water and eaten sprouts, they would not have wasted precious gas, I thought in frustration while listening to the tape. But it was protein. What a lucky turn.

Although Irena sold soybeans all day, she found time to spend with her friends Anula, Bella Barbash who she knew from Tarnopol, and Marilka, who was half-Polish and half-German. They attended Soviet school together until the Germans came. Then Anula and her parents suddenly fled Lwów for Russia.

One day, Bella announced that the *kehila*, the Jewish Community House, was having a clothing drive and invited my mother to help collect for the sick and poor. First, they went to an elegant part of town where they thought wealthy Jews still lived, but came up empty handed. After a while, my mother noticed a pattern similar to what she had observed when she and Anula were Jewish Scouts in Kraków after the *Anschluss*. Just as less affluent Jews agreed to take in German Jewish boarders, Jews residing in Lwów's humbler abodes gave more generously to the poor. "Nevertheless, before we finished our collection, the Germans shot the sick and the poor," my mother observed in her oral history.

This statement, slid into her narrative, at first made me feel ashamed of both cities' well-to-do Jews. But then I realized that embedded in her comment was the shocking truth that my mother either saw or heard Nazis shoot people she had just called on. Having conducted oral history interviews myself, I was trained to regard tone and body language themselves as information. I also knew from reporting to note what a source avoided and wished to leave unsaid. My mother spoke of the German reprisals with little affect and immediately distracted her interviewers from the atrocity by segueing on to the need to find work and the work she found. The Germans began registering all Jewish residents between the ages of sixteen and sixty and required them to present work certificates from their employers. It was imperative to find work, or risk being dragged away to Czwartaki or Janowska, two labor camps within the city limits. (Janowska later became a death camp.)

My mother and Bella obtained work cards and found jobs chopping vegetables for the cook at a school for *Volksdeutsche* girls (girls of German descent), the very school their friend Marilka now attended. I cannot imagine what that must have felt like to my mother as she peeled rotten carrots in the basement.

Chapter Seventeen

More Insisting

A crisis erupted in the Goldberger family when the Nazis announced the formation of the Lwów Ghetto in the fall of 1941. First my mother spoke not of her own reaction to the news, but of the plight of Bella's mother:

> I remember what apprehension there was about getting Mrs. Barbash to ghetto. Mrs. Barbash was much older than my mother. Bella was her last child—child of a menopause. And I remember making her up, putting rouge on her cheeks and sneaking her through the gate. And I think being on the outside more than my parents, I had a feeling that we would not survive the war as Jews.

Later in her testimony, my mother said she told her parents, "There is not a chance we will survive as Jews. Unless we get false papers, this was the end." She had begged her father not to stick so rigidly to his philosophical beliefs. To her, they were out of context. Now she again entreated him to request a loan to buy the papers.

How did that heated discussion go, I wondered. What reasons did Izydor give for not buying papers? My mother had recorded only the outcome, the punchline, so to speak. I reconstruct their argument:

"You really have the arrogance to think you can fool the authorities?" Izydor says. "And you want me—us—to try, too?"

"Yes. Like you did during the Great War, when you fooled the Italians!" my mother replies.

"What has that to do with betraying your origins? Your forefathers?" Izydor sputters. "The enemy wins when you stoop to lying about who you are."

What would Teofila have said? According to my mother, the family always made decisions together, democratically, with each member having an equal vote. In my mind, I hear Teofila's response. "This is no time for such pride. And since when are our ancestors so holy? Not long ago we didn't celebrate the high holidays because Mama and Papa couldn't visit from Berlin." To this, Izydor lowers his eyelids in embarrassment.

Because she sold all day on the black market, my mother heard people talk and was more aware of ominous events than her cooped-up parents. In her testimony, she said:

> What has puzzled me for many years—how did my perception of the death of my people evolved.... I think being on the outside more than my parents, I had a feeling that we would not survive the war as Jews. As a matter of fact, I told [my father] that we must have false papers and he was convinced he raised a snake. He really thought that there was something terribly wrong with me. My parents did not have the sense of danger I had. I also might have been aware of it because in 1938 or 1939 in the spring, I read a book that my father also read, but I came to different conclusions. The title was *Made in Germany*...the book told what was going on—then—in concentration camps. That might have been the reason why I—I believe that Hannah Arendt mentioned that children not burdened by experience and education had sort of an open slate and saw the reality, easier, some of us did, than our elders.

The book my mother and my grandfather Izydor disagreed about was *Murder Made in Germany* by Heinz Liepmann. I try to reconstruct their debate:

Irena appeals to Izydor's intellect by revisiting their earlier debate about Liepmann's message, reiterating that he showed that the Germans planned to destroy the Jews.

"That was part fiction," Izydor retorts.

"No! It *is true*. Liepmann says so," Irena persists. Then, she quotes his Foreword: "'Not a single word was not spoken in my presence; not one character whom I did not know personally, not one incident I did not see with my own eyes.' Father, we simply have no choice. We must get fake papers."

With Teofila right there, Izydor can hardly counter argue that they—really meaning his wife—did not look the part; of all of them, she looked the most Semitic. But perhaps he is that candid and Irena retorts, "But we don't have Yiddish accents. And we speak Hochdeutsch (Literary German)."

"That is not enough of an advantage," Izydor responds.

Teofila sides with her daughter. "She's right. We should try to buy false papers. I'll look into it."

"Where will we get the money? Tell me that."

"We can borrow from our American relatives," my mother suggests, as in her oral history. "They won't refuse."

Is this when Izydor, utterly exasperated, concluded there was something terribly wrong with her? "What's the matter with you? Have I raised a snake? I won't let them think of us as poor relations."

Listening to the tape, I thought, What is the point of all that reading if you don't heed the warnings? Ridiculous, idiotic, foolish pride, I thought, as my teenage mother must have, too.

"But Father, our lives depend on it."

To no avail. "Even if we borrow to pay for papers, there are bad forgers and opportunists. They will take advantage and betray us."

There was one more option: to seek help from Teofila's half-Jewish cousin Gushchinka, who was in Kraków. She had a bureaucratic office job, but that was a cover; Gushchinka and her fiancé were with the

Armia Krajowa, the Polish underground resistance known as the AK. Teofila wrote to Gushchinka asking who in Lwów could be relied upon for false papers. My grandfather reluctantly agreed to ask relatives in America for two hundred dollars. But while the Goldbergers awaited their false papers, the situation in Lwów deteriorated rapidly and became extremely dangerous for young girls. The Nazis and their collaborators were kidnapping them and forcing them to work in brothels, or worse. Teofila and Izydor decided that my mother had to leave Lwów as soon as possible. My mother was reluctant to leave, but Izydor dug in his heels and insisted.

Sheltered and isolated on the Aryan side, he might have only heard rumors or read warnings in the press. One Jewish underground newspaper reported pogroms in Lwów during which Ukrainians dragged thousands of Jewish women out of their apartments, raped them in the streets, and cut off their breasts. I wonder whether my grandparents spared my mother these details and felt it was better for her to know only about forced prostitution.

Perhaps my mother protested that collaborator pimps only went after Jewish girls, and that her false papers would shield her. Wouldn't she have reasoned that the threat would be the same wherever she was? In their response, it seems likely that my grandfather would have again withheld some of what he heard or read—that after being forced to work as prostitutes, Jewish girls were shot a few days later. Or he might have said that the Ukrainians were particularly vicious and that my mother would be better off in western or northern Poland.

Teofila wanted her to join Aunt Lucia and her family in the Warsaw Ghetto. My mother said she refused because she felt ghettos were for burning. The alternative was to stay with Izydor's sister, Aunt Gusta, who was still practicing medicine in Tarnów, not far from Kraków. Although the Nazis had occupied Tarnów since September 1939 and had established a ghetto in March 1941, Jewish physicians and their families were still allowed to live in the Aryan part of the city. Gusta was my mother's favorite aunt and her role model. My mother was also very fond of Aunt Gusta's daughters, Annetta and Olga, then ages eleven and nine, with whom she had played on many holidays in Zakopane.

But Tarnów was almost five hours away. I'm sure my mother protested that it would be very risky for her to travel without false papers. Teofila would have reassured her that as soon as the papers were ready she would send them. Having lived in Berlin during World War I, she knew she could count on German efficiency; the mail would be reliable. Wherever my mother went, though, it was essential that she have a job. Accompanying Aunt Gusta's return letter, therefore, was an official statement saying that she needed a medical assistant.

My grandparents used some of the borrowed money for the fare on a truck to Tarnów in the middle of the night of December 23, 1941. "I still see my mother in the doorway," my mother said on tape, "and the last words she said were, 'When the war is over, you go to your Uncle Max in New York.' And I thought that was the most remote possibility ever."

Being forced by her parents to leave them in Lwów and unable to participate in decisions as she usually was able to do, but could not after she left, was unacceptable to my mother. She never got over losing her parents and blamed herself for not being there to protect them. This is the saddest and most painful incongruity of my mother's wartime experience. Although she had to obey her parents and departed very reluctantly, and even though she did the leaving, she must have felt abandoned. When my father suddenly died, I believe his loss threw my mother back in time to the deep despair she felt when she realized she would never see her parents again and was utterly alone. To succumb, though, was not an option; she had to rally to survive and carry on as her parents would have wished. Twenty-seven years later, widowed at forty-five and in agony at again being alone, my mother seemed, to me, to have lost her resilience. I was desperate for her to resurrect the tenacious combatant I knew she was. The fighter who got her through the war.

Chapter Eighteen

A Sonata in Brooklyn

December 7, 1941. The silence from Lwów is unbearable. My father longs for a scrap of information from his family to drown out the crushing quiet. Yet he also fears their news, dreads knowing. His imagination amplifies their hushed lives.

So, too, does mine, now.

Nothing entices sleep, so my father dresses and goes down to the common area of the Jewish Hospital for Chronic Diseases, where he is now a pathology resident. The room is empty, which is not surprising since it is 3:00 in the morning on a Sunday. He sits on the bench of a beaten-up, barely in-tune upright piano and begins to play. The famous triplets of the "Adagio Sostenuto" come easily, as do the brooding chords of the baseline—descending, dissatisfied groans. Then comes the dotted quaver, a warble or an uneven trill tolling like a bell in a tilted steeple.

Mollie, my father's girlfriend, is visiting her parents; she and my father are not getting along. He invited her on a trip to California, and had even, in passing, mentioned vacationing someday in Europe. But he canceled the West Coast excursion when the Archives of Internal Medicine accepted his first research paper and the editors wanted more data and changes to the draft right away. That, along with Mollie's impatience about the situation with Rose—even though he had told her about it when they started dating—created tension.

Ordinarily and during daytime, my father and his new friend, Bob Root, another doctor and a refugee from Czechoslovakia, played chess to relax. They were so well-matched that they became chess partners, sometimes snatching games between rounds. But it is the wee hours and Bob is married.

All seems to him the deepest, darkest nadir since the *Anschluss.*

My father returns his attention to the piano. He has played Beethoven's "Moonlight Sonata" many times before, having studied it as a teenager with his piano teacher. The first movement was the most excruciating, yearning music he had ever heard. Sadness sustained, unchanged, over time.

Some think Beethoven's sonata, which he dedicated to a student with whom he was infatuated, is about unrequited love. But others say the dolorous first movement has nothing to do with failed romance and everything to do with death. The great composer wrote it after holding vigil at a friend's deathbed;it is a funeral hymn that evokes a somber, meditative state of mind.

As my father's fingers move across the keys, he tries to smother his woes. His mind flits from appreciating the beauty of the musical turns of phrase as they flow by, to rumors of Nazi atrocities committed in his hometown, to happier times as a student in Vienna, the enlightened city of music. While there, he had made sure to take an evening off from his studies to hear the great Artur Schnabel perform the sonata. Although my father admired Schnabel's playing, he felt in retrospect that Schnabel had rushed the first movement. How in character it was, therefore, that Schnabel had moved with alacrity in 1933 and escaped the Nazis when Hitler took control of Germany. The pianist fled for England and, ultimately, the United States. My father wondered why it was, what it was, that this renowned interpreter of Austrian and German culture had heard and seen that caused him to act so swiftly. What enabled him to be alert and responsive while many other Jews, like his parents and Milek, were deaf to the danger, unable to act?

Both having emigrated in 1939, my father and Schnabel are now in the United States—yet they remain stateless. Both have left their parents behind. Grief, the great equalizer.

My father's hands rest on the keys He tries to breathe slowly. What good are the late 18th-century Illuminati and their reputed influence on Beethoven and his ilk? So they had their progressive vision. Had it ever amounted to much? Was their contribution still true and clear and valid in the face of all the evil now inflicted on the world? My father must believe the brotherhood of humanity will endure, will withstand the assault.

And yet, where is his brother, Milek? Where are their parents?

With a clack, my father shuts the lid over the keys.

The next morning, my father tells himself he will be tired later and arrives on time for grand rounds. Among the cases: a sixty-seven-year-old patient with chronic congestive heart failure; a forty-four-year-old with Parkinson's disease; another admitted for atherosclerotic heart disease and cardio insufficiency and suffering from pneumonia. Pneumonia—that is the subject of my father's research paper. He and his colleagues have found a new way to diagnose the disease. My father has high hopes that it will save many lives.

My father is finishing a late lunch when a nurse runs into the cafeteria shouting that the Japanese have attacked a naval base in Hawaii. She just heard it on the radio. The room vibrates with the frantic voices of the attending doctors. Several run to telephones. One calls relatives in California. Another tries to reach a buddy stationed in Oahu but cannot get through. My father overhears one colleague worrying that a new naval hospital under construction in Pearl Harbor may have been hit. Another says the hospital ship USS Solace had just steamed into port and hopes she has not been stricken.

There's a lull for a few minutes as people think perhaps the attack is a horrific rumor. But half an hour later, NBC interrupts its broadcast of the Giants and the Dodgers football game to confirm the attack. Within ten minutes they learn that in a second raid Japanese planes have pummeled Pearl Harbor.

When the chaos subsides, my father dials Sydney, but he is not in. In the late afternoon, my father and the other interns huddle at the nursing station radio. One by one nations declare war on each other. At five o'clock, NBC interrupts its broadcast of auditions at the Metropolitan Opera to announce that Japan has declared war on the United States and Great Britain. Later, Canada declares war on Japan.

That night, NBC reports the first casualties—104 young men killed. Medical officers are treating sailors everywhere—on ships, in the old 250-bed Naval Hospital, at first-aid stations in barracks. They set up cots on the docks to care for those rescued from the water or evacuated from ships. Doctors treat shock and severe burn cases; sailors who swam in hot oil. There are flesh wounds, gunshot wounds, wounds caused by shells and shrapnel, wounds produced by fragments of bombs and metal, and traumatic amputations. But the staff of the Jewish Hospital for Chronic Diseases does not yet know these details.

By 10:45 the next morning, NBC reports 3,000 casualties, including 1,500 fatalities. Overhearing this, a young nurse begins to weep. My father approaches and gently asks what's wrong. Her kid brother is stationed at Pearl Harbor on the USS Arizona.

My father puts his arm around her shoulders and tries to comfort her. "I know how you feel."

At noon President Roosevelt addresses a Joint Session of Congress, which the staff catches on the nursing station radio.

Then someone yells that Sydney is on the line.

"So we're at war with Japan. How long 'til we declare war on Germany?" asks my father.

Sydney ignores the question. It's rhetorical anyway. "I want to enlist right away. Fight in Europe."

"Me, too," my father agrees. "I have to find out if I can interrupt my residency."

My father's residency will take another two years to complete, and he is not sure how the Army would regard him without that training. Later, he seeks advice from the Chief Resident.

"Do nothing until you have your medical license and residency behind you," says the Chief without hesitation. "You owe it to the war effort to volunteer when you are most qualified."

Such is the scene my mind's eye envisions, enhanced by facts and medical memories of the date that lives in infamy.

Chapter Nineteen

Resistance

In 1911, when my paternal grandmother Michaela Leder Lauterstein Fränkel was a bride, she wore her long cherry blonde hair in two braids wrapped around her head like a halo. Or so it must have seemed to her adoring husband Ojzer. Not only was Michaela very beautiful, she was interesting to talk to, Uncle Sydney said in his interview with my cousin Anita. But because Michaela was orphaned, she might have been at a disadvantage in the matchmaking arena; she probably had no dowry, or only a small one, and was two years older than Ojzer and several inches taller. Perhaps that is why she's seated in their wedding photograph. Then twenty-four, she would have been considered old; women were usually married off by their mid- to late-teens. Given these few facts, which went against the stereotypical rules and norms of the day—that a woman should be younger and shorter than her husband and contribute a dowry—I think theirs was a love match.

My mind invents a scene before the Great War. Michaela looks out the window of her and Ojzer's first apartment at Kazimierzowska Street 39. Having a few minutes to herself because baby Sydney is napping, she brushes her long locks while watching the traffic on the same avenue the Nazis will speed through during the next war. But her world is tranquil now and she is looking forward to a new baby. Because she is expecting, the Fränkels will soon move to a larger, quieter apartment in Number 7, Passage Fellerow, where my father and Milek will be born.

The tiny lane leads to that underpass to the opera house that I tried but could not enter virtually, a passageway my family traversed often.

I wonder, knowing what rascals the brothers were, whether Michaela dreamt of having a little girl. But as her boys approached manhood, Michaela knew a more loving family was not to be had. Husband and sons hung on every word as she told stories of her childhood in Zuków and the teachings of her Rabbi. Whenever Ojzer was away on business buying furs in Leipzig or some other city, he returned with gifts for Michaela—a muff and a matching hat, soft leather gloves, or jewelry. He always thought of her. When vacationing at the finest spas—Franzensbad and Marienbad in Czechoslovakia, and Karlsbad in Germany—the Fränkels would stroll together on the street, the boys forming a little parade as if to announce Michaela. Sydney told Anita that passersby turned to admire her flowing blonde hair and soft, sweet smile. When she entered a café or restaurant, patrons rose to glimpse the beautiful, happy woman his father cherished, the mother of his three beloved sons.

After World War I and upon returning from Vienna, Ojzer and Michaela bought Rejtana 5, one block south of Passage Fellerow. Maybe Michaela knew and was entranced by the building's romantic, musical history. In the early 19th century, Mozart's son, Franz Xaver Wolfgang, fell in love with a Polish baroness, a singer whom he accompanied at musical soirees. But she was married to an older man. Mozart fils moved from Vienna to Lemberg to be near her and lived in a house on the very same lot as my grandparents' house. It is possible, according to urban archaeologists at LvivCenter.org, that Rejtana 5 was built around the staircase of Mozart fils's house. For the next twenty years, the lovers were never apart. Enterprising Franz Xaver Wolfgang founded the city's first music school and performed throughout Europe, playing both violin and piano. Maybe Michaela mused about him and his music school when Sydney and my father played both composers' violin and piano sonatas.

The pleasure of sipping tea while sitting on their balcony, watching passersby through the Secessionist, cast-iron filigree must have seemed very distant in both time and space to Michaela in June 1941. The prospect of enduring yet another upheaval after two invasions must have been terrifying. But Michaela did have, in a way, the daughter she may have always wanted; Milek's bride. Feiga was blonde and blue-eyed, too, so it was decided that together they would pose as Catholic Poles. But Vos toig shainkeit on mazel? (What good is beauty without good luck?) Perhaps Michaela and Feiga stayed at the address I had found in Milek's Polytechnika file and Ojzer took a room somewhere else. In any case, together Michaela and her daughter-in-law endured the ever-intensifying grip of the Nazi vise.

When Michaela was in her late forties, her braided hairstyle, so typical of 1930s eastern Poland, gave way to a graying bob cropped at her chin. In her mid-fifties, upon the Nazi invasion, would her blue eyes and fair hair save her? Could she really pass for a Catholic Pole? I suppose she was reasonably certain her fluent Polish and German would not betray her. But reasonably certain was not good enough. I wonder why her accent was not an issue while Ojzer's was. Both spoke Yiddish and were from the same rural region, but perhaps her German was better because her family was based in Lemberg and visited Vienna often. Maybe Michaela left Zuków after Eisig's death and lived with relatives in Lemberg, where more German than Yiddish was spoken. Ojzer thought she could manage it, but how good was his ear? He mixed languages and accents into a linguistic stroganoff. And that was dangerous.

Some time in 1941, the Gestapo arrested Uncle Milek. Because he was a mechanical engineer, the Nazis forced him to run a factory that manufactured coal gasification engines. According to Uncle Sydney, Milek oversaw eighty Jewish laborers and was told that if anybody escaped, he would pay with his life.

Even more calamitous than the work edict, however, was the ghetto, located in the northwestern part of the city and isolated by railroad tracks and an embankment. The neighborhood was the city's worst slum and had been slated for demolition. Most of the one-story buildings were moldy and decrepit, had no electricity, and no sewage or water system. The Germans forced Ukrainians and Poles to vacate the run-down area, finding it ideal for overcrowding Jews and then tormenting and annihilating them. The Jews had four weeks—between November 16th and December 15th—to move to the quarter. Tens of thousands of Jews complied before the deadline.

The entrance to the ghetto was under a railroad trestle, which was manned by Ukrainian police, the SS, and the German security police, who had been recruited from the Einsatzgruppen and other units of German killers. They rounded up Jews and forced them into the old public bath building, which had been converted into barracks for the German and Ukrainian militias. Anyone emaciated, shabbily dressed, ill, or aged was dragged there, where Ukrainian guards beat them to death. Others were taken to Lonsky Prison where they were stripped naked and shipped aboard freight cars to a forest and executed. At a school, hundreds of elderly Jewish women were forced to stand in line while a Ukrainian woman wielded a spiked ball on a chain. She swung it as she walked down the line, crippling whomever she struck. They writhed on the floor in pools of blood.

At the same school, young and healthy Jews were assembled and required to watch the elderly being forced by guards to dance and sing. Afterwards, the guards continued to force the younger Jews to watch as they tortured the elderly and ill to death. Then the young Jews buried the bodies in the schoolyard.

The next day, the young Jews were sent to the Special Labor Bureau where they were selected by SS men who commanded slave labor camps in Eastern Galicia. They executed anyone they found not able-bodied enough for labor. This vicious escapade became known as the "Aktion under the Trestle." The ghetto entrance, itself, was called "The Bridge of Death."

The Ukrainian police broke into homes, and on the pretext of searching for the elderly, extorted money and valuables from the Jews. There were many suicides. It is estimated that 10,000 Jews lost their lives during this series of aktionen, which lasted until the middle of December. For the first time the victims included many women.

That fall, the Nazis also began building Belzec, the first killing center. In March 1942 they started gassing Jews from Lwów and Lublin with carbon monoxide gas generated by diesel engines. By the time the death camp was liquidated in June 1943, 434,500 Jews and an undetermined number of Poles and Roma had been annihilated there.

As much as Milek must have hated the Nazis for exploiting him and his fellow laborers and seethed from the humiliation, it was probably nothing compared to the torture of being separated from Feiga. We were told that one night, perhaps in the spring of 1942, he could stand it no longer and snuck away from the factory barracks. Stealthily he moves along a circuitous route, hoping to throw off anyone who might follow him, constantly looking behind and sensing no one. What bliss it will be to hold Feiga in his arms, to smell her hair.

He steps over the threshold and embraces his bride. Michaela, at once joyful and petrified, sees the couple's adoration and has not the heart to admonish her son. He parts before dawn.

The next day, the screech of brakes on the cobblestones and barking dogs fill the air. The door of the downstairs vestibule is flung open. The stomping up the stairs means only one thing. The Gestapo has arrived to arrest Michaela and Feiga.

Michaela is prepared. She reaches for the locket on a chain around her neck and removes two cyanide tablets Ojzer had given her when the Nazis marched in to Lwów. She offers one to her daughter-in-law, but Feiga does not extend her hand. Instead, she curves both arms and hands around her belly, cradling it.

Nazis kick in the door, burst in, and scream, "Raus Juden, Raus (Get out, Jews, get out)!"

Michaela looks the first Gestapo officer in the eye. Then at the gun he points at her heart.

I have lived through both wonderful times and harrowing ones, she thinks. I was orphaned, but found a husband to love and who worshiped me. My sons adored me and I them.

She remembers the touch of Ojzer's hand as he caressed her cheek, and the tender expression in his eyes when they parted.

Michaela returns her gaze to the killer's face. She stares into his eyes as if she, herself, is taking aim.

Bridge of Death? No.

Belzec. Never.

She bites hard into the poison.

Chapter Twenty

The Stamp of Life

In the middle of the night of December 23, 1941, my seventeen-year-old mother boarded a crowded truck in Lwów bound for Tarnów. Her false papers were not yet ready. She brought only her work card and her aunt's letter, which would have made my mother's trip legal but for typhoid fever and dysentery epidemics raging in Lwów's terribly overcrowded ghetto. It was therefore forbidden, on pain of death, for any Ukrainian, Pole, or Jew to leave the city. My grandparents had gambled that right before Christmas the Nazis were unlikely to patrol the roads as thoroughly as usual. Nobody stopped the illegal travelers. Polish winters are very, very fierce and the truck was not heated. After standing for five hours and enduring the bitter cold, my mother arrived in Tarnów on the morning of Christmas Eve.

Tarnów is known for its traditional Polish architecture, which was strongly influenced by Austrians, Germans, and Jews, who had lived there since the 16th century. The entire Old Town, built during the Polish Golden Age, is preserved—defensive walls, tenements, homes, and houses of worship. There was a school, a synagogue, a Calvinist prayer house, Roman Catholic churches, and twelve guilds. The medieval system lasted well into the 18th century; Tarnów was owned and controlled by three successive noble families until the Habsburg Empire absorbed Galicia in 1772. Unlike Kraków, the town was captured by the Russians during World War I, then liberated by Polish Legions. In the 1930s, half of Tarnów's population was Jewish, the fourth largest in Poland. When the Nazis arrived on December 8, 1939, they immediately incorporated Tarnów's 50,000 vanquished citizens into the Reich's Generalgouvernement. The next day, the Nazis destroyed most of Tarnów's synagogues and drafted Jews into forced-labor projects.

After getting off the truck, my mother probably walked from the town square to her aunt's apartment building, which was not in the Jewish section. In her testimony, she described her impression upon entering the apartment: "The parquet floors were clean. The maid was there. One of the rooms was occupied by a German clerk, the other room by a refugee doctor. It was a huge apartment. My two little cousins were there.... Officially I was my aunt's office assistant. I don't think I was very useful."

The building where my great-aunt Gusta had lived with her husband Wilek, also a doctor, and two daughters Annetta and Olga was a beautiful turn-of-the-last-century structure built by another doctor. The place was indeed large, but only some rooms were in use when my mother arrived because fuel was scarce and the entire apartment was impossible to heat. Before the war, Aunt Gusta and Uncle Wilek had practiced medicine in the left wing. They shared a small waiting room, a second room had been Aunt Gusta's pediatrics clinic, and the third, much bigger room was Wilek's office. Now, under the German Occupation, everyone except Wilek lived in that room. He had gone undercover with false papers and was working in a brush factory near the salt mines south of Kraków. No longer practicing at her home office, Aunt Gusta treated children in an orphanage near the ghetto. While she was at work, the girls were cared for by their nanny, Antosia, who slept in a corner in the kitchen.

In 2016, Ed and I got the address from my mother's octogenarian cousin Olga Mandel Kapeliuk, a Hebrew University professor emeritus of linguistics. While we took photos and shot footage outside the yellow-brick building, our guide struck up a conversation with the landlord who was about to drive off in his Mercedes-Benz. She convinced him to show us his second-floor apartment.

We walked through the carport, admiring its beautiful orange stained-glass cornice that evoked sunrise. In the partly renovated stairwell, I climbed the stairs gripping the original art nouveau banister as my mother would have that winter morning. I passed several geometric, stained-glass windows lighting the way. As I crossed the threshold, I had the strange feeling that I was entering the same apartment my mother had lived in from Christmas 1941 to June 1942, and standing on the same gleaming, herringbone parquet floors. Did she turn to warm her hands by the fireplace decorated with floral tiles? When the landlord plinked a few notes on an antique piano he said belonged to his sister, I felt certain my great-aunt was its owner but restrained myself from saying so. Was someone playing when my mother arrived?

Opposite the kitchen a small terrace overlooked Plac Sobieskiego, a plaza surrounded by yellow and blue houses. I was sure I was gazing from the same terrace she had in the winter of 1941–1942. These intuitions were later confirmed when I shared images of the apartment with Olga.

To the right of the terrace, a glass canopy juts from the first floor like a lady's fan, covering the bay window of the café below. The frosted white glass reminds me of river ice. I envision my mother standing on that terrace, teeth clenched. Everyone was teetering on fast-moving ice floes back in late 1941.

And yet, Tarnów was relatively calm that December because many Jews still believed they could surmount Nazi persecutions with ransom money and bribes. In part this was perpetuated by the Judenrat (Jewish Council), a governing body in every ghetto that carried out the Nazis' orders. The Judenrat had its own police to enforce orders. The Nazis dictated which Jews to arrest, which to send to work, and so on. If the Judenrat did not do the Germans' bidding, the leaders were imprisoned or shot. In Tarnów during the early war years, the head of the Judenrat advised Jews to work, pay whatever the Nazis extorted, and conform to Nazi edicts. So when German soldiers on the Russian Front suffered from the cold and the Nazis ordered the Jews, on penalty of death, to relinquish their furs, boots, and skis, they complied. They were biding their time, hoping for rescue.

Tarnów was the first Polish city where the Nazis forced every Jew to wear an armband—a white, wide ribbon with a blue Magen David (Jewish star). The Nazis instituted this humiliation on Tarnów's 25,000 Jews as early as October 1939. Another first: 728 prisoners, 708 Christian Poles, and 20 Jewish Poles were deported from Tarnów to Auschwitz where they were tattooed with the numbers 31 to 758. The first 30 numbers were for German criminals, prisoners brought from other camps to set up Auschwitz.

Relative calm in Tarnów lasted for six months until June 10 when the Nazis decreed that Jews doing essential war work must get their work cards stamped. Anyone unemployed was "resettled." Neither my mother nor Aunt Gusta could contain their agitation because by then, they understood the meaning of this euphemism. In her oral history, my mother described getting her stamp:

> I remember passing the desk of Grunoff, Head of Gestapo. He was a young, extremely handsome man, but there was madness in his eyes. Completely petrifying experience. Somebody shuffled me in to the Labor Office. It's a funny thing—there was a mirror there. And as I walked in, or was pushed in, I realized I was completely pale green. I maintained my composure, got out my documents and got a stamp. I did not know this was a stamp to live. I thought it was just a question of staying in Tarnów.
>
> That day, they rounded up at least 10,000 Jews in Krakow, took them to the cemetery, made to dig their graves in the cemetery, and shot them. One escaped. So we knew.

While transcribing my mother's testimony, I could not quite catch the name of the terrifying Gestapo chief my mother had passed in the Labor Office. Grunoff, Grunov, Gruenov, Grünow? I wanted to know more about him. Was he tried at Nuremberg? Spelling his name phonetically, I searched the historical record of the handsome, blond monster my mother described, but found nothing.

On JewishGen.org I found a history of the Tarnów Ghetto with a devastating title: "The Suffering and the Destruction of the Tarnów Jewry: The Annihilation of the Jews of Tarnów," by Dr. Abraham Komet. But I read with pride of my great-aunt Gusta, "the woman doctor Mandel" who cared for children in the "orphan home." In September 1942 all the Jewish orphans, their teachers, the director of the orphanage and his entire family were gassed. I was so upset that I did not notice a photograph of six young-adult Jews in front of a ramshackle ghetto house. The next time I returned to the printout, I thought I saw my mother standing in the shack's doorway, but the woman was too blurry for me to be sure.

Further in was an account about the villain: "Gerhard Grunow, the famed Hitlerist hangman," arrived in Tarnów on December 9, 1941. The new enforcer with the elaborate title Kriminalassistent der Abteilung Gestapo der Sicherheitspolizeiaussendienststelle (Criminal Assistant in the Gestapo Department of the Security Police) chose the day the United States declared war on Japan for his first display of authority. To intimidate Tarnów's Jews, he arrested 100 and shot 17. He set the rest free, presumably to demonstrate his power as well as to "lull vigilance to sleep," according to Komet.

The new year began with an order for all Jews to register with the Gestapo. The master race wanted a master list. Then followed an outbreak of typhus, spread by German soldiers returning from the Eastern Front. Meanwhile, Jews from surrounding shtetlach (villages) were "relocated" to the ghetto where the population swelled to 40,000.

Just before Passover, Grunow and fellow Nazi Wilhelm Rommelmann happened upon a young girl in an alley who sold poultry and was carrying a slaughtered chicken in a basket. Wielding revolvers, the Gestapo men chased her and demanded that she reveal who had butchered the chicken. When she pointed out the home of the Jewish ritual (kosher) slaughterer, they broke in and butchered him and his two sons. According to another report, with bloody hands, Grinov (a spelling variation I had not thought of) and Rommelmann then entered the residence of a neighbor. Everyone in the household began to recite Shema Yisrael, the prayer Jews traditionally say as their last words, but the murderers merely wanted a dish of warm water and a clean towel. After washing their hands, they left. Not yet used to such criminal acts, the Jews of Tarnów were so terrified they stopped eating meat.

A few weeks later, fifty-six Jews who had arrived from Lwów, as my mother had, were murdered: a rabbi who had returned from the Zionist Congress in Geneva and was slated to be the next chief rabbi of Tarnów died of a heart attack while being dragged over the threshold of his home; another Jew was shot because he did not stand up when a Gestapo officer entered; Josef Hudes was simply shot for no reason. My mother had a friend, Ted Hudes, whose poodles used to scamper on our lawn in Forest Hills. Was Josef Ted's father? Or an uncle? A brother? It seemed that with my personal background, at any moment I might come across an un-anonymous victim.

Finally, I found a description of the edict for the special stamp of life, as my mother had called it:

> After the 10th of June 1942 the Gestapo men stamped two sorts of seals on the work cards. One seal was a swastika and was called hoheits (territory); the second with a Latin letter "K." The unemployed and children received a white card. No one knew the actual significance of this mysterious letter "K."

An account on Deathcamps.org by the Aktion Reinhard Camps group of historians described yet another seal with the letters "SD" for those who could prove they were employed doing essential war work.

These different seals increased the agitation and anxiety of the Jews. Speculation abounded. People began to speak of deportation, but they did not know whose fate was more secure: those whose seal contained the swastika, "K," or "SD." "The mystery was clarified after registration ended a week later; the letter 'K' meant deportation as well as—death," wrote Komet.

None of the types of stamps mattered. It was all a manipulation by the Nazis to confuse and terrorize Tarnów's Jews so that they could more efficiently annihilate them. With these stamps, the Nazis refined their sort in preparation for the first Tarnów aktion. The mass murder began on the morning of June 11 and continued through June 18. They shot Jews in the market square, into pits in the Jewish cemetery, and in the forest. Others were shipped by rail to the death camp Belzec. There they immediately were gassed, and their bodies thrown into a giant, bloody, oozing pit. Two years later, in an attempt to destroy the evidence, the Nazis had slave workers exhume the victims' remains and grind the bones into powder.

Toward the end of their bloody rampage, the SS dragged Jews out of their homes and killed even those with work cards bearing the proper seal my mother had obtained. The SS extinguished 18,500 Jewish lives—75 percent of the entire pre-war Jewish population of Tarnów.

After two days of Jewish bodies being thrown into mass graves, relative quiet befell Tarnów. Then the Nazis rounded up all remaining Jews, including doctors, to the ghetto on the outskirts of town. Until then, the ghetto had not been sealed, but as my mother, Aunt Gusta, Annetta, and Olga walked toward it, they would have seen a new, two-meter-high wooden fence topped with barbed wire. After passing through it, they moved into a one-room apartment with nine other people.

A second, two-day aktion, the Kinderaktion (Children's Aktion), followed in late July. The Nazis ordered Jews out of their houses, forced them to remove their shoes, and hounded the barefoot victims with rifle butts and whips all the way to the market square. Then the Nazis tore children from their parents and shot the children in a nearby shed. Some older Jews were selected for forced labor. The rest were deported to Belzec.

Then there was a lull. Perhaps even the Nazis needed a break from aktionen.

"So we knew." An echo of my mother's words persists in my mind. But it occurs to me that she was probably aware of only a smattering of incidents. I'm glad. Had she not witnessed or heard about them all because she was still living in Aryan Tarnów? I hope so. It is possible that only the Jews confined to the ghetto heard such horrific news. Or did she deliberately omit atrocities because she knew her daughters would be terribly disturbed by them? I will never know.

It is chilling to contemplate how easily my mother could have been among the murdered. And how—according to Hitler's plan—my sisters and I were never supposed to have been born. But the precision genocide of the Third Reich was not quite infallible.

Chapter Twenty-One

Aliens in the Catskills

When my great-grandparents arrived in Washington Heights, NY, in the winter of 1941, a joke was circulating among German-speaking refugees.

"Two Dachshunds meet in Central Park. They sniff one another and one asks where the other is from. 'Vienna,' he says. The first replies, 'I'm from Berlin. How do you like it here?' Both complain about the wurst (sausage) and the apartments. They agree that Central Park is not quite the Tiergarten, Berlin's most popular park, nor the Volksgarten, the People's Garden in Vienna adjacent to the Hofburg Palace. Despite all they bemoan, the Viennese concedes that life here is not too bad, considering the alternative. The Berliner agrees, but adds, 'What really bothers me, though, is that in Berlin I was a Rottweiler.'"

Sara might have heard this joke from fellow matrons gathered outside a butcher shop or a bakery on Nagle Avenue, where they regularly gathered to exchange news and chat. After tittering and bidding her neighbors goodbye, Sara would have hurried home a few blocks to 65 Hillside Avenue, a six-story, Art Deco building. When Max, Stefi, and Vera arrived in the fall of 1938, they rented a two-bedroom, and Max was pleased to have found another apartment in time for his parents' arrival.

Had Sara recounted the Dachshund joke to Heinrich, he would not have been amused. My mother never said anything negative about her grandfather, but Vera, Max's daughter, told me he was grumpy and "not nice." Like so many immigrant men living in Washington Heights, he found it difficult to adjust to American life, although for different reasons. They struggled over how to handle their Germanness at a time when Germans were the enemy, and yet hoped to assimilate. In contrast, despite having lived in Berlin for thirty-five years and becoming a German citizen in early 1933, and despite having changed his first name, Heinrich did not consider himself German. Both he and Sara still identified as Polish Jews, and since Polish was their mother tongue, they must have spoken German with Polish inflections at the very least. In contrast, most Polish Jews in New York City claimed Yiddish as their native language, and although they had been Polish citizens, were not strongly nationalistic. They considered Jews with Polish nationalist leanings assimilationist traitors. German Jews barely disguised their contempt for Yiddish with the result that many American Jews thought German Jews were distancing themselves from Judaism.

Given this friction and as twice-refugees (having fled Kraków for Berlin at the beginning of World War I), the elder Finkelsteins navigated with difficulty in their new neighborhood. They did not fit.

The recent wave of German Jews had not come to the United States for economic opportunity, as had the German Jews who arrived in the mid-19th century. The newest newcomers had fled Nazi Germany because the alternative was persecution and death. Many had witnessed Kristallnacht or had been imprisoned in the first concentration camps, or both. While they felt nostalgia for the life they had left, their break with the Old Country was harder to reconcile; they had felt a part of German society, and it had cruelly discarded them. They rejected the word "refugee," yet they realized they were exiles and could never return.

At eighty, Heinrich was also experiencing the usual losses that come with advanced age. During the past four years, his three brothers had passed—I. F. died in Stockton in 1938, and Maurice of Antwerp and Paul of New York died the following year. As the last remaining brother, Heinrich must have felt his age.

Trying to keep up with current events, he probably read *The New York Times* and *Aufbau*, the weekly journal founded by Albert Einstein, Thomas Mann, and other German refugees. The paper influenced the thinking of German Jewish immigrants, 78,500 of whom had arrived in America between 1938 and 1940, compared to 30,000 in the five years before the Nazis came to power. *Aufbau* was filled with readers' letters describing their problems adjusting—everything from the difficulties of earning a living to gauging the culture to keeping up morale. Heinrich would have seen this in Max, now in his mid-forties, who did not return to law school and study for the bar and gave up his profession. Instead, he earned a living as a diamond broker, benefiting from the connections of his cousin, Frederic Finn (né Finkelstein), who imported diamonds. And yet, Max was doing relatively well, although Stefi, too, had to work. Many men could find none and others who had been professionals in Europe toiled in clothing factories, or as bakers or salesmen.

While Heinrich fretted about his daughters in Europe and being the poor relation in America, Sara tried to adapt. When not focused on her husband, she corresponded regularly with Cousin Fillmore in California, crocheted doilies, and embroidered a linen tablecloth I store in my dining room.

When Heinrich went for a checkup with his internist that spring, his doctor reminded him that previously the summer heat had taxed Heinrich's heart. This time the doctor prescribed leaving town during the hottest months. Because Max and Stefi had summered in the Catskills before, that was the obvious destination. But the United States government considered the elder Finkelsteins "enemy aliens." Each had to fill out a form called "Alien's Declaration of Intention to Travel," which included:

1. Home telephone number: none
2. Employer: none
3. Business address: none
4. Nationality (if stateless, give last nationality): Austrian with German passport
5. Alien Registration Number: (appears above photograph inside certificate of Identification): 7594341
6. Purpose of trip: recovery of health (80 years of age)
7. Destination: Haines Falls, Catskill Mountains, N.Y.

8. While away from my permanent residence, I will be at: The Fenimore, Haines Falls, N.Y.

At the bottom, Heinrich and Sara signed a line labeled "Signature of Alien."

The Catskills, a natural paradise, had a brutal history. In 1609, when Henry Hudson sailed up the river that today bears his name, 10,000 Native Americans lived on either side of its banks. From the east bank, the Mohicans held land from Long Island to Connecticut and Albany. From the West, their home extended from the Catskills to Schenectady until the territory of the Mohawks. The Mohicans battled the Mohawks, who hunted, danced, and loved in the Hemlock forests and on the craggy plateaus of the valley named for them that lies between the Adirondack and Catskill mountains.

The Mohican terrain overlooked lakes, wild ravines, and lofty peaks. The slopes resembled giant terraces stepping their way to a deep gorge, Kaaterskill Clove, which the lakes fed. There, the mesmerizing Kaaterskill waterfall drops 260 feet and empties into a creek. European settlers hailed the stunning area as a primeval Eden unsullied by progress.

Sandwiched between Kaaterskill Wild Forest and Hunter Mountain is the hamlet of Haines Falls, where Hudson River School painter Thomas Cole depicted landscapes. He painted four scenes he imagined in James Fenimore Cooper's novel, *The Last of the Mohicans*, including the final confrontation between settlers and Native Americans. The landscape is jagged, dangerous and frightening, with boulders ready to tip and crash onto climbers' paths. A sense of loss permeates all four paintings—the lost American wilderness, a murdered maiden, and, with the death of the last Mohican brave, the annihilation of that tribe.

My great-grandfather rocks in a chair alone on the veranda of the Fenimore Hotel in Haines Falls. Max, Stefi, and Vera are hiking the magnificent falls. Sara naps upstairs in the elder Finkelstein's room.

Heinrich leafs through the July 3, 1942, *New York Times*. On page six—not deep in the paper, as some conveniently claimed accounted for why Americans knew nothing of the atrocities and extermination—he reads the headline: "Allies Are Urged to Execute Nazis." A little below is the subhead, "Report on Slaughter of Jews in Poland Asks Like Treatment for Germans. Curb on the Reich is Sought" in order to save millions from certain destruction. The article describes a report recently received by the Polish Government in exile in London saying 700,000 Jews have been slaughtered in German-occupied territories. The report recounts the extermination of Jews through gross mistreatment at concentration camps, starvation in the ghettos, and unbearable conditions of forced labor. All the cities where Heinrich's daughters and their families are, or recently have been—Lublin, Lwów, Tarnopol, Tarnów, Warsaw, and Złoczów—are listed.

In Galicia, where the killings began a year ago, Heinrich reads, Jewish men aged 14 to 60 were herded into public squares and cemeteries, forced to dig their own graves, and then machine-gunned and grenaded, the report claims. Children in orphanages, the elderly in almshouses, the sick in hospitals, and women in the streets were all slain. The Nazis also rounded up and deported them to clandestine destinations in nearby woods and massacred them. In Lwów, 35,000 Jews were reportedly murdered, as were 5,000 in Tarnopol and 2,000 in Złoczów.

Sweat dots Heinrich's forehead. The report estimates that 25,000 Lublin Jews were taken to an unknown destination and have not been heard from since. Some are thought to have been detained in the suburb of Majdanek. In the Warsaw Ghetto during a bloodbath one night in April, the Gestapo entered homes, dragged out Jews and killed them. Elsewhere, murder was more methodical; ninety Jews at a time were gassed in chambers on wheels, *The New York Times* reports.

"The criminal German government is fulfilling Hitler's threat," the article concludes, and that regardless of who will win the war, "all Jews will be murdered." It implores the Polish Government in exile to protect those threatened with annihilation and calls upon the Allies to retaliate in-kind against Germans living in Allied countries.

Heinrich lets the newspaper drop onto the porch. He stares out at the lawn and then at the hemlock forest ahead. A forest not unlike the ones where his children and their children might be facing gunfire at this very moment.

Heinrich lifts his eyes to the mountains. Alone and unable to think of much else, despair creeps into his consciousness. He pines for Zakopane and peacetime excursions with his children and grandchildren. He remembers Irena's enthusiasm for wildflowers, especially for a rare, yellow trumpet-shaped flower with violet dots. Together they had found a patch growing on limestone. But when he stooped to pluck and gather them into a bouquet, Irena said with a curtsy, "*Danke, lieber Großvater, aber sie sind so viel schöner, wenn sie noch am Leben sind.*" ("Thank you, dear grandfather, but they are so much prettier when they are alive)."

It was obvious to him now that he and Sara were wrong to have spurned I. F.'s offer three years earlier to adopt Irena. Looking up into the Catskill sky with its series of white cloud puffs, he imagines someday giving Irena a fine string of pearls.

Heinrich eyes a cluster of dandelions on the Fenimore's lawn and frowns. The yellow flower, *Gentiana punctata* had once been an ingredient for Underberg, a German bitter based on a secret, proprietary family recipe. In the mid-19th century, this popular liqueur was lauded for its digestion-stimulating and calming effect. But production had ceased in 1939 due to a lack of raw materials.

So much had ended that year.

Heinrich licks his lips as he remembers the Underberg flavor, and then reaches for his seltzer to wash away the bitter taste.

Chapter Twenty-Two

The Fighter

My purpose in visiting Tarnów in 2016 had been to see my great-aunt's house and get a general sense of the city. During our hour-long car ride from Kraków, I told our guide, a woman in her forties, about the important role Catholic Poles had played in my mother's survival. I also said my mother had gotten a special stamp on her work card at Gestapo Headquarters. Somehow the guide, Ed, and I got into a discussion about contemporary anti-Semitism in Poland. She insisted there was none, but I pointed out why we felt there was; our hotel provided tourism information encouraging patrons to visit Auschwitz, stating that 74,000 Poles had perished there without mentioning that 960,000 Jews did, too. Our guide justified this omission because Jews died only in Birkenau, a subcamp and extermination camp. Had the hotel's literature omitted the fact of these deaths in describing Auschwitz-Birkenau, *that* would have been incorrect. She could not understand why we took umbrage and vehemently held her position.

I was irritated as she started fiddling with her phone, but it turned out that she was looking for the address of the old Gestapo Headquarters. She announced that it was now an apartment building and that we were going there. I was surprised. It had not occurred to me that the building still existed.

Gestapo Headquarters was only a ten-minute walk from Aunt Gusta's house. When I got out of the car, I reenacted my mother's arrival, shooting with my iPhone as I reached the first of two forbidding, cast-iron doors. I wonder whether my mother's composure would have faltered had she been confronted outside by two guards. The second doorway was as dungeon-like as the first, with medieval-looking, black studs reaching toward the street. Did my mother realize, as she passed by, that Jews cowered behind the barred basement windows? I, myself, could not stand the sight of the gray, murder-infused place.

Near one entrance, the guide pointed out a commemorative plaque, a sort of demented tic-tac-toe configuration referencing the metal grids that protected the building's basement windows behind which Jews were imprisoned in cells. I turned away to see a resident leaving through the second door. I strode toward it, grabbed the doorknob, and slipped inside. I shot footage of the vestibule's blood-red and black speckled wall tiles where mailboxes are attached. What? Was this décor some weird joke, I thought, as I panned back and forth. Beyond the staircase my camera caught the silhouette of a cat as it padded toward the backyard. Hopefully when my mother lurched up the eight steps in June 1942, the main hall was too crowded for her to glimpse that backyard, where, after being tormented, Jews were routinely shot.

Feeling spooked, I returned outside to get Ed and our guide. We descended to the basement, where, she said, the tiny cells that had held captives are now storage rooms for the apartment dwellers above. How soundproof were the wooden doors, with their horrible grid-covered portals, I wondered. Did anyone on the street hear the wails of the captured Jews? Did my mother? Probably not. They were likely drowned out by the desperation of their brethren on the sidewalk as they clamored for a stay of execution, a little more time in the exterior dungeon.

Upstairs and outside again, I stood in the very backyard where Jews stood before firing squads. My eyes hovered over the wall and the weeds. In my mind's eye, blood seeped between blades of grass into the soil. How can people live in such a place?

I was unable to focus on the conversation during the rest of the tour. I was only mildly interested in the *Mikvah* (Jewish ritual bath), now a restaurant, and the remains of the great synagogue, a lone brick arch of the bima. I thought about the part in my mother's testimony when she remarked that she was "not very useful" at her "official" job as a medical assistant. I counted the years her life had been in danger. Anger and sorrow burbled inside of me because my mother's youth had been stolen.

Contemplating the message embedded in what she said and avoided, it seemed to me that having to mentally revisit her terrifying Gestapo Headquarters experience, my mother resorted to irony and understatement. But she was not merely deflecting; she knew her job was a ruse and so from the moment she arrived at the Gestapo Headquarters to standing on line to finally receiving her stamp, she was terrified that an officer would call her on her deception.

Forty years later, clad in her pink paisley dress to which she had pinned her silver horse broach—Teofila's last gift—my mother sat before the Fortunoff archive's video camera. Her amethyst necklace and matching, dangling earrings caught the camera lights. And even though she had been safe for decades, all the jewelry in the world could not mollify the feeling of mortal, intolerable dread.

In one of her college papers, my mother described the Tarnów Ghetto in late summer 1942. She wrote it upon the twentieth anniversary of the events described. There were seven drafts, including carbon copies, the pages all jumbled. Below is most likely the final version she submitted for Professor Jameson's Sunrise Semester class, ENG W14, in 1962:

> The afternoon sun lost some of its midday brightness and now shone warm and golden in the pale blue September sky. The tranquility of the beautiful Polish autumn day contrasted sharply with the mood of the Jewish teenagers standing in the corner of the almost empty square of the Tarnów ghetto. I was a stranger here and my presence in the group of the local elite was due to the respect my aunt has [sic] enjoyed here for many years. The conventions and the snobbery seemed ludicrous in view of the topic of our conversation. On the local black market, the price of poison had skyrocketed

in the last few days, I reflected enviously. In 1942, only the rich can afford to die when they choose to do so and escape German tortures. The rise in the price of poison indicated that the murderous, SS Sonderkommando was again expected in Tarnów soon, killing on its way thousands of Jews in the neighboring towns.

Two months ago, no one had suspected that killing [sic] of 10,000 helpless people within three days was possible. The Germans had announced then a "resettlement" of Jews not productively employed in Tarnów. The mood in June had been quite different from the present one, I recalled. Then the fear of the unknown spurred me to the daring move. I had smuggled myself into the labor office with a group of factory workers employed by the German military. Suddenly confronted with the row of Gestapo officials, I froze with fear. In the mirror on the back wall of the office I caught a glimpse of my very pale green image. I gathered the flickering remnant of my 17-year-old courage, and in my best German said to the nearest Gestapo officer, "I am a medical assistant." He smiled faintly as he reached for my dusty pink identity card and put on it a swastika stamp. A few days later, I found out that this swastika was a stamp of life, for a while anyway. The SS men rounded up all those with empty identity cards and proceeded with their "resettlement" plans. A little boy escaped from the cemetery and told me about the mass graves of the 10,000.

This September afternoon we had no illusions and no hope. The anxiety of two months ago was changed now into frozen panic. Next to me stood a delicate, beautiful girl. Her blue-black hair framed her fine-featured, suntanned face and her graceful neck, falling in soft waves to her shoulders. Elegant in a gray summer dress,

Lili drew intricate designs in the soft yellow dust of the square with her sandal. On the other side of the square, the Jewish militia, pompous in their insecurity, bossed the Jewish workers entering through the ghetto gates.

Only two days ago, Lili's sweetheart, Stan, was the head of the militia. The favorite of the head of the Gestapo, the notorious Gronoff, Stan was an important personality in our ghetto world. Two days ago in midst [sic]of what seemed a friendly conversation, Gronoff took out his gun and shot Stan. In the sunny square, Lili quietly drew pictures with her elegant sandal. Her slim figure would have looked well in any of the fashionable resort places. Only her eyes betrayed the tragedy. Her narrow, black eyebrows tensely arched, gave her almost black eyes an expression of intolerable pain. Like many others in the ghetto, Lili was resigned, wished to be dead.

The Germans, methodical in their destructiveness, took first our guns and furs. No one objected, then—it seemed a small matter indeed. Then they took our homes and step by step, our freedom of movement outside of [sic] ghetto. But when they began taking away the ones we loved, suddenly stripped of our humanity, we found that life had lost its meaning. To many of us the fight for life seemed pointless.

Looking at Lili I shuddered. I would kill Gronoff even with a kitchen knife, I thought in a fury. If I must die, I will die fighting. My absurd notion was quickly chilled by my more sober reflections. What right did I have to be a hero? If I attacked Gronoff on one of his terror-spreading, wildly shooting sprees in the ghetto, not only would I die, but the Germans would kill everyone in our street. As it was, my little blond, blue-eyed

> cousins still could be sent out of the ghetto to hide with our Christian friends. My aunt might survive since the Germans did not kill doctors as a rule.
>
> In the little dusty garden the sunflowers were turning their ripe faces towards the setting sun. I wished I could be a mole and crawl underground until the end of this madness... In a few days, the Radio London [sic] will announce once again: "In the last days of September, in the town of Tarnów, the SS Sonderkommando killed another 10,000 Jews..." Why don't they send bombers here and kill the SS men and Jews alike! Oh! What a relief it would be to die from an Allied bomb...
>
> The children were playing Gestapo and Jews, a "resettlement" game. Little ones ran shouting and giving out stamps...

Not knowing whether the assignment had been to write an essay, short story, or a fragment of a memoir, I wondered whether Stan and Lili were individuals or composites. Did my mother give them fictitious names? I searched for Lili among Tarnów survivors' oral histories at the U.S. Holocaust Memorial Museum and the Fortunoff Video Archive for Holocaust Testimonies. None of the women could have been her. I considered whether Lili was a stand-in for my mom, then decided against that; although she, too, was dark and her black hair fell in waves to her shoulders, my mother was neither frail nor petite. She clung to her will to live. The details were so precise that I accepted her account as authentic. But who remains to remember Stan and Lili? Am I the only one alive who knows that they, like innumerable other wartime, young Jewish lovers, existed?

Whatever the genre, for this extraordinary eye-witness account of the mood and events in the Tarnów Ghetto, Professor Jameson gave my mother a B minus. His comment: "I'll leave it to you whether you rewrite this or not. The mechanical errors are not so numerous."

I was so repelled by what I read and heard about Gestapo Commander Grunow's rampages through the Tarnów Ghetto that it took me four years to seek his records in the German State Archives. Within a week I received his Application for Employment in the *Sicherheitsdienst* (Security Service known as the SS) for the Colonies. *Colonies?* Oh, right, I thought, the Third Reich regarded conquered nations as "colonies." Grunow had filled out this form in 1937. After graduating from high school, he had gone into hotel management, having trained on American ships as a clerk and steward in the United States, Central and South America, and the West Indies. As a result of his time overseas, Grunow became fluent in English and knew some French. "How does a man switch from placing chocolates on people's pillows to putting bullets in their heads?" Ed wondered. Ah, one of the great mysteries. When Grunow returned to Germany in 1933, the year Hitler came to power, Grunow quit hospitality for the police force and became an assistant detective. At the time of his SS application, he had a wife, toddler, and four-year-old.

A photograph depicted the devastatingly handsome monster just as my mother had described him. His fine, chiseled bone structure and features—from his symmetrical, straight nose to his chin, cheekbones, and mouth—bore an uncanny resemblance to Paul Newman's (which is especially ironic because Newman was half Jewish). Only the lunatic ogre's eyes were the exception. I found a black and white photo of the great actor to compare the men. Whereas Newman's eyes exuded warmth, twinkled, and were slightly tilted down, Grunow's lay flatly horizontal. The future *SS Obserscharführer* (High Commander) gazed not at the camera, but just above its lens. At what? His vision of future elevated carnage?

The Poles tried and hanged him in 1948 in Tarnów. I wished my mother had lived long enough for me to find out and tell her. But she was not vengeful and I don't think she would have felt satisfaction.

The fact that my mother had lived in any ghetto in Poland was news to me. She simply told me she left Tarnów when her false papers arrived. Perhaps my mother never spoke of the Tarnów Ghetto because she felt humiliated by being forced into it.

I stood in Tarnów's former Wolność Platz, which the German occupiers called Magdeburger Platz, the teen hangout within the ghetto in August 1942. Today the square would have been unrecognizable to my mother. Dark gray flag stones pave the spots outside the Jewish Police headquarters where, my mother wrote, Grunow fatally spilled Stan's blood and Lili traced designs in the sand. Known as the Square of the Victims of Stalinism, today a monument at the center depicts a woman, symbolizing Poland, standing atop a cracked granite pedestal to represent the division of Poland upon the outbreak of WWII. Three eagles, one wounded, fly from her outstretched arm.

But something so much more important to me has endured. I contemplate my mother's words: "To many of us the fight for life seemed pointless.... If I must die, I will die fighting."

Shortly after the murder of 10,000 other Jews in Tarnów, false papers for my mother arrived from Teofila and Izydor in Lwów. The papers enabled my mother to pose as a Catholic Pole. My grandparents wrote that they, too, had false papers, and were posing as the aunt and uncle of my mother's alias. They were among approximately 2,000 Jews in Lwów posing as Aryans with the help of forged papers.

My mother showed some of her false papers during her oral history interview. Most important is a Proof of Baptism signed on September 5, 1942, by a priest at Lwów's St. Nicolai Church. Three others are report cards. One pale pink, the other faded green, were from a Polish public school for the 1935–1936 academic year. The third is in Cyrillic. The fact that it was issued in Lwów on July 6, 1940, by the District Department of the People's Education, means that the student attended school during the Soviet Occupation, as did my mother. Included with this report card is a receipt from Ukrainian Secondary School #104 certifying that the student passed state exams and was promoted to the 6th grade. The last document is titled "*Arbeitskarte für Arbeitskräfte aus dem Generalgouvernement Polen un Bescheinigung über eingezahlte Lognerparnisse.*" This is my mother's work card from the General Government for the Occupied Polish Region, or *Generalgouvernement*, the administrative agency the Reich imposed on the conquered territory.

Folded in two, the card creates a cover page. On the lower left corner are two of my mother's fingerprints.

I reluctantly examine a stamp of the German national emblem. The Reichsadler is an eagle with wings spread and perched atop a small, wreath-encircled swastika. No matter the size, swastikas always frighten me and I must avert my eyes. Those spidery Indian Sanskrit symbols—appropriated and bastardized by the Nazis into *Hakenkreuz*—are now ruined for the world. I turn to the photograph, a three-quarters shot that shows my mother at age seventeen wearing a dark blouse with two strings looped loosely into a bow at her neck. Her full lips curl slightly, but I cannot read the expression in her eyes. It seems deliberately opaque. Her combed back, black hair reveals her left ear, a requirement for all German-issued identifications. Why was this compulsory? To prove that she was *not* Jewish, for according to Hitler's great theory and contribution to the pseudoscience of phrenology, Jews have attached ear lobes. Ha! He was so obsessed with this idiotic non-correlation that he sought a photograph of Stalin's ear to ascertain that his adversary was not a Jew.

Underneath the photograph of my masquerading mother is her signature: "Danuta Milewska."

My mother scrutinizes these papers upon receiving them. Perhaps she asks herself whether she could get used to answering to that name, but decides it would be easy. Nor does she feel challenged to remember her new birthday, June 20, 1925—not November 29, 1924. But when she sees Danuta's grades, a wave of irritation hits. "You will be amazed," she told her interviewers, "it bothered me that she was an 'F' student." All her life, my mother's intelligence had been valued and cultivated, but now in Autumn 1942, she realized she would have to play dumb to fit the identity of the girl named in the papers. My uppity mother.

The strong conviction she had in Lwów, that a false identity was essential to survive, persisted, yet apparently she could not immediately recover from the news from Kraków and the previous two Tarnów *aktionen*. She saw misery and despair everywhere, but had no intention of digging her own grave so that the Nazis could shoot her into it. As she said in her testimony:

> I made the decision that the best way to die was to walk out of the ghetto because they would shoot you on the spot. The occasion presented itself [when] a friend of mine, Palek Fass, arranged for man who was delivering hay to his factory—young man of about 20—to take me out of ghetto. I did not ask my aunt. I didn't ask her permission. I was ready and I left within five minutes. There was one route by which you could get out—it was on the way to the hospital—and I was sure that I will never make it to the railroad station.

Recounting her escape on tape, my mother neither dwelled on the danger nor on the extraordinary courage and defiance it took for her to leave. Her tone was almost matter of fact, consistent with what I had always known of her: exemplary bravery, daring, resourcefulness. These qualities along with resilience and *joie de vivre* were what I admired most about her. She was a fighter. And she taught her children to fight.

My mother was fascinated by James Fenimore Cooper's tale of the fate of the Native Americans. In *The Last of the Mohicans*, after Magua kidnaps her, Cora refuses to cooperate and tells him to kill her if he wishes. On the edge of a jagged precipice with arms outstretched toward heaven, Cora cries, "I am thine! Do with me as thou seest best!"

At the moment of her decision, my mother, like Cora, decides that she will die when *she* chooses to die. And like Uncas, the last Mohican, she sees herself as the last of a doomed tribe. But my mother remembers Teofila saying, as she had so many times before and on the train when they fled Kraków, "Remember, you are your daddy's daughter and he was a war hero. Be brave like him."

As Irena approaches the ghetto gate, she discreetly removes her armband and stuffs it in her skirt pocket. And then, a cool resolve: *If I must die, I am ready. Shoot me now.*

Somehow, my mother slips through the gate unnoticed by the guards.

Chapter Twenty-Three

In Transit

There were several routes my mother could have taken from the ghetto to the train station where she was to meet the hay farmer. I estimated a half-hour walk. What went through her mind as she proceeded? Were Nazis swarming the streets or was it relatively quiet? If stopped and searched, I worried retrospectively, would they not have found her armband? No, she would have had to discard it because she also carried her false papers. What if she arrived at the station and the hay farmer was not there? Where would she go? Maybe she figured she would just shuffle back into the ghetto with the zombie-like, exhausted Jews she had seen returning while she was leaving.

She arrived at the train station and saw the peasant standing by his horse-drawn wagon. Ever so quickly he helped her climb on to the wagon bed and covered her with hay. Prostrate on the gritty planks of wood, she inhaled the musty scent and listened to the clomp of the horse's hooves. She dared not move, afraid a change in position and the vibrations of the wheels might disturb the grassy blanket and expose her.

The young peasant brought my mother to his farm on the outskirts of town where he lived in terrible poverty with his parents and four siblings. The youngest was five years old. My mother commented in her oral history, "I was wondering if these people were absolutely out of their minds to hide me. All of them would have been shot if I was found there." To ask for shelter when, according to German law, you were guilty just by being a Jew, was to endanger those who helped you. Another kind of murder. She reiterated to us over the years that she couldn't understand why the farmer and his family put themselves in jeopardy. She wasn't sure she would have done so, now that she had her own precious children.

The farmer had an older brother, an officer in the Polish Army who unfortunately was not among the 85,000 Polish soldiers who had escaped to France; he had to hide because the enemy hunted down, then captured or murdered, the rest of the 800,000-strong Polish force.

"He took interest in me," my mother told her interviewers. "He told me what was going on outside of [the] ghetto. He said, 'You are too dark to survive in western Poland. You must go to Germany.'" The Reich needed workers and he was suggesting that she volunteer to be a slave laborer.

"You were too dark?" one incredulous interviewer asked.

"Dark, yes, because in the western part of Poland they were all blond and blue-eyed. It was propitious that my papers were from the East." By this my mother meant she could more credibly pose as a non-Jew from astern Poland because, having intermarried with the local Armenian minority, their complexions and hair tended to be darker.

Going to Germany was, nevertheless, completely counterintuitive. My mother risked being found out wherever she was, but the consequence of hiding in plain sight in Germany was unknown, whereas she was sure the officer was right about being unmasked in Poland.

But as a dark-haired *Ostarbeiter* (Eastern worker) in enemy territory, wouldn't my mother encounter the same problem? Apparently, the Germans were so desperately short of workers because many men were fighting on the Russian Front, that no one asked questions when the vanquished volunteered.

The Nazis had devised an intricate economic system on which the future of The Reich depended. Although the Weimar German government had signed the League of Nations' Slavery Convention in 1926, the Nazis ignored it and began their forced labor program fourteen years later. At first, they did not want many foreigners to enter the Reich because they feared espionage and abhorred the contamination of Aryan blood. But they escalated the program after the attack on the Soviet Union in 1941, and their subsequent economic and military needs overruled racist concerns.

In 1942, Minister of Armaments and War Production Albert Speer and General Plenipotentiary for Labor Deployment Fritz Sauckel organized the forced labor of millions of foreigners and incorporated them into Germany's war economy. Their policy combined exploitation with racist repression; extermination through hard labor forced upon foreign civilians, prisoners of war, and concentration camp inmates. Although the Nazis never referred to their program as slavery, calling forced laborers *Arbeitsvolker*—people deemed fit only for labor—they envisioned a slaveholder society after their expected victory.

This system of slavery was different from the United States, where plantation owners used slaves for an agricultural economy. Germany integrated foreign workers into its industrial war economy, creating a mixture of state and corporate slavery. Foreign workers were used by government contractors—including Bosch, Daimler-Benz, Demag, Henschel, IG Farben, Junkers, Krupp, Messerschmitt, Philips, Siemens, Thyssen, and Volkswagen—that profited from the labor of *Arbeitsvolker*. German subsidiaries of American companies, such as Ford Motor Company and General Motors, also profited from slave laborers. Furthermore, the state—through its Labor Office, police, *Wehrmacht*, SS, and security guards whom these government contractors employed—carefully registered and controlled foreign workers. In contrast, in the United States the plantation holders themselves owned and commanded their slaves.

Germany's early attempts to recruit Czech and Polish volunteers were unsuccessful. Later, they impoverished the defeated by requisitioning property and food, thereby promoting inflation and unemployment. Civilians of occupied countries had no choice but to work for the Nazis; the alternative was starvation. Besides the Slavs, they conscripted Dutch, Belgian, and French civilians. The Nazis called all these workers "volunteers," but only 10 to 20 percent, or 1.3 to 2.6 million, really were volunteers. When my mother "volunteered," she became one of 12 million workers toiling in Germany for one of the largest systems of forced labor in history.

It was not that my mother's false papers were useless; on the contrary, they were invaluable, especially if the enemy did not know the Polish people well. Furthermore, because my mother's papers were from Lwów, if the Gestapo wanted to check them, it would take more effort than if her papers had originated from Kraków, the seat of the Reich's *Generalgouverenment.*

The *Generalgouverenment* rewarded Poles for tipping off the Gestapo about Jewish imposters. Poles daily denounced Jews. Neighbors ratted on Gentiles who sheltered Jews. When the Jews' money ran out, even those who had sheltered them betrayed them. Bands of children denounced Jews on the street for candy.

On September 10, a second, two-day *aktion* befell the people of Tarnów. The Nazis loaded 10,000 Jews into cattle cars and shipped them to Belzec where they were all murdered. Unbeknownst to my mother hiding on the farm, just before the *aktion* Aunt Gusta contacted her daughters' nanny, Antosia, who smuggled them out of the ghetto. When Annetta and Olga arrived at the Mandels' apartment, Antosia hid the girls under a quilt on her bed. (Polish winters are very cold, so Polish quilts are puffier than ours; you sink into them and therefore can easily hide small children.)

Because Aunt Gusta worked in a hospital just inside the ghetto gate, she slipped through and survived the *aktion.* She got her daughters and fled to Guschinka and Aunt Fryda. Guschinka was the half-Jewish cousin of my mother who had joined the Polish resistance and helped Teofila find the right contacts in Lwów for obtaining false papers. Gusta knew Guschinka and Fryda no longer lived in Kraków's Old Town and had moved to Lagiewniki, a Kraków suburb. When Aunt Gusta and her daughters arrived, Guschinka began arranging for their false papers. While awaiting the papers, Gusta and her children moved to a farmer's hut in a nearby village. When the false papers came through, they fled to Warsaw.

Meanwhile, the farmer escorted my mother to the Labor Office where she signed up. Like her escape from the ghetto, timing was of the essence. My mother continued on the oral history tape:

> It was [the officer's] brother, the same one who took me out of [the] ghetto after the killings did die down, who took me to the Labor Office where I volunteered to go to Germany as a slave laborer. Polish doctor examined me, looked at me, and asked if I was volunteering. I said yes. He approved of what I was doing. And we workers went by train to a camp in Kraków.

It amazed me that not only had the brothers aided and advised my mother, but that one even accompanied her to register. I had heard all my life about the altruistic officer-in-hiding but did not know that his brother, the farmer, had risked his life *twice*. Why did the family save my mother? It is possible that the fellow who ran the ghetto factory paid the farmer, or strong-armed him by threatening not to buy his hay. But I doubt that any Jews in the ghetto had such leverage.

My mother always emphasized that Poles had helped the Jews. She was aided by a nun in Lwów who taught her the catechism, and a priest who might have signed a copy of her alias' Certificate of Baptism, if it was a forgery and not the original. My mother argued that the Catholic church helped in clandestine ways. She said the Pope had signaled the church's resistance by switching the language of Mass from Latin to Polish so that priests could communicate righteousness to their congregants without the Germans understanding. Priests emphasized to their flocks the importance of loving their neighbors, implying that they should help Jews. It was also one way to defy the occupiers. I conclude, therefore, that my mother benefited from those two brothers' Christian kindness and courageous acts of resistance. When my mother first told me of the officer, I felt grateful; as I got older and heard the story again and again, I wanted to express my gratitude. With that in mind, I once asked if my mother knew the family name. Pained, she said with the most plaintive moan, "No. I do not know it." She furrowed her brow and frowned while I sat silent and surprised. It crossed my mind, though, that perhaps the officer preferred to be anonymous. If she had been caught, under torture she might have revealed his name and endangered the whole family.

As I prepared to visit Tarnów in 2016, I entertained the fantasy that by searching old maps of Tarnów's suburbs I might locate the hay farm, meet the family, and thank them. Stranger things have happened since World War II; the five-year-old sister could still have been alive, albeit well into her seventies.

In her oral history, my mother described her disguise:

> The story I said [was] that I came from Eastern Poland and that my parents were sent to Siberia, that I cannot find work here, so I might as well go to Germany. And nobody asked any questions. They needed workers....
>
> When I went to that Labor Office, I masqueraded completely and did not look at all, and was not dressed at all, as a girl from middle class. I characterized myself like a girl from [a] village with a notch of pretense. Because in my class [in Lwów] there was a girl [Katia] who was a daughter of an organ player. She was idiotic in her sense of superiority toward the other peasants. And I thought that was the right character to portray. And that's what I did. The objective was to keep my shoes. A lot of girls were barefoot.

It was a relief in this grim story for me to imagine my mother as a brilliant improv actress. I loved that she poked fun of her self-important, hierarchical classmate. But then my mother's loneliness intruded and returned me to the danger she faced moment-to-moment:

> When I arrived in [the] Kraków camp for slave laborers, I realized right away I cannot visit my non-Jewish cousin because someone would say, "How come you're so black?" So I put on my Eastern accent and enormous amount of vulgarity to convince them I simply was from different district. I remember a girl who had bleached hair, and we exchanged glances, and I was sure she was Jewish. And I said, "Let me get out of here

> immediately." So I slept during the day when I was not so conspicuous.

Here my mother refers to Cousin Guschinka, whom she longed to visit. But my mother feared that her dark skin and hair might cause a neighbor to question the connection and denounce them both. My mother's hesitation was fortuitous. In the late 1920s, Fryda, who was German, lost her husband, my mother's great-uncle who practiced medicine in Tarnów. After his death, Aunt Gusta inherited his practice and Fryda moved to Kraków to be close to her dead husband's other relatives. The enterprising widow used capital she inherited to build a row of attached houses for Polish Army officers. As landlady, she lived in one of the apartments and raised Guschinka there. When the Nazis arrived, they offered Fryda the opportunity to register as a *Volksdeutsche* (one whose race, language and culture had German origins but who was not a German citizen). As a *Volksdeutsche* Fryda would have had more privileges than a mere Pole, but she refused. The Nazis requisitioned the Polish officers' quarters and evicted her and Guschinka. My mother did not know they were displaced to a suburb. Had she tried to visit them in Kraków's Old Town, she would have risked her life for nothing.

As for the Jewish bottled blonde, my mother told me she, too, had considered dyeing her hair. When I naively praised the disguise, my mother impatiently replied that it was not smart because she inevitably would have run out of peroxide. "What if I was unable to buy it or barter it later on black market?" she asked.

The isolation and persistent tension my mother endured—constantly avoiding any association with another Jew and trying to remain inconspicuous despite her looks—was great, indeed.

I admired my mother's resourcefulness in mimicking the mannerisms of her uncouth former classmate from Lwów, improvising and refining her imposter act as necessary. But I wanted to visualize the stage where these players debuted. What was the transit camp like? I corresponded with the guide who had shown us Tarnów and asked her to locate the camp. She sent a picture of an enormous school building that reminded me of the Puck Building off Houston and Lafayette in New

York City, with its imposing arched windows and red bricks. Located in the old Jewish quarter of Kraków called Kazimierz, the transit camp was a few blocks from the Progressive Tempel, where my mother's parents had been married eighteen years before, and just up the street from the New Jewish Cemetery where my mother's great-grandparents, Abraham and Laija Finkelstein, lay buried. I think of Abraham in his top hat, his trusting, laughing eyes, and what they did not see forty-three years later a few blocks away. I am grateful for that, at the very least.

Chapter Twenty-Four

In the Belly of the Beast

Every beautiful woman, I have observed over the years, harbors persistent dissatisfaction about some aspect of her appearance. In my beautiful and glamorous mother's case, on the rare occasions when she complained, she bemoaned having heavy legs like her mother. "Why couldn't I have inherited my father's shapely calves and narrow ankles?" she asked. But she never alluded to a dime-sized, pebble-deep crevice on her right shin. I once asked her how she got the scar. She scowled and said she had an infection long ago. Clearly, she did not want to talk about it.

My mother also disparaged her hands. She would spread out her fingers and palms face up and say, "See the lines? Here, and here? Scars." She traced them with her right index finger. "My hands were completely black from hoeing and carrying burlap sacks."

"I don't see them," I answered. "They just look like your hands." My mother sighed in exasperation, then changed the subject to how surprised and pleased she was that my hands were just like Izydor's. I had his thumbs, whereas Ivy had one double-jointed thumb like Teofila.

In late September 1942 while my mother was in the Kraków transit camp, the Germans called for slave laborers to work in Bavaria, a state in southeastern Germany. Recalling the many adventure stories she had read about Indian mountain trails in the American Wild West, my mother responded in hopes of escaping to Switzerland via the Bavarian Alps.

My mother and several other girls boarded a steel-gray passenger train bound for central Germany. They passed through Beuthen, which had been the last stop and border check between Poland and Germany, but there was no longer a state line—all was part of the Greater Reich. Ironically, this was a great relief to my mother because her papers were scrutinized one time less. To keep calm, she joined in with the other girls who were singing Polish folk songs.

As they passed through former Czechoslovakia, my mother was amazed at how much richer the country was compared to Poland, despite being occupied. Hours later, as they entered Germany proper, my mother sensed no inkling of war. In parks, mothers sat enjoying the sunshine while their babies safely slumbered in strollers and their older children romped in the playgrounds. The only hints of warfare were German soldiers' uniforms—a blurred blue-green Aryan force speeding to the East on the opposite track.

My mother sits in a Third Class car, finding it hard to tolerate the stifling end-of-summer heat. As the train approaches a bend, she leans out the window just a little and glimpses the thin, silvery, curved rails—the warped parallax of the tracks. In the mid-September light, they seem to shimmer and morph and stretch ahead as they guide her to the unknown. The locomotive snorts and expels steam as the train lurches forward into the belly of the Teutonic beast.

The volunteers disembarked in Schweinfurt, where my mother was puzzled to see rubble and ruins. Why had the Allies repeatedly bombed this city and not Tarnów, as she had so often hoped? She asked around and learned that since 1940, the Allies periodically tried to destroy the local ball bearing factory because this mechanical part was essential to tanks, other military vehicles, trains, and planes.

Surprisingly, the Labor Office allowed slave workers to choose their locations even within Germany, so my mother declined a job in Schweinfurt and waited for one in a rural area less likely to be targeted. She still wanted to be near the Alps. She noticed, with immense relief, that Germans in this region had dark hair, as she did. Bavarians looked different from the blond, northern Aryan stereotype because they had mixed with the Romans and other Mediterranean peoples. My mother felt a little less pressure because she could blend in, but there was a new reason to feel conspicuous—everyone spoke a Bavarian dialect she could not imitate, having spoken formal, literary German all her life.

Through the centuries, nobles and kings had built forts and magnificent castles on lushly forested hills overlooking lakes and rivers that nourished the stunning Bavarian countryside, giving the region an almost magical aura. Walt Disney was so entranced that he modeled the Magic Kingdom castle on Mad King Ludwig II's 19th-century romantic neo-gothic fantasy castles in southern Bavaria. It was into this fairytale-like landscape that my mother traveled from Schweinfurt to Hollstadt, where the Labor Office had dispatched her to a farm. According to a form attached to the second page of my mother's *Arbeitskarte* (work card), her "employer" was Kilian Laudenbach. I searched the farmer's family name and found that his descendants still own farmland just beyond this hamlet of barely 1,000 people.

Upon her arrival, my mother wrote to her parents, who were still living on the Aryan side of Lwów, to tell them where she was. As planned, my mother addressed them as if they were her Aunt Zośka and simply "Uncle" (Wujėk in Polish). Even posing as their niece, my mother could disclose few details because she assumed the Gestapo intercepted all workers' letters.

How would my grandparents have received the news that my mother was in Germany? I tried to put myself in Teofila's frame of mind. She would have become quite hysterical when she read that my mother had left Aunt Gusta. *How could she do this? What possessed her? Who could possibly have convinced her she would be better off there?* Teofila might have cried as she paced their hovel. It probably took several hours for Izydor to calm Teofila, perhaps arguing that in this peculiar war, counterintuitive strategies made more sense. He would have reminded her of the completely illogical outcome of the choice Russians' offered to refugees—to stay or return to western Poland—which had resulted in many other refugees being deported to Siberia.

My mother—now called Danuta—struggled to meet farmer Laudenbach's demands as she toiled in his fields harvesting potatoes, turnips, and threshing grain. My mother commented to her interviewers with characteristic caustic understatement:

> I was *not* a very good slave worker. I was not strong enough. I was not conditioned from early childhood to hard labor. So the peasant was eager to get rid of me as soon as it got cold.

I recognized the hurt in her tone. She only briefly mentioned that Laudenbach had worked her hard. I knew she had omitted crucial information from her oral history. In 1958, my mother sued the German government for damages for deprivation of liberty. She informed the German court:

> While I was employed by the farmer Kilian Laudenbach, I became sick. I had a purulent outbreak over my whole body, abscesses, from which scars can still be seen on my body. Although the farmer noticed the outbreak, he did not send me to a doctor. I was afraid to ask him for permission to visit a doctor. This is because I always had to keep in mind that I am a Jew and I did not know how things would turn out if I were to stop working for the farmer due to a sick note.

It must have been terrifying when sores appeared on her skin in November 1942, a month after her arrival. How awful to be all alone wondering what the condition was as spots spread across her entire body and exuded pus. They had to have been visible on her arms, neck, and legs, yet Laudenbach ignored the abscesses. What kind of man does not spare a worker even for a few days? My mother knew. "He himself was a man who limped and could not be in the army so he had a tremendous need to produce for the Fatherland," she remarked superciliously on his Teutonic zeal. How hard it must have been to ignore the relentless sores. Better to suffer and remain inconspicuous. The worry that she could be disfigured by pocks must have sped through her like the contagion, but taking the long view, as ever, she probably consoled herself that the scourge did not attack the chiseled features of her face.

I surmised from her deposition that the scar on my mother's shin was owed to a particularly persistent pustule. At first, I thought it strange that no diagnosis appeared in the deposition, but then I decided that had there been, the court might have required my mother to prove she had that specific disease. Without medical records this would have been impossible. It may have been Anthrax, a bacterial infection well-known since the 18th century. When I saw pictures of black skin ulcers and read that they have a 24 percent chance of causing death, and realized that farmer Laudenbach probably knew this, I had to look away, unable to stomach investigating and contemplating it further. But my mother did not have that luxury. For the rest of her life, every time she rolled on nylons she was forced to remember Laudenbach's fervor.

After the harvest, Laudenbach started to construct a house and ordered my mother to carry bricks day in and day out. The malady, the cold, and the heavy work exhausted her. In late November, when winter weather no longer permitted further construction, he dismissed her. She immediately saw a doctor in Hollstadt who gave her salve for the sores. They healed gradually.

My mother's next assignment was as a maid for the Ress family in Hollstadt proper, where quaint half-timber houses, similar to England's Tudor architecture, were painted in warm earth tones and creams. Red brick tiles covered all the roofs. It was all so clean and orderly. Uniform.

Not everyone thought alike in Hollstadt, though. The Resses operated a small dry goods store in the center of the hamlet on the main street. The other villagers knew the family was anti-Nazi. Their lithe twenty-five-year-old daughter, Antonia, had visited the United States in the 1930s. Perhaps that accounted in part for the family's liberalism. Toni, as she was known, ran the store. The Resses treated and fed my mother well, but when their politics became clear, the Labor Office penalized the family by removing my mother. Besides, her job was too good for a slave laborer. Two for one for the Third Reich.

Chapter Twenty-Five

Castles and Fairy Tales

The Labor Office transferred my mother from Hollstadt to the neighboring village of Bad Neustadt an der Saale, which dated back to the reign of Charlemagne. According to legend, the first Holy Roman Emperor founded the "new town spa" as a valentine for his wife and that was why a medieval wall enveloped the village in the shape of a heart. Their imperial palace, The Salzburg, was a ten-minute walk across a charming stone bridge. Built on a hill on the far bank of the Saale River, the castle had a fine view of the Holy Roman Emperor's local domain. A more recent castle, constructed in the 12th century on the foundation of the old one, still stood on the site.

About 10,000 villagers were living in this beautiful resort when my mother arrived in the spring of 1943. Besides a spa, tourism, and small farms, there was a new Siemens factory, Schuckertwerke AG Elektromotorenwerk, at the village's northern edge by the railroad tracks. The plant was built in 1939 for the manufacture of refrigerator motors, but within a year it began to produce electric motors for other purposes.

My mother was assigned to the Oppelt family, peasants who had taken over a Jewish home. Just off the main square, the three-story house was modest and narrow. No doubt my mother eyed the palimpsest of a removed mezuzah as she knocked on the door. Farmer Oppelt was gruff and crude, his wife sickly and shrewish. Their older sons were away at school. The youngest, a seven-year-old, seemed hungry for attention.

When my mother told her Fortunoff video archive interviewers that she had worked in the Oppelt's nursery, they assumed she meant a nursery school. It was a *gärtnerei*, which translates poorly into a market garden, but really means a truck farm or small produce and flower nursery. After my mother clarified that she was a farm hand, she was asked to describe her work. My mother looked down, hesitated, and changed the subject. "I think I should, perhaps, before I do that, mention that in Würzburg at the time lived a cousin of my mother who was married to a German gentile," she says. I watch her display a photograph of herself and Thea Schaller seated on a balcony. I am appalled by my mother's appearance—her exhaustion, her puffy face and arms. She caresses a Dachshund against her white blouse and plaid vest. Pinned to her blouse I recognize the silver horse brooch with a ruby eye that Teofila gave my mother when they parted.

After Teofila regained her composure over my mother's whereabouts, Teofila wrote to her cousin Thea, who lived with her husband Willy in nearby Würzburg, presumably asking Thea to look after my mother. Thea's husband, Willy Schaller, was the concertmaster of the local philharmonic. Despite great pressure, he had refused to divorce his Jewish wife. She invited my mother to visit on Sunday, June 13 (the photograph was, amazingly, dated), during the Pentecost.

On the oral history tape, an interviewer asks, "You went there [to Würzburg] as a Polish peasant?"

My mother elaborates:

> Imagine. Illegally. What was absolutely amazing about it was that Thea wrote to me that she would have red gloves so that I could recognize her. But the family resemblance was so striking that I didn't need any red gloves. But I became aware that it was extremely dangerous. I was a Polish national and it was obvious I could have been her daughter.... So I left with her the watch that my mother gave me and tried to minimize the contact. I thought it was dangerous.

Thea and my grandmother Teofila also looked alike, as I knew from photos in my great-grandparents' collection. Their taste was similar, too; Thea wore the same style of wide-brimmed hats that Teofila favored. She had a similar aquiline nose and heart-shaped face. But their smiles were different.

The scene of the Schallers and my mother sitting on the terrace, sipping tea and cuddling their adorable Dachshund, belied the fact of war. Would it have intruded into their conversation? What did they talk about? I checked for events that had been reported that week. The holiday fell on the six-month anniversary of the catastrophic defeat of the Germans by the Russians in Stalingrad, so Hitler's propaganda minister, Joseph Goebbels, used the occasion to announce that Germany had overcome that setback. He declared "the winter crisis over," and called for austerity and bravery in the face of shortages and unrelenting Allied bombings. Although this year's harvest was good, he said meat still had to be rationed at 100 grams (3.5 ounces) per person a week. The hundreds of thousands of foreign workers "who we are proud to say have followed the flag," also need to eat, he said. "That all impacts the food situation." Then he appeased begrudging Germans by reminding them that those workers also increased Germany's military strength. He was preparing the Germans for an Allied invasion and warned that attacking the enemy would "cost us much blood and tears."

To distract his countrymen from the bad news, Goebbels ranted about the Jews, as he had done just after the Battle for Stalingrad: "The goal of Bolshevism is Jewish world revolution.... A Bolshevization of the Reich would mean the liquidation of our entire intelligentsia and leadership, and the descent of our workers into Bolshevist-Jewish slavery." He passionately demanded more of his countrymen—that they commit to "total war." In his June, pre-Pentecost address, he echoed that with: "We are dealing with a band of crooks who are striving for world domination, and who want to subject Europe to Jewish world rule. The only reason they went to war against us is because we were the last bastion in the way of their infernal Jewish-plutocratic-Bolshevist goals.... They reach for war to rule poor nations and take from them the little they do possess. This is a criminal conspiracy."

Pure projection, I thought as I read both speeches on Calvin University's German Propaganda Archive (https://research.calvin.edu/german-propaganda-archive/). I was struck by the incongruity that while Goebbels accused Jews of plotting to enslave Germans, it was my Jewish mother posing as a Catholic who toiled for Germans.

Perhaps my mother and the Schallers discussed Goebbels's June speech and debated whether the Battle of Stalingrad marked a turning point in the war. Or maybe they kept the conversation light and Willy had entertained my mother with music. Willy was an extraordinary musician. I met him in the late 1960s when he visited several years after Thea died. He strolled around our dining room and kitchen playing his violin. It was quite dramatic and entrancing. But perhaps while he played in his villa, my mother was considering the association and concluding that she had to relinquish it because it was too dangerous; all it took was for one person to conclude that since my mother resembled Thea, she, too, must be Jewish.

I found it terribly sad that despite Teofila's efforts, my mother could not benefit from the comfort of even a distant relative. My mother returned to Bad Neustadt to "follow the flag," as Goebbels had put it, to manage her horribly lonely highwire act.

Not long after her visit to Würzburg, the Gestapo came for the Schallers. As she told her interviewers, "Shortly after, they were arrested. Willy Schaller was on the way to Dachau. She [Thea] was imprisoned until liberation and—"

My mother again interrupted herself to reflect once more on appearances, her fear that her dark looks made her conspicuous and her relief that she "sort of fitted in to the family Oppelt looks wise, which was very convenient." She added that when she ran errands, or on her days off interacted with the villagers, they noticed her manners and concluded that she came from a better social rank than the Oppelts, who were not well-liked whereas she was. "It is interesting how in Europe a class situation played [a] role in such absurd times," she mused. She was to exploit the Germans' hierarchical nature in the coming months.

But my grandmother Teofila had not written to her cousin Thea because of casual or passing concern about my mother. My grandparents were very much disturbed by my mother's letters and her state of mind. They sensed that she was not disclosing what was really happening to her. They were right; my mother dared not communicate daily hardships for fear that the Gestapo was intercepting and reading their letters. She could not tell them how the Oppelts treated her compared to her only other nursery co-worker, a crippled Belgian prisoner of war named Camile Krüger. Farmer Oppelt observed POW rules and was lenient with Camile, as my mother stated in her oral history, and instead used her for the heavy work. Evidently, because the Reich considered Eastern slave laborers more subhuman than Western ones, Germans felt free to starve and work them to death. From 6:00 a.m. until 8:00 p.m., my mother cultivated vegetable crops and flowers, whereas Camile worked from 6:00 a.m. to 5:00 p.m., she testified in her oral history. Every Friday, she and Oppelt lifted 50-kilo baskets of vegetables onto a truck. Later, she swayed from the effort and had difficulty walking.

After toiling all day long in the produce nursery, my mother had to cook dinner and wash the dishes. Other Polish female slave laborers, including Stasza and another girl also named Irena, went for leisurely walks around Salzburg Castle after dinner. They would invite my mother to join them, but she was always too exhausted. She also feared she might answer to her true name when people addressed the other slave laborer named Irena. Every night as my mother got ready for bed, she was terrified that if she dreamt, she might cry out and reveal her true identity.

"My father apparently was worried I was near [a] nervous breakdown," my mother stated. "But what is amazing to what degree my father tried dispassionately to keep my sanity long distance." A little later, she said, "What he did not know, [was] that by the time afternoon came, I was so tired that I could not control my reflexes anymore." She meant her muscles, of course, but her error does not matter; her desperation and their cruelty and exploitation are clear.

When my mother discussed her correspondence with her parents, she held up to the camera a yellowed April 1943 letter in which her father did his best to comfort and guide her.

> …the chaotic style of your letters and the sadness they reflect tell us that you are inwardly "disorganized." You have to apply a method, which is based on the following: If I am nervous and spiritually "uncombed," there must be a reason for it. So I search and search for it—and when I discover this reason—I become aware. Is this reason really valid enough to poison my life? Surely you will arrive, my dear, at the conclusion that actually these are only the extraordinary circumstances that occur during wars and during this one especially, which evoke this condition of strained nerves. This manifests itself so much more intensely, because the organism, overtaxed with hard labor, is not as resistant as usual to the whims of strained nerves.… So rather a good mood and optimism should prevail in your disposition (state of mind) over the "shakiness" so to say, of your spiritual balance.…

Perceiving that her nerves were frayed and worried about her sadness, Izydor used all his powers of persuasion to coach her long-distance into living one day at a time. He urged her to recognize that things could be much worse, and by referencing a German philosopher tried to instill hope that the war would soon end.

> Try to create this particular little world of thoughts, which go, more or less, in this direction: "I take the present life as each day brings it, that is, I consider it as a necessity. Everything that is, is necessary," says one German philosopher. "Everything that is necessary is good, hence the conclusion: everything that is, is good."

I wondered which philosopher he meant. While a student at Hampshire College, where we designed our own concentrations, or majors, I had studied philosophy of mind, theory of knowledge, and philosophy of science in relation to psychology. Pleased and intrigued by my interest in philosophy, my mother intimated that her father had an analytical mind, and wondered whether that might be hereditary. But I had not studied political philosophy. My husband Ed, who has a doctorate in political theory, did. He searched the ceiling-high bookshelves in our dining room and pulled out his copy of Wilhelm Friedrich Hegel's *Elements of the Philosophy of Right*. It seemed that my grandfather had reached back to his days as a law student when he was studying contracts and must have read the 19th-century philosopher's discourse on the nature of the rights of individuals and the state. In the Preface, Hegel states, "What is real is reasonable," and "what is reasonable is real" and that "what is real" is created by reason. And so Izydor was bending Hegelian philosophy to comfort his daughter.

How had my destabilized and overworked mother reacted to this? Did she, in frustration, slap down her father's letter and dismiss his highfalutin philosophizing? She did not know he was paraphrasing Hegel, and I doubt that if she had, she would have cared. It smacked of the same impractical reasoning that, to her, did not seem to apply during extreme times—like when the Goldbergers were starving in Tarnopol and Lwów. Izydor had refused to engage in the black market because that would have violated a concept of Hegel's known as *Sittlichkeit* (ethical order), in which an ethical life and moral consciousness combine with a community's customs and laws. Izydor could not in good conscience violate *Sittlichkeit* for the sake of his family. His self-consciousness, as Hegel would have called it, his "sound reason," knew "what is right and good" just as it immediately recognized a valid law.

But here and now during this mid-20th century war, was it necessary and good that she had to toil to the point of exhaustion? Necessary and good that her parents had insisted she leave Lwów? Necessary and good that she suffered unbearable anxiety about them? How could it possibly be necessary, right, and good that the Nazis were slaughtering Jews everywhere?

My sister Ivy believes our mother loved Voltaire because he refuted and ridiculed Gottfried Wilhelm Leibniz's view that "all is for the best" in "the best of all possible worlds." In trying to account for injustice and suffering in the world, Leibniz postulated that God is "a perfect existence," and makes decisions based on reason, therefore, the universe that God chose to exist is the best world that could be. Voltaire countered this philosophy by depicting Candide's painful disillusionment as he witnessed and experienced great hardship and catastrophe during his travels. Candide and his friends endured misfortune, from earthquakes to political villainy, including slavery. As a result, they rejected Leibnizian optimism and turned inward to cultivate their own Epicurean gardens.

My mother's delight in *Candide, or Optimism* when we read it together, rested in its refutation of both Leibniz and Hegel's ideas, as her father quoted the latter in his letter. After all, if you accept that "what is reasonable is real" then you accept that the amount of suffering in the world is reasonable because that is the best God could manage.

After the war, my mother repeatedly translated my grandfather's letters—which he wrote in Polish—into English, but was never satisfied. I believe she was trying to work through terrible loss as a teenager, trying to come to grips with having been senselessly deprived of her parents. The *process* of examining the letter word-by-word was what mattered. It was a little like what I did when I transcribed my interviews with my sources; I heard their tones of voice, I got into their heads in a more intimate way than just reading a transcript someone else had created. With these cues, their personas came to life and their intentions became clearer. In later years, when she was troubled and lonely, the meticulous exercise of translation comforted my mother and mollified her feeling of deprivation that her father was not present to guide her, as he had done long-distance during the war. Still another possibility is that she was testing her interpretation as a teenager against her objectivity as an adult whose primary language was now English. Translation is, of course, an art, and the meanings of words and phrases can be inexact and filled with nuance. In another translation of this paragraph my mother used tender and more emotional language:

> You must apply to yourself a method in which the point of the matter is as follows: If I am nervous and emotionally upset, there must be a reason for that. I look therefore, for that reason. I look and look, and if I do find it, I visualize it to myself. Is this reason important

> enough that I should let it embitter my life? Surely you will, my beloved, arrive to the conclusion that strictly speaking, only extraordinary situations which occur in time of war—and during this war specially—evoke a state of temporary strain on nerves…

What strength it took to revisit the letters. And yet I think she found the task comforting. The entire letter, and this version of the second paragraph in particular, always bring tears to my eyes. Although he could not completely reach my adolescent, enslaved mother, through time my mother's father began to reach me. Reading these words, my mother's father, until then unfamiliar to me, becomes my grandfather Izydor. I keenly feel his vast love for his only child, and I reciprocate with love for him. Confined day after day in the besieged city of Lwów perhaps without heat or enough to eat, enduring the fear of discovery at any moment, my grandfather made no mention of his hardships. Instead he channeled his skills as a litigator to save his daughter, deploying every logical and philosophical argument he could formulate. Never mind his trials; with composure and fortitude, he strove to encourage her to disassociate from *her* daily hardships. The heartache, the worry, and stress must have been torture, and yet he overcame them to buoy her up. I see the beauty of adoration and evolution in partnership; the parent endeavoring in every possible way to ensure that his progeny would survive.

I knew so little about this learned and thoughtful man, who was at times extraordinarily logical and yet also irrationally impractical. Yet I began to recognize how he had influenced and shaped who my mother was and therefore how she had raised my sisters and me.

My mother selectively heeded her father's advice, accepting his recommendation to disassociate from the day-to-day hardship of literally toiling in someone else's garden. But I am sure that when she read *Candide*, the irony of having been assigned as a produce laborer in a nursery was not lost on her. This tension between hypotheticals, rational thought, and practical versus ethical behavior permeated my mother's narrative about the war and her struggle to accept the loss of her parents.

During her interview, my mother finally steeled herself to describe not just her work and conditions but starvation at the Oppelt nursery:

> I worked 16 hours a day. My parents didn't know that, but what I really ate only potatoes and vegetables because whatever fat and other things were given to me they somehow managed not to give it to me. So vegetable and potatoes I had.

My mother is faltering, her words are choppy. She cannot blurt that she was treated brutally, as if she was an ox. Her grammar is a casualty of the emotional strain of recollecting this trying time.

She jumps ahead to one of her triumphs. "Later on, I won a suit against the German government, documented by that picture," she says as she holds up a photograph dated October 23, 1943. The shot shows her with her friend Stasza, who was lucky to have been assigned as a slave worker for a photographer. "My dress conceals the fact that actually I could have been a concentration [camp] victim, I was so skinny," my mother states matter-of-factly. I examine the photo with my magnifying glass. No, the contrast between my gaunt, anemic-looking mother and plump, healthy Stasza is not, in fact, concealed. It is blatant and shocking. My mother's dress is two sizes too big. It might as well have been hanging on the picket fence behind her and Stasza. My mother's head and jaw appear too wide to be supported by her thin neck. Her bust is flat, her shoulders angular. Her wide hips and legs, which she always complained to us were too heavy, here seem skeletal. Did she even menstruate? I ask myself. Nevertheless, my starving eighteen-year-old mother forces a grin as she squints at the camera.

I return to my mother's trial file and deposition:

> When I then worked at Oppelt in Neustadt in a gardening nursery, I was very much exploited. The Oppelts had my food ration card. Based on the food

> card, I had a right to butter, sugar, and possibly also other things. The Oppelts, however, withheld all this from me and gave me only bread, potatoes, and vegetables to eat.
>
> As a result of the deficient nutrition and the hard work, I grew weaker and weaker and became emaciated.
>
> Although I had a right to the food based on the food card and although not having it caused my health to suffer, I did not dare to approach the Oppelts and demand that this be given to me because I was afraid that I would then be handed over to the Gestapo or another agency that could recognize me as a Jew.

When did the Oppelts confiscate my mother's food card? I was not about to research whether it took three or four months to reduce my mother from the bloated yet undernourished teenager who visited Thea and Willy in Würzburg to a skeletal one. But because of the new sacrifices demanded by the Reich, the Oppelts had the perfect excuse for persecutory parsimony. Did Herr Oppelt spit out, "Give me your food ration card?" Or was it more insidious? I conjure Frau Oppelt rifling through my mother's few belongings, and snatching her card while she was weeding a potato patch.

Deprived of her full rations, which were supposed to include protein, my mother wasted away. As during her days working for Farmer Laudenbach, she did not dare to ask for anything, given the ever-present possibility of being unmasked; she was paralyzed by fear that the Oppelts would summon the Gestapo, which, if it suspected her true identity, could check her papers in Lwów.

After the war, my mother ran an ad in a Belgian newspaper seeking Camile as a witness to testify for her lawsuit against the German government. She told this to my sisters and me and recapped their correspondence for her interviewers: "He [Camile] wrote to me that he was considered an invalid as a result of the work at Oppelt nursery." This, despite having been treated leniently compared with my mother. The Court sought verification that Camile was indeed a POW, but the clerk in Bad Neustadt somehow could not or would not confirm that fact. His deposition was therefore not accepted.

It took me three years to get up the courage to contact the Oppelts, who of my mother's four "employers" had been the most vicious. One day I discovered the website for their flower business. I sent an email asking whether the Oppelts' youngest son was still alive. If so, I wondered whether he recognized her based on the photograph on her false papers, which I attached. I was not surprised when there was no reply.

A month later, my mother's friend Krysia Nabel died at age ninety-five. Also from Kraków, they had known each other since grammar school, although Krysia was a little older. Their friendship resumed when they ran into each other in Bad Neustadt after Liberation. Krysia and her husband Edek also had false papers and had worked on a farm only a half-hour away. Because of the dual bond of having survived as slave laborers and as the remnants of Kraków's Jews, the Nabel family became very important to mine. Growing up, my sisters and I considered Krysia and Edek our aunt and uncle and their sons, Bill and Gary, our cousins. While Ivy and I paid a shiva call to Bill, we learned that the Torah scrolls of the synagogue of Bad Neustadt had been brought to the United States after the war because there was no longer a congregation. This information proved to be an important lead that enriched my mother's story.

I found a website, "Unfolding Communities: The Lost Jews of Bad Neustadt," (http://www.judaica-badneustadt.de/bn/) with a map of the tiny village showing the locations of the synagogue and former Jewish homes. The Israeli professor who had built the website put me in contact with Günter Henneberger, a high school history teacher in Bad Neustadt, so that I could communicate with the son of my mother's "employers." In his late seventies, he claimed not to remember her, though he did remember Camile. Not quite a dead end.

Also through Günter, I contacted the Resses, the anti-Nazi family my mother had worked for in Hollstadt, the neighboring hamlet. Günter acted as a go-between for me and the granddaughter of a cousin of the Resses' now-deceased daughter, Toni. I confirmed their liberal politics and added a few more details to this segment of my mother's war years. Sometimes a disheartening experience is counter-balanced by an equally heartwarming one.

The historian also sent a photo of the Oppelts' tiny house, which was sandwiched between two others on the village square, so quarters had to have been cramped. Seeing it, other worries crept into my mind. Where had my mother slept? Had she had enough privacy? Was there another reason for her shaky nerves besides the unrelenting farm work? Why was Frau Oppelt so hostile? Ivy said my mother had not lived with the family and stayed in their barn. That did not quell by concerns. Why, if the Oppelts were in another building, had she been afraid of revealing her identity while dreaming? My mother never explained what exactly had caused her equanimity to falter. Were there other causes for the breakdown she suffered? Not that physical hardship, anxiety about her parents, the stress of concealing her true identity, loneliness, and the danger of being discovered were not enough. Yet it struck me that my mother never described Herr Oppelt and only characterized his wife. Her poor physical and mental health suggested a less than happy marriage. Frau Oppelt's cruelty toward and resentment of my mother seemed disproportionate to the mere presence of a young girl toiling in her midst. After all, Frau Oppelt had the power. Aware of the plight of so-called "comfort women" for Japanese troops in China, I began to suspect more than loneliness and physically demanding work. I considered whether my mother was the victim of sexual predation. At the very least, it seemed plausible that, given my mother's youthful allure, Frau Oppelt considered her a sexual threat. Entirely at the mercy of those people, however, it was not far-fetched to weigh whether my mother was also at the mercy of a sex abuser.

Under the Nazi miscegenation laws, German men who fraternized with slave laborers were sent to concentration camps. Were a female laborer to become pregnant, she would be urged to have an abortion. If she wished to give birth, she would have to work until the due date. If the child was deemed suitable according to racial criteria for Germanization but the mother was not, the child would be put up for adoption and raised by a German couple. Otherwise, the child would be placed in a boarding home for foreigners' babies, where it had a 50 percent chance of dying from malnutrition.

So there were miscegenation laws in Germany. Laws were broken all the time.

I scoured the literature on sexual violence against women during the Holocaust and found an extensive bibliography on the United States Holocaust Memorial Museum's site. Many women, Jewish and otherwise, were sexually exploited during the war, so it is a small leap to assume that my mother was, too. After reading about sex abuse in the Third Reich, I reframed the question: Why would my young and beautiful mother *not* have been abused? It seemed odd to assume that she was the exception and survived untouched. What a repulsive irony, then, that despite my grandparents trying to spare my mother from sexual servitude in Lwów, she may nevertheless have landed in the power of a man who knew how to bend the anti-miscegenation laws and keep himself satisfied.

Of course, my mother could have revealed none of this in her correspondence with her parents, both because she suspected it was not private and because her plight would have devastated them. But she unwittingly left clues that she was abused, which my sisters and I sensed but could not pinpoint until we were in our fifties and our mother already gone. Michelle described reading the memoir of a Holocaust survivor who readily admitted to being sexually exploited, and suddenly recognized similar behaviors and reactions in our mother. We could not prove what we felt and yet it seemed highly probable.

I am convinced that it is important to give voice to this possibility, not just as part of my mother's story, but for all women in similar situations today. In wartime, women are more vulnerable to sexual abuse than in times of peace. It's highly likely that my mother—a beautiful young woman with no civil rights—was also at risk, and if so, the experience may have been too painful to revisit. Had she been alive today in the #MeToo era, I believe my mother might have spoken out. I disclose this to expose all the dimensions of trauma foisted upon the persecuted and displaced, especially women during war.

On June 10, my mother received another letter from her parents, which predated her visit to the Schallers. My grandfather wrote:

> ...maybe, after all, you will try to come to an order within yourself. It is possible to check the strained nerves a little. In your last two letters, your nervousness is very intense. That this is influencing your work negatively you write about yourself, and this is very sad. Even though I realize precisely that you work very, very hard, even so I dare to maintain that you should be very satisfied with this situation because you are not in C.C. [Concentration Camp] or with T. [Tuberculosis] because that is much, much worse. Have it always in your mind and construct for yourself even artificially—a state of mind, which after thinking it over, will bring you to [the] conclusion that your situation is good, because it could be much worse. That after all, this is temporary, that this is nothing else, only a hard trial of life. This practical examination you must pass, and I am sure you will pass. Try to think as little as possible about the things not connected with your work. Every such thought toss aside immediately—remembering this letter and the one before. Try to admire nature, the growth of flowers and vegetables. After all, you loved flowers so much. As a little girl, you did not permit them to be picked, maintaining that flowers are alive and that it would hurt them. Look forward all week long towards the Sunday that you will be able to spend among nature. After all, you were always so impressed and happy with beautiful views and you had for the beauty of nature great understanding. Did this all change in you now? It is possible that even hard labor has ousted all your likings?
>
> When you go to sleep, be happy that another day has passed and shortened the time of war—that it is nearer to, not further from the end, and when you wake up in

> the morning, think immediately about that: again is a day starting after which flow and end a whole 12 hours that bring you nearer normal and peaceful times.
>
> When everything is going to be peaceful and quiet, next year in summer, we will take a trip to climb the Tatra Mountains. Then we'll take the train to the tip of Kasprowy. From there I will take you down to the Valley of Five Lakes and then to the Eye of the Sea. You probably think this is nonsense, but it will give you hope. I am sure that on that trip you will be thinking, "How could I have been so nervous and worried, as is happening now?"
>
> Do not forget that you are young and good looking, that you have the ability to win other peoples' sympathy, that you are not crippled, and that in general the future should smile at you. Smile at the future a little and immediately it will be much easier. In order to be able to survive and not to sink into melancholy, you cannot permit yourself to think about matters that influence your nerves negatively, but be very energetic. Put them aside and try to think about the work and its proper finishing, and about what is so much more beautiful than this present.
>
> I wish with my whole heart that you should be able to accomplish this. And everything will be all right.
>
> All my kisses to you, Uncle

My grandfather Izydor's April letter had brought tears to my eyes, but this one broke my heart. My grandfather's hope. His dream of an excursion eternally missed. My mother's disappointment and unending sorrow. Unable as he was to reach my mother through philosophy, so was he effective when he wrote of nature and the beauty of the Tatra castle in the sky.

As she reads and rereads, my mother envisions hiking with her parents along the edge of the placid lake, watching the clear water of the Eye of the Sea meet the pebbles on the shore. When she closes her eyes, she is a trout undulating through the icy lake, diving to the depths where it is safe. With pewter-neutral scales and bland eyes. Inconspicuous.

Or she simply turns her attention to Teofila's note, just below Izydor's letter, in which she, too, did her utmost to comfort her daughter:

> Beloved Danusiu,
>
> ...It's very important that you know you can tell us what is bothering you. You have to remember that six months ago what was bad is now 50% better. Your leg is better. You can speak up, only you have to work hard. I know it's not easy. You got used to the physical labor, and also to the expectations of the people over there. Also you are receiving my letters more often now, and finally you are equipped with some clothes, unlike a few months ago, when you were missing the simplest things. So these are six things, six pluses I counted, and they should influence your frame of mind. It is not good to pick at wounds. Try to heal—even superficially.
>
> I want you to feel better and I want you to have things to wear.... There are clogs with cloth straps available, but I don't know if you'd like them. So I am still looking for slippers and I'll send better ones next time....
>
> Janusz has an infection and suffers from arthritis. I don't go out often now, because Tadzio doesn't like it.
>
> My Darling, write letters and have hope.
>
> I kiss you sincerely – Your Zośka

This seems to be a reply to my mother's peevish response to a carefully packed parcel. Whereas in Lwów she had been logical beyond her years and as assertive as a grown woman, in Germany when writing to her parents she sometimes regressed to a rebellious adolescent. Apparently, in an earlier letter she barely acknowledged the plaid vest and skirt; she disliked the slippers and said so. She complained that she was unable to concentrate as she planted vegetables and flowers in the nursery. As for clogs, when they were fashionable in the sixties, Ivy and I asked our mother for them. "Clogs! You want to wear clogs?" she replied shrilly. No, she had not wanted clogs with straps. Wooden shoes? Certainly not.

There was constant tension at the Oppelts'. My mother felt the lady of the house was deranged. When my mother developed a toothache, dental care was denied. My mother also described an incident that revealed why she hated whenever Ivy and I wanted to bake a cake—or anything, for that matter. She always found reasons why we should not—we would mess up the kitchen, she was on a diet, we could use our time better studying, and so on. If we answered back, she raised her voice. Apparently, this was due to Frau Oppelt, who, though sickly and never exerted herself, occasionally baked pastries. Once when my mother had offered to assist, Frau Oppelt said in the haughtiest tone, "Your help is not needed. We don't want the hands of a filthy Pole so *intimate* with our flour."

My mother did not describe her reaction. But I see her yank her head away as if she had been slapped and dart out of the kitchen. I seethe, filled with impotent rage. She was good enough to cook dinner and clean up after a whole day's work, but not to bake pastries? My lingering emotions were so volatile whenever I recalled this that I had to distract myself. What were those damn pastries? I searched for a typical Bavarian tidbit. *Dampfnudel*, popular in southern Germany, calls for flour, yeast, salt, butter, eggs, and sugar. I suppose the lady of the house did not want my mother to benefit from any crumbs.

But perhaps my mother strode to the nursery, calmed herself, and did not allow that woman to disturb her equilibrium. "This crude creature cannot insult me. Cannot humiliate me." My mother may have convinced herself to be thankful she did not have a personality and life like Frau Oppelt. Instead, she would have been glad that she herself was not cruel and deranged. With that, she would have thought of four positive things, four "pluses," as Teofila instructed. But I don't bake because every time I consider it, I recall what that disturbed Nazi farmer's wife and her husband said and did to my then teenage mother.

How could my grandmother Teofila have thought my mother could speak up, given the ever-present threat of the Gestapo? The gulf in understanding must have exasperated my mother.

More important, though, what did Teofila mean that Janusz was unwell? I believe he was the Pole they relied upon for food and to deliver their mail. My mother said she and her parents sometimes wrote in code. Perhaps Teofila was suggesting between the lines that his job was getting riskier. Even more foreboding was Teofila's comment that Tadzio forbade her to go out. I was confused about who Tadzio was, but this statement in code indicated that the streets of Lwów were far too dangerous for Jews. Clearly the situation in Lwów was getting worse.

All my life I heard a variation of the refrain, "If only I had been with them. I wish I could have stayed with them. If I had stayed, I would have made sure Mamusia never went out." No doubt my devastated mom thought that then.

By June 1943, most of the 250,000 Jews who had lived in or fled to Lwów from western Poland and middle-Europe were dead, either murdered during *aktionen*, worked to death at Janowska Camp, or had been deported by train to the extermination camp Belzec. Of Poland's large cities, Lwów endured the most *aktionen* because, although given individual names—Petliura Days, *Aktion* under the Bridge, Telephone *Aktion*, The Great *Aktion*, and so on—these mass-murder operations were continuous. Elsewhere, they usually occurred in one- to three-month intervals.

About 10,000 Jews remained in the Lwów Ghetto, which was declared a *Judenlager*, meaning a Jewish Camp. On June 1, the Germans and Ukrainians sent 7,000 Jews to Janowska Camp where they murdered them. The Jews in the *Judenlager* resisted with arms, killing nine and wounding twenty Germans and Ukrainians. In retaliation, the Nazis blew up buildings to force out the Jews. They were taken to the sandpits on the outskirts of Janowska Camp, machine-gunned, and their bodies burned on pyres. One last stand occurred at a bakery. Jewish workers there bought automatic rifles and grenades from Romanian soldiers, allies of the Germans who had passed through on their way to the Eastern Front. The Jews opened fire and mowed down the startled SS and Ukrainians who called for reinforcements. During the prolonged struggle, the Jews shot twice as many persecutors as their own number. But those 3,000 Jews were annihilated anyway.

Although they lived on the Aryan side, Izydor and Teofila doubtless were informed of these events by Janusz. A few weeks later, they sent much briefer letters:

> Lwów, July 2, 1943
>
> My Darling,
>
> … I haven't seen Janusz's mother for the past few days. Since his health is not getting any better, I don't want to burden them with my visits.
>
> Nothing new here…Gobekowie asks you to send letters to them to the address of Aunt Fryda (Elfryda) Kraków, Łagiewniki, Rydla 74.
>
> Janusz received your letter, but he is too weak to write to you. Don't write to him, so he doesn't feel bad that he can't write back to you, because of his health. When you write to Fryda, put down your address clearly, in the letter, not on the envelope, because the envelope can get dirty, and she doesn't know your address. I would like to send you a package, but I am not sure what you would like.
>
> I kiss you sincerely – your Zośka
>
> My Dear!
>
> Your aunt wrote to you about everything that is important already. So I only send my greetings and kisses.
>
> Your Uncle

I do not know who Gobekowie was, but I distinctly remember my mother deciphering the rest of Teofila's encoded message and instructions: That Janusz was ailing really meant he could no longer help her parents and their friend, Dr. Robert Feldman, with whom they shared their lodgings; "Janusz is too weak to write" meant that her parents were no longer able to correspond. That is why my mother was to write instead to Aunt Fryda, Guschinka's mother. The instruction to include her address only inside, not on the "dirty envelope" because Fryda "does not know where you are" was to further emphasize that Izydor and Teofila did not expect to be able to communicate.

As my mother stated in her oral history, "Well, of course, I knew they were in mortal danger."

After a pause, she added, "That was the last letter."

Chapter Twenty-Six

Holocausted-Out

Driven as I was to excavate whatever information I could, I often felt weighed down by the material and needed to take breaks. Sorrow and mental fatigue would suddenly swamp me as I traversed the miasma of the Holocaust.

In the late 1980s, I was on the Board of Second Generation of New York, a grassroots organization for children of Holocaust survivors. We members, children of the remnants of the European Jews, called ourselves "2Gs." I was brought into this local chapter of the International Gathering of Children of Holocaust Survivors as older children of survivors began having their own nuclear families and started handing over the reins to younger 2Gs.

At first, I was the keeper of our list of 300 or so names, updating and maintaining it, and sending out announcements of our events. Later, my friend Marian Weisberg and I were responsible for programming. We offered documentary screenings and panel discussions relevant to children of survivors, refugees, and anyone whose family had been displaced by the Holocaust. One especially memorable event was a discussion with Yale Strom and his cinematographer, Oren Rudavsky, who had recently returned from Poland, about their film-in-progress, *The Last Klezmer* (1994). Strom was filmed playing his violin on the streets and in squares of various towns. While he bowed, passersby whispered Sabbath invitations or slipped paper scraps with their addresses into his coat pocket. After watching excerpts of the film, we all talked about "going back" to our parents' countries of origin, unconsciously parroting them even though for most of us such a visit would have been our first.

I also participated in one of several kinship groups. At these informal gatherings, we discussed what we had in common, exchanged complaints about our parents, and tried to understand them better. There was much anger and frustration, but we also felt great empathy for our parents because of all they'd been through. In the face of silence, many of us shielded our parents from articulating and reliving painful memories. We were therefore aware of the uniqueness of our legacy but in many cases, due to our parents' silence, lacked specifics. Some of us discovered that our parents were more protective than American-born parents; ours were wary of mass movements and did not permit us to attend political demonstrations. My mother forbade us to go to the Vietnam War Moratorium, for example. We were locked in a cycle of protection due to past trauma known only to our parents, in some cases creating distance and a void. We were witnesses of the witnesses, but through a filter.

Children of Holocaust survivors are hardly a monolithic group, although we share common characteristics, like our interest, as mentioned before, in well-made shoes because of their importance to our parents' survival. There are, or were, many different combinations and permutations among our parents: two concentration camp survivors married one another; a partisan married a camp survivor; a child hidden in a convent married an American Jew; a Kindertransport child married an American, and so on. In my case, my mother, a Holocaust survivor not in the camps, married a refugee.

Furthermore, we hailed from different nations, socioeconomic backgrounds, and various levels of religious observance. Our parents were different ages when the war began; their post-war attitudes were influenced by whether they perceived the onslaught as a child, teen, young adult, or married an adult who perhaps already had lost their own nuclear family. I found that I had less in common with those whose parents were Hungarian, or Orthodox, or had both been in Auschwitz, for example, than with assimilated Polish Jews. But the feelings of loss and mystery were the same.

Some survivors had adjusted better than others. I was appalled to hear one kinship group participant describe parents who sat in front of their television for hours watching video "snow," or TV static, too depressed to rise and tune in to a working channel. I realized that I did not quite fit in because my parents were traumatized in different ways from concentration camp survivors. Sometimes, of course, I did not want to fit. Nevertheless, I made several good friends and lots of acquaintances.

Occasionally, Marian and I became overwhelmed by the topic of a presentation, or the discussion that followed. After one screening and discussion, I blurted to Marian, "I can't take this. It's too much. I'm Holocausted-out." We laughed. This became our shorthand for legacy-induced freak-out. When it crept up, we slowed down, took breaks, and lengthened intervals between meetings. At its worst, though, I reverted to how I felt after my father's death and my mother's divorce from her second husband. I wanted to get away from the Holocaust and blend in. The war, the war, the war, the war, the war. I was sick of it.

Sometimes during my quest, shifting my attention to another side of my family provided a respite. Other times, turning to another unsolved mystery did nothing to stanch the stench of the Holocaust and its repercussions. There were junctures during my research where I became blocked.

As I learned the details of the Nazis' systematic destruction of European Jews, I had to find an outlet for the rage and sorrow that engulfed me. The cruelty that lurked in a horrifying anecdote triggered the most vehement disgust. I became short-tempered and high strung. Then I had to get away and distract myself, otherwise I felt sure I would crash and burn. Meditation and breathing exercises helped, as did Pilates and long walks. I also turned to literature, art, music, and my husband.

When Russia began massing troops on Ukraine's border in February 2022, I plunged into the BBC's 1995 production of Jane Austen's *Pride and Prejudice* to immerse myself in another era. I watched and rewatched, studying the acting, camera angles, costumes, interior decoration, and other elements of the series. Sure that I had a mad crush on Mr. Darcy a.k.a. Colin Firth, Ed made little jealous and snarky remarks. Ignoring them, I called his attention to Austen's subtle satire and keen character portrayals. In his usual nurturing way, when I mentioned the annotated edition of the book, Ed ordered it for me. I immersed myself in that, too. Anything to get my mind off the aggression of yet another madman and a war that made me feel my relatives had died in vain and that tragic loss of life and culture were repeating.

On my sister Michelle's suggestion, I took watercolor classes at the 92nd Street Y. It was not the first time I had painted with that medium; when I was coping with the unwelcome but necessary sale of my parents' home in Amagansett, I said goodbye by painting our view, Three Mile Harbor, and other Springs and Sagaponack scenes.

When our teacher assigned portraits, I chose to copy black and white photos of my smiling grandmother Teofila sporting her wide-brimmed hat, and my dreaded great-aunt Lucia gazing sternly, pursing her heavily lipsticked mouth, and wearing a terse, white blouse buttoned to her chin. I sketched their features lightly with a hard pencil and then filled in their skin tones, guessing their complexions. When I applied blue paint to Teofila's irises and black to her pupils, an eerie feeling gently sidled over me for an instant, as if she was gazing at me. I added eyebrows and suddenly she and my sister Ivy resembled one another.

When not in visual escape mode, I followed Ivy's suggestion to join the Association of Classical Musicians and Artists (ACMA), a self-run organization that provides opportunities for amateur and professional chamber musicians to practice performing. Monthly concerts are held at the Opera Center of New York, where the halls are small and not intimidating. We also could audition annually to perform at Zankel Hall or Weill Recital Hall. If we did not want to participate in a formal coaching program, like Mannes' Extension Program or at the 92nd Street Y, both of which I had done, ACMA was a great alternative.

I organized a trio to perform Franz Doppler's "Andante et Rondo, Op. 25" for two flutes and piano. Who was Albert Franz Doppler? A native of Lemberg born in 1821, when it was part of the Austro-Hungarian

Empire. I wondered whether my father knew of this virtuoso and composer, who formed a flute duo with his younger brother. Together they caused a sensation throughout their tour of Europe. Like most of his pieces, "Andante et Rondo" reflects Hungarian influences; the first movement has a traditional romantic lyricism while the second is jaunty and light-hearted. I had gravitated to an era before Lwów's Jews were destroyed and, though the Dopplers were not Jewish, I must have felt in my bones their earthy Hungarian peasant-dance thromping, and bird-like Galician flourishes hovering above.

I harbored nostalgia for an unknown era before exterminationist anti-Semitism. In the case of Austen, I contemplated the title of her masterpiece; how we are all guilty of prejudice and pride, even if it's a matter of degree. What would genteel Austen and her contemporaries have thought, I wondered, of Germans entrapping Jews behind barbed wire fences and then gassing them? I went on to read *Daniel Deronda* and asked the same questions about its author George Eliot. With the Doppler it was more personal; had my father lived longer, would we have gotten good enough to play that piece together?

But like a black adder, the Holocaust always slithered into my psyche. It was not that I was obsessed with the Holocaust. It pursued me. It relentlessly beckoned. During every decade of my adulthood, I had approached the Holocaust either by trying to talk about it with friends and colleagues, initiating and abandoning research, or writing about it. Each time I either failed and clammed up, or people made surprising and hurtful statements that silenced me.

While in college, on the few occasions I did talk about my parents' wartime experiences, people did not want to listen. The first time I spoke about my family and the Holocaust to a peer was during my first year at Hampshire College. One evening, a woman in my dorm invited me to chat. "You don't say much about yourself," she remarked. I opened up, answering her questions in detail. She was taking the Holocaust course, the first of its kind to be offered to undergrads. She had grown up in Manhattan and attended one of New York's high schools for gifted students, was much tougher and far more mature than me, and had a boyfriend at fifteen. The next morning she said, "You laid a lot of shit on me last night." Even though I got the slang, I felt reprimanded. I thought she had initiated our conversation because she was genuinely interested. I thought we were making friends. But evidently she had changed her mind. Maybe I was "too heavy," to use another vernacular of the day.

"Heavy" was our shared 2G experience and yet it was still difficult for some of us to talk in the group. I remember attendees just listening and never contributing. There were many reasons for their silence. Some were quiet for weeks and then felt safe enough to speak, while others were protecting their parents' privacy. When we discussed concentration camps, I kept quiet and listened.

Attitudes of children of Holocaust survivors toward their parents' reticence have evolved since World War II and Liberation. In the 1980s, 2Gs balked at their parents' refusal to discuss their wartime experiences. A movement was born as they refused their parents' silence and expanded their familial need to a demand for broader recognition of their legacy. They wanted the world to acknowledge what had happened to their parents and to them.

Over the years, when I revealed my legacy, people made remarks that hurt, angered, and silenced me. A colleague said the European Jews behaved like sheep and went to their deaths without fighting. When I said I didn't have grandparents, a date corrected: "You did, but you didn't *know* them." An academic in one of my writing groups said about the protagonist of a novel I was writing who was a child of survivors, "She thinks she's special." Another, after hearing about my summers in the Hamptons, commented, "Except for Hitler, you had a charmed childhood." The same person could not absorb that my mother feared her "employers" would use ill-health against her and summon the Gestapo, which would investigate and determine her papers false. When I raised my suspicion that Oppelt sexually abused my mother, she asked, "Couldn't your mother have just refused Oppelt's advances?" And after I explained that Oppelt's wife absconded with my mother's food card and as a result my mother starved, the same person insisted that "there must have been something else going on about that food card." In her denial, she could not acknowledge that my mother was trapped and that if she had not cooperated, the consequences could have been lethal. Or maybe she was deafly applying peace-time norms to a wartime context.

At first I found such remarks not just hurtful and infuriating, but stunning failures of empathy. They made me feel isolated and that I ought to shut up. I could not understand why it was so hard for people to realize that the same could have happened to their relatives, or to them, if they had been in Europe then. But maybe fear and pain are at the root of denial. It's easier to poke holes in what has been written or said, easier to be skeptical and put the onus of proof on the teller. Now I see that such remarks were not always consciously cruel; the speakers didn't realize the impact their words would have. They were made out of ignorance and resentment at having to face what my sisters and I had to grow up with. They may have been due to the speakers' own pain, anger, and feelings of helplessness.

I have heard other children of Holocaust survivors say they did not have grandparents. It takes a sensitive and skilled listener to recognize what underlies such word choices. To 2Gs it *feels* like we did not have grandparents because we never knew ours. Psychically, the two are equivalent. This and the loss of other relatives and their culture differentiate us from our friends and peers whose parents were American-born. The way I dealt with my grandparents' absence was to think of them as distant relatives. That was my attempt to mollify my sense of loss, my parents' loss, and their silence. And in a way, 2G experiences *are* "special" in that they are different and difficult for others to grasp. Sometimes it has felt impossible to bridge the gap. But I don't believe in solipsism (in the philosophical sense, that knowledge of anything outside one's own mind is unsure and can't be effectively communicated). So I keep trying to connect and explain because I believe humans are meant to share experiences and with that, perhaps heal.

I *want* the specific circumstances of my parents' wartime experiences known because I believe we are wired to understand and empathize with the plights of individuals, whereas we have more difficulty attaching meaning to the suffering of millions. In this spirit, I recall my mother's words about the atrocities that took place in the Republic of the Congo in the early 1960s. She commented that it was easier to weep about one death than for the entire starving province of Kasai. "Individuals respond to individuals, not to multitudes," she wrote. That is why even she, who survived the Holocaust, felt concentration camp prisoners upon Liberation as shown in newsreels were strangers, and that the characters Sol and Herman in the story she wanted to translate were not.

My parents did not want us to be cloistered in a separate Jewish community. They wanted us to know about other cultures and races and have friends from different backgrounds, which is one reason why we went to UNIS. Perhaps another reason for not living an insular Jewish lifestyle was because that made it hard to gauge the mood of the world and attitudes toward Jews. Maybe my parents learned from the war that there is danger in homogeneity. They were inherently curious, sophisticated, and inclusive, though, and would have valued variety anyway, had there been no war.

Since Liberation in 1945, psychologists have examined the impact of the Holocaust on survivors, including enduring massive trauma and adapting to life challenges afterward. In the 1980s I became aware of psychological studies of Holocaust survivor families. Clinical psychologist Yael Danieli described four ways of coping among Holocaust survivors as they interacted with others, including their children. She called these "posttrauma adaptational styles." They were linked to survival strategies the survivor had used during the war, Danieli said, that later generalized to a way of life, a style of being in the world.

The four posttrauma styles according to Danieli are: victim, fighter, numb, and "those who made it." These became integrated into the survivor's personality, defenses, views of him- or herself, and of the world. The victim style includes sadness, worry, mistrust, fear of the outside world, and symbiotic clinging within the family. The fighter style consists of intense drive to build and achieve, compulsive activity, and banning weakness or self-pity. Pervasive silence and depletion of all emotions, minimal tolerance to stimuli, and expecting children to grow up on their own characterizes the numb style. "Those who made it" includes denying survivors' Holocaust experiences, assimilation, and single-minded pursuit of higher education, social and political status, fame and wealth, or all of these.

My mother fit into the fighter style Danieli described, but she also possessed some characteristics of the victim style—sadness, worry, and symbiotic clinging within the family, especially in her later years. My father, though a refugee, fit loosely into the "those who made it" category, but he never denied survivors' Holocaust experiences. Assimilation and pursuit of high education were very important to him. Social and political status or fame and wealth were not his goals; he was not a social climber but a healer, and he wanted us to succeed and be comfortable.

Danieli and her colleagues observed that these styles inevitably influenced how survivors parented and so affected their children's development. The adaptational styles therefore became intergenerational. In other words, as a result of their traumatic wartime experiences, survivors passed on to descendants their styles or ways of being. Both my parents modeled to my sisters and me the fighter style qualities of intense drive to build and achieve. So it is not that children of Holocaust survivors simply inherit the effects of traumatic experience, but it is that we learned by example from our traumatized parents' styles of coping.

In my case, that translated into a strong sense of justice, especially as a journalist. My mom's example enabled me to excel as a young, female reporter in a male-dominated industry. Eventually, it drove me beyond reporting into activism as a vocal feminist when I experienced and observed discrimination on and in my beat. In my reporting, I was doing what my mother did—fighting for justice and equality.

There is now an extensive body of psychological literature on Holocaust survivors and their descendants. It feels a little odd to be studied and able to confirm based on personal experience some of what has been clinically observed about us. It does help me feel less like I don't fit anywhere, but my ambivalence about this legacy remains. The fighter family ethos may propel those of us brought up in its midst to accomplishments, but we also have difficulty relaxing and doing nothing. I'm not sure that means we are "compulsively active," as the experts say.

But there was little room in my upbringing for lassitude, weakness, or self-pity.

Psychologists studying 2Gs also have found variations on the impact of intergenerational trauma depending on the parents' circumstances of survival: A concentration camp survivor's child might have lower resilience than an escapee's child, and surviving alone put offspring at risk for more anxiety and depression than surviving in the company of relatives. A survivor's age and education made a difference. So did the passage of time, as the long-term impact of the Holocaust on a survivor's health became apparent later in life.

Certainly, isolated in Germany from those who loved her, my mother suffered from surviving entirely on her own. She took audacious risks to do so. And, uncanny as it seemed to me after reading Danieli's comment about time and survivors' physical well-being, my mother later paid for her courage and circumstances of survival with her health. But I can't conclude that my sisters and I have experienced greater anxiety and depression compared to our peers with American-born parents. Those symptoms are ubiquitous, regardless of legacy.

Some psychologists have said there is no hierarchy of suffering in the Holocaust, but people slip into pecking orders anyway. I saw that plainly with a survivor of the camps, who when I explained that my mother had false papers and was a slave laborer in Germany, snapped, "That's *not* the same thing." That was the end of our conversation. And yet a family's feelings of loss do not diminish based on how the survivor survived. My mother's parents are no less dead or missed than those of camp survivors who knew their parents' fates. Same for my refugee father regarding his mother. Trauma and loss are indiscriminate.

People remark that the way I convey my mother's wartime stories shows that I identify with her. Quite right, although it is a matter of degree. Some children of Holocaust survivors feel that they, too, are survivors. But I was never so identified with my mother as a Holocaust survivor and my father as a refugee that I did not feel a separate identity. Instead, I see my legacy as different from my peers whose parents are American-born Jews.

As a result of my upbringing, for example, I see, and have always seen, the world as unstable both politically and economically. My mother placed little value on money, saying, “Money is here today and gone tomorrow,” because that is what happened to her grandparents and so many others. But I do not want people to feel sorry for my family because of material and emotional losses. I would like people to acknowledge the brutal persecution my relatives were subjected to. The key to healing our wounded planet is to nurture those who have experienced trauma. That’s why it’s important to have conversations, painful as they are, about victims of persecution and to know the specifics of what they endured.

In the last decade, authoritarian regimes have risen around the world. Many Americans who formerly believed democracy was safe and enduring now acknowledge its fragility and agree that we must cherish and safeguard our democratic institutions. When we learn from the past, we stand a chance of reversing the inequities that plague our planet and preventing them from persisting in the future.

Holocaust survivors have said that they felt no catharsis when they told their stories. What matters, they have said, is that someone cared to listen. I feel the same way.

Chapter Twenty-Seven

Walking

During the Miocene Epoch millions of years ago, volcanic eruptions displaced the land along what is now the border between southwestern Ukraine and northern Hungary. The Earth heaved and spat up streams of lava and deposited boulders, forming a huge east-west crescent. The volcanic band became part of the Carpathian mountain range that stretches from Central to Eastern Europe: from Austria to Poland just south of Kraków where the highest part of the range is known as the Tatras, and through Ukraine to Romania. The Volcanic Carpathians separate the Tysa Lowlands of Hungary to the south from a series of valleys and older mountain ranges behind. Through them laces the Tysa River and its tributaries, depositing pebbles and rocks so that fields of stone punctuate the troughs.

This formidable natural barrier, its inhabitants, and those who patrolled it were all that separated Ojzer Fränkel from destruction—or another chance to live.

For two-and-a-half years he had toiled as a forced laborer in a shoe factory and lived in the execrable ghetto under unbearable conditions. It amazes me that he survived the many continuous *aktionen*. Certainly during that time, his great despair upon hearing of Michaela's suicide was compounded by losing track of Milek.

At some point, an opportunity arose that enabled Ojzer to resurrect his original plan to hide in his attic. Uncle Sydney said a friend of

Milek's, a young communist—I'll call him Viktor—was still living on the fourth floor of Rejtana 5. Viktor agreed to supply food to Ojzer and about nine other Jews, were they to hide in Rejtana 5's attic. A couple on the floor below knew Jews were hiding above and agreed to keep the secret. But what was the timeframe and what had convinced Ojzer to take such an extraordinary risk?

In August 2016, when Ed and I arrived at Lviv's train station at dawn, we were met by a driver who brought us to the Hotel George. I chose the hotel because of its proximity to the street where my father had grown up. Lviv was the hardest city for me to visit and the most nervously anticipated. We had journeyed along the same route as my mother and my grandparents when they fled Kraków on September 3, 1939.

Despite being sleep-deprived from the all-night train ride, after we unpacked, anxious energy propelled us to Kurbasa Street, the Ukrainian name for Rejtana Street. Ed and I scouted it out and I shot video and still images with my iPhone. The only change since my virtual visit two years earlier was that the street was closed off to vehicles and the stores on either side of the door had changed. To the left was a dentist's office, to the right a computer store.

After I finished shooting, I turned to Ed, who was on the opposite side of the street looking up. I followed his gaze and saw that the roof was not flat but slanted up about 10 degrees away from the street toward two chimneys. Between two top-floor, gabled windows of the neighboring home we saw the sidewall of my grandfathers' building and a grid-covered window. We were staring at the window of the attic where my grandfather hid for almost a year.

As we walked back to the hotel along the main drag, a cobblestone street now known as Svoboda Avenue, formerly Legionow Avenue, I thought of my grandmother Teofila. On which cobblestone street had she been denounced?

The next day, we returned to my grandfather's house with Alex Dunai. He walked right up to the cast-iron door and tampered with the lock. To my surprise, it opened and I crossed the threshold into the vestibule, which was still decorated with Majolica tiles and deteriorated paintings of seascapes with peeling, ghostly cypresses on the coast.

Stepping over broken floor tiles that camouflaged the Polish name of the street, we climbed the creaky wooden staircase to the top floor. Each landing was strewn with piles of boxes, old furniture, and junk covered by faded, flowered tablecloths. Behind one pile peeked a cornice with the same elegant carved leaf and grapes motif we had seen downstairs, but glossy with brick-red, slopped-on Soviet paint.

As we approached the attic, I saw two new doors on either side of the landing. In the center was a set of metal doors clamped shut with a large, heavy padlock so old it could have been my grandfather's. Any of the doors could have led to the secret attic. The tenant in one top-floor apartment was afraid to let us in because she was alone, so we descended to the third floor. An elderly Ukrainian woman emerged having just showered. While Alex chatted her up, I discretely slipped my phone out of my coat pocket, touched the video record button, and hoped for the best. She said she had been living in the building since the 1970s and was told by old-time tenants that the house had become a brothel during the war and that the theater next door became a cabaret. There was even a red lantern outside the front door, she said. She also had discovered gynecological records in her apartment vouching for the good health of the women. At that point, I believed the entire story because such details are unlikely to have been invented. Then she added that she thought the house had been a brothel before the war, though she wasn't sure. But I was. I managed to suppress an ironical guffaw.

I was more focused on the basement. Despite being fairly certain that it had been renovated and my grandparents' jewels gone, I needed to know for sure. The Ukrainian woman agreed to show it to us, but she asked us to return in an hour so that she could get dressed. We then asked two guys from the computer store to take us down to the basement, but the bulb was burned out, so we left to buy a new one. Upon returning, we asked the staff of the dentist's office, which abutted the theater, if we could see their basement. It had been renovated.

We returned to the Ukrainian woman, who led us down to the basement where we screwed in the bulb. There was no flooring, just dirt! She opened an old, white door to her storage space. A stench greeted us from the sewer. All we could see was an old water heater and junk piled behind it. Encouraged, though, that during the intervening years no one had poured concrete in the central part of the cellar, I thought there might still be a chance of finding the jewels. I asked where the gas lines were, but the lady said that during the Soviet era each apartment was outfitted with its own gas meter. Alas, the only clue to the loot's location was gone.

Hoping to find clues in old structural or construction drawings, when we returned to the United States I asked Alex to find blueprints of the house. I also requested the deed in case I wanted to prove ownership. He never found one but he did find drawings of all the floors from 1948, but they revealed nothing about the gas lines.

Alex had not told the Ukrainian lady who I really was. To prevent her from concern that I was there to reclaim my family's property, he just said my relatives had hidden in the sewer. She then volunteered that there were two secret passageways from the cabaret to the attic and to the basement. That way the girls could accommodate their clients after a show.

I immediately understood that these passageways were clues as to how Grandfather Ojzer had managed to escape the attic when he and the other Jews were found out by the Gestapo. They could not have swung down balcony by balcony to the street where the Gestapo's cars would have been idling. The only way they could have eluded the Gestapo while it stormed up the steps would have been through the upper floor passageway.

The revelation struck Alex, too, who later commented on the reactions of other Lviv tourists when he told them of my grandfather's escape. "The story how he was hidden and how he was using this path to go from one building to another to escape from the Nazis, to the people it makes a bigger impression than [if] I would read them a book, or they would read an article about Holocaust."

Here is my version, combining what my uncle Sydney said with what I discovered, of how my grandfather escaped to his attic:

Ojzer took the extraordinary risk of returning to Rejtana 5 because Viktor must have informed him through a messenger that the rest of the building had been turned into a brothel. The place would have been busy; the women had a steady supply of clients from the Bagatela Cabaret next door.

After all he had seen in the workcamp and ghetto, Ojzer was inured to the news that his beautiful building was a house of ill repute and felt neither outrage nor shock, only a glimmer of possibility. Who would think to search for Jews in the attic of a whorehouse? But my grandfather was both altruistic and practical; he would have wanted to help his friends and he might not have been able to afford to pay Viktor alone. Perhaps they, too, had squirreled money away in various hiding places. Today's dentist office had been a grocery store, so Viktor could carry food up to his place and then smuggle some to them. The couple on that floor agreed to let the fugitives use their bathroom, Sydney said. But the attic was really a crawl space, which seemed right given what Sydney said and the rise of the roof Ed and I had seen. In the cramped garret, Ojzer and the other Jews had slept in shifts, half standing while the rest slumbered. Certainly the fugitives had to have been both physically and psychologically very strong to withstand such a scheme.

When rumors circulated of yet another pending *aktion*, Ojzer might have seized the moment for his daring plan. He and his friends escaped from the factory barracks at night and scaled the series of fences that connected adjacent backyards. They climbed over the low dividing wall Ojzer and his sons had years ago forced their neighbor and rival to rebuild to a more reasonable height. One by one the escapees snuck into the stairwell through the first-floor window, stole up four flights to Ojzer's camouflaged closet, and climbed up to the attic.

Shut into darkness, there was not much to do but try to adjust to the crowded quarters and to wait and listen. I visualize Ojzer late that first night, hearing the hum of car motors and voices from the street below. A cabaret show must have just let out, he concludes. And then, muffled footsteps not far from the closet below. They seem muted, as if behind more walls. Ojzer cocks his head in the dark. As the steps grow louder, he discerns a woman's high heels and the heavier tread of a man. The pair laughs loudly.

When Ojzer sleeps he often dreams of his birthplace, Busk, which means "stork" in Ruthenian. A myth of the town's origins recounts that a great white bird guided the wife of its founder out of a thick forest on a hill. He ordered a fortified ancient settlement to be built there and named it in honor of the *busko*. Others said the village's name was related to its geography and ecology. Busk is situated on the banks of four rivers—the Bug and its tributary the Pełtew (the same river that flows under Lwów's opera house) the Sołotwina, and Rokitna. The town was also surrounded by ponds and watery moors. After the spring snowmelt, the waterways flooded and the town looked like an island, so it became known as the Venice of Galicia. Then slowly, slowly the water receded, leaving behind marshes. These boggy meadowlands were an attractive nesting ground for storks, hence the *shtetl*'s name.

Ach, it was a terrible, filthy swamp, Ojzer thinks when he awakens. But there were gems in the squalor. Near Busk he had met and courted his beloved Mechla while home from Lemberg visiting his family for the holidays. She dazzled him with her fine looks and intelligence. She was a good listener, refined and clever. Although born in Zukow, an even tinier *shtetl* nearby, she was hardly provincial because her father was originally from Lemberg and a member of a large, influential family there.

Besides oil tycoons and hoteliers Max and Simon, another of Michaela's nine uncles had been mayor of Łyczaków, a town southeast of then Lemberg. He also had been awarded the *Order Wojenny Virtuti Militari*, Poland's highest honor for heroism and courage. They were quite a crowd, that generation born to Abraham Lifschütz and Chuwe Leder Lauterstein—oil prospectors and hoteliers, real estate holders, a war hero.

But that must seem like eons ago to Ojzer, confined in the dark.

Ojzer would have had ample time to ruminate about many other matters. While still working at the factory, perhaps he had discreetly asked around hoping for a nugget of news about Milek. Perhaps he learned that, as an engineer who had specialized in energy and automobiles, Milek's skills were particularly useful to the Reich.

Germany was at a disadvantage when it came to energy because it had few domestic oil fields; before the war, it had relied on their meager output, oil from imports of crude, and the synthesis of petroleum products from coal. But Hitler's vision demanded more and more fuel. The *autobahns*, the Volkswagen, the *blitzkrieg* strategy that used bombers, fighter planes, tanks, trucks—all depended on oil.

The 1930s saw a high-stakes race to maintain a technological lead in hydrogenation, a method for attaching hydrogen molecules to coal at high temperatures and pressures so that it liquefied into gas. In 1935, however, an American breakthrough in gasoline production surpassed Germany's more complex, cumbersome, and expensive method. The resulting high-octane fuel meant the Allies could fly planes with more powerful engines at higher altitudes, outdoing the *Luftwaffe*. By the autumn of 1942, oil blockades were causing a fuel shortage and the Reich had to restrict civilian consumption; only doctors, midwives, policemen, and high government and Nazi Party officials were allowed to drive.

The Nazis faced a choice: either secure the Russian oil fields of Baku Grozny and Maikop in the Caucasus, or build more hydrogenation plants. When the Nazis failed to capture Baku's oilfields and refineries, they constructed coal gasification plants in Germany where they stepped up synthetic fuel production. In all likelihood, Milek was slaving in one of them. Agonized at the prospect, Ojzer vowed to find his son as soon as the war was over.

On another night, Ojzer overhears the same sort of traffic, only worse. A couple arrives, again from where he is not sure. The officer seems to be off balance and the prostitute tries her best to keep him on his feet. Suddenly, Ojzer hears a revolting splatter and then senses a sickening, sour smell.

"*Verdammt noch mal* (Bloody hell)! I've puked and now the landing is slippery."

The woman bursts into laughter while they descend the steps.

Ojzer tries to contain his disgust. *This is my house. Mine. My wife and I made our home here.* His mind flashes back to the day they moved in. Walking up to their new apartment, he had reached for Michaela and caressed her on the stairs; she had smiled and cradled his cheek in her hand and said, "My darling. Tonight. Tonight." Ojzer recalls the alluring fragrance of her neck, still feels the sensation on his fingertips when he stroked it.

A song repeats in Ojzer's head:

I sit in my home
and think only of you
A grave opens up inside of me
when I hear a knock at the door.
Because my heart is drawn only to you
No one knows what's in my heart
Oh! It's bitter, my pain
This love breaks my bones
If I would have wings,
I would fly to you
If I would have a magnet
I would attract you
No one knows what's in my heart
Oh! It's bitter, my pain
This love breaks my bones

*Author unknown

Ojzer sighs. *A grave opens up inside of me.... I cannot even molder away next to my Mechla. She wasn't tortured—of that I can be sure. At the very least.*

And then one night, a pimp unwittingly gives away the secret.

"Marta, your customer awaits you," Ojzer overhears the pimp say, apparently speaking to Marta through the door to her room. "He's impatient. I'll escort him through the passageway."

Ah! So, someone has done construction work while I have been gone. In the dimness, Ojzer had many hours to contemplate what this could mean for him and his companions should there be a raid. That secret hallway could save them.

But all this could be wrong, or at least off the mark. Maybe Ojzer himself was responsible for those fissures between Rejtana 5 and Rejtana

3. He could have been well-aware of the money-making connection between the two buildings.

The key questions were when and how Ojzer had escaped his attic and crossed the Carpathian Mountains to Hungary. I was stuck again.

A clue arrived on a Sunday morning in 2016 with *The New York Times*, which ran an obituary of the sole survivor of a ship filled with Jewish refugees called the *Struma* that had been torpedoed in December 1941 on the Black Sea en route to Palestine. I studied the *Struma* and began to learn the history of other illegal refugee ships to Palestine. In August 1944 a flotilla of three—the *Mefkura*, *Bulbul*, and *Morina*—set sail from Constanța, Romania, but the *Mefkura* had been attacked and sank. Was this the ship Ojzer had not taken? I contacted the Central Zionist Archives and requested a record of my grandfather's arrival between late 1943 and 1944. The Archive sent a form Ojzer had filled out indicating that he left Lwów on October 4, 1943, and arrived in Budapest in May 1944. I also found an early 1950s document in the Arolsen Archive, formerly the International Tracing Service, that Ojzer had filled out to request remuneration from the German government for all he had suffered. He said he had been arrested in September 1941 by the Gestapo, lived in "GH Lemberg," which I assumed was the ghetto, and lived illegally for a while in Poland. Now I was able to piece together the puzzle.

Ojzer must have worked in various labor camps and factories for over two years until his daring escape to his attic in early 1943. By August 1943, the Soviets had advanced 800 kilometers west from Stalingrad and the Front was half that distance from Lemberg. Viktor would have warned Ojzer and his companions that the Soviets would liberate the city soon. Ojzer certainly was not going to live under their brand of tyranny again. He might have thought: My beloved Mechla is dead. My youngest son is missing. For what should I remain here? I must see my precious Izak (Sydney) and Dolek (David) again. *Meyne zin. Ale mayne kinder.* (My sons. All my children.) For them, I will save myself and leave my country of fifty-six years.

By the summer of 1943 the ghetto had been liquidated and Ojzer and his cohort would have been ten of eight hundred Jews still secretly defying the Nazi declaration of a *Judenfrei* (free of Jews) Lemberg. Like Ojzer, most were scattered in hiding places throughout the city—"The Remnants," as they would later be called. Fueled by his desire to reunite with his sons, spurred by defiance and rage, Ojzer and his group meticulously mapped out their escape.

Through Viktor, Ojzer and his attic mates lined up guides to help them traverse the Carpathians and bring them to safe houses nestled in forests along the way, according to Uncle Sydney. Budapest was far away—a 574-kilometer trek equivalent to the distance from New York City to Richmond, VA, and that was as the crow flies, not hiking up and down ravines and cliffs during winter. Ojzer's plan was to walk at night and sleep by day. On a good night, he hoped to cover 12 kilometers.

On October 4, 1943, the Gestapo officers must have stormed up the steps of Rejtana 5 while Ojzer and his companions scrambled down from the attic and through the passage to the cabaret. But after almost a year in the dark, all was blurry. Ojzer blinked and tried to focus as they found their way to the women's rooms. Besides his house, prostitutes were using two floors above the cabaret that had once been a small hotel. In preparation for a raid, Viktor had paid off several of the women to hide the escapees. Ojzer and his troop were only permitted to stay until things quieted down. They had to leave that night.

A woman handed Ojzer a bundle containing a ragged shirt, baggy trousers, a three-quarter length coat, and an eye patch—the disguise Uncle Sydney reported and that Ojzer probably had asked Viktor to prepare. Half-blind already, Ojzer wanted the patch to conceal as much of his face as possible. He also shaved his beard and fashioned a large, handlebar mustache. Most important of all, he probably asked for a decent pair of boots. Thus, outfitted as a Ukrainian peasant, he crouched in a corner and waited until dark.

Ojzer did not ask Viktor to retrieve the jewels from the basement, perhaps because Milek might return in need of them. On the Central Zionist Archives form Ojzer stated that he arrived in Budapest in late May 1944 after an eight-month trek. He was right on time for the Nazis—they had just taken Hungary—so he fled to Constanța. I knew from my mother that on the dock, he met a woman with three children who needed an extra ticket. My altruistic grandfather, father of three sons, gave her his ticket and somehow got on another ship. But which one? The *BulBul* or the *Morina*?

I knew many illegals in Palestine were immediately confined in Camp Atlit, which the British built. Guessing that my grandfather was interned there, I asked the Central Zionist Archives for a list of prisoners, which it provided. It happened to be sorted according to the ships on which they arrived. On the *Morina* passenger list I saw my grandfather's name! I deduced that originally, he was supposed to have sailed on the ill-fated *Mefkura*, but after aiding the mother of three switched to the *Morina*. It docked in Istanbul, having evaded a mere squall. But an "M" next to his name indicated he was married, and below his name was his wife, Francesca, age thirty-eight! No one ever said anything about a wife in between my grandmother Michaela and my step-grandmother Rifka. All these secrets. What was with the Fränkel men and their surprise women?

I never proved how my grandfather got from Turkey to Palestine, but reports by the JOINT Distribution committee (a Jewish charitable organization that helped rescue Jews and support survivors) said the flotilla survivors either took a train from Istanbul or walked. I did determine that Ojzer was in Camp Atlit for several weeks, because I have his passport, which the Polish Consulate in Tel-Aviv issued on August 29, 1944. I assume that his niece, who had made Aliyah in the 1920s or 1930s, helped get him out. It must have taken many months, if not years, for Ojzer to recover from the trauma and tragedy at sea from which he had been spared.

My mother told me other stories of my grandfather's selflessness; he had pulled a friend out of a burning synagogue, eluding the Nazis by running around to the back door and bursting it open, for example. Unfortunately, I no longer remember the details. But I always think of my grandfather as generous and heroic because he tried to help that mother of three. And now the tale is buttressed with historical facts.

Chapter Twenty-Eight

Dixieland, England, D-Day, and Normandy

While my mother was slaving for Laudenbach, the Resses, and the Oppelts in Bavaria, my father completed his residency, passed his medical boards, and enlisted in the U.S. Army. In May 1943, he traveled to Little Rock, AR, as a medical officer-in-training at the U.S. Army Medical War College, Camp Joseph T. Robinson. There he was to take a six-week course at the 29th Medical Field Service School—basic training combined with rehabilitation techniques for the wounded. A three-week officers' training program would follow at the 12th Chemical Warfare School, and then he would be a first lieutenant.

Serving accelerated my father's naturalization process and the prospect of becoming independent from Rose. Above all, my father chose to serve in the European Theater because he wanted to vanquish the Nazi terror.

Situated on wooded hills just north of Little Rock, the capital of Arkansas, Camp Robinson was originally a training post for the Arkansas National Guard during World War I. The federal government had the right to reclaim the post in an emergency, so the army repossessed it in 1940 and enlarged the camp. By May 22, 1943, when my father arrived, it was a city unto itself with a population of 50,000.

Lying in his bunk in a hutment after a long journey by rail, my father reads about the post's history in the camp Handbook of Information. He is stunned by a note on a map of Little Rock that restricts White soldiers from entering certain neighborhoods: "Only Negro personnel may enter the area in Little Rock defined as 'between Seventh Street, exclusive, and Eleventh Street, inclusive, north and south respectively, and Spring, exclusive, and High, inclusive, on the east and west respectively'...etc." The Army is prohibiting White soldiers from visiting neighborhoods of color. At Unity Hospital, he had worked side-by-side with staff who were people of color. He must have been disappointed and embarrassed by that note.

Before finding the manual I had worried about my dad as a Jew in the land of the Ku Klux Klan. Clearly he had left one form of prejudice on the Continent for another in the land of the free.

Of all the mysteries I solved, unraveling my father's tour of duty in the U.S. Army from the fall of 1943 to December 1945 took the longest and required the most diligence. My father left a large collection of war photos, so that is where I began. He crawls under barbed wire, smiles in plane cockpits, stands or sits smoking a cigarette in front of a tent with a white cross on its roof, waves from the front seat of an earth mover or gestures at the deep mud, standing triumphantly on the tail of a downed Nazi plane.

Most images had no dates or locations marked because that was forbidden, lest they fall into enemy hands and provide information about the Allies' strategy. In some pictures, however, my father poses in front of signs and landmarks. My father, his chess partner Captain Bob Root, and two other buddies stand before Mont Saint-Michel's quicksand; in Paris he poses for the camera with a woman I dubbed "Big Hair" with the Palais Garnier in the background (dated September 1944); on the steps of the WWI memorial and ossuary at Verdun, France; by a café in Liège and a fountain in Maaseik in Belgium.

As per his separation papers, my father was assigned to the 50th Field Hospital. But the photos told a different story than that unit's reports. My mother said my father had treated the wounded during the Battle of the Bulge. How, then, could he have made summertime excursions to Mont Saint-Michel and a September visit to Paris without taking several furloughs and traveling so far west between 1943 and 1945? I could not solve the puzzle. Also, according to my mother, my father had gone to Dachau in southern Bavaria in search of his brother Milek shortly after the concentration camp was liberated in May 1945. Again, unless he had taken time off, I did not see how my father could have traveled that far from the 50th Field Hospital's northern Germany location in early May. Finally, my mother also mentioned my father's last assignment in late summer 1945 as commander of a POW hospital in France, which I vaguely remembered was near Lille. But two detachments of the 50th had operated POW hospitals in Winzenheim and Bad Kreuznach, Germany. And they had closed in July.

I was stuck and switched to Grandfather Ojzer's story, which yielded an unexpected tip concerning my father's tour. According to my mother, after he arrived (illegally) in Palestine, Ojzer wrote to the president of the United States asking that his two sons be informed of his whereabouts. Maybe the Roosevelt and Truman presidential libraries had a record of this correspondence. Archivist Virginia Lewick of the Franklin Delano Roosevelt Presidential Library found no correspondence from my grandfather. In my disappointment, I remarked that I was also having trouble mapping out my father's tour of duty. She suggested that I contact the National Archives (NARA) in St. Louis, which houses Army personnel records. Although most had been destroyed by a fire in the 1970s, Ms. Lewick said the staff had reconstructed some charred files and that it was worth a try. I filled out all the forms, wrote a check, and forgot about that lead.

Six months later, NARA, St. Louis, sent my father's discharge card, which listed information shrouded in military acronyms. From what I surmised, they contradicted my father's separation papers so I asked NARA's staff to translate the acronyms. I learned that my father had been a medical officer with the 93rd Medical Gas Treatment Battalion.

At dusk on April 22, 1915, in Ypres, Belgium during World War I, German troops rolled 5,730 heavy cylinders to the Front. They opened the containers with trepidation, hoping the prevailing winds would carry 128 tons of escaping chlorine gas away from them and toward enemy lines. As the gas released, a pungent, nauseating smell permeated the air. The dense gas quickly sank into trenches filled with French and French Algerian troops. The soldiers gagged, their eyes smarted, and they writhed on the ground. Within ten minutes, 6,000 died from asphyxia and tissue damage to their lungs. Many more went blind. Others turned and fled. Not all German soldiers escaped unscathed, but they did have gas masks.

Six hours later in a nearby wood, the Germans set fire to a chemical that released sulfur chloride. A thick, greenish-yellow cloud blew toward the French and Belgians, who were bewildered and unable to see a yard ahead. The cloud of death forced nauseated soldiers to heave and suffocate. Their deaths were slow and the agony indescribable. Then the Germans charged and drove the French back past their trenches.

Thus was modern chemical warfare born. The enemies lobbed chemical rounds at one another for years. In 1917, the Germans deployed a new and more lethal chemical agent: mustard gas. It became known as the "King of Battle Gases" because, when uniforms were soaked in it, severe skin blisters erupted. Mustard gas also damaged victims' eyes and traumatized soldiers and civilians alike who suffered from "gas fright."

When the United States Army arrived in France in the summer of 1917, it was completely unprepared for chemical weapons. During the inter-war period, the War Department created the Chemical Warfare Service to develop poisonous gas, gas alarms, and masks. But President Roosevelt abhorred the use of toxic agents and did not support the Service. As 1942 unfolded, however, the War Department reasoned that the enemy might again resort to gas. If it did, the Department wanted to beat the Germans at their own game, but poisonous gas was to be used only as a deterrent. The United States wanted Germany to fear its readiness to retaliate, so it mobilized and trained troops to function in gas and smoke. It also trained doctors and medics to treat and decontaminate troops with five special units called Medical Gas Treatment Battalions.

Attending neurology and psychiatry lectures in medical school just twenty-three years after the Germans introduced chemical warfare, my father had to have been keenly aware of the devastation it caused. Perhaps that made him more easily recruitable for the gas treatment battalion, or perhaps he volunteered. In any case, in August 1943, my father left Camp Robinson to attend a three-week course on how to treat gas casualties at the Chemical Warfare School at Edgewood Arsenal, Maryland. When his training was complete, he was as ready as the mascot on the service's special insignia: a fierce green dragon with red eyes, red claws, and a red-tipped tail. But its motto, *Elementis Regamus Proelium* (Let us rule the battle by means of the elements), probably did not jibe with my father's allegiance to the Hippocratic Oath. He would have worried whether the original policy of deterrence was turning into something else.

Next, my father shipped off to Camp Livingston in Alexandria, Louisiana, where he and several other first lieutenants shared the latest in medical treatment and techniques with the battalion of 44 other officers, one chaplain, and 457 enlisted men. It was divided into four units, a Headquarters Detachment and three Companies: A, B, and C. Each Company had a staff of 135: five doctors, one dentist, medical technicians, supply people, drivers, surgical assistants, and three administrative officers.

In early September, the entire battalion went on a six-day bivouac in the wilds of Kisatchie Forest and its bayou, complete with snakes and alligators and sweltering heat. The purpose was to practice setting up a clearing station and treating gas casualties under simulated battle conditions. The battalion was also subjected to overhead fire. Was that when my father was crawling on his belly, rifle in hand, in one of his many photos?

It must have been very difficult for my fair-skinned father to protect himself from the Deep South's sun. The insects—not to mention the many reptiles that surfaced in the murky waters to eye the men—must have made my father's lobster-red skin crawl. On the other hand, as he pushed on through the extraordinary humidity, nature lover that he was, he might have found the birds and the kudzu-draped trees exotic and wondrous.

I'm certain the hardship was worth it to him. He wanted to fight for his haven and do whatever was required because of all he witnessed in Europe. He believed in American democracy; he was not just fighting to free his parents and brother but to defeat the Nazi terror. With his medical and language skills he had much to offer the service. He loved our country and wanted to fit in although he recognized its many flaws, especially racial hatred in the South and bias in the North.

I had to know more about what he witnessed while serving, but could not locate Company C's unit history in the European Theater. Online I discovered the history of Company A's tour of duty, which helped because the two Companies' histories overlapped a little in Normandy and Brittany. But there was no information about Company C in Belgium and Germany so my father's whereabouts in late 1944 and 1945 remained murky. Finding C's unit history preoccupied me for many months.

In the fall of 1943, members of the five Medical Gas Treatment Battalions boarded a troop train bound for New York to Camp Shanks in Orangeburg, the army's largest embarkation center known as "Last Stop USA." Everyone got twelve-hour passes for a day on the town and piled into buses to Times Square. Perhaps wanting to see Mollie one more time, my father hopped on the subway to Brooklyn and called on her at work to hug and kiss goodbye. Maybe he hoped distance would enable them to see if they truly missed each other. Then, once he was free of Rose, he would know whether he and Mollie had a future together.

My father had another important errand, though. He was expecting his Certificate of Naturalization to have arrived and to his great joy, it was waiting for him at his New York address. His name and vital information were printed on an elegant sheet of paper:

> Be it known that at a term of the District Court of the United States held pursuant to law at New York City on October 21, 1943, the Court having found that David Allen Frenkel then residing at 86 East 49th Street, Brooklyn, Kings, New York, intends to reside permanently in the United States....

To the left was a photograph of him in uniform and an embossed seal of the United States overlapped his signature. His delight was matched upon opening another manila envelope that contained reprints of his first published research paper: "Diagnosis of Lipoid Pneumonia by Aspiration Biopsy," with co-authors Dr. Louis Nathanson and Dr. Mendel Jacobi, in *Archives of Internal Medicine*, Volume 72, Number Five, November 1943.

On a corner torn from a brown paper bag, he dashed off a note to Sydney asking him to place the precious naturalization certificate in my father's safe. Then he returned to Manhattan to rejoin his battalion.

At Pier 90 they boarded the *Gray Ghost*, previously known as the *SS Queen Mary*. Then one of the world's three largest liners, she had been retrofitted to a troopship. The carpeting, china, crystal, silverware, Art Deco tapestries, and paintings had been removed. Leather covered the woodwork in the staterooms, the cabin-class dining room, and other public areas. The staterooms now slept soldiers in triple-tiered, wooden bunks.

The Medical Gas Treatment Battalions and 15,000 other servicemen set sail for Scotland on October 26. As *Gray Ghost* steamed past the Statue of Liberty, my father must have felt a mixture of pride and wonder; just four years ago he had sailed in the opposite direction as a refugee with little else but his education and hopes. Here he could rise on his own merits, unfettered by how he worshiped god, if he worshiped at all. So much had occurred in such a short time since he left the Continent. But he regards the future with a young man's optimism and certainty that he is on the right side, that his new country's mission in the world is to defend and spread democracy and freedom. That more than any other country, it has graciously welcomed and embraced him. That strangers may realize their potential and their dreams, to seize possibilities according to this true American ideal.

Returning to Europe as an American with other American soldiers to free the Continent from the tyranny of fascism, my father looked toward the Atlantic with a well-defined sense of purpose. This time his voyage was smooth and uneventful.

I wanted to know more about the 93rd Medical Gas Treatment Battalion because it was the key to my father's tour of duty in Europe. In early 2017, I corresponded with military archivists and historians, including one at the U.S. Army Medical Department's Office of Medical History who kindly sent *The Medical Department: Medical Service in the European Theater of Operations*. Five footnotes within this tome referenced annual and semiannual reports of the 93rd probably stored in NARA, Maryland. I realized that I had gone as far as I could without hiring a historian to visit NARA's collection on my behalf. But Steven B. Rogers, the historian I hired, made five trips, leafed through many boxes of 93rd documents and turned up nothing.

Meanwhile, I reread the history of Company A and noticed that the authors thanked Patrick Yack, whose father had served in Company C. I called Patrick, the executive director of Florida Public Media. He had searched at NARA, Maryland, but had not succeeded in getting Company C's history. Like me, Patrick had a snapshot taken in England of his father, who had been a medic, standing in front of a plane called "The Pride of Minnesota." The plane was about to be painted gray and retrofitted with hospital equipment for transporting wounded troops. Patrick and I quickly bonded, having in common enigmatic fathers who were mum about their wartime experiences.

I returned to the World War II medical history book, reread the footnotes, and asked Steve to please try again. Steve found the 93rd battalion documents in the back of a box (Record Group 112, Entry UD 1012, Box 278). I was ecstatic. Inside were one hundred pages of detailed accounts by the Battalion commanding officer, Colonel Joseph Palmer, and the historian of Company C's service: from Normandy to Brittany to just outside Paris; to Étain below the Bulge; to Belgium; and finally southern Germany. The documents were filled with specifics of the stamina and bravery of medical officers and personnel as they leapfrogged across northern France, chasing the Front and caring for the wounded in field hospitals on airstrips.

On November 2, 1943, *Gray Ghost* steamed into the Firth of Clyde, Scotland. My father stands on the deck as the ship weaves her way between the Isle of Arran and the Scottish mainland to upper Firth, a spectacular introduction to the United Kingdom and its contrasting shorelines. Blue mountains jut down into the even bluer loch waters, wide swaths of sand and pebbles stretch along other parts of the coast. The main entry point for Allied merchant shipping, military personnel and equipment, the Firth teamed with activity. From it, ocean convoys were dispatched to the European and Mediterranean Theaters of Operations.

Gray Ghost docked at Gourock and the troops immediately boarded trains for England. The 93rd's destination was Camp Ramsden Heath, Oxfordshire. The campsite included a former British Army Hospital on one of the highest hills in the area, which meant chilly winds and low temperatures with heavy frost and snow. But the worst of it was that from that elevation they could see the beating London was taking from the *Luftwaffe*.

Colonel Palmer ordered an officers' club to be set up for recreation and relaxation. There they could distract themselves by watching films, using athletic equipment, and reading books from the library.

During the following weeks, the Battalions attended lectures on European Theater of Operations regulations and on British customs, laws, and traditions. They also imparted to other medical personnel their expertise treating gas exposure. At the American School Center and Shrivenham, for example, they lectured on the admission of gas casualties, triage, and treatment—that is, how to decide which soldiers who had been attacked with gas could return to combat, which to send to other treatment units, and so forth. The 93rd's officers discussed scenarios and prepared skits in which soldiers presented symptoms and doctors diagnosed and treated them. They did seven or eight roadshows attended by 350 medical officers.

Although anticipation of gas attacks must have been horribly stressful, all these treatments were hypothetical. It was not yet known how the Germans would respond to the still secret amphibious invasion of Normandy.

My mother was well-aware of the long-lasting fear of poisonous gas and commented tersely in her oral history about the terrible irony of Polish citizens' concern upon the 1939 German invasion: "At the time, the biggest fear was that of the poisonous gas, which in retrospect seems absolutely ludicrous." She meant not only its deployment during WWI but the Nazis' innovative use of gas-filled trucks to asphyxiate rounded up Jews, and later in concentration camp "showers" on Jews and other minorities also deemed inferior.

Colonel Palmer wished to gain the confidence of British local military personnel and citizens, so in December the battalion threw a Christmas party served at the officers' club for children from the surrounding towns. A lieutenant officiated as Santa Claus. Judging from a series of photographs in his collection, my father was enchanted by the children enjoying their first American meal.

The Company lived in a tent hospital. Everyone pitched tents, dug ditches, and knocked in pegs. Great for Dad's back, I thought as I read the unit history. They slept on folding cots and ate, read, and wrote by lantern light. The Army brought in concrete mixers to lay floors, but they did not always keep away the mud. At 6:30 a.m. everyone washed in water so cold that they postponed rinsing their faces until later in the day.

By early 1944, the United States Army was preparing for the Normandy landings. As large numbers of U.S. servicemen gathered, hospitals became essential on England's southern coast. In June, Company C and the Headquarters Detachment of the 93rd Medical Gas Treatment Battalion were in Southampton. On June 7, the day after D-Day, they awaited the first Utah Beach casualties. Colonel Palmer was the port evacuation officer charged with removing patients from the Landing Ship Tanks and distributing them to holding units and transit hospitals. As the LSTs arrived at wharves and landing ramps, doctors boarded them to recheck the triage that LST doctors had done during the return voyage from Normandy. Teams of Company men carried patients on stretchers and helped the walking wounded to ambulances parked nearby, shuttling between the docks and hospitals. Medics removed as many as 175 stretcher cases in less than half an hour.

My father worked around the clock, at times handling one casualty per minute. After being on duty at the docks for sixteen hours without a break, he might have snatched some sleep and eaten hurried meals from mobile kitchen trucks. He patched up others well enough to be transferred to nearby station hospitals and treated those so gravely wounded they could not be moved. There were fewer casualties than expected, however—about one hundred a day—and my father probably wondered grimly about loss of life on the beachhead.

On June 10, the first wounded German POWs arrived. Knowing that my father was fluent in their language, Colonel Palmer would have assigned these cases to him. They were panic-stricken. According to the unit history, a German prisoner became aggressive when touched and would not permit anyone to examine his wounds.

I narrate the scene my father would have faced had the patient been his:

"*Was ist die Angst* (What is the fear)?" David asks in German. No reply. "*Du kannst es mir sagen. Wir helfen Ihnen.* (You can tell me. We will help you)." After further coaxing and reassurance, the POW confesses that he fears he will be used for experiments.

Stunned, my father asks in German, "Who do you think we are?"

He reassures him and the other Germans that they will be treated humanely in accordance with the Geneva Conventions. My father is deeply disturbed; their dread implies that Nazis are experimenting on captured Americans. Given the clashes in medical school and the Nazis' view of science, though, my father is not completely surprised.

I like to think that to distract themselves, he and his staff mused about past USO shows they'd heard about. A photo of my father sitting on a bleacher, looking relaxed and surrounded by dozens of soldiers, inspired this little scenario in my head. "What are the odds we'll see Bob Hope or Jascha Heifetz?" my dad asks his colleagues. He yearns to hear the great Polish violinist, whose recordings he often listened to and who emigrated to the States between the 1910s and 1920s. With fellow émigrés Arthur Rubinstein, Bruno Walter, and Lotte Lehmann, he raised money for British War Relief by giving a benefit concert as early as 1941. Weeks after the attack on Pearl Harbor, Heifetz performed his first stateside USO concert and urged Americans to invest in war bonds. Possessing fine comedic timing, he had entertained the troops as Jack Benny's straight man in a famous skit for NBC in 1942; Benny, a fine violinist in his own right, downplayed his talent while Heifetz caricatured the stern *maestro* for the sake of the gag. Right now, the violinist was on tour entertaining troops in Italy and was expected to perform in France the next year.

Company C received casualties from Normandy throughout June. In mid-July, with the rest of the 93rd, it crossed the Channel to Utah Beach. Through the sand and up dusty roads the battalion marched for 13 kilometers to its first bivouac in Foucarville, half an hour south of Cherbourg. The day was warm, so the men—clad in gas-proof garments with winter underwear (incredibly), field jackets, and equipment—sweltered as they marched.

Corpses and rubble were strewn throughout the countryside of little farms separated by 4-feet high hedgerows. These made it difficult for tanks to cross, and everywhere my father saw signs warning "Mines cleared by hedges only" to discourage shortcuts across the farm fields.

Sore-footed and weary, the battalion reached its destination that evening and erected tents to the crackle of distant gunfire. Although the men witnessed the shattering force of modern warfare throughout the Cherbourg Peninsula, a major concern dissipated; the Germans, though in retreat, were not deploying chemical weapons. The Headquarters Detachment and companies of the 93rd therefore attached to various evacuation and field hospitals as needed. They were to be pioneers in a new field—the speedy evacuation by air of wounded soldiers to General Hospitals in England or the Continent.

As the American Army took Saint-Lô and moved further into the Continent, all five medical gas treatment battalions leapfrogged across northern France to keep up with the Front and the continuous flow of patients. Some battalions moved to a different bivouac every month. It was grueling, bloody work.

For their next assignment, the 93rd Headquarters Detachment and Companies A and C convened at Biniville, a hamlet in the middle of the Cotentin Peninsula. There they teamed up with the 8th Field Hospital and established a holding unit for casualties. After army engineers carved out roads and passageways, the hospital units raised their tents to accommodate 900 patients. C-47 troop carrier airplanes—like the painted over "Pride of Minnesota"—evacuated the wounded via an airstrip just smoothed by engineers. Transport planes were on a tight schedule, so the medical team had to be prepared to rush patients to the planes at a moment's notice. Fifteen ambulances did the job.

Many patients arrived directly from aid stations. A soldier wounded in the morning would reach the hospital unit a few hours later and arrive at a General Hospital in England that same afternoon. From July 19 to August 10, a mere 22 days, my father's unit evacuated 5,786 soldiers of all nationalities to England and transferred 472 soldiers to General Hospitals on the Continent.

After the breakthrough at Saint-Lô and as General Patton's Third Army pressed through the Brittany Peninsula, admissions began to lag as my dad's hospital was too far behind the fast-moving frontlines. On August 11, Company C was sent to Courtils at the base of Cotentin, where both peninsulas meet. There they augmented platoons of the 12th Field Hospital and set up another holding unit, which evacuated 650 casualties. Fighting diminished in Brittany as the Allies liberated the rest of Normandy and approached Paris.

In mid-August, with demands on the hospital abating as the frontlines moved east, my father and his buddies took leave to visit newly liberated Mont Saint-Michel. The famous, strange little tidal island had been a strategic fortification since ancient times. Owing its safety and tactical value to quicksand and extreme tides that made it sometimes inaccessible, the island successfully resisted occupation for 1,200 years. Until the Nazis besieged it.

My father, his chess partner Captain Root, and two other servicemen pose on the beach to the left of the newly liberated mount on the horizon jutting from the sea toward the heavens like a religious palace, a cluster of spires reaching for peace through faith. In another photo, my father and the two unknown colleagues stand next to the turrets of the island's battlements, marveling at the views of the freed coastal village of Pontorson and the indomitable sea.

Chapter Twenty-Nine

Doppelgänger

Chartreuse, yellow, orange, red, purple, lilac, and white. So many zinnias to water, fertilize, inspect, and admire. What my mother loved most about these tall, daisy-like flowers was that their stamens also resembled little flowers. Blossoms within blossoms—nature's *Matryoshka* dolls. In Forest Hills, she had specialized in roses, but they refused to grow in the sandy East End soil of my parents' summer home. She compromised by coaxing dune roses to climb the cliff. In the springtime, all emerging buds seemed miraculous to her and she called us outside to visit them.

Look," she would say, stooping and pointing to a delicate young-green tip. "Eeee-*heee*!" A chirp of delight. She had the same effusive reaction to cypress seedlings that popped up in our lawn. We transplanted those to our cliff, too, hoping their roots would stabilize the soil. Emboldened, my mother made flower beds between our deck and the edge and inserted arrowhead-shaped seeds and bulbs into soil she had enriched with peat and dark dirt imported from mid-Island. The result: countless zinnias and lilies in our garden in East Hampton.

The exercise and the earthy scent made her feel alive and alert. Later, as she drove up our crunchy, gravel driveway after shopping at the IGA, the zinnias and lilies—elegantly balanced on their slender stalks—welcomed and waved to her in the mid-summer light.

My mother was weeding such a flower patch one late-summer day in 1943 when her friend Olga, another Polish slave laborer, stopped by the Oppelt nursery. My mother recounted their conversation:

> She said, "Danush, everybody says in Hollstadt your brother came." I said to myself, Oh that's not good. I said to Olga, "I don't have a brother." She said, "Come and see for yourself if you never had a brother. This man looks just like you." This was very bad news. If he looks like me, he must be Jewish. "He came with a hat and a watch," she said, "and a suitcase." I stayed clear of Hollstadt.

The slave laborers had a loosely organized support system in Hollstadt, the first hamlet where my mother had worked. Run by Jan Ryda, "an elder" Czech all of thirty-eight, he gathered the group to celebrate major holidays. He was usually very supportive in a quiet way, but was puzzled by my mother's absence. As the winter holiday season approached, Jan sent her a note. "'Danka, what on earth is the matter with you?'" my mother recounted in her oral history. "You have not been here for months. We expect you Christmas."

My mother and her friends Olga and Stasza went to Hollstadt and stayed over the holiday in a room near a church. When my mother entered the church, she immediately spotted the man Olga had described, a lanky fellow named Staszek with green eyes and black hair, who indeed could have been her twin. They were introduced:

> He immediately said to me, "You don't sound like [you're] from Lwów. You sound like you're from Kraków." I was caught off guard, and I said, "I need that like a hole in the head." Spontaneously, he said. "You're not from Lwów." Wherever he came from, whoever he is, he certainly should not have said that I have a Kraków accent. The Polish peasants didn't [recognize urban accents].

Other workers were unaware of Poland's regional inflections and Stasza was too busy making eyes at Jan, and he at her, for them to notice Staszek's gaffe. Nevertheless, my mother declined future invitations. Before Easter, however, Jan wrote again announcing that he and Staszek would be coming to Bad Neustadt for the holiday. During that visit, Staszek and my mother strolled around the medieval castle on the hill of Bad Neuhaus, which overlooked the village. He was so overworked that, like my mother, he swayed as he walked. He said he and his two brothers were from Słomniki, a village near Kraków, and had gotten false papers before bribing their way to Bavaria. "The only thing that betrayed him that he was not a peasant," my mother told her oral history interviewers, "was that he said, 'You know, Danka, it could be much worse.'" A typical Jewish adage. An echo of Izydor.

I met Staszek Merin when I was a teen. After the war, he and one of his brothers settled in Hartford, Connecticut, near my mother's friends, my surrogate aunt and uncle Krysia and Edek Nabel. When we visited during summer vacations, we always went to the Merin Brothers coat factory. There my mother selected for herself, and when we were old enough, for my sisters and me, winter coats cut from the finest camel hair cloth. On one such expedition my mother taught me about "the hand of the cloth." She scrunched up a fistful of material and watched it unfurl. "See how it springs back? No wrinkles," she said. "That's how you know it's good-quality wool."

I believe Staszek supplied such fine department stores as Lord & Taylor and B. Altman and Company. In the winter, we visited Staszek's showroom on Fashion Avenue, where my mother bought us navy blue spring coats. But one winter my mother abruptly stepped away from a rack and strode out of the showroom without buying. When I asked why, she said, "Did you see how Staszek lost his balance?"

"No."

"He's been drinking. I could smell it on his breath." A new, shameful reason for his shaky equilibrium. She walked briskly to the elevator. Although irritated, my mother did not sever ties with Staszek. They remained friendly for the rest of their lives.

Curious to learn more about the Merin brothers' wartime travails, I searched the internet and found Staszek (whose given name was Leonard) and his brother David's obituaries. I was surprised to read that they had been in Płaszów, the concentration camp depicted in Steven Spielberg's movie *Schindler's List.* There they had worked as tailors, mending Nazi uniforms. Somehow, they escaped to Germany.

I went on a tear researching the castle on the hill overlooking Bad Neustadt, which my mother said Charlemagne had built. In fact, the castle was newer than Charlemagne's 10th-century citadel. The current castle is an irregular pentagonal enclosure that protects a series of inner courts. Along the smallest side at the southwest and the adjoining south wall stands a hunting lodge, and beyond that, a row of residential buildings.

As they circled the castle's perimeter, Staszek and my mother were unaware that these quarters were still in use by the family of Baron Karl Ludwig Freiherr von und zu Guttenberg, scion of a German noble line that reached as far back as 1149. Nor could they have known that the owner of the castle was not at home because, in 1941, he had joined German counterintelligence in Berlin. Part of the Nazi resistance, he participated in the failed July 1944 assassination attempt on Adolf Hitler. Arrested by the Gestapo and interrogated under torture, Baron Guttenberg revealed nothing. The Gestapo executed him in late April 1945. The plotters' politics were not uniform; some were conservative nationalists, others, like zu Guttenberg, monarchists. Some wished a return to Germany's 1914 boundaries and wanted to keep Poland, and they were more concerned with military victory than with atrocities in the east and the fates of the Jews. But my mother and Staszek would never know that the Baron was the enemy of their enemy. Oh, the heartache that what I discovered I cannot share with my mother.

My mother liked Staszek, but he was voluble and therefore a hazard. She told me he had a crush on her and did not want to encourage him. Fortunately, after Easter he returned to Hollstadt, so my mother no longer had to concern herself with his indiscretion or worry about being associated with him should his true identity be discovered.

The Oppelts continued to starve and overwork my mother. Malnutrition set in. To make matters worse, a toothache plagued her. She asked for permission to see a dentist. Denied. Did she, remembering Grandfather Izydor's advice, console herself, thinking, *This is nothing but another hard trial of life. An exam I must pass.*

My mother realized she "would not survive as a healthy person," as she said in her oral history, if she continued to work for that family. When my emaciated mother ran errands for the Oppelts, or on her weekly days off, the villagers noticed she was gaunt and overworked. There was talk; they made known their disapproval of the Oppelts. The townspeople's heightened empathy was double-edged, though, because my mother's plight made her more conspicuous. Looking for a way out, she reasoned that the Germans' defeat in Stalingrad and the Soviet Front subsequently moving west presented an opportunity for her to find another "employer" and increase her chances of survival.

She hatched a plan to buttress the ruse of her identity and use public opinion to her advantage for support, should she try to switch to a better job. Planting half-truths, she exploited the Germans' respect for hierarchy. Irena is in the town market, for example, striking up a conversation with a cheese shopkeeper who always cast admiring glances her way. Does she mention how much her father enjoyed just the type of *Allgäu Emmentaler* the cheeseman made? Then segue to Izydor's heroic World War I acts in the Dolomites and inform the shopkeeper that her father was a decorated captain?

"My father served in the Austro-Hungarian Army and received a silver medal for bravery." At the 11th Battle of Isonzo, as I found out from the Austrian State Archives.

"Silver, you say? Oh yes, that battle was very important," the cheeseman acknowledges, beaming at her with admiration. While they're speaking, two *hausfrauen* enter the shop, overhear, and maybe later they'll tell their friends.

"Yes, and he tricked the enemy into thinking he was accompanied by an entire battalion near the caves. But it was just him and his valet."

"Well, my dear, his efforts paved the way for our triumph at the 12th Battle of Isonzo." Another admiring glance.

If my mother's father was a war hero and a decorated officer, it followed that she could not possibly be Jewish, for very few Jews held such rank in the German and Austro-Hungarian armies. So if anyone suspected she was Jewish, this half-truth would have derailed them.

Perhaps as the cheeseman gave my mother change for Frau Oppelt, he surreptitiously snuck a wedge of *Rauchkäse* into my mother's hand. Ah, a little respect. And precious protein.

I return to the photo of my starving mother standing next to her friend Stasza, the other Polish slave laborer. It was taken on October 16, 1943, which I determined was a Saturday. They probably had the evening off, and perhaps were on their way to meet friends. My mind drifts through the rest of the weekend. Although she never said so, my mother probably attended church the next morning and every Sunday. I have a hard time imagining her at Mass. Church would not have been a haven for her because if she made a mistake while pretending to pray, a congregant could have become suspicious that she was Jewish. But perhaps the nun in Lwów effectively taught my mother the catechism and she would not have stumbled.

If my mother had believed in the Catholic God represented in the Bavarian church, she might have prayed for forgiveness for her bratty response to her parents' packages, prayed for a way to apologize to them. In reality, she could not have prayed to any god. For her, this was a time of bereavement, yet she was unable to surrender to her sorrow because she had to maintain her charade. Doubly strained by her grief, and having to camouflage it and her true identity, she would have longed for and been deprived of support from others while mourning.

I wonder whether Mass reminded my mother of happy times before the war, when she and the family maid went on long Sunday morning walks. Because tuberculosis was greatly feared, children had to take in fresh air, and on these outings the maid introduced my mother to Kraków's many magnificent churches. Thus they were more familiar to my mother than synagogues, which she and her parents never attended. Out of curiosity, my mother first visited a synagogue on her own at age thirteen.

Kneeling in church, alone with her thoughts, did she feel grief, or comfort, or both?

My mother was unpredictable regarding churches and Christian observances. She was once very hurt after a conversation with a neighbor in East Hampton who asked how she had survived. The woman, then in her mid-eighties and from a wealthy, social register Episcopalian family, was a former schoolteacher and poet who celebrated the beauty of nature as God's blessing. My mother was quite fond of her and, with pleasure, received her book of poems about East Hampton and asked for her autograph. But when my mother described her ruse in Germany, the woman asked, "And afterward you didn't choose to remain a Catholic?" As if, even after the Holocaust—maybe especially *because* of the Holocaust—anything was better than being a Jew? And so I rebel at the notion that my mother had to kneel with Stasza, Olga, and the other Irena, and sing beautiful Christian hymns among the German congregants while my grandparents decayed in Lwów's dirt, or their ashes alighted on its steeples.

In my mind's eye, as my mother kneels, her thoughts wander back to her parents. Four months have passed since she last heard from them. Nothing. Not one letter. Nothing all summer and fall.

I imagine these are her racing thoughts: What has become of my parents? Were they captured in the apartment on the Aryan side? Abducted as they fled through the streets? Snatched in an alley? Who caught them? The Gestapo? A Ukrainian? A Pole? A band of adolescents in exchange for a fistful of hard candy? Were my parents shot then and there? How deep did their blood seep into the cracks between the cobblestones?

I can only hope that back at the nursery, my mother found solace despite the backbreaking work. I see her hovering over a flowerbed, crumbling a handful of moist soil and sifting the dirt through her fingers, the way you might cradle a clump of sand and then, with your finger, shave off the fragile, crispy, outer layer. Like the little mounds of sand encased in water-molded crust that submitted to my fingers as I sat on our beach below our cliff, shearing off granules with my index finger, or gently blowing on them to see how thin the encasement could get before it crumbled. The way you pluck a small ice sheet from a crunchy snowdrift and brush off the flakes until you see how thin and brittle the ice-shroud really is.

Silently, mournfully, my mother realizes she is an orphan.

How often did my mother reread her parents' correspondence, hoping she had misunderstood the code, trying to convince herself that they really were alright? Or perhaps she found no other interpretation than the first and cried herself to sleep. Did she dream of them? In her nightmares, did she envision them being rounded up and deported together on a train? No, her father is facing a firing squad. Her mother is alone in a boxcar on the way to a concentration camp. No, they escaped east on foot to Russia—that explains the silence. All the while in her dream she desperately crisscrosses Galicia, searching.

After she awoke and the nightmares faded, I hope she closed her eyes and envisioned the Tatra Mountains on a spring day at the moment her entire family assembled for a photograph with snowy-peaked Kasprowy Mountain in the background, when she had knelt in the front row and smiled joyfully.

Or perhaps, afraid to fall back to sleep, she tried to comfort herself repeating Izydor's words:

> *My situation is temporary, only a practical test I will pass.*
> *It is an aberrant phase in what will be my long life.*

Chapter Thirty

These Hands

On January 4, 1944, Soviet troops advanced west across the pre-war Ukraine border with Poland. My mother believed the Soviets would soon reclaim Lwów, which would mean that even if the Gestapo was suspicious of her, it could no longer investigate in Lwów and prove her papers false. After almost two years in the Oppelts' thrall, my mother was desperate for another job; the situation was "unbearable because of the people involved," she told the oral historians. Now was the time to act, otherwise she would not survive beyond her nineteen years. Buoyed by news of Soviet advances, the fact that the Germans were fighting on two fronts (the other being Italy), and that public opinion in Bad Neustadt was in her favor, my mother went to the Labor Office.

My mother told my sisters and me that she displayed her palms to the *Kommandant*, an SS officer, to show how scarred and blackened they were from rough harvest and produce work. "These are not the hands of a lazy person," she said in *Hochdeutsch* (literary German). "Nevertheless, the Oppelts are still not satisfied. Perhaps you can give me a job at a factory because it's obvious that the woman for whom I work is not pleased with me." In her testimony she added that this "was not the case at all. I just used psychological warfare and got myself [a] job in Siemens-Schuckertwerke because I knew nobody could check that I was Jewish." In other words, the Oppelts were perfectly content to indefinitely exploit and starve her.

I suppose the *Kommandant* scrutinized my mother and weighed his options. Probably from his point of view, *Ostarbeiter* were lucky to work for the Reich and eat scraps. A few months earlier, he could have shot her without a moment's hesitation for such an audacious request. As she stated in her oral history, "Later on, of course, when I worked for [the U.S.] military government in charge of other foreign workers' files, I knew that [the Germans] shot people on the spot for what I did."

But she was lucky. "With the victory in Stalingrad, things changed [a] little bit for the better. The Germans were not so sure that they would conquer the whole world. You had a feeling—'Ah, they want to be remembered on your good side,'" she explained to the oral historians. The *Kommandant* assigned my mother to an assembly line at the Siemens-Schuckertwerke Elektromotorenwerk factory. Now she was one of 50,000 slave workers out of the company's 244,000-strong workforce. "That was so much better because I worked there only twelve-hour days," my mother remarked with a whiff of sarcasm.

She moved into the company camp, which housed *Ostarbeiter*. French, Belgian, and Czech workers lived outside the factory grounds in rented spaces or private apartments. The *Ostarbeiter* were permitted to leave on their days off, which were every eighth day, but had to get passes from the camp director to exit through the gates. A curfew required that they return by dark.

Men and women slept in separate barracks, dingy and austere rooms that housed twenty-five workers. Although heated and winter-proofed, the barracks were infested with lice, rodents, and other vermin. My mother slept on a rough wooden board. Splinters wedged their way into her skin. Before bedtime, if you could call it that, my mother tried to ward off head lice with denatured alcohol, which was ineffective and burned and scarred the skin behind her ears. When the lights were out, mice scurried across the floor.

I wrote to Siemens informing their archivist that my mother had been one of their slave laborers. My email included her assumed and real names, a copy of her work card, and a request for pictures of the facility where she worked. I also asked the archivist to tell me what the print on the back of the card said. He confirmed my documents with their list of Neustadt "employees" and said the words on the back pertained to general regulations and rules concerning the use of the identity card. Well, like what?

Here is the German-English computer translation of the back of my mother's Siemens work card:

> This ID serves as proof of the affiliation of the owner to his company office when entering and leaving the work premises and when staying in them. It only applies while the service is being carried out. Outside of the office, it may only be used in official matters to prove company affiliation, but not for general identification purposes.

With terms like "service" and "affiliation," Siemens exhibited its euphemisms.

> The holder must carry the ID card with him during the service and show it to the company representative when entering the office and when leaving at other than the prescribed exit times without being asked, otherwise on request.
>
> The holder must report the loss of the pass to the issuing office immediately; before the holder leaves his office, the ID card must be handed in to the issuing office. Violations and misuse of the ID card are punishable by law.

Law. Nice to know that the beneficiaries of slave labor had such respect for racist rules.

Instead of wartime images, the archivist sent several sterile 1938 pictures of the factory and workers. Why had he not sent any from the war years? I read with satisfaction on the company website that by the end of WWII the Bad Neustadt plant was western Germany's sole producer of electric motors because the Soviets had seized the rest of Siemens' factories in what became East Germany. Furthermore, Siemens' overall losses during WWII amounted to 2.58 billion reichsmarks, four fifths of its total assets.

Every day my mother reported to work at one of the huge, white, one-story factories. The sanitized photos showed that each worker had a station with tools on the right and parts to be assembled on the left. From 6:00 in the morning until 6:00 at night my mother toiled assembling little electric motors. What were they used for, I wondered. In fact, Siemens supplied electrical parts to concentration and death camps.

But the company did issue my mother a food card. Each barracks had a dining hall, although nutritious food was still very scarce. On days off, my mother scrounged for extra food. If, for her food stamps, the miller in Bad Neustadt gave her flour and a few marks, she walked 6 kilometers to the baker in neighboring Hohenroth and exchanged the flour for bread. Then, instead of her weekly ration of one loaf, she might obtain several. On a lucky day, she traded the extra loaves for margarine at Heustreu, another village 5 kilometers in the opposite direction. She said her nutrition improved, but I cannot imagine how she could have gained weight, given all that walking.

My mother did not say whether she was alone on these long, long walks but if so, she had plenty of time to think as she trudged along. One of her favorite poems was Percy Bysshe Shelley's sonnet, "Ozymandias," which depicts the ruins of a tyrannical pharaoh's statue. We read it together when I was in middle school:

> I met a traveler from an antique land
> Who said: "Two vast and trunkless legs of stone
> Stand in the desart. Near them on the sand,
> Half sunk, a shattered visage lies, whose frown,
> And wrinkled lip, and sneer of cold command,
> Tell that its sculptor well those passions read
> Which yet survive, stamped on these lifeless things,
> The hand that mocked them and the heart that fed:

And on the pedestal these words appear:
"My name is Ozymandias, King of Kings:
Look on my works, ye Mighty, and despair!"
Nothing beside remains. Round the decay
Of that colossal wreck, boundless and bare
The lone and level sands stretch far away.

While she walked, if she feared Hitler might prevail, she could remind herself of the temporary nature of power and the fall of the Roman Empire. Such an arrogant boast: "Look on my works and despair." Never. *No matter how tired and hungry I am.* "Nothing beside remains." All has crumbled—his empire and the monuments to him—demolished. That is what comes of imposing murderous ideology on the world.

Nothing surrounds the ruins. The remains, themselves, nothing. Nothingness. And so, perhaps with poetry my mother willed away Hitler and the destruction he wrought.

But this is speculation.

In fact, the endless quest for more food in winter and early spring of 1944 took its toll and my mother developed a sore throat, swollen glands, and a fever. A village doctor prescribed medicine and bedrest, but Siemens did not accept his diagnosis and orders. The company relied on another doctor, as my mother's sworn deposition for her 1958 legal action against the German government reads:

> When I was then later transferred to Siemens-Schückert, I got a sore throat, and this kept recurring, and I had a temperature and felt hot. When I could stand it no longer, I went to a doctor in Neustadt…named Dr. Schmidt. He gave me medication and ordered bed rest.
>
> The factory management, however, did not recognize the orders of Dr. Schmidt. They had a different doctor come, who, as I vaguely recall, was named Dr. Weigandt and who worked in a military hospital. This doctor

> only took my temperature and because it did not go over 38°, I had to keep working. I did not receive any medications.
>
> So I trudged along with this sore throat and temperature until the liberation occurred.
>
> After the liberation, I went to Würzburg. There I was treated by an American doctor, Dr. Roth.
>
> At that point I did everything I could to escape Germany as quickly as possible.
>
> When I came to America, I was treated by a heart specialist, Professor Dr. ZAK, because a heart defect was in fact discovered which was due to the illnesses in Germany, in particular the long-standing temperatures.

"I did not receive any medications." Why was my mother's deposition about her medicine so understated, vague, and passive? She also had not mentioned Dr. Weigandt in her oral history. Yet I knew otherwise. My mother told me quite explicitly what had really happened, although it had taken probing.

"The Siemens doctor said I had no temperature, but that was because I was already taking medication."

"Then what happened?"

"Siemens doctor sent me back to work."

"Couldn't you take the medicine anyway?" My mother was silent. "When no one was looking, I mean?"

"HE TOOK IT!" she screamed. My mother rarely lost it like that. I was taken aback.

"He confiscated your medicine?"

"Yah."

I didn't dare ask anything further. I shudder to think what went through my mother's mind at the time. How does a doctor deny a colleague's diagnosis and demand that an obviously ailing nineteen-year-old surrender her medication? Yes, he was probably under pressure to maintain a certain quota of workers, but what about his conscience?

Until Liberation, my mother was unaware that she was suffering from rheumatic fever, which occurs several weeks after an untreated strep throat infection, and in turn, attacks the heart. It was better that way; if she had known, she might have panicked. She did not describe her symptoms, but I looked up rheumatic fever: night sweats, a ringed abdomen rash, headaches, swollen ankles, knees, hips, abdominal cramps, and nosebleeds. How did she get through each day, hampered by even one of these symptoms?

On the other hand, my mother, daughter of a WWI hero, had learned from her father's example. She would have recalled her mother's entreaty as they had fled Kraków: "Remember who you are. Be brave like your daddy." She was exceedingly courageous. But it was difficult and there were long-term consequences.

Men in the Siemens camp noticed how pretty my mother was, and she overheard them wonder about her. "Somebody always figured, 'Ah, what's wrong with her? She doesn't have a boyfriend.' So that was a problem," she told her interviewers. Men were dangerous and she was wary of them. Although she had adored her father, she knew he was a ladies' man so perhaps she was guarded and looked seriously upon romantic entanglements.

Even though fraternizing with slave workers was forbidden, German men made overtures:

> One of the engineers wanted to take me to the movies, which was not allowed, and he wouldn't take no for an answer. As a result, management at the factory decided that something had to be done about Danuta Milewska. And I was approached that actually since I speak German well, and obviously since I was different from the other Polish workers, I should apply and state that I am of German origin. Which amused me no end. And I refused on the ground that I really was of no German origin, which displeased them no end.

And which briefly entertained me—my mother a *Volksdeutsche*, an ethnic German who could be re-patriated during the Reich? Six months before, on one side of town, Frau Oppelt persecuted my mother as a dirty Pole. Now, on the other side, a German master builder was so captivated that he exalted her. If they had only known who she really was.

One of the Siemens photographs shows a factory wall on which hung a huge clock. Irena chooses not to watch. Instead, exhausted by months of illness and toil, she again wishes for Allied bombs, as she had in the Tarnów Ghetto. *Why do they not target this factory, like the one in Schweinfurt? Demolish it! Just do it.*

My mother did not know that the Allies' priority was to bomb coal gasification and hydrogenation plants throughout Germany. Perhaps these raids killed my uncle Milek. In May 1944, a massive and successful raid crippled five Siemens plants and other attacks continued into the spring of 1945. But none took out my mother's factory.

The big factory clock reads 2:45 p.m.

Nothing beside remains.

4:45 p.m.

"Round the decay of that colossal wreck, boundless and bare."

The hour hand approaches six o'clock. The minute hand trails it by long, distended seconds.

"The lone and level sands stretch far away."

Chapter Thirty-One

Dear Mr. President

The sack of grapes winemaker Doron was hauling to his press seemed unusually heavy in the Negev Desert summer heat, but he persisted. His wine was renowned in his settlement and he made a good living. To ensure that, he had devised and built an elaborate complex—a central treading floor, several collecting vats, and a split-level of six surrounding rooms. Doron dumped the grapes into the upper rooms, which he had paved with intricate mosaics. Each had a drain so that the prized fermented musk trickled into the lower-level cell, and from there conveyed to the treading floor and the vats. The taste was distinctive and Doron's celebrated press became known as "Khirbat Deiran," or "Vineyard of Doron."

Fifteen hundred years later, in 1890 while Palestine was part of the Ottoman Empire, Polish Jews purchased the land above Doron's buried Khirbat Deiran from a Christian Arab. One of the Jews proposed the name "Rehovot," which means "wide expanses." He had drawn on a passage in Genesis 26:22 for inspiration: "And he removed from thence, and digged another well; and for that they strove not: and he called the name of it Rehoboth; and he said, For now the Lord hath made room for us, and we shall be fruitful in the land."

The Polish settlers were part of a wave of immigration known as the First Aliyah, during which European Jews returned to the Promised Land. But for generations, that land had enabled Arabs to tend their animals in an economic system in which ownership of the land had not been the norm. The land purchase meant a disruption to their livelihoods and lifestyles. Disputes broke out while the European settlers planted vineyards, almond orchards, and citrus groves.

My grandfather Ojzer's niece, Golda, had settled in Rehovot during the Second Aliyah (1904 to 1914). I believe Golda got him released from Camp Atlit and took him in.

Ojzer sits in Café Freulich next to a cranky fan that barely alleviates the desiccating late-August desert heat. He dabs his brow with a damp kerchief and squints as he composes a letter on onion-skin paper. As he pulls on his mustache, he sucks in his breath. According to my mother, he writes:

> Dear Mr. President,
>
> Two of my sons are in America. At least one must be in your army. Please tell him that his father is alive and well in Palestine. I thank you, Mr. Commander-in-Chief.
>
> Sincerely,
>
> Ojzer Fränkel

Ojzer puts his letter in an envelope, seals it, and addresses it. Then, undaunted by the blistering heat, he walks to the post office.

With great impatience, he awaits a reply.

Chapter Thirty-Two

The Battles for France and Belgium

The French Second Armored Division liberated Paris on August 25, 1944. Ordered to Le Bourget Airport just north of Paris, Company C, the Headquarters Detachment, and the 8th Field Hospital staff arrived a few weeks later while cheering Frenchmen welcomed them.

Enemy bombs fell as the units battled fields thick with mud to get the hospital operational. Nevertheless, the Company received patients within a few days. The wounds soldiers endured were more severe than in Biniville and required a great deal of surgery, so more surgical teams were called in. The rest of the 93rd arrived and doctors in two tented operating rooms performed surgeries around the clock. During this short stay, the unit evacuated 2,424 wounded to the United Kingdom; 1,303 wounded to General Hospitals in the communication zone; and 550 patients to General Hospitals in and around Paris.

While my mother was toiling at Siemens, the exhausted staff of my father's Company got passes to Paris. My father may have been twice blessed; in early September, the U.S. Army offered every Jewish G.I. and officer a three-day furlough to attend *Rosh Hashanah* services on September 17 even though the city was still off-limits to most G.I.s. It was the first *Rosh Hashanah*—after four years of German occupation—openly observed without fear.

Had he accepted this opportunity my father could have attended services at the Grand Synagogue, also known as the Rothschild Synagogue and the largest Jewish house of worship in France. About one hundred Jews of all ages gathered outside as trucks of Jewish soldiers arrived from all over the country. The congregants cheered wildly and greeted the men with tears, hugs, and kisses.

Three years before, the Germans—hoping to kill as many Jews as possible—had placed bombs in Paris's thirteen synagogues after *Kol Nidrei* services. The next evening, after the Day of Atonement and the Jews had returned home, the bombs exploded. The Germans did not understand that *Yom Kippur* begins at sundown the evening before the Day of Atonement. Thus their ignorance foiled their nefarious plan; the bombs detonated in empty synagogues, but six were demolished. The Germans certainly compensated for their mistake. Maybe my father is thinking, "This *Yom Kippur* will be the most excruciating Day of Atonement and mourning ever because of so many missing Jews."

Fatigued from living in tents and tending the wounded for months, my father spent his next two days in Paris relaxing in cafés, meeting women and going to the opera, sometimes with "Big Hair" on his arm, sometimes not. What jubilation to be in this city again, not as a fugitive but as an American. Did he long to explore Paris with a woman he truly loved at his side? Did he think of Mollie, with whom he still corresponded, and wonder how she was celebrating the new year?

Perhaps when my father returned to his field hospital, a letter from Sydney awaited, announcing that he had married his girlfriend Beate Friedberger and that they were expecting a baby in April. I know my father was delighted with the news—he loved babies, and would have been thrilled to become an uncle. A new life in the wake of all the destruction was to be celebrated. But Sydney probably also reported that he and the detective had made little progress regarding Rose and her lover. But I suppose David realized that after the baby's birth, Sydney would have less free time to help the detective, for at about that time my father seems to have written to Mollie asking for her help.

In mid-September, the ill-fated invasion of the Netherlands, called Operation Market Garden, commenced. The largest airborne operation in history, it included 34,600 men of the 82nd and 101st Airborne Divisions, the British First Airborne Division, and the Polish First Independent Parachute Brigade. All landed in Holland with the intention of entering Germany. They hoped to circumvent the north end of the Siegfried Line. Also known as the West Wall, Hitler had built this network of barbed wire, ditches, huge cement antitank barriers, and bunkers to defend Germany's western border. To reach it, Allied fighters had to capture bridges across the Rhine.

The battle raged until the end of September and the Allies lost, suffering enormous casualties as they vainly attempted to take the main bridge of the town of Arnhem. I had the fantasy, or nightmare, that after the fierce battle, my father treated a Polish private and learned from him of the bravery of the Polish Brigade under Brigadier General Stanisław Sosabowski. When the general escaped to Paris after the Germans invaded Poland, he joined the Polish government-in-exile and commanded 6,000 Polish troops. At Arnhem, they tried three times to cross the Rhine to assist the surrounded 101st Airborne Division. Unfortunately, the ferry they hoped to use had been sunk, so the Poles crossed the river in small rubber boats under heavy fire. Nevertheless, they reached the opposite bank and reinforced the embattled British paratroopers.

I wonder how my father would have felt about this. On the one hand, he could have been proud of the valor of his countrymen and their bond with the Allies. On the other, in his experience most Poles were rabid anti-Semites and he might not have commended them; his allegiance was now entirely with his new country.

On September 20 my father's unit moved east again and split up in Soissons. Company C's destination was Étain, where it joined the 7th Field Hospital to help treat the many casualties of the failed mission. In October, there was a lull in the action. After the Allies' swift progress through northern France, the Netherlands, and Belgium toward the German border, they stalled partly due to problems getting supplies to the frontlines.

Could they sustain their success as they approached Germany? The troops exuded bravado and cockiness. Little did my father and his colleagues know that in a few weeks they would face the bloodiest battle of the war.

The Ardennes cover 11,200 square kilometers of rolling hills and ridges. French folklore is full of legends about these woods, which are said to be enchanted because of a magical horse named Bayard. Charlemagne coveted and yet eventually tried to kill Bayard, who, it is said, continues to roam the forest. But if the Ardennes was enchanted, it also was accursed. Because of its strategic location, the Belgian portion was constantly fought over. During World War I's Battle of the Ardennes, Germany successfully attacked France. After the Battle of France in 1940 when the Germans crossed the Meuse River, a French general declared that he could no longer protect Paris. And yet, the Allies continued to believe the forest unsuitable for large-scale military operations. They were therefore caught off guard on December 16 when the Germans attacked with hundreds of Panzer tanks in an effort to split the American and British armies and capture the Port of Antwerp.

My father, still with the 7th Field Hospital in Étain, treated a torrent of wounded during the fierce campaign, which became known as the Battle of the Bulge. The epic struggle lasted from December 16 through January 25, 1945. "This is undoubtedly the greatest American battle of the war and will, I believe, be regarded as an ever-famous American victory," said British Prime Minister Sir Winston Churchill.

On Christmas Day, someone in my father's unit marked the moment by carving "Merry Xmas, France 1944" out of the crusted snow covering their tent. My father sits on a stool looking drained, and stares at the camera as a buddy takes his photo. The entire staff is no doubt exhausted from treating the many casualties of the Battle of the Bulge. The G.I.s and other officers answer letters from girlfriends, wives, and family in the States. My father can only write to Mollie, a few staffers at the two Brooklyn hospitals where he had worked, Bob Root, and Sydney. There has been no word from other relatives for years.

That night, enemy aircraft strafe and bomb roads to the airstrip. Every night, enemy action can be heard uncomfortably near. The Battle of the Bulge rages and rages in the grueling, bitter cold. One day during triage, when my father and his staff are cutting away uniforms from bleeding and battered G.I.s, he feels a crunch under his boot. He stoops and grasps an oval, black-painted brass badge. Above two embossed crossed swords is an imprint of a German M35 helmet with a swastika. The pin is a *Verwundetenabzeichen* (wound badge), the Nazi equivalent of a Purple Heart. But for the swastika, it is just like the badges from World War I. My father is deciding what to do with it when several ambulances arrive with a fresh load of torn-up young men. He slips the badge in his trousers pocket and gets to work.

This is my version of how my father acquired the badge. Long ago, after showing me my father's Army dog tags with the "H" for "Hebrew," my mom and I discussed whether or not to throw them away. She did. Now I regret that they are gone. But we saved his gold-plated U.S. Army Medical Corp lapel insignia. His souvenir of the toll the war took on the defeated Nazis—the reward for Teutonic bravery captured and held by "inferior hands"—this, too, she kept.

On the evening of January 25, when the battle was finally over and the Allies victorious, my father chain-smokes through the night. In his many photos, a cigarette invariably hangs from his lips, so why should this night be different from other nights? Yes, they had won, but the cost was huge. According to conservative estimates, the American Army sustained 75,000 casualties compared to the Germans' 80,000 to 100,000. The German forces were so weakened they could no longer wage offensive warfare. But my father needed no statistics. He had seen it all. Enough amputated limbs, lacerations, stitches, and morphine. Enough shell-shocked men, enough shrouded bodies sent home. Enough. Enough.

After the Battle of the Bulge, Company C moved to Metz, where it prepared buildings to be used as a hospital and established living quarters at the École Nationale Professionnelle. What a luxury after many months at war to shower and sleep indoors. Eight days later they moved again, this time north to Verviers, Belgium. In conjunction with the 46th Field Hospital, Company C set up and operated a rail evacuation holding unit. They were again relieved of tent life and stayed in an old school on Place du General Jacques, a charming oval village green in the center of town. Verviers is known for some interesting fountains. I was amused to discover Fontaine David, named for a beloved 19th-century mayor. Thinking I remember a shot of my father in front of that fountain, I rummage through his three albums of war photos and envelopes of other shots I never placed. I come up empty handed. Oh, my dad and fountains. And now me.

The voracious war demanded more and more men, and the units' privates were transferred for infantry training. There were no replacements, leaving the staff shorthanded. And then a change of command in late March. Captain Keating, the Commanding Officer of Company C, was transferred to the 50th Field Hospital, which was stationed in nearby Liège. Perhaps this was when my father also joined that hospital.

At about that time, my father received letters forwarded by the Red Cross. I see him immediately recognizing his father's handwriting. Overjoyed to know Ojzer is alive, he tears open the envelop. My father loved his resourceful, *chutzpadik* father and his hands shake as he reads Ojzer's brief description of his escape from Lwów. Dread turns to horror as he continues reading and learns how and when Michaela died. I'm sure Ojzer would have tried to describe her suicide gently but based on post-war correspondence I had translated from the German, he was neither an eloquent nor subtle man and his sharp pain would have made him blunt. Yet there is no right way to tell a son such news.

Next, Ojzer disclosed that he left Lwów unaware of Milek's whereabouts and that he was forced to oversee a coal gasification plant. In another letter that July, Ojzer implored my father to find out whatever he could about Milek. Ojzer also said he hoped my father would visit him in Palestine soon.

How did my father get through the days that followed, as he made rounds, waited for a soldier's thermometer to register his temperature, or removed stitches? Did he dwell on his mother's last moments? Had she been very frightened, or did it all happen quickly? Had the cyanide worked as efficiently as it should have so that she had felt no pain? Or had some black marketeer cut it, so that its potency was reduced? In his mind's eye her throat undulates with her last lethal swallow. In my mind's eye, too.

While shaving in the morning, while buttoning his shirtsleeves, while smoking a cigarette and flicking an ash into the springtime breeze, my father tries to repress flashes of ire. His thoughts turn to his brother, the sweetest, the kindest soul. Why did he have to suffer? If Milek had missed his wife on another day, perhaps the Gestapo would not have followed him and both women would be alive. Submerged in medical emergencies and surrounded by death, my father finds it impossible to mourn his mother the way he knows he should. He clasps her to his heart as he tries to stifle his rage and sorrow.

Grief seeps out at unexpected moments, as it does for my fevered mother in church or working in the factory. When my father gazes at the back of an army engineer directing G.I.s in tractors to smooth mud to become a runway, and wishes instead the man was his younger brother. When the image of a mechanic refueling an airplane's engine pollutes my father's mind with the irrational hope that in a mirror image on the other side, his brother is doing the same. When my father tunes out a colleague's remarks about the Germans' fuel shortage and imagines Milek starving and toiling in some filthy fuel plant.

My father would never have questioned his mother's decision to take her life. He was not judgmental, so perhaps he would have seen the act as one of resistance by which she had bravely seized control in the only way left so that she would not be victimized further. Eventually my father lived his life the way she would have wanted him to, though, by squandering nothing, thriving and suffusing it with the *joie de vivre* she had had, in honor of her. That, he knew, was the best way to celebrate her life, one of which she would have approved.

Despite his heartache, my father would have nurtured the optimism he practiced as a healer, always looking on the bright side no matter how severe a wound or how debilitating a disease. This no doubt helped him get from one day to the next and not dwell on the unknown. And so later, when another engineer directing G.I.s to level a grade brought forth thoughts of my father's persecuted brother, my father could shunt them away by asking to drive the earthmover himself, and got a friend to document it with his camera. Sometimes my father sat in the cockpit of a plane and posed as the pilot. When the Company came upon a downed plane with a swastika on its tail fin, my father climbed onto the stabilizer and had a photo taken of that, too. It was one of the few photographs of his large war collection in which he smiled.

Shortly before leaving Belgium for Germany, my father and three buddies visited Maaseik and toured bombed-out Liège. A photograph suggests that along the way they came upon a beaten-up, abandoned bus for transporting German troops, bearing the motto, "*Sieg oder Sibirien* (Victory or Siberia)."

After posing in front of the broken-down bus for a camera shot, they pile back into their jeep and continue on to Liège, where they down beers and relax at Café de Chene by the Meuse River. Click.

"You ready to brave those Dragon's Teeth?" says one buddy, using the nickname for the reinforced concrete, pyramidal blocks the Nazis deposited along the Siegfried Line to prevent American tanks from breaching it.

"Are you kidding? I want ten teeth and ten photos," says another. Click. Click.

"Just wait 'til those pearly whites get a load of our green monster," my father chimes in, referring to the gas treatment battalions' mascot. They chuckle as they leave the café.

On the way to all-but-destroyed Aachen, the first German city the Allies had taken in October, my father gets his wish. Embedded in the Siegfried Line, Aachen was at the top of the bulge. As the seat of Holy Roman Emperor Charlemagne—founder of the First Reich according to Hitler, and in whose cathedral all German kings were crowned—Aachen was an important symbol of the Nazi regime. Its capture was therefore of immense psychological value to the Allies. Another Charlemagne bailiwick. One for each parent's tale, for symmetry.

My father and his friends approached the city from the south. At the line near the suburb of Kopfchen, my victorious father poses among seven long rows of hip-high "Dragon's Teeth." A side arm holster slung over his right shoulder, he looks pensively and directly at the camera. He does not smile as he steps into Germany.

They come upon a sign posted by the U.S. Army announcing a new, military airport: "Advanced Landing Ground: Y-46 Aachen." Next to it is another sign that quotes Hitler: "Give me five years and you will not recognize Germany again."

In the background lies the flattened town.

Chapter Thirty-Three

Liberation

On Friday evening, June 6, 1944, a French POW in Bad Neustadt clandestinely tweaked the antenna of his contraband radio. After fiddling for several minutes, he found the frequency he wanted. A mix of crackle and news emanated from Radio London into his room. Moments later, he jumped up and ran to the open window across the street from the workers' barracks at the Siemens factory.

"Danka, the Allies landed in Normandy," he yelled. "They were not pushed back into the sea!"

"At that moment, for the first time, I began to plan to live," my mother told her oral history interviewers. She could imagine her future as a person with rights, dignity, and free will. She put it this way:

> The day-to-day existence abruptly changed with hope. I don't think that I allowed myself any kind of daydream, but—this was the important thing—there *is* a chance that I may live and I began to look at my situation as temporary, which I could not do before.

And yet, when asked about the outstanding events between D-Day and Liberation, my mother answered, "Nothing really changed. The only thing that might have changed was that the Germans were getting friendlier."

One of the interviewers did not quite catch my mother's meaning. "Friendly?" she mistakenly echoed.

"Friendli*er*," my mother clarified, emphasizing the last syllable. The interviewer asked how she sensed this, and she replied, "Some of them were friendlier. Some of them were friendly all along and supportive. But you can't really pinpoint this down."

That fall, my mother acted on her mother's instruction to write to Aunt Fryda in Kraków. In late November a postcard arrived from Fryda's daughter, her beloved cousin Guschinka. Her news was not good. Fryda was very ill and being treated in the hospital for typhus, pneumonia, and a weak heart. Guschinka did not expect her mother home for Christmas. "I am walking without thinking clearly, but I am still working," she added. Then she included a new address for her fiancé: Marian Puzio—34087, Block 37, Buchenwald.

Buchenwald Concentration Camp! Oh my God, I thought when I first got the postcard translated. Then I found this disclosure peculiar and inscrutable; why would Guschinka have given my mother this detailed information? And on a postcard, not an enclosed letter. Wasn't that risky? I decided that postage for a letter was too costly and disclosing that a friend was in a camp might not have been uncommon among Polish Catholics. The only explanation I could come up with for giving Marian's address at the camp was to communicate indirectly that both he and Guschinka were no longer working for the AK (Polish Resistance).

Guschinka also wrote that she had no news from her aunts. Trying to decode this prose the way my mother had when she received her parents' final letter, I interpreted it to mean that Guschinka, too, had not heard from Teofila and her sisters, Lucia and Isa. But she had heard from "Aunt Gunia," which I believe was a pseudonym for Aunt Gusta, the pediatrician my mother had stayed with in Tarnów. As she read, my mother must have savored a moment of joy that Gusta was alive, but that was dashed when Guschinka added, "Gunia cannot come to the farm since she lost Genie." I surmised from this diminutive that one of my mother's little cousins was dead. My mother had told my sisters and me that during a gun battle, Annetta peeped above a windowsill to see what was going on. "I don't know why Annetta did not stay low like she was told," my mother lamented. A sniper shot her and she sank to the floor. "It was terrible. Aunt Gusta and Olga could not move to help her." They, too, were tormented as Annetta's moans became weaker and weaker while she bled to death a few feet away. The horror of it stays with me: Aunt Gusta and Olga huddled in a corner while bullets whiz through the window and land in the pool of Annetta's blood. Because I knew Gusta and her daughters had fled to Warsaw posing as Catholics, I deduced that Annetta had died during the Warsaw Uprising.

My mother must have been filled with dread and dismay for all her aunts; back in Lwów in 1941, when my mother's parents insisted that she leave, my mother refused to go to Aunt Lucia in the Warsaw Ghetto. "I felt ghettos were for burning. I don't know why I knew it," she said in her oral history. Staying with Aunt Isa, who was in the Kraków Ghetto, was not discussed. It is possible that in the autumn of 1944 when she heard from Guschinka, my mother did not know that after the Warsaw Ghetto Uprising in April 1943, the ghetto was liquidated. But she probably heard through Radio London of the uprising of the whole city of Warsaw, which began on August 1, 1944, and lasted sixty-three days.

Some Poles hid Jews, but the Nazis exposed them during house-to-house clearances, ferreting out three hundred Jews hiding in what remained of the city. Aunt Gusta and Olga were not among them. Somehow, they fled with the 700,000 expelled Poles and escaped to a farm in central Poland. I do not know how Lucia, her husband, and their daughter Franca survived. Aunt Isa and her husband Tobek were lost, but their daughter Rena was liberated by the Jewish Brigade. In fact, she was rescued by her brother Lolek, who had gone to engineering school in Palestine and returned to Europe with the Brigade.

An operation of the Polish AK, the Warsaw Uprising was timed to coincide with the retreat of the Germans and the arrival of the Red Army, which the Poles hoped would liberate the city. Despite Churchill and Roosevelt's pleas to help the Poles, the Red Army refused to advance into Warsaw. In the meantime, the Germans regrouped and defeated the Polish Resistance. To make matters even worse, Stalin denied the Allies air clearance but after a delay they flew in anyway. By the time Warsaw fell on October 2, the Germans had destroyed 85 percent of the city.

Living alone on a farm in a Kraków suburb was taking its toll on Guschinka; nevertheless, she attempted to comfort my mother by commiserating: "I understand you well what loneliness means and counting only on yourself." Guschinka asked my mother to confide about what was bothering her. Then she apologized that she could not send twenty-ninth birthday wishes to Isa but added that "she probably feels from a distance what I (Guschinka) wish her." At first, I thought this was about Aunt Isa, but because the Kraków Ghetto was liquidated between June 1942 and March 1943, Guschinka probably already knew Isa was dead. Instead, I decided the initial "I," the first letter of my mother's real name, was paramount. Clever cousin. She had found a way to encrypt her best wishes upon my mother's approaching twentieth birthday on the 29th of November. The cipher was necessary because that date, of course, did not match the birthday of my mother's alias, Danuta Milewska.

On April 6, 1945, as American troops approached Bad Neustadt, Radio London instructed civilians to avoid railroad stations because they would be bombed. The Siemens factory was next to the tracks so the frantic slave workers sought shelter nearer the village. In her oral history, my mother commented:

> ...[we] were not allowed to go into the shelter because it was only for the Germans, which was idiotic. Across the river were already American troops. Some people had the perception that things were changing. Others had none, as is usually the case. The Liberation—the most idiotic thing that I did before Liberation was that I stayed in factory.

Initially I was surprised that my mother chastised herself for not heeding Radio London's warning. But actually, self-blame was in character; when it came to keeping a step ahead, anticipating, and strategizing, she was a perfectionist. After bombs struck and killed several workers, my mother and some friends ran from the factory across the bridge over the Franconia Saale River to Bad Neuhaus. Then they clambered up the hill to the castle. A map of the village and photos of the mount revealed a steep hike if you were fleeing from the northwest to save yourself, as they were.

"We were watching the dogfight of two planes," my mother told her interviewers.

I hear and see it now: The air is filled with the roar of two aircraft swooping and diving murderously, shooting and ducking as they fire at one another. Irena presses herself against the cool gray sandstone of the castle wall. While the planes growl at one another and the pilots ready themselves for another joust, my mother runs for cover under the arch of the main gate. The din of the swarming fighters, a series of shots—and then one plane suddenly pitches and yaws violently. Something is wrong with its wing. Is it the American plane? Or has the Yankee outwitted the Nazi? As one plane tumbles to Earth, the spectators spot the unmistakable iron cross on its wings.

And then the moment my mother had awaited for six years:

> Suddenly we looked down, and there were American tanks in Bad Neustadt. We were across the river. Absolutely unbelievable feeling. And German soldiers were fleeing.

There she stood on that hilltop literally at the precipice of freedom. Did she watch in stunned silence? Did she and her friends cheer and applaud? My mother's wartime travails, which had begun with warplanes, were ending with them.

Asked to elaborate on her feelings, my mother either could not or would not articulate them. Instead, she continued to detail events, but reaching back almost forty years and revisiting the trauma made her narrative choppy:

> It wasn't until [the]next day that I was liberated. I still tried to get to the shelter. I couldn't get in. The bridges were bombed. The Saale River is a very tiny river. And then Americans came.

Twice? *Twice* excluded from the shelter? The petty rigidity and inhumanity of the villagers shocked and galled me. But what exactly happened when my mother arrived at the shelter? Was it full or were the villagers too terrified to let anyone in? Or did the villagers turn her away because she was not one of them? According to my mother, although the Germans were about to be vanquished, they persisted in their prejudice and strict adherence to rules. She sought refuge and was barred twice. They showed total disregard for the lives of those they deemed fit only for labor. Just as her life meant nothing to Dr. Weigandt, it meant nothing to the citizens of Bad Neustadt safe in the underground shelter.

Later that day, my mother and Stasza met American troops from the Ninth Air Defense command. Again, she remarked on the incongruity of war:

> The troops that came were long-legged, they moved quickly, and luckily they were Pennsylvania troops and they spoke Polish. (She smiles.)
>
> This was the third invasion I experienced. It was very different from the Soviets who were quiet and well-informed. The brutal one of the Germans. And here were these young men completely not informed about Europe. They did not know who we were—that there was a whole cadre of displaced persons. And they became very interested because some of us spoke Polish. And of course they fed us royally. We were invited to eat in the kitchen and I was given pot roast and peaches. And one of the soldiers told me, "Look at the sloppiness, peaches with meat." I said these people have no idea what has been happening here in Europe.

My mother was surprised that, compared to other conquerors, these troops knew little about the hardship and starvation throughout Europe. With these words, her unconscious disappointment seeped through. She did not wish to state outright that the Allies' arrival was overdue, inadequate even, because she would seem ungrateful. Instead, she marveled not at the bravery of American soldiers but at their ignorance, just as she had faulted the Allies for not bombing Tarnów, and repeatedly asked why they had not destroyed the rail lines to Auschwitz. But she told me what she really felt; upon Liberation she was both elated and terribly disappointed because it was too late for her parents.

My mother returned to the Siemens camp where Russian former slave workers were celebrating by drinking wildly, especially the men. They imbibed anything in sight, my mother said, including denatured alcohol, so they went blind and berserk. "I had to escape," she told her interviewers, and again sought refuge in Bad Neuhaus where she got a room with an elderly couple in exchange for cleaning. "Back to slavery. Nothing changed."

Not long after Liberation, my mother read in a newspaper that some Jewish girls with false papers went to the U.S. government in Würzburg to regain their identities. My mother wanted her name back, too, and needed several witnesses to prove who she was. That very day my mother ran into her look-alike, Staszek Merin, strolling with Edek Nabel, whom she knew from Kraków. His wife, Krysia, had been a grade or two ahead of my mother in grammar school. As I mentioned earlier, the Nabels later became my surrogate uncle and aunt. They also had obtained false papers and worked as farm slave workers just 19 kilometers east of Bad Neustadt, but neither they nor my mother knew of each other's proximity. The Nabels agreed to help my mother prove her identity, but she needed more witnesses to certify an affidavit. It would take time.

Word quickly got around Bad Neustadt that my mother was not Danuta Milewska and was, in fact, Jewish. Most townspeople, including Toni Ress, the daughter of the liberal Hollstadt family for whom my mother had worked as a maid, were shocked. My mother stated with satisfaction:

> I remember they said, "Well, we knew that your father was an officer, and we knew you went to *gimnazjum*, but we did not know that you were Jewish," which means that my whole strategy of telling half the truth worked very well.

Still unwell and plagued by fever, my mother's priority was her health. She traveled to Würzburg where, according to her trial deposition, she was treated by a U.S. Army Medical Corps doctor named Roth.

She moved in with Thea and Willy Schaller, the relatives she had visited in June 1943 and who had recently returned to Würzburg from Dachau. The city was just beginning to recover from tremendous damage inflicted in mid-March by the Royal Air Force when a firestorm consumed the historic center and killed five thousand civilians. People were calling Würzburg "*Grab auf dem Main* (The Grave on the River Main)."

But despite that, I saw joy and recovery in post-war Würzburg photos of parties and weddings my mother attended with Thea and Willy, co-workers, and their new American friends. I recognized one man because, in my mother's overflow box of photos, he appeared in a shot with his wife and baby. Below, a short note was signed "Bob Root." I knew that Dr. Root and my mother became acquainted somewhere in Germany, that they became fast friends, and played chess. With this in mind, I reviewed my mother's trial deposition and suspected a typo—that Dr. Roth was really Dr. Root. I believe it was Captain Root who heard with his stethoscope that my mother's heart valves were damaged from nine-months of streptococcus, and that he diagnosed and treated her for rheumatic fever, possibly with penicillin, then a new and rare drug. He probably monitored her health over the next year.

On Ancestry.com I discovered that Dr. Root's original name was Rosenfeld, which he changed when he arrived in New York from Czechoslovakia via Genoa in early 1940. He had served in the 53rd General Hospital of the U.S. Army Medical Corp. Like my father, he had a medical degree from the University of Vienna Medical School, but they had just missed each other; Dr. Root graduated the year my dad arrived. I could not find the unit history of the 53rd General Hospital. Perhaps that was his last assignment and he was with another hospital in Würzburg. I was upset to discover that he died suddenly in 1954 at age forty-eight in New York City.

After my mother recovered, she worked for the U.S. Army. Because of her language skills in German, Polish, and Czech, she was with the

Denazification Department of the U.S. Military Government handling Jewish claims and requests for information.

In Würzburg, my mother fell in love with a Czech named Jan who had been a slave worker in Nuremberg. I only know of Jan because my sisters and I found a postcard from him and had it translated. Although the postcard was not overtly romantic, I vaguely remember my mother mentioning a Czech boyfriend who was not Jewish and who she had considered marrying, but offered no details. She must have announced her engagement to her relatives in New York because her cousin Vera wrote a congratulatory reply. Wistfully, Vera commented that she had not yet been lucky enough to take that step herself.

My mother pondered a career. She seriously considered staying in Germany because the Germans were financing the educations of displaced persons and she wanted to study medicine. But Jan had family in England who were encouraging him to move there. She was conflicted.

Then one day, she either received a letter from her parents' friend Dr. Robert Feldman, or he found her on a Displaced Persons List and visited. He informed her of their fates. "I knew my parents died in July 7 [1943]. At least my mother did," my mother said in her oral history. "Gestapo took my mother and [my] father disappeared. And that was all. And that I never really did get over."

The paucity of detail regarding Teofila and the lack of resolution in the case of Izydor may have made their deaths even harder to accept. Unanswerable questions arose in my mother's mind about Teofila: How could Mamusia have gone out? Why did father allow it? It was too dangerous. She looked more semitic than me. And then the endless self-blame even though her parents forced her to leave them and thereby helped save her: If I had been there, I would never have permitted my mother to go on the street....

Less certain that Izydor was dead, my mother imagined different scenarios—maybe he had not fallen to his death from that train. Maybe Ukrainian peasants had not found him and bashed in his head. Maybe Ukrainians *had* found him and *not* bashed in his head. Maybe no one found him and he died of exposure. Maybe he had jumped off the train and running along in a zigzag, dodged German and Ukrainian bullets, and ended up somewhere in Russia. Maybe. There was a chance he was still alive.

My sisters and I grew up with these lamentations.

My mother could not accept that her parents had vanished. There was no resolution, no finality.

As the extent of the atrocities and the extermination of Europe's Jews became known, my mother found it intolerable to remain in Germany. She wanted to be a physician like Aunt Gusta, yet she also wished to heed Teofila's parting instruction: "When the war is over, go to your Uncle Max in New York." Maybe the tension from being unable to reconcile these desires affected her relationship with Jan and she grew unsure of her feelings for him. She told me that he did not emigrate to England, but instead entreated her to go with him to California. In the end, she broke off their engagement. She never said why.

By January 1946, my mother was planning to emigrate to the United States. Her supervisor's letter of recommendation for political clearance stated that she had worked for six months for the U.S. Military Government, that its investigation of her statement of severe racial persecution was correct, that she performed her job in "a superior manner," and that her work and personal conduct was "of the highest type." The letter concluded by recommending her "case for application for an immigration visa."

On March 31, 1946, the U.S. Army issued a certificate declaring that my mother was born in Berlin, a Polish national, named her parents and her father's occupation, and stated that she had been a forced laborer for agriculture and confined in a labor camp. It listed her assumed name and stated that she had been issued a foreigner's passport with her real name. The witnesses were Dr. (of jurisprudence) Eduard Nabel, Krysia Nabel, Professor (of music) Willy Schaller, and the mayor of Bad Neustadt.

Having been born in Berlin, Irena Georgina Goldberger applied for a visa under the German-Jewish quota rather than the more rigorous Polish-Jewish quota. That way, she was likely to receive a visa to the United States relatively quickly. But there was trouble satisfying the authorities that she was born in Germany, as I found in a May 16, 1946, document confirming my mother's birth in Berlin and the registration number but declaring that further details could not be given "because civil status registers were relocated and had not yet come into the possession of the statute." My mother worked around the chaos and bureaucracy by requesting that Max verify her birth and the exact location. He did so in a June 14, 1946, Affidavit in lieu of a Birth Certificate, vouching that he lived in Berlin at the time of Irena Georgina Goldberger's birth, visited the mother and newborn child, and that his niece was born two months after his daughter at the same address and cared for by the same physician.

Nothing remained of the doctor's clinic at Kaiserallee 30, Berlin-Wilmersdorf, nor of my great-grandparents' apartment building at 86 Prinzeregentstrasse in the same district. Nothing. Lone and leveled Berlin. A colossal wreck, boundless and bare.

But my mother's five years masquerading as someone else had come to an end.

While awaiting her visa, my mother told Bob Root over a game of chess that she planned to join her family in New York. He, too, was hoping to return to New York soon. "When you arrive, I would like to introduce my chess partner. He's Polish, too. Right now he's the commanding officer of a U.S. Army POW hospital in France."

On her way home to the Schallers, my mother came upon a huge pile of Navy sweaters in the back of a truck that the military was giving away. It was hard to find good-quality wool—good quality anything, really. She paused before the dark, almost black, navy-blue American wool. My mother took several sweaters and had a peasant woman unravel them and knit her a new sweater.

My mother told me she instructed the woman to knit a blue and white pattern of squares across the top, from shoulder to shoulder. "I said, 'I would like you to knit it in the seed stitch.'"

"Seed stitch?"

"Yah. How do you say it in English—I mean rice stitch. Somehow chessboard pattern was on my mind," she said, still amused years later that she had sensed unconsciously then that the pattern represented something significant in the future.

My mother walked up the gangplank of the *SS Marine Perch* on July 18, 1946. One of the first liberty ships to bring Holocaust survivors to the United States, it was filled with displaced persons, mostly young, single Jewish survivors like my mother, now age twenty-one. Of the 545 Jews aboard, almost half had received support from the Joint Distribution Committee. The agency had aided them by handling immigration papers, arranging transportation, and paying for or advancing travel costs from a United Jewish Appeal $100 million fund (about $1.4 billion today). Another 275 passengers were American citizens, mostly repatriates.

The ship was sparsely outfitted—no piano, no movie projector, and no library—so the passengers had little to do but hang about, sunbathe, and gossip. Among the repatriates was a nineteen-year-old who had been visiting her aunt in Bremerhaven. The American niece spent fourteen years in Germany, most in concentration camps, and was coming home to reunite with her mother. There were sixty-five Jewish orphans, including six orphaned Polish siblings. Their mother had died of starvation and their father had succumbed to tuberculosis in a slave labor camp.

One rumor circulating throughout the ship that utterly threw my mother related directly to her eastern Poland wartime experiences. The talk was of a Ukrainian on board who was said to have led the massacre of Jews in Złoczów. This was one of the towns where my mother and grandparents had stayed while zigzagging across Galicia. I fact checked: A summertime *aktion* in which 3,000 to 4,000 Złoczów Jews were murdered shortly after the Germans invaded Soviet-occupied eastern Poland; in August and November 1942, two more waves of killing; two months later, 7,500 to 9,000 Jews from the surrounding area were concentrated in the Złoczów Ghetto, which was liquidated the following April.

In one of her college essays, my mother described her astonishment that a notorious murderer was in her midst on the *Marine Perch*. Didn't the American authorities, so thorough in my own case, check this man out, she asked. One day during the voyage, speaking in Ukrainian she engaged the man and his wife in casual conversation. They exchanged the names of the towns they originally were from. Indeed, the couple came from Złoczów.

"Oh, I know your town very well," my mother said. "We lived there for a while."

The friendly exchange halted. The startled couple looked at her with horror. My mother thought they betrayed themselves with the expression in their eyes, that they seemed petrified that she had witnessed the massacre and might recognize the man as the leader. My mother quickly backpedaled, adding that during the Soviet occupation she and her parents had left Złoczów for Lwów. The man and his wife were obviously relieved.

My mother was dismayed that "her monumental mistake in judgment" allowed her to slip into such an exchange. She had supposed that on a ship ferrying mostly survivors to the United States she was finally safe. How could she have endangered herself, she asked, berating herself for her mistake. She would not assume anything until she reached New York.

For the rest of the voyage, my mother clung to her group of survivor friends. She feared that the man, of whose guilt she was certain, would turn on her. "I was afraid he would throw me overboard and silence me forever," she wrote. My mother was so shaken she did not feel free to tell anyone about the episode. But she made a vow to herself: I will not hate this man, or any other killers, for then they win. I will not be debased by putting energy into hate. Surviving the war has been a gift. Every day I have lived since the Tarnów Ghetto has been a gift. Every future day will be a gift.

Passengers rushed to the railings, clamoring to see. Some cheered and kissed one another, others stood silently, reverently, incredulously as they saw the Statue of Liberty. Although my mother had not felt entirely safe, might never feel unscathed, she was thrilled to behold Lady Liberty welcoming her to the land of the free. The unutterable feelings of a year ago on the castle hill in Bad Neuhaus—that the cost of peace had been too high, that liberation had taken too long so as to seem almost too late—that taint finally gave way to joy. This beacon, this Mother of Exiles, as Emma Lazarus had written, was a longed-for contradiction of the ruined statue of the Ozymandias of my mother's imagination. In contrast to that symbol of the hubris of humanity, here she saw that art and literature outlasted lust for power and the destruction it spawned.

Gazing at the lantern shimmering in the sunlight, watching seagulls circling as if to bask in its glow, my mother inhales the harbor air and exhales with the deepest, most grateful sigh. It is July 26, 1946—2,519 days since she fled Kraków as a fourteen-year-old, 1,676 nights since she bade her parents farewell as she left Lwów. Her six-and-a-half-year journey was about to end, although her odyssey meant she could never return home, that she would have to find or make a new one. She had come of age as she conquered obstacles along her wartime path, had mastered her doubts and agitation with the help of her father's coaching from afar. Now she was fulfilling her mother's final instructions. She had made it. The New York skyline beckoned.

Chapter Thirty-Four

Dachau

On March 28, 1945, my father's Company left Verviers for Ober-Olm, near Mainz, Germany, to set up and run an air evacuation holding unit with the 28th Field Hospital. Near Bingen, the lead vehicle of the convoy made a wrong turn. Suddenly, enemy shellfire struck, launched by a German pocket of resistance on the east bank of the Rhine. Everyone ran for cover in trenches and ditches along a road parallel to the river. For two hours, my father and his cohort covered their ears and crouched and shook with each hit. Luckily no one was wounded and they continued on to Ober-Olm, where they set up a three-hundred-bed hospital and began accepting patients.

A week later, the Company and hospital were again on the road bound for Herzogenaurach, near Nuremberg. On the way, the convoy passed Würzburg a few weeks before my soon-to-be-liberated mother would move there to live with Thea and Willy. Senseless tragedy struck when a jeep in the convoy had an accident and a captain died in the collision.

While mourning their colleague, the Company set up a holding hospital in a field despite a shortage of vehicles, men hauling gravel for the roads amid torrential rainfall. Many patients were Allied soldiers—newly released prisoners of war. Gaunt and lice-infested, they described horrific conditions in the POW camps. It was just the beginning of the appalling stories the Company would hear.

The end of April and early May brought momentous political and military news: Hitler had taken his own life and the Seventh Army had liberated the concentration camp called Dachau. The threat of raging epidemics among the 32,432 former prisoners was so great that the camp was quarantined. The 116th and 127th Evacuation Hospitals tried to treat the infected, but a Typhus Commission called for thirty inoculating teams to control the scourge. My mother told me my father had been to Dachau so I assume he responded to the call out of duty and altruism, and to search for Milek.

When confronted by the cynicism of the slogan on the iron gate, "*Arbeit macht frei* (Work will set you free)," my father might have been bewildered at first and unable to fully absorb the implications. The saying had been familiar to German-speaking people since 1873 when the German Nationalist and linguist, Lorenz Diefenbach, had coined the phrase in a novel.

It soon became clear that German and Austrian Nazi physicians had conducted painful and often deadly experiments on thousands of prisoners. One "researcher" was my father's former professor of internal medicine, Hans Eppinger, the liar and kleptomaniac who had treated Stalin. His experiment derived from a dispute over how best to make seawater potable, with Eppinger arguing that either the kidneys would adapt, or the concentrated salts would be expelled in urine. Eppinger and Eduard Pernkopf, the Nazi Dean of the Medical School, wanted to reward a colleague, Wilhelm Beiglböck, for serving on the Eastern Front and in Dachau while continuing to publish. Aggressive experiments were a way to climb the professional ladder, so Eppinger appointed Beiglböck to test desalination techniques on ninety Romani prisoners. The purpose? To determine whether prisoners would suffer severe physical symptoms or death within six to twelve days. Forced to drink only seawater, the prisoners suffered such severe dehydration that they licked the floors they had mopped.

The fearful German POWs my father had treated in England after D-Day must have known what their compatriots were up to. But my father was wrong about the victims; they were helpless civilians, not Allied POWs.

Hundreds of prisoners died or were permanently disabled by these experiments. The Nazis had stated in 1938 their intentions for medical science and practice, and yet what they had implemented was beyond any sane imagination. My father no doubt understood the bigoted intent of the University of Vienna administrators and that the Nazis would link racist theory with science, but neither he nor any of his colleagues anticipated that German and Austrian doctors would go this far, violating the Hippocratic Oath and sinking so low.

What went through my father's mind as he left the camp and passed through the gates for the last time? "*Arbeit macht frei*" was not that different from Virgil's "*Labor omnia vincit* (Work overcomes all)." The fact that my dad taught us Virgil's version reveals his resolve to not permit the Nazis to co-opt or pollute a motto that had given him courage; it nurtured the perseverance that had enabled him to survive before, during, and after the *Anschluss* so that he could heal those the Reich had abused.

Devastated by the conditions of the former prisoners and what he imagined had happened to his brother, perhaps my father was thankful for the first time that his mother had not met such a fate. Surely, all my father saw left him deeply sorrowful. I can only conclude that he was so horrified, so chilled by the experience that he did not talk for days afterward, and during that interval resolved never, ever to discuss it. For it was unspeakable.

Back in Herzogenaurach, my father continued searching for Milek on Red Cross lists and in displaced persons camps and wrote to authorities asking for information. All for naught.

Company C remained in southern Germany until late July, finally moving north again through Würzburg—where my mother was now living and working for the U.S. Army—to Haimbach. In the stifling heat, the staff of the Company packed up their equipment—supplies for forty men and cars for personnel—to return to France by rail. My father looks frankly into the camera lens as he and his buddies pause for a smoke before their train starts its journey west. Surely, slouching in his white undershirt and slacks, legs dangling from a boxcar, the appalling incongruity of this manner of travel from Germany does not escape my father.

At Camp Sissone, my father received another letter from his father in German, which I had translated.

> Rehovoth, July 10, 1945
>
> Lieber Sohn!
>
> I received your letter of May 15 today. I am glad that you typed the letter because that way I can read it myself. My dear son, first of all I would like to congratulate you on your becoming an uncle to your niece Mechla [a reference to my cousin, Anita Michaela Frankel]. *I hope I will see you happy. Amen.* I am very sorry that up to now you have not received a sign of life from our dear Milek. I am upset about it. Who knows what happened to him. Let us hope he may live somewhere in Germany or Russia. Dear son, I am sorry that I have to give you bad news about the problem I have with my right ear. I suffer from headaches, dizziness, and have consulted a doctor for diagnosis. Everybody agrees that I need an operation, but I will not make a decision in a hurry. But if not, I might die in a short time, since my leg is in bad shape. I told my doctor that I would undergo surgery under the condition that you would assist. I do not know how the outcome if it will be. So my dear son, if you wish to help me with my problem, you will have to ask your Mr. Commandant to grant you a leave, so that you will come and visit me. Should that not be possible, I am telling you that I would rather die than have the operation without your presence. I enclose a letter from my family doctor and emphasize that you can tell your Mr. Commandant that I am out of 130,000 people the only one who was able to survive from the German tyranny. I hope that your Mr. Commandant is also a

> father and will have pity on me and grant you a leave. I thank him in advance.
>
> I send you greetings and kiss you.
>
> Dein Vater

After my father finished reading, he probably felt it best that they be alone when reunited. Even though in a moment of brash happiness he had invited Mollie to join him, he realized that he and his father would need time to mourn together, to experience their sorrow in private without concern for anyone else's needs. Clearly, Ojzer was in too much distress, both emotionally and physically, to meet Mollie. My father wrote her that he very much hoped they would visit Palestine together "some other time."

Chapter Thirty-Five

Un Château

In the 12th-century, a crusader named Hélon Villers built a Templar (knights' Safe House) with a stream behind it, and a church at a crossroads in Picardy. Near Soissons and not far from Paris, Villers "Monsiegneur" Hélon's Templar eventually became a château and the church attracted inhabitants. By the next century, a village was established in the founder's name. Over the centuries, several lines of aristocrats owned the château and surrounding acres; family members of the owner during the French Revolution were executed. The grounds were then sold off and the château turned into a shoe factory. A banker bought it in the late 19th century and a general acquired it before the century turned. The property became a billet for German soldiers in the First World War. During this war, the Nazis imprisoned French POWs there. When they had free time, the superior Aryans lounged in the property's caves and scribbled cartoon-like drawings depicting German fairy tales and fantasies on the stone walls.

It was to Villers-Hélon, with its extraordinary château 62 miles northeast of Paris, that my father arrived in August 1945 as a captain and the new commander of a six-hundred-bed POW hospital.

As with my father's entire tour of duty, I knew nothing of his experience commanding the POW hospital. A typo on my father's résumé stymied my search of the Station Hospital until I found two photos taken in France that my father could label because the war had ended. In the first, my father kneels and caresses a puppy. To the left is a wooden structure and in the background stand trees. On the back of the print I read, "David and Duke, Villers-Herlon [sic], France September 1945." On the back of the second shot my father had written, "David in a group of officers, 8278th Station Hospital." The number on my father's résumé was off by two digits!

Google corrected the name of the village Villers-Hélon and I found myself virtually wandering through the medieval hamlet. The only two structures that could have accommodated six hundred patients were the château and the *pigeonnier*, or dovecote. I assumed that the U.S. Army had requisitioned the château for my father's POW hospital, or that it was a tent hospital in a field. The dovecote seemed unlikely; it probably did not have a roof, but I could not tell for sure because its wooden gates were locked shut.

Then I found several old postcards of the château and learned that an early 19th-century owner was the godfather of Alexandre Dumas. A perfect excuse for a detour to read about the great author's life and visits to the château on the other side of the forest from his home in Villers-Cotterêts.

The most recent owner, the late entrepreneur Anthony C. Tirri, had written a book about the château's history and restoration, titled *History of the Chateau de Villers-Helon and its Return to Splendor*. I was correct about its role in WWII:

> The Chateau was used from 1940 through 1945 as a field headquarters...When the Germans retreated in 1944, they, following military protocol of not leaving cover for the advancing troops, destroyed a portion of the west wing of the Chateau and tossed a grenade into the living room.

In the ancient stone walls surrounding the Château they installed rifle ports. Before the Nazis left, they stripped the Château of valuables including furniture and paintings by the 18th-century French romantic artist Hubert Robert. From the dining room walls they peeled off three of his murals. Also an architect, Robert had designed the garden in the

1790s. Today his works grace the galleries of the world's finest museums, including the Louvre. Hopefully art historians active in art restitution are investigating what happened to the ones the Germans stole.

When the Americans arrived in Villers-Hélon, they requisitioned the château and continued to use it as a military headquarters, hospital, and prisoner of war camp. On the grounds they poured twenty-four concrete pads for tents and showers.

How many people have fathers who treated the vanquished enemy in a French medieval castle? I'll never know what my father felt as he tended to German soldiers, knowing what had happened to his mother. Was the experience fraught with ambivalence for him? I found the record of a POW of my father's generation, a doctor from Weimar who I believed would have been a grateful patient. But I had dark thoughts about others for whom the war would never be over, like a Hitler Youth who didn't want to be touched by a Jew.

When not treating patients, there would have been little to do in this beautiful, feudal village, where the only other buildings besides the château, dovecote, and church were a town hall and school. An important resource in olden days, birds were valued for their eggs, flesh, and dung, and a dovecote symbolized status and power, a privilege regulated by law and granted only to noblemen.

My father walks along the main street toward the 16th-century lime and sandstone dovecote. The building seems abandoned, nevertheless David envisions it filled with birds. Pigeons that even Jews can own now that Hitler has been defeated. My dad sends an imaginary winged emissary to bring a message of love and hope to Milek, wherever he is. A dispatch soul to soul.

Chapter Thirty-Six

A Reunion and a Kibbutz

In mid-September 1945, my father got his furlough and flew from Paris to Palestine with twenty other U.S. servicemen making pilgrimages to the Holy Land. After landing at the large British airport near Lydda, now Lod, he went straight to Tel-Aviv. On the beautiful drive into the city, he watched low hills with their stubby edge-of-the-desert trees turn into Judean hills dotted with Arab villages.

It is hard for me to imagine the reunification of my father and grandfather after six years of trauma and loss. Judging by the expression on my father's face in a photo taken in Palestine, it must have been difficult. He looked very hurt and older than a man of thirty-two, who ordinarily would have had everything to look forward to. My father had lost the parent he favored and his relationship with Ojzer was sometimes contentious. In later letters to my parents, Ojzer states that his sons were the impetus for his survival. Not wanting to "burden him, the victim," my uncle Sydney said he did not ask questions; instead, he listened to whatever Ojzer wished him to know. I suppose my father did the same. Yet any imagined scenario of the first meeting of these two suffering men seems presumptuous.

I do think my grandfather would have described his triumphant trek from Lwów through the Carpathian Mountains to Hungary, though, for we are the heroes of our own stories, as my therapist sister

Ivy says. Sitting in the kitchen of his Tel-Aviv apartment, Ojzer may have narrated his tale to my father this way:

"On a good night, I walked 12 kilometers. Sometimes I had the help of a guide, sometimes not. There were many close calls—some peasants I lined up to give me food and shelter backed out in the last minute. I was lucky if I found a cave where I could sleep during the day. That winter of '43 to '44, I made it through three blizzards, *cholera jasne* (a plague upon it all). One night a snow-laden tree collapsed and nearly crushed me. Many times I was pursued. But here I am."

My father had hiked the Carpathians as a boy. He knew the terrain could be very rough—troughs carpeted with stone fields especially treacherous to traverse at night, not to mention sudden blizzards in the freezing winter. Who knows how many enemy soldiers and wolves Ojzer, son of Leiser, flax merchant and wolf strangler of Busk, encountered and thwarted?

By late February of 1944, Ojzer crossed the Polish-Hungarian frontier and at dawn overlooked the Tysa Lowlands. No longer a nocturnal, hunted, wandering Jew he walked to Budapest during the day and slept at night, like a normal human being.

Ojzer made it to Budapest by early spring 1944 just when the Germans invaded Hungary, formerly an ally, and proceeded to murder its Jews. Ojzer fled again and eventually made his way to Romania's coast on the Black Sea. Perhaps along the way he met his second wife, Francesca, but she was never included in the subsequent narrative my mother shared with us.

"I was standing on a dock in Constanza with a thousand other Jewish refugees," he tells my father, "including three hundred orphans. It was the night of August 3, 1944. I had a ticket for the *Mefkura*, a small, rickety, Turkish motor schooner. Everyone was weary. Mossad agents and the Zionist Organization in Romania organized the charter. There were two other ships, the *Bulbul* and the *Morina*."

"Were they any better?" asks my father.

"The vessels had been refitted. Various middlemen—dockworkers, Romanian undersecretaries—everyone was paid off. So much money they got. And somehow the boats were not equipped with sextants."

"Not even proper navigation instruments!"

Ojzer nods. "I heard the *Mefkura* was in such bad shape the insurance company only covered her for war risks, not sea risks. Anyway, people were exhausted by the anticipation and uncertainty of the voyage. Turkey had just stopped dealing with the Nazis. They already were disrupting Turkish shipping on the Black Sea. Everyone was scared to death they would block our passage.

"I am standing on that dock. Everyone is so tense. I see a woman with three pale children aged about five, seven, and nine." He pauses and closes his eyes. "She is crying to her sister about being one ticket short." Ojzer's voice falters. "'I can't possibly abandon one of my darlings to save two,' she says. 'I can't imagine staying here either. Surely we will all perish.' Now her sister is hysterical, too, and says she'll stay behind. I'm listening to this and thinking I must do something." Ojzer opens his eyes and looks into my father's. "It was too much for me. I gave her my ticket."

"Oh *Vater*," my father says with a mixture of admiration and pain. "But what about you?"

"She was such a lady, such a *mensch*, she asked me that, too. I just said, 'I'll make my way.' I got a spot on the *Morina*. At midnight the second night, some unknown boat, maybe a submarine, ordered the *BulBul* to halt. The captain identified her and she was allowed to pass. But I heard later the *Mefkura* captain wouldn't say who she was. All of a sudden, a flare lit up the *Mefkura*'s deck. Her captain shouted to the passengers to put on lifejackets. But before they could, the other vessel fired on her. She split in two."

The *Bulbul* passengers told him later they wanted the crew to lower the lifeboat, but there was a scuffle. Nobody spoke Turkish and the captain thought they wanted to seize the lifeboat. The *Bulbul*'s passengers could hear cries for help as the *Mefkura*'s passengers struggled in the freezing water. "But the captain of the *Bulbul* waited. We on the *Morina* were too far ahead to hear, but a *Bulbul* passenger thought he heard shouting in German from the attacker's deck. We were seething when we learned the *Mefkura* sank."

According to news reports and Jewish JOINT Distribution Committee records, the *Bulbul* finally steamed back to rescue survivors and picked up five of the *Mefkura*'s 379 passengers. "Only *five*. Including a pregnant woman and her husband, both champion swimmers who had been in the water for five hours," Ojzer said. "Another was a teenage girl who said she had heard Germans in the attack boat taunting drowning survivors saying, 'Look at the Jews who are swimming to Palestine.'"

As they were helped aboard, the *Bulbul*'s passengers rushed to the captain and beseeched him to extend the search. He would not. They gestured to lower the lifeboat again.

"I am thinking, *The mother and her three children must have survived. They had to have survived*," Ojzer tells my father and looks blankly at him. "And then I wanted to know what kind of monster is this man? And I asked God what would have satisfied Him. What?" Ojzer raises his hands toward heaven. "Why? Why was my *mitzvah* not enough? Why not at least those three children? And their lovely mother." He sobs uncontrollably. "Their beautiful, wonderful mother."

And my father knows what Ojzer really means: What about the darling mother of *my* children?

As the *Bulbul* and the *Morina* entered the Bosphorus, a squall prevented the *Bulbul* from sailing into Istanbul's harbor and the *Morina* arrived alone. The *Bulbul* hugged Turkey's southwestern coast and dropped anchor in the remote port of Igneada. JOINT rushed food and supplies to the seaside village. It arranged for the *Bulbul*'s passengers to travel over the mountains on ninety carts, each drawn by two oxen, to a town called Vize.

JOINT also sent workers to help. One commented to some women that they seemed calm after having witnessed such a catastrophe. A woman in her twenties responded that she had grown tough, really tough. "Violent death has become familiar and therefore is no longer frightening," added another. An older woman remarked, "Hitler taught us to die without noise."

From Vize the *Bulbul* survivors traveled in trucks to Çerkezköy, a small city 105 kilometers west of Istanbul. As they were about to board a train to Istanbul, passengers were asked for their passports. The previous calm erupted into anxiety. In their panic, they forgot they were no longer in German-occupied Europe where no papers meant extermination. But the Turkish authorities allowed them to board the train without incident.

Although safe in Istanbul, Ojzer must have suffered from flashbacks of the calamity at sea; again and again in his mind's eye, artillery shells split and lit up the water, pink and red and orange with destruction. If he slept, he would have awakened feeling like he was suffocating as his lungs filled with saltwater. Or maybe he saw the faces of the woman's three children sinking, arms outstretched, the youngest taking on Milek's features and disappearing into the infinite.

From Istanbul, the survivors traveled either by rail or by foot to Palestine. Whichever way Ojzer got to the Promised Land, he arrived on August 14 only to be detained near Haifa in Camp Atlit, a holding pen for illegal refugees. The British Mandate for Palestine established the 25-acre detention camp at the end of the 1930s to prevent Jewish refugees from entering Palestine. Between 1934 and 1948, 222,000 Jewish immigrants were interned there surrounded by barbed wire and watchtowers. They became known as "*Ma'apilim*," or illegal immigrants.

Ma'apilim Ojzer Fränkel passed through the disinfection barracks. From one of the one hundred housing barracks he would have sent word through the guards to notify his niece, Golda, where he was. She must immediately have arranged for his release because two weeks later he went to the Polish Consulate in Tel Aviv which replaced his lost Polish passport.

His passport photo, scotch-taped to the torn and taped-together document, shows how gaunt Ojzer was. Gone was the paunch; he had lost more hair, and darkness ringed his eyes. He still sported a mustache, although it was grayer. Yet I admired my grandfather's vigor, his astuteness, his energy at age fifty-seven. I have no idea how, why, or when my grandfather's second marriage dissolved, but I do believe my father was glad Ojzer found Rifka, his third wife and our step-grandmother, of whom we were so fond. I think my father was grateful Grandpa Ojzer was not alone, did not resent his stepmother, and sensed she would tend to Ojzer's needs.

I conjure Ojzer and my dad sitting on the Tel-Aviv apartment's chunky, art deco balcony, so unlike the filigree ones in Lwów. The conversation turns to women. Maybe Ojzer asks, "Nu? Anyone special in your life?" My father tells him that the detective and Sydney have obtained proof of Rose and Joe's adultery and so now he has a way to escape her thrall. Perhaps my father also admits he and Mollie seem out of sync; something is amiss that disturbs him.

"If it is not right, it is not right. You will know when you have found your *bashert* (your intended)," Ojzer states reassuringly. He applauds my father's strategy to shed his sham marriage and pooh-poohs any concerns my father might have about his eligibility as a divorced refugee. Ojzer points out that with so many young men lost, plenty of women will accept a good-looking, divorced young doctor who wishes to marry again. "Remember the monster we both faced down," he says, "and that you are a war hero."

In demonstrating his contentment in his third marriage, Ojzer encouraged my father by example. Ojzer's joy at becoming a grandfather was obvious in the way he scrutinized the photos Sydney sent, how touched he was that the baby was named for his late wife, and his blessing in his letter that my father, too, should be happy. But was my father ready? Did Ozjer underscore what my father felt—desire to start afresh, to rebuild the fractured family with a family of his own? My father knew how a doting husband behaved—he had only to observe his father. Did my father admit to himself that he wanted children who would adore their mother the way he and his brothers had adored Michaela?

My father would have understood that Ojzer's medical conditions and percolating anxieties about them were the cost of the physical and emotional stress he had endured. Although I believe he tolerated the patriarchal tone of his father's letters and was used to his Hapsburgian requirement of filial obedience, I do not think my father appreciated it. Based on how he raised my sisters and me, he felt the approach outdated and unnecessary. But given how he looked after Ojzer when he became ill ten years later in New York, visiting him in the hospice and making sure he received good care, I'm sure my father was and always had been a dutiful son. However, his subtlety, tact, and affection suggest that he emulated his mother's parental style. He might have been a little ashamed of Ojzer's insistence and pushiness in writing often to American authorities. There was no way to know whether Ojzer's letters had even moved the military's bureaucracy and accelerated authorization of my father's furlough. On the other hand, my father might have concluded that if pushing the system had helped his father endure the wait, then it was worth it.

I envision my father in a waiting room while Ojzer is in recovery. Seeing a rabbi pass by, my father catches up and approaches the learned man, introduces himself, and explains his visit to Palestine. He asks a question about Milek that has plagued him since *Yom Kippur*.

"Rabbi, if we have not given up hope and do not recite *Kaddish* on his behalf, is that right, if in fact he is gone? And if he lives, but we never discover where, should we still pray for him?"

The rabbi explains that *halakhah* (Jewish law) emphasizes the importance of being absolutely certain a person has died before observing mourning rituals. But *halakhah* also asks that the families of the missing maintain hope that they will return.

"How long should we hope?"

Without a recovered body, the rabbi says, the family would normally seek an eyewitness to the death. But in this case, as it is unlikely a witness can be found, mourning could begin when the family gives up hope of recovering the body.

There was, as yet in 1945, neither a *Yom Ha'Shoah* (Holocaust Memorial Day) nor the more recent *Yom Hakaddish* (prayer in remembrance of Holocaust victims whose exact date of death is unknown), nor general *Kaddish* day, on the tenth day of the month of Tevet.

My father, not yet ready to give up, would still have had hope.

Assured that after his surgery Ojzer was convalescing as expected, my father saw some sites and visited a kibbutz called Givat Brenner, just south of Rehovot. There he and some army buddies met the United States Senator from Florida, Claude Pepper. A staunch New Dealer and a liberal, the senator looked favorably upon social democratic experiments in Europe like those in Red Vienna, earning him the friendly nickname "Red Pepper." During the pre-Cold War period of the 1930s and until the mid-1940s, such views were not unusual because of the United States' alliance with the Soviet Union. American liberalism espoused the "Four Freedoms"—Freedom of Speech, Freedom of Worship, Freedom from Want, and Freedom from Fear—while simultaneously working toward more equal distribution of wealth and greater opportunity for the underprivileged. The Depression and the war allowed the Roosevelt administration to experiment with leftist ideas without being associated with totalitarianism.

Pepper's purpose in traveling to the Middle East in late summer 1945 was to renew trade between the United States and the region. It was fitting that he took an interest in kibbutzim and Givat Brenner, in particular. Founded in 1928 by pioneers from Italy and Lithuania, the kibbutz was one of the oldest and most innovative in Palestine. In 1938 it opened the first kibbutz tuberculosis sanatorium and a vegetarian convalescent home. During the war it supplied the British armed forces with jam. Now this kibbutz was home to over one thousand people.

My father was invited to join the senator and his aides for tea, perhaps because he was a doctor. The senator shared what he had learned in his earlier interviews of *sabra* and refugee children. He thought it interesting that all children from infancy lived in their own quarters attended by nurses. When parents returned from work, he said, they visited their children, but the children slept separately with their small group.

My father saved three photographs with the senator, his entourage, and himself sipping tea. In a fourth photo, in the Claude Pepper collection at Florida State University's library, my father strides with them through the kibbutz's newly plowed farm fields. While Palestine and its kibbutzim modeled on socialism and Zionism had some attractive features, my father knew he was not a Zionist and not a pioneer. Although Palestine fascinated him, he remained a diaspora assimilationist. He had experienced enough hardship and had fought for the United States. Now he wanted to enjoy the rewards it offered.

After two weeks, his furlough was over. In my mind's eye, Ojzer presses his gold watch into his son's palm—much as he did the pouch of diamonds six years earlier in Lwów when they parted.

When my father returned to the hospital at Villers-Hélon in October, a nurse handed him a letter from Mollie. She chastised him for having invited her to Palestine and changing his mind. "You should not make such rash promises, which you can't keep," she wrote in her letter. The next paragraph was about Rose, whose mother was critically ill and in a hospital. But somehow Mollie learned that gangster Joe's wife had caught up with him and Rose and "they had it out."

Mollie closed with snarky references to my father's good looks and jealously suggested that he was a Casanova who, en route to Palestine via Paris, had pleased many French ladies. Maybe she was right. Or maybe my father, displeased by her flippant, angry tone, concluded they had been parrying for too long. When it's right, you know it's right.

In January 1946, my father returned to the States and mustered out of the Army at Fort Dix, N.J. But he faced another fight; armed with evidence gathered by his detective and Sydney, my father's lawyer began to negotiate his divorce from Rose.

Meanwhile, having seen so much destruction and death during the war, my father decided to switch specialties. Despite his successful start in pathology and having co-authored in 1944 a second paper on lipoid pneumonia, he wanted to do something inherently positive that was not always directly linked to disease. As an intern, when he had first assisted a birth in the delivery room at Unity Hospital, he had been in awe of the miracle of life. Training to become an obstetrician and gynecologist would further delay opening a practice, but he knew it was the right choice. He got a preceptorship in obstetrics and gynecology at Unity Hospital and began attending courses at Columbia Physicians and Surgeons. He was thrilled to have a found a mentor, Dr. Samuel L. Siegler, an obstetrician and gynecologist. An expert on infertility and an attending at Unity and Brooklyn Women's Hospital on Eastern Parkway, he was also the founder of the International Fertility Association and the New York Fertility Society. My father was proud to be affiliated with someone of his stature.

In July my father and Rose's divorce was finalized in Dade County, FL. He flew home, unfettered.

At the same time, my mother was on a Liberty ship, approaching New York City.

Chapter Thirty-Seven

Chez Éclair

On the top shelf of my office closet I had for many years stored a metal lock box in which my father kept cash that patients with no bank accounts had paid him for his services. In one box were two unlabeled audio cassettes my mother had saved. One preserved a medical school lecture my father had presented about a surgical technique he had devised. I vaguely remembered that the other tape was more personal so I had never listened to the entire recording.

In 2020, Ed and I bought a vintage cassette player so that after fifty years I could once again hear my father's voice. Finally, I would be privy to the story I had been too shy to ask about as a five-year-old standing by my father's hospital bed. The mystery cassette contained the beginning of an unfinished novel he had dictated into his Norelco recorder while recovering from one of his back surgeries. To pass the time, my doped-up dad recounted the memories of an ailing protagonist whose mind meanders back to 1947, when he was thirty-three years old and full of life. He is about to enter a café with his friend George where they are to meet a young lady. Refugees from Central Europe frequented a pastry shop, which he described as "a poor imitation of a Viennese café." In the back were "marble tabletops, straight chairs, but the cakes looked delicious." As my father dictated into his novel-in-progress:

> I felt, "Let's see now who I am going to marry." I thought it was all a joke when George told me about

> her. But he was so convincing. He said, "Yes, you will. You'll see. You will. She's beautiful. She's fine."

The café was Éclair on West 72nd Street, which a Czech refugee opened in 1939. The characters are, of course, thinly disguised stand-ins for my parents. Their mutual friend, George, is Captain Robert Root, my father's chess partner and the U.S. Army doctor who treated my mother in Würzburg. He was also my father's Brooklyn roommate, somewhat older, and much more serious. They often played chess surrounded by beautiful roses and hedges in the garden of the large hospital where they were both interns. The stone benches weren't very comfortable, but good enough, my dad had dictated and then continued:

> We got everything we wanted—tranquility, chess, sunshine, and fresh air. We could concentrate on the big game. Patients came down for walks and paraded past in their pajamas.... While waiting to meet George near the café, I glanced at my golden watch given me by my father some years ago. I knew it was not quite accurate but I looked at it just the same, adding or subtracting the minutes so as to approximate the time. But I wouldn't part with it. I'm used to it. A good watch. A fine companion. It is nearly timeless. Literally timeless. It does not keep good time.
>
> She sat at the table somewhat slumped. She was new in this country. She looked around and I guess she expected me. But did she? I caught her eye. I caught her glimpse and our eyes met. It must have been some time before I took my eyes off her because she blanched and then she rouged a bit, lowered her long eyelashes, as if saying, "Well...."
>
> George and I approached and he introduced us. I made a stupid remark, like, "How do you like this country?" Or, "How long have you been here?" She didn't

> understand a word I was saying. She smiled and looked at my tie, my face, my light gray suit. I thought, *I know what you are thinking about*: "So that's the fellow, is it?" What does a girl think when she meets a fellow the first time? The introduction. Does she think, "Where will this lead?" Or does she think that at all?
>
> I had not much in mind at the time. I was go lucky, like a butterfly jumping from flower to flower. Was this one of the flowers? Was I to be stuck, or was I to be caught? Chained. Well, I was caught. Caught I was. I was caught, but I never did regret it.

My mother's version of the fix up was quite different and terse: "I took one look at your father and said to myself, 'He'll do.'" My mother paused. "When he asked to see me every Saturday night, I said, 'You can have every other Saturday night.'" She tilted her head back and smiled a little, mocking her own hauteur.

"What did he say?" my sisters and I wanted to know.

"He didn't like it."

I pictured the alluring, mysterious coquette she had been. "But weren't you worried he would find someone else?" I was in early adolescence.

"I wanted *him* to worry that *I* would."

Certainly in life, as in chess, you must think several moves ahead, my mother was teaching me. Yet she also knew that life and love are fragile and full of serendipity. Years later, she said that when my father smiled—the most charming, winning smile as they sat across one another—she felt very much at ease. Somehow he seemed familiar, though then she did not know why. She told me she realized much later that my father had the same smile as her mother, my grandmother Teofila. She said that I, too, have that smile.

My mother added that throughout their courtship my father insisted on speaking English, which she was only just learning. "He did most of the talking. So your father had no idea who he had married." She did not think he appreciated her intelligence and abilities until later, revealing his admiration for and reliance on her when they went to the theater, for example, by asking her interpretation of the play.

She did not elaborate on the small talk that evening when they first met. So I fill it in: They shared their love of music, the opera houses in Kraków and Lwów, and their favorite museums. My father, a Dodgers fan, would have been eager to introduce my mother to American culture and pastimes.

"Have you been to a baseball game yet?"

"This game with stick?" she asks. "No, not yet."

He might have told her about the impressive Diego Rivera murals in Mexico City and the beauty of the countryside during his trip from Veracruz to the bustling metropolis in the early summer of 1939. My mother must have realized that he was there during the invasion of Poland and could not get much news. She always told us she felt that it might have been a little easier to be in the thick of things than to be tormented by vast distance, other peoples' accounts, and one's imagination.

Had she asked about his relatives' survival, he would have described how his father made his way to Palestine and had just opened an appliance store in Tel-Aviv, noting that demand for appliances will increase as the population grows. Remarking on his father's business savvy, he adds, "During the war he was resourceful in ways others did not think of." Even during the Soviet Occupation of Lwów, my father says his father had managed quite well as the buyer for a supermarket co-op, Food Factory Number 4.

How interesting life is! Here before me is the son of the practical man I had hoped Father would emulate so that we could eat better. "I believe our fathers knew one another," says my mother, adding that Izydor was the assistant bookkeeper at the same co-op. My father, too, is struck by the coincidence.

"If I had stayed, we surely would have met," he says somberly.

The conversation repeatedly returns to family. Two generations ago both their families were very large—so many great-aunts and uncles, so many cousins, my mother states. "But my parents chose to have only one child. It was fashionable then." Whereas throughout her childhood she had longed for a sibling, during the war my mother counted it a blessing not to have had one; she did not think she could have withstood the pain of losing a brother or a sister. Now, in peacetime, she wants to have several children so they can play together and keep each other company as they get older. "It's important for children to have siblings," she says in Polish. "At least two."

Yes, if something happens to one, my father thinks, the remaining two will have each other. "Many of my army friends want to rebuild their lives and have families."

"*Tak, życie musi iść dalej* (Yes, life must go on)." *Nektar życia jest słodki tylko wtedy, gdy dzieli się z innymi.*" She is quoting Adam Mickiewicz, the greatest Polish poet of the 19th-century.

"In English we would say, 'The nectar of life is sweet only when shared with others.'"

In the subway my father speeds from Washington Heights toward Crown Heights, Brooklyn. His watch shows that about three hours have passed since he and my mother met and just thirty minutes since they parted. Alluring Irena, with her jade green eyes that matched her dress, which showed off her soft contours. Refined, intelligent, elusive Irena. Is she my *bashert*? When will I know?

Sitting in her aunt and uncle's apartment, my mother continues to think a step ahead—as she did to survive, and as my father had done to escape Europe. Bob had told her David was divorced and twelve years older. No matter. She understood the impossible risks and choices one had to make. He was attractive, already established, sophisticated and worldly. The stigma back then of divorce was of no concern.

Still in the subway, my father again checks his unreliable watch and thinks of Irena, this time with certainty. There is no more time lose. Finally, after years of struggle, it is their moment. *Never mind butterflies and flowers*, he tells himself. *Soon we will savor the nectar of life together.*

For a while.

Epilogue

David and Irena's marriage lasted twenty-three years. It was a good marriage with the usual day-to-day ups and downs, but atypical because of the trauma and the enormous losses they suffered. There was constant illness, in large part due to stifled sorrow and untreated post-traumatic stress disorder. Although my parents were the lucky ones, they did not escape strains that truncated their lives and denied them the longevity they might have enjoyed had they lived during peaceful times.

Both my parents played chess throughout their lives, just as they jousted courageously during the war. For my father chess was a distraction from the chaos and danger he faced day-to-day in medical school, and later became a way to relax between treating patients. He used bold strategic planning to get out of Europe, taking the formidable risk of marrying Rose in haste. A wartime photo shows my father and other medical officers in a forest leaning over a table, perhaps mapping the layout of one of their many field hospitals. No doubt Dad was thinking many steps ahead about all the options. On the other hand, given his sense of humor, my father may have been posing as a general pretending to discuss future tactical maneuvers of his next campaign. My mom, too, lived by her wits: her audacious escape from the Tarnów Ghetto; the risk she would not take by asking for medical treatment; the risk she took to request a transfer to Siemens when the timing was right. All these moves rested on preparing for the right moment, evading danger, and taking the chance that she would be overlooked by the enemy.

Even though my mother played chess far less often than my father, chess was an essential link and played an important role in their meeting. They had in common my father's chess partner and respect for the skills of the game. It seems fitting that although very much alone on the board after the war, they met and married in America to start new lives. They were a strong team. Their understanding of one another's losses as remnants of European Jewry did not have to be articulated. It was a good match.

I have always admired both my parents for their extraordinary resilience, but in writing this memoir, I came to appreciate these qualities even more. Discovering the historical specifics of what they endured enabled me to use my imagination to envision their experiences: my father playing ball after school in the nearby park then scampering home, my mother hiking Zakopane or ambling in the Planty with her parents and Arko, Teofila completing a needlepoint clutch bag that Sara saved, or my grandmother Michaela gazing at her street from her filigree balcony. And yet, despite trauma, loss, and the burden of survival, my parents were able to love, enjoy life, and create a happy home. My sisters and I felt deeply cherished. My parents tried to recreate a semblance of extended family by welcoming any surviving relatives, and close friends who became adopted relatives, to our home for visits short and long.

There are many kinds of resistance, as I hope this book shows. My mother's decision to walk out of the Tarnów Ghetto expecting to be shot was such an act. The suicide of my grandmother Michaela was her final expression of free will; by deciding for herself how to die, she resisted. My grandparents Izydor and Teofila resisted by parting with their only child to save her, and then with their letters emotionally supporting her from afar. My father resisted by fleeing and returning to fight in the European Theater.

That is how intellectually I understand these events. Emotionally, it still pains me to think of them; it has been excruciating to imagine my grandmother Michaela and my grandparents Izydor's and Teofila's final moments. The heartbreak when I was young—on behalf of my parents and my own—was so severe that it took years for me to face what I knew and dig deeper.

I am grateful for the fifteen years I knew my father and all he taught me. He succeeded as a loving and responsible father. What I remember most, though, was his sense of humor. A raconteur, my father regaled friends and family with jokes and amusing anecdotes. He had such a gift for languages and astute observation of demeanor that he could mimic peoples' tones of voice and physical idiosyncrasies. He loved music and played the "Moonlight Sonata" or "Für Elise" as written, but when he felt too confined, relaxed by improvising with whimsical, jazzy musical jokes. He singled out a figure, exaggerated it to the point of caricature, and then laughed his head off. His renditions were quite convincing and I was not always certain which was the original. What a charming and courageous way to respond to Germany's perhaps greatest composer—with affection and generosity in the wake of what that culture wrought a century later.

But my father missed so much that would have engaged his curious mind. When the first "test-tube baby" was born in 1978, I wondered how he would have reacted. What would he have thought of in vitro fertilization so common today? How he would have enjoyed playing chess on a computer with a remote challenger, or conversing on cell phones. I still think of flute duets we might have played.

After my father's death, my mother struggled valiantly and reinvented herself from housewife to bookseller, to stockbroker and then real estate broker. Ultimately, the untreated rheumatic fever she contracted as a slave laborer in Nazi Germany compromised her heart and shortened her life. At age sixty-seven she had heart block, that is, her heart's electrical system failed, a consequence of rheumatic fever. A pacemaker kept her heart going thereafter. A few years later, her aortic valve—diseased because of the fever—was replaced. When she was diagnosed with breast cancer at age seventy-two, her weakened heart could not withstand the full course of chemotherapy her oncologist prescribed. Had the physician Siemens used allowed her to finish the medication the village doctor prescribed, she might have lived twenty years longer. Instead, the consequence of confiscating her medicine inflicted its lethal damage fifty-four years later. In her old age, my mother should have enjoyed all her grandchildren and great-grandchildren: my niece and nephew Davida and Bret Hogan's son Oliver, their daughter Ava, my nephew and niece Andrew and Alison Sidrane's son Henry and daughter Shana, and my niece, Juliana Torres. Instead, the unchecked breast tumor attacked the rest of my mother's body and she died in 1997 at age seventy-three.

Let no one minimize the long reach of the tentacles of war.

In her later years, my mother often felt isolated and sad. She missed and mourned the loss of the culture and values she was born into. She said at the end of her oral history:

> Once you choose how you're going to die, a lot of things become much less important. Certainly money, certainly certain quest for prestige doesn't seem important. Never was. I tried to raise my children to be decent people. I say I was successful.

I believe both my parents were. We had a wonderful childhood because our parents were so attentive and we felt so loved and treasured. Looking back on it now, I see that they thought a lot about how they were going to raise us.

But my mother carried unending sorrow. "I also feel alone," she added, "There are very few Polish Jews left. And who can you tell these stories to, for God's sake? And it is now really that I have feeling of deep regret that the Polish Jews are no longer here."

Despite her cancer diagnosis, my mother told Michelle that every day she had lived since Liberation had been a gift; she had had fifty years of daily gifts. To Ivy, she modeled emotional courage and the ability to face life's tragedies head-on with a philosophical approach. Shortly before she died, my mother said to me, "I've had a good life. I have three children who love me."

My mother's memory of events during World War II was near perfect. I read the books she mentioned in her Fortunoff oral history and checked her recollection of historical dates and facts. The only inaccuracy was her timeframe for the Battle of Stalingrad, so crucial to her decision to request a new job. I believe her dates were off because

Nazi propagandists deliberately obfuscated and withheld the news from the Germans.

When *Schindler's List* was released in 1993, my mother was startled by a revelation. She went alone to see the film many times. Then she read the book. She recognized many Krakówer names on the list—old families like the Rosners, musicians who had serenaded Kraków's citizens for centuries, for example. Yet, a little baffled, she added, "Somehow all these years I imagined that many others not on that list also survived." Because she had left as a teenager in 1939, her memories of Kraków were frozen in time, the way you might still envisage the youthful face of a friend even though in reality he or she has grown old and wrinkled. Despite what my mother knew intellectually, the catastrophe that befell the Jews of her hometown left a vacuum.

To write *Family Treasures Lost and Found*, I may have gone further than my parents would have wished. But the cost of silence and omissions is not just that the facts of survival remain incomplete and frustrate the children of the displaced, but that the world can shrug off the toll of war. Reticence makes it easier for others to belittle or condone the consequences of war: murder, persecution, starvation, rape, and other suffering.

It also means that heroic deeds of those who helped are lost to history. I once asked my mother if she knew the name of the Tarnów Polish officer-in-hiding, and with the most sorrowful moan, she admitted she did not. He may, however, have wanted to remain anonymous; had she been captured and tortured, my mother could have jeopardized him and his family. And so in 1961, she could not have returned to Tarnów to thank them, nor could I thank their descendants seventy-four years later when I visited Tarnów.

The same is true of the nun in Lwów, anonymous members of the AK who indicated where and how to obtain my mother's false papers, and the young communist who fed Ojzer and his attic cohort. The righteous had to determine how far they would go to help, and still live with their consciences. The world needs their examples. We need more people capable of altruistic acts of resistance.

My mother badmouthed neither the Germans nor the Poles. She always defended the Catholic Church and maintained that the aid of nuns and priests who helped Jews was underestimated. She said the Pope had signaled the church's resistance by switching the language of Mass from Latin to Polish so that priests could communicate righteousness to their congregants without the Germans understanding.

She was amused and pleased when Karol Wojtyła was elected Pope John Paul II. He was from Wadowice, the same town as my grandfather Izydor. It is not a coincidence that a Polish Pope came to power as Lech Walesa's Solidarity trade-union movement was challenging Poland's Communist Party, she said. After my mother explained this to me, I asked about her Polish nationalism. How could she support the Poles when they had murdered returning Holocaust survivors, or threatened them so that they would leave forever? My mother emphasized that nevertheless it is important to acknowledge those who did help.

I often think of my father's words during that drive through Brooklyn shortly before he died and how he gestured with a panoramic sweep toward burned-out buildings. You must have a profession. Earn a living. Make something of yourself. Make the world a better place.

Tikkun Olam. The world needs healing.

I've tried to heal the world a little by sharing my parents' stories, however incomplete. In writing this book I hope in some small way I've both heeded my father's final instructions and fulfilled my mother's wish that I tell her story. I looked to the past so that I could understand the present with more clarity.

I hope my quest will inspire others to investigate their family histories. At first, I intended to honor my lost relatives by gathering information so that they would not be forgotten, but the affection and respect I came to feel was a comforting surprise. I learned that it is possible to love people you've never met.

My more global hope is that by recounting the uncelebrated triumphs of those who struggled eighty years ago, this memoir will promote greater understanding of and empathy for today's refugees, the displaced, and their unspeakable suffering.

Family Treasures Lost and Found: A Documentary

Just as I have encountered people who were reluctant to hear about the Holocaust or responded with aggression when they learned of my legacy, so too have there been deeply sensitive friends and colleagues. While I was researching material in this memoir, I shared my discoveries. Relatives and friends listened raptly to the twists and turns I navigated to find my grandparents' house in Lviv, for example, and to retrieve documents containing scraps of information about the lost.

One long-time friend and colleague enthralled with my online sleuthathon was documentary filmmaker Marcia Rock, New York University Associate Professor of Journalism and director of the NewsDocs program. Whether during intermission at the opera or a concert, or over dinner, or on the phone, Marcia listened with fascination to my process of discovery. For four years Marcia and I collaborated on two documentary versions of *Family Treasures Lost and Found*, she as director and I as producer. As Associate Producer, my husband Ed contributed enormously with his Photoshop skills, restoring and removing spots from over one hundred family photos, helping with historical research, reviewing cuts, and much more. Some discoveries were omitted from the film because they were too detailed and could not be visualized. The challenge for all storytelling, regardless of the medium, was to find the right balance between the emotional impact of the Holocaust stories and the details of my investigative quest.

We released *Family Treasures Lost and Found* as a seventy five-minute documentary for general audiences and edited a series of five-part series of short segments ranging in length from 15 to 30 minutes for classrooms (https://www.familytreasuresfilm.com). Both versions are an innovative way to teach the Holocaust. The series of shorts is ideal for high school classrooms and we have written a discussion guide for teachers that includes suggestions for topics to examine and homework assignments. All three materials and this memoir will also be useful to museums, Jewish Community Centers, synagogues and churches, Holocaust Resource Centers, and other organizations that offer professional development for social studies teachers and family history workshops.

Both versions of the documentary and my memoir demonstrate how a reporter thinks associatively, follows leads, uncovers facts, and tells stories. I hope readers and audiences, especially students who are our future, will appreciate the importance of unfettered journalism, for we cannot protect democracy without it. In addition, by showing how I used newly available digital archives, people will recognize the democratization of information, for these carefully maintained resources make research affordable and accessible.

Finally, I hope that these offerings will promote understanding that to the victims, war is never over because they and their families continue to suffer from the trauma and loss of past generations. May these works galvanize youth to try to heal the world. May empathy guide you.

Author's Note

For additional information, including a bibliography, discussion questions, glossary, etc., please visit the memoir website, www.KarenAFrenkelMemoir.

Acknowledgments

In addition to my quest, writing this book has been a journey unto itself. Many people enthusiastically supported me throughout its long gestation. At various stages, the manuscript benefited from several fastidious editors. I thank them for their great sensitivity and thoughtfulness. They include the team at Post Hill Press, managing editor Caitlin Burdette, Rachel Paul, who edited the final manuscript, acquisitions editor Debra Englander, and publisher Anthony Ziccardi and the whole staff.

This memoir began as a narrative non-fiction account—an historical novel with characters based on real people—my relatives. Very special thanks go to Mindy Lewis, memoirist, editor, and teacher, who edited the final draft of that account while we both struggled with post-Covid fatigue. Mindy suggested that I rewrite the account as a memoir and enroll in her online memoir class to transition to that genre. I therefore appreciate her for both mentoring me and editing this memoir.

Friends and colleagues also read sections of drafts of the account or memoir, or the entire parade of manuscripts, and generously offered feedback. Special thanks to Blanche Wiesen Cook and Clare Coss, who championed this work from its inception and showed the way with their exemplary activism. "Unpack your heart, be bold, enjoy the process," Blanche declared. James Maurer, my editor during our years at *Communications of the ACM*, the membership magazine of the Association for Computing Machinery, carefully read and commented on the narrative non-fiction manuscript. Howard Lovy meticulously reviewed a late-stage manuscript and suggested what to cut. Walter

Andrejewski, Nancy Finnerty, Suzanne Gannon, Barbara Grossman, Valerie Oppenheim Neal, Julia Ittah, Mitch Levenberg, Elisa Petrini, Marcia Rock, Susan Jackson Rollins, and Eve Sandler were also thoughtful readers. Thank you all for your feedback.

I also want to thank Stephen Naron, Director of the Fortunoff Video Archive for Holocaust testimonies at Yale University for his enthusiasm and generosity regarding my mother's oral history, excerpted in both this memoir, the documentary, and the five-part documentary series.

Many historians helped during the research phase and located documents. Alex Dunai, who is also a guide and genealogist, probed the State Archival Service of Ukraine in Lviv. His thorough search yielded precious information about my paternal grandmother, Michaela Lifschütz Fränkel, including where she grew up, when she and my paternal grandfather married, the births of my father and his brothers, where they lived in Lemberg/Lwów/Lvov/and Lemberg again, and much more. Alex's finds also enabled me to build the very large Lifschütz family tree. During our 2016 trip to Europe, he escorted my husband, Edward Volchok, and me into my paternal grandparents' house in Lviv where he helped divulge its secrets.

Our resourceful Tarnów guide, Eliza Emrozinska, brought us to the former Gestapo headquarters, the former ghetto square, and convinced the landlord to show us my Great-aunt Gusta Mandel's former apartment, where he now lives. Eliza also sent me a picture of the former Kraków transit camp for slave laborers.

I am also indebted to Mark Halpern, an authority on researching Jewish roots in Galicia and Board member of JRI-Poland (Jewish Records Indexing)-Poland.org, and GesherGalicia.org. He advised me about hiring a researcher familiar with Warsaw AGAD and suggested how to research the oil business of Drohobycz and Boryslaw.

Historians Herbert Posch and Katharina Kniefacz of the University of Vienna, who created the Memorial Book for the Victims of National Socialism, answered my many questions about campus life during my father's medical school days as the Nazis rose to power, and emailed many invaluable documents about the university's history. They also sent information about the Hotel Continental, which the Lifschütz side of the family owned.

Historian Lewis Barger of the U.S. Army Office of Medical History emailed me *The Medical Department: Medical Service in the European Theater*, by Graham A. Cosmas and Albert E. Cowdrey, a tome crucial to uncovering my father's tour of duty. He also suggested that I hire an historian to search the National Archives and Record Administration (NARA), Maryland. That historian and consultant, Steven B. Rogers, retrieved the rich unit histories and annual reports of the 93rd Medical Gas Treatment Batallion, Company C, in which my father served. They were almost missed, though, due to a kink in the finding aid. Credit is also due to Sanders Marble, Army Medical Department Center of History and Heritage, U.S. Army Medical Command, who also suggested where those records were ultimately found.

Information about the villagers of Bad Neustadt and Hollstadt came through Professor Moshe Caine, Hadassah Academic College, on his wonderful site, "Unfolding Communities - The Lost Jews of Bad Neustadt." I thank him and history teacher Günter Henneberger of Bad Neustadt, for identifying and sending pictures of the Oppelt house and for contacting the family on my behalf. Günther also spoke to his student, Hanna Zwierlein of Hollsadt, whose grandfather shared memories of his neighbors Antonia Ress and her father Alois Ress.

A bit of vehicular lore rolled in from John Heitmann President, Society of Automotive Historians and Professor of History, University of Dayton; he identified my great-great-grandfather Herman Lewy's car as an early twentieth century German-made Argus.

Many archivists tirelessly searched for documents on my behalf. I am grateful to all for their thoroughness and suggestions, which lead to many discoveries: Arkansas National Guard Museum, Raymond D. Screws; Association French Lines Centre de documentation, Hélène ten Hove; Central Zionist Archives, Simone Schliachter; Claude Pepper Library, Robert Rubero; Department de l'Orientation et de la Recherche-bibliographique; Deutsche Bahn Stiftung Museum; Christina Block; Jagiellonian University archives, Pawel Gaszynski, Igorzata Klimas; Jewish Museum of the City of Vienna, Christa

Prokisch; Lviv Center for Urban History and Lviv Interactive; Austrian State Archives; Siemens Archives, Siemens AG, Frank Wittendorfer, and Siemens Historical Institute, Christoph Frank; the State Archival Service of Ukraine in Lviv; U.S. Army War College Library at Carlisle Barracks, Carlisle, PA, Shannon Schwaller; U.S. National Archives and Records Administration (NARA): Franklin D. Roosevelt Presidential Library, Virginia Lewick; The Harry S. Truman Presidential Library & Museum; Staff of NARA, College Park, MD, Marie Carpenti, Robin Cookson, Tab Lewis, Jaclyn Ostrowski, Kenneth D. Schlessinger, and Eric van Slander; Red Cross Archives, Susan R. Watson; Warsaw AGAD Archives, Witold Wrzosinski. Ancestry.com and Newspapers.com, GesherGalicia.org, and JewishGen.org, were also important to my sleuthathon.

My mother left my sisters and me boxes stuffed with her, my father's, my grandparents' and great-grandparents' documents in Polish, German, and snippets of Yiddish and Ukrainian. I thank the following for their translations: German: James Maurer, Gregory Divers, Lorena Balensifer Ellis, Hanne Leibmann, and Halina Weinrausch; Hebrew: Shula Wiener and Emil Kon; Polish: Walter Andrejewski, Ivona Kwiatkowska; Ukrainian: Ali Kinsella; Yiddish: Amanda (Miryem-Khaye) Seigel of the New York Public Library's Dorot Jewish Division. Thank you, Arthur Flug, former director of the Kupferberg Holocaust Center at Queensborough Community College, and Yuri Shevchuk, Senior Lecturer in Ukrainian at Columbia University, for recommending translators.

Librarians have also helped enormously. Thanks go to Library of Congress's Regina Frackowiak, The New York Academy of Medicine Library's Arlene Shaner, and The New York Public Library's Paul Friedman.

Thank you, Laurie Lindquist, publicist of Reed College, who connected me with Reverand Robert Palladino expert calligrapher and typography authority, who helped me determine the font of my great-grandmother's calling card.

For the art: Bretton and Kim May of Goldenlight Visions who digitized family portraits and photos with great precision and color fidelity;

Michael Lugo Holmes re-purposed the animated maps of escape routes he created for *Family Treasures Lost and Found*, the documentary; Don Morris transformed the poster for the documentary into the book cover. Thanks to all these talented visual artists.

A family tale, by necessity, requires collective family effort. Because our clan was far-flung, I needed experts to help me gather missing branches. During my family history romp, I unexpectedly found six relatives through a series of professional connections. Jérôme Segal, Sorbonne University assistant professor and a researcher and reporter in Vienna, kindly connected me to a distant cousin of my father's, Enrico Lamet (né Eric Lifschütz, now deceased). Thanks to Enrico, I connected with Rose's cousins, one of whom supplied photos of her. Rose's son (now deceased), graciously imparted information about his mother and the Harmatz family. I also thank Mel Corren of Temple Israel, Stockton, CA, for putting me in touch with the long-lost branch of California Finkelsteins: Fillmore Marks, Jr. and his sons, Brad, Will, and Doug. Fillmore told me all he knew of his line and his sons generously supplied footage and images of two of Temple Israel's past presidents, their grandfather Fillmore Marks, Sr. and our great-great-uncle, Martin P. Stein. They also supplied many other images and newspaper clippings about them, I. F. Stein, and their forefather Mozes Marks, pioneering émigré from Kraków to old Stockton and older brother of my great-great-grandfather Abraham Finkelstein. The Marks brothers also introduced my sisters and me with two other cousins, Jessica Baer Mears and Janet Broude.

I also thank my cousins by marriage, Arthur Beckman and his wife Nina Skaya, for visiting the United States Holocaust Memorial Museum on my behalf and checking the International Tracing Service/Arolsen Archives for my lost relatives, including my uncle Milek Frenkel and my great-aunt Isabela Finkelstein.

My first cousin Anita Frankel, journalist-turned-therapist, generously shared her three-hour audio interview with Uncle Sydney conducted when he was in his mid-70s. She also shared her graduate school term paper about our family, which included a Fränkel family tree and two family photos. I thank her profusely as I do my mother's cousin,

Olga Kapeliuk, for her memories and for help building the Goldberger and Trammer family trees. Barbara (Basia) Müller shared written memories of her half-Jewish mother, Guschinka Trammer Szemelowska, who helped save her Jewish relatives. Guschinka's text includes genealogies of the Goldbergers and Trammers of Wadowice and Tarnów. My mother's cousin, Marcel Goldberger, M.D., whose father Arthur was my grandfather Izydor's brother, has had great input as well, and opened his beautiful home to me as a refuge from the chaos and clutter of Manhattan whenever I needed it. Heart-felt appreciation to them all.

My sisters Michelle Frenkel Sidrane and Ivy Frenkel gave me their encouragement and valued input during all phases of my investigative genealogical adventure. Michelle suggested numerous family histories and memoirs pertaining to the Holocaust, hinting that I might chronicle our family's story. She read several drafts and offered incites not only as my oldest sibling, but as former President and Publisher of Crown Publishers and Executive Vice President of Random House. Ivy encouraged me to tell the Holocaust tales as well as the story of my "treasure hunt," as she put it, and imparted her sensibility and opinion as a therapist on the role of trauma and loss in our family. Because I did not know our only surviving grandfather, Ojzer, who died when I was three, I relied on my sisters' sparse memories of "Grandpa Frankel," as we called him, or "Grandfather Ojzer," as I referred to him here. I cannot thank them enough for their love and support.

Finally, my beloved husband Ed responded with unbounded enthusiasm to this project from the start. It has been most touching to watch him try to become acquainted with in-laws he never met, imagining how they coped with events and wondering what it would have been like to converse with them. Not only did Ed read and comment on all drafts and enter changes when my arms gave out, he tirelessly scanned, digitally retouched, and enlarged family photos so that I could see my relatives close-up. He made our 2016 visit to Europe a fabulous experience.

Karen A. Frenkel, December 2024

About the Author

Karen A. Frenkel is an award-winning technology and science journalist, author, and documentary filmmaker. Frenkel is the producer of the documentary *Family Treasures Lost and Found*, a companion to this memoir (www.familytreasuresfilm.com). She is co-author with Isaac Asimov of *Robots: Machines in Man's Image.* Her previous award-winning documentaries appeared on public television: *Minerva's Machine: Women and Computing*, winner of the 1997 Exceptional Media Merit Award (EMMA) for Best Television Documentary (Small Market), and *Net.LEARNING*, winner of the National Education Reporting First Prize Television Documentary Feature. Her many articles have appeared in magazines, newspapers, and websites, including *The New York Times, Bloomberg Businessweek, Forbes, Scientific American, MIT Technology Review, Discover, Science Magazine, Essence, U.S. News & World Report*, FastCompany.com, *The Village Voice*, and *Communications of the ACM.* For more information please visit www.karenafrenkel.com and https://www.familytreasuresmemoir.com.

www.ingramcontent.com/pod-product-compliance
Ingram Content Group UK Ltd.
Pitfield, Milton Keynes, MK11 3LW, UK
UKHW021711190726
13853UKWH00001B/489

9 798888 459560